The Promise of Happiness

The Promise of Happiness

SARA AHMED

Duke University Press   Durham and London   2010

© 2010 Duke University Press
All rights reserved
Printed in the United States of America on acid-free paper ⊛
Designed by C. H. Westmoreland
Typeset in Whitman by Tseng Information Systems, Inc.
Library of Congress Cataloging-in-Publication Data appear on the
last printed page of this book.

For Audre Lorde

For teaching me so much about everything

CONTENTS

Acknowledgments   ix

Introduction: Why Happiness, Why Now?   1

1. Happy Objects   21

2. Feminist Killjoys   50

3. Unhappy Queers   88

4. Melancholic Migrants   121

5. Happy Futures   160

Conclusion: Happiness, Ethics, Possibility   199

Notes   225

References   283

Index   301

CONTENTS

ACKNOWLEDGMENTS

I WOULD LIKE TO THANK the Arts and Humanities Research Council (AHRC) for funding my research leave in 2007–8; my department, Media and Communications, Goldsmiths College, for allowing a lengthy absence; as well as my colleagues and friends at Goldsmiths, especially Lisa Adkins, Lisa Blackman, Gavin Butt, Nick Couldry, Natalie Fenton, Mariam Fraser, Angela McRobbie, Rachel Moore, Simon O'Sullivan, Beverley Skeggs, Richard Smith, and Gareth Stanton. My appreciation to the Department of Women's and Gender Studies at Rutgers University for providing a calm and stimulating place to complete this book and to Mary Hawkesworth for making my visit possible. For helping New York live up to its promise, thanks to Ann Pellegrini, Jasbir Puar, and Sarah Schulman. For friendship, thanks to Clare Hemmings, Shona Hunter, Jonathan Keane, Catharina Landström, Elena Loizidou, Mimi Sheller, and Elaine Swan. For the creation of an intellectual home, thanks to all those who participate in Black British Feminism, including Suki Ali, Heidi Mirza, Gail Lewis, Ann Phoenix, Nirmal Puwar, and Shirley Tate. For intellectual inspiration over many years, thanks to Judith Butler. For excellent advice and suggestions, thanks to Ken Wissoker, Courtney Berger, Molly Balikov, Fred Kameny, and the editorial team at Duke University Press. For ongoing support and solidarity thanks to Lauren Berlant, Sneja Gunew, Elspeth Probyn, Sasha Roseneil, and Terry Threadgold. For helpful feedback on chapters and papers, thanks to Sarah Franklin, Kristyn Gorton, Elena Loizidou, Heather Love, David Glover, Ali Rattansi, Róisín Ryan-Flood, Simon O'Sullivan, and Sarah Schulman.

To those who have contributed killjoy anecdotes and happiness references, I am grateful. I have been lucky to have the opportunity to share my research with audiences at the University of British Columbia, Carleton University, University of Cincinnati, City University of New York, Cornell University, University College Dublin, Durham University, Edinburgh University, Florence University, Goldsmiths College, Hampshire College, University of Illinois, University of Kansas, Kent University, London School of Economics, McGill University, New York University, University of Oslo, Queen Mary and Westfield College, Rutgers University, UC Santa Cruz, University of South Australia, Sussex University, Syracuse University, University of Turku, and York University (Canada).

To my family for your kindness, especially my mother Maureen Fisher and my sisters Tanya Ahmed and Tamina Levy. Thanks to Mulka for being part of my life and to Yvonne and Meredith Johnson for being part of his. For providing the grounds for optimism, and even happiness, thanks to Sarah Franklin.

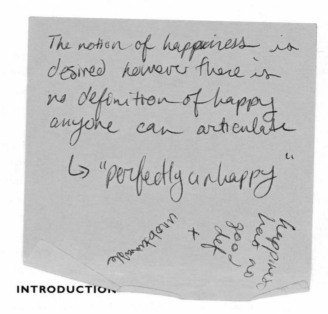

Why Happiness, Why Now?

HAPPINESS IS CONSISTENTLY DESCRIBED as the object of human desire, as being what we aim for, as being what gives purpose, meaning and order to human life. As Bruno S. Frey and Alois Stutzer argue, "Everybody wants to be happy. There is probably no other goal in life that commands such a high degree of consensus" (2002: vii).[1] What they are describing is perhaps a consensus that happiness is the consensus. Do we consent to happiness? And what are we consenting to, if or when we consent to happiness?

Even a philosopher such as Immanuel Kant, who places the individual's own happiness outside the domain of ethics, argues that "to be happy is necessarily the wish of every finite rational being, and this, therefore, is inevitably a determining principle of its faculty of desire" ([1788] 2004: 24). And yet Kant himself suggests rather mournfully that "unfortunately, the notion of happiness is so indeterminate that although every human being wishes to attain it, yet he can never say definitely and consistently what it is that he really wishes and wills" ([1785] 2005: 78). If happiness is what we wish for, it does not mean we know what we wish for in wishing for happiness. Happiness might even conjure its own wish. Or happiness might keep its place as a wish by its failure to be given.

Happiness: a wish, a will, a want. In this book I wonder what it means for happiness to be thought in such terms. The question that guides the book is thus not so much "what is happiness?" but rather "what does happiness do?" I do not offer a definition of happiness, or a model of authentic happiness. Nor do I offer a set of instructions on how to achieve happiness: I do not have one to offer, and if anything I write from a position of skeptical disbelief in happiness as a technique for living well. I am interested in how happiness is associated with some life choices and not others, how happiness is imagined as being what follows being a certain kind of being. The history of happiness can be thought of as a history of associations. In wishing for happiness we wish to be associated with happiness, which means to be associated with its associations. The very promise that happiness is what you get for having the right associations might be how we are directed toward certain things.

Happiness shapes what coheres as a world. In describing happiness as a form of world making I am indebted to the work of feminist, black, and queer scholars who have shown in different ways how happiness is used to justify oppression. Feminist critiques of the figure of "the happy housewife," black critiques of the myth of "the happy slave," and queer critiques of the sentimentalization of heterosexuality as "domestic bliss" have taught me most about happiness and the very terms of its appeal. Around these specific critiques are long histories of scholarship and activism which expose the unhappy effects of happiness, teaching us how happiness is used to redescribe social norms as social goods. We might even say that such political movements have struggled *against* rather than *for* happiness. Simone de Beauvoir shows so well how happiness translates its wish into a politics, a wishful politics, a politics that demands that others live according to a wish. As she argued: "It is not too clear just what the word *happy* really means and still less what true values it may mask. There is no possibility of measuring the happiness of others, and *it is always easy to describe as happy the situation in which one wishes to place them*" ([1949] 1997: 28; second emphasis added). I draw on such critiques of happiness as a way of asking questions about the happiness wish. We need to draw on such critiques *now*, as a way of responding to the worldliness of this *now*. Why happiness, why now? We could certainly describe this *now* as a "happiness turn." *The Promise of Happiness* is written in part as a response to this turn.

The Happiness Turn

What do I mean by "the happiness turn"? It is certainly the case that numerous books have been published on the science and economics of happiness, especially from 2005 onward.[2] The popularity of therapeutic cultures and discourses of self-help have also meant a turn to happiness: many books and courses now exist that provide instructions on how to be happy, drawing on a variety of knowledges, including the field of positive psychology, as well as on (often Orientalist) readings of Eastern traditions, especially Buddhism.[3] It is now common to refer to "the happiness industry": happiness is both produced and consumed through these books, accumulating value as a form of capital. Barbara Gunnell (2004) describes how "the search for happiness is certainly enriching a lot of people. The feel-good industry is flourishing. Sales of self-help books and CDs that promise a more fulfilling life have never been higher."

The media are saturated with images and stories of happiness. In the UK, many broadsheet newspapers have included "specials" on happiness and a BBC program, *The Happiness Formula*, was aired in 2006.[4] This happiness turn can be described as international; you can visit the "happy plant index" on the World Wide Web and a number of global happiness surveys and reports that measure happiness within and between nation states have been published.[5] These reports are often cited in the media when research findings do not correspond to social expectations, that is, when developing countries are shown to be happier than overdeveloped ones. Take the opening sentence of one article: "Would you believe it, Bangladesh is the happiest nation in the world! The United States, on the other hand, is a sad story: it ranks only 46th in the World Happiness Survey."[6] Happiness and unhappiness become newsworthy when they challenge ideas about the social status of specific individuals, groups, and nations, often confirming status through the language of disbelief.

The happiness turn can also be witnessed in changing policy and governance frameworks. The government of Bhutan has measured the happiness of its population since 1972, represented as Gross National Happiness (GNH). In the UK, David Cameron, the leader of the Conservative party, talked about happiness as a value for government, leading to a debate in the media about New Labour and its happiness and "social well-being" agenda.[7] A number of governments have been reported to be introducing happiness and well-being as measurable assets and explicit goals, supplementing the Gross Domestic Product (GDP) with what has become known as the Genuine Progress Indicator (GPI).[8] Happiness becomes a more genuine way of measuring progress; happiness, we might say is, the ultimate performance indicator.

Unsurprisingly, then, happiness studies has become an academic field in its own right: the academic journal *Happiness Studies* is well established and a number of professorships in happiness studies now exist. Within academic scholarship, we have witnessed a turn to happiness within a range of disciplines, including history, psychology, architecture, social policy, and economics. It is important to witness this turn, reflecting not simply on happiness as a form of consensus but on the consensus to use the word *happiness* to describe something.

Some of this work has been described under the rubric of "the new science of happiness." This is not to say that the science of happiness is itself new; many of the key texts in this area offer revivals of classical English utilitarianism, in particular, the work of Jeremy Bentham with his famous maxim of "the greatest happiness for the greatest number." As Bentham explains in *A Fragment of Government* "it is the greatest happiness of the greater number that is the measure of right and wrong" ([1776] 1988: 3). Bentham is himself drawing on an earlier tradition, including the work of David Hume as well as Cesare Beccaria and Claude Adrien Helvétius. The science of happiness shares a history with political economy: just recall Adam Smith's argument in *The Wealth of Nations* that capitalism advances us from what he might call "miserable equality" to what we could call "happy inequality" such that "a workman, even of the lowest and poorest order, if he is frugal and industrious, may enjoy a greater share of the necessaries and conveniences of life than it is possible for any savage to acquire" ([1776] 1999: 105).

Of course, nineteenth-century utilitarianism involves an explicit refutation of such a narrative, in which inequality becomes the measure of advancement and happiness. Bentham, following Alexander Wedderburn, describes the principle of utility as dangerous for government: "a principle, which lays down, as the only *right* and justifiable end of Government, the greatest happiness of the greatest number—how can it be denied to be a dangerous one? dangerous to every Government, which has for its *actual* end or object the greatest happiness of a certain *one*" ([1776] 1988: 59). Despite this belief that every person's happiness should count equally (the happiness of many refuses to elevate the happiness of any one), the utilitarian tradition did uphold the principle that increased levels of happiness function as a measure of human progress. Émile Durkheim offered a forceful critique of this principle: "But in fact, is it true that the happiness of the individual increases as man advances? Nothing is more doubtful." ([1893] 1960: 241)

One of the key figures in the recent science of happiness is Richard Layard, often referred to as "the happiness tsar" by the British media. Layard's important book *Happiness: Lessons from a New Science*, first published in 2005, begins as a critique of the discipline of economics for how it measures human growth: "economics equates changes in the happiness of a society with changes in its purchasing power" (ix). Layard argues that happiness is the only way of measuring growth and advancement: "the best society is the happiest society." One of the fundamental presumptions of this science is that happiness is good, and thus that nothing can be better than to maximize happiness. The science of happiness presumes that happiness is "out there," that you can measure happiness and that these measurements are objective: they have even been called "hedonimeters" (Nettle 2006: 3).

If the science of happiness presumes happiness as being "out there," then how does it define happiness? Richard Layard again provides us with a useful reference point. He argues that "happiness is feeling good, and misery is feeling bad" (6). Happiness is "feeling good," which means we can measure happiness because we can measure how good people feel. So "out there" is really "in here." The belief that you can measure happiness is a belief that you can measure feelings. Layard argues that "most people find it easy to say how good they are feeling" (13). Happiness research is primarily based on self-reporting: studies measure how happy people say they are, presuming that if people say they are happy, they are happy. This model both presumes the transparency of self-feeling (that we can say and know how we feel), as well as the unmotivated and uncomplicated nature of self-reporting. If happiness is already understood to be what you want to have, then to be asked how happy you are is not to be asked a neutral question. It is not just that people are being asked to evaluate their life situations but that they are being asked to evaluate their life situations through categories that are value laden.[9] Measurements could be measuring the relative desire to be proximate to happiness, or even the relative desire to report on one's life well (to oneself or others), rather than simply how people feel about their life as such.

It matters how we think about feeling. Much of the new science of happiness is premised on the model of feelings as transparent, as well as the foundation for moral life. If something is good, we feel good. If something is bad, we feel bad.[10] The science of happiness thus relies on a very specific model of sub-jectivity, where one knows how one feels, and where the distinction between good and bad feeling is secure, forming the basis of subjective as well as social well-being. Cultural studies, as well as psychoanalysis, may have an important role to play in these debates by offering alternative theories of emotion that are *not* based on a subject that is fully present to itself, on a subject that always knows how it feels (see Terada 2001). Cultural and psychoanalytic approaches can explore how ordinary attachments to the very idea of the good life are also sites of ambivalence, involving the confusion rather than separation of good and bad feelings. Reading happiness would then become a matter of reading the grammar of this ambivalence.

Happiness research does not simply measure feelings; it also interprets what it measures. Measuring happiness primarily generates knowledge about the distribution of happiness. Happiness research has produced databases that show where happiness is located, which are largely predicated on a compara-tive model. Happiness databases show us which individuals are happier than others, as well as which groups, or nation-states are happier than others. The science of happiness makes correlations between happiness levels and social indicators, creating what are called "happiness indicators." Happiness indi-cators tell us which kinds of people have more happiness; they function not only as measures of happiness but also as predictors of happiness. As Frey and Stutzer argue in *Happiness and Economics*, social indicators can predict how happy different kinds of persons will be, creating what they call "happiness psychograms" (2002: 7).

One of the primary happiness indicators is marriage. Marriage would be defined as "the best of all possible worlds" as it maximizes happiness. The argu-ment is simple: if you are married, then we can predict that you are more likely to be happier than if you are not married. The finding is also a recommenda-tion: get married and you will be happier! This intimacy of measurement and prediction is powerful. The science of happiness could be described as per-formative: by finding happiness in certain places, it generates those places as being good, as being what should be promoted *as* goods. Correlations are read as causalities, which then become the basis of promotion. We promote what I call in the first chapter "happiness-causes," which might even cause happiness to be reported. The science of happiness hence redescribes what is already evaluated as being good as good. If we have a duty to promote what causes happiness, then happiness itself becomes a duty. I will explore the significance of "the happiness duty" throughout this book.

This is not to say that happiness is always found. Indeed, we might even say that happiness becomes more powerful through being perceived as in crisis. The crisis in happiness works primarily as a narrative of disappointment: the accumulation of wealth has not meant the accumulation of happiness. What makes this crisis "a crisis" in the first place is of course the regulatory effect of a social belief: that more wealth "should" make people happier. Richard Layard begins his science of happiness with what he describes as a paradox: "As Western societies have got richer, their people have become no happier" (2005: 3). If the new science of happiness uncouples happiness from wealth accumulation, it still locates happiness in certain places, especially marriage, widely regarded as the primary "happiness indicator" (see chapter 2), as well as in stable families and communities (see chapter 4). Happiness is looked for where it is expected to be found, even when happiness is reported as missing. What is striking is that the crisis in happiness has not put social ideals into question and if anything has reinvigorated their hold over both psychic and political life. The demand for happiness is increasingly articulated as a demand to return to social ideals, as if what explains the crisis of happiness is not the failure of these ideals but our failure to follow them. And arguably, at times of crisis the language of happiness acquires an even more powerful hold.[11]

Positive Psychology

Given that this new science rests primarily on self-reporting, it involves an important psychological dimension. Within psychology, we can also witness a happiness turn. Much of this work is described as "positive psychology," which begins as an internal critique of the discipline. Michael Argyle argued that "most work on emotions in psychology has been concerned with anxiety, depression and other negative states" (1987: 1). Or as the editors of the volume *Subjective Well-Being* argue, following Ed Diener, "Psychology has been preoccupied less with the conditions of well-being, than with the opposite: the determination of human unhappiness" (Strack, Argyle, and Schwarz 1991: 1). While the science of happiness "corrects" the tendency of economics to focus on economic growth at the expense of happiness, the psychology of happiness "corrects" the tendency of psychology to focus on negative feeling states at the expense of happiness.

We can start with Michael Argyle's classic *The Psychology of Happiness* (1987). He defines the project of his book as follows: "This book is primarily concerned with the causes and explanations of positive happiness, and how our understanding of it can be used to make people, including ourselves, happy" (1). We can immediately see how happiness becomes a disciplinary technique. Positive psychology aims to understand "positive happiness"—by providing explanations of its causes—as well as to use this knowledge about happiness to create happiness. Positive psychology aims to make people happier. Positive psychology is positive about positive feeling; it presumes the promissory nature of its own object.

At one level, this seems a wise council. Surely, feeling better is better, and we all want to feel better? Surely, all knowledge should be transformative and predicated on an impulse to improve life worlds and capacities for individuals? What is at stake here is a belief that we can know "in advance" what will improve people's lives. Making people happier is taken up as a sign of improvement. The very "thing" we aim to achieve is the "thing" that will get us there. Positive feeling is given the task of overcoming its own negation: feeling positive is what can get us out of "anxiety, depression and other negative states" (1). To feel better is to be better—positive psychology shares this presumption with the economics of happiness. Here there is a stronger argument: to feel better is *to get better*.

Argyle relies on self-reporting as an objective measure of the subjective: "We shall rely to a large extent on subjective reports of how people feel: if people say they are happy then they *are* happy" (2). He then describes certain institutions as good insofar as they are likely to promote happiness: "the greatest benefits," he suggests, "come from marriage" (31). Happiness involves developing a certain kind of disposition: "Happiness is part of a broader syndrome, which includes choice of rewarding situations, looking on the bright side and high self-esteem" (124). Individuals have the project of working on themselves, governing their souls, to use Nikolas Rose's (1999) terms. Such projects are described as forms of "enhancement" and include "mood induction techniques," which can "become a habit" and thereby "have more enduring effects" (203). In contrast, unhappy people are represented as deprived, as unsociable and neurotic: "Unhappy people tend to be lonely and high in neuroticism" (124). Individuals must become happier for others: positive psychology describes this project as not so much a right as a responsibility. We have a responsibility for our own happiness insofar as promoting our own happiness is what enables us to increase other people's happiness. One of my key concerns in this book is to explore what follows from the idea that we have a responsibility to be happy for others, or even simply from the idea that there is a necessary and inevitable relationship of dependence between one person's happiness and the happiness of others.

Unsurprisingly, positive psychology is now a huge popular as well as academic field: many cross-over books now exist that instruct people on how to become happier, forming a generalized culture of expertise. Take the work of Martin Seligman, who has written books on positive psychology and also runs the Positive Psychology Center at the University of Pennsylvania.[12] Like Argyle before him, he offers a critique of psychology as it has made "relieving the states that make life miserable" more of a priority than "building the states that make life worth living" (2003: xi). He describes the role of positive psychology as providing "guideposts" for "the good life" (xi). Happiness is often described as a path, as being what you get if you follow the right path. In such descriptions, happiness offers a route, and positive psychology helps you to find the route: "This road takes you through the countryside of pleasure and gratification, up into the high country of strength and virtue, and finally to the peaks of lasting fulfillment: meaning and purpose" (xiv). Happiness becomes a form of being directed or oriented, of following "the right way." Seligman does not simply describe happiness as a reward, as being what follows a life well traveled, but also as being a quality of a person. Happiness is a kind of trait. He closely identifies happiness with optimism (see chapter 5). Happy people are more optimistic as they "tend to interpret their troubles as transient, controllable, and specific to one situation" (9–10). Seligman also suggests that happy people are more altruistic: "when we are happy, we are less self-focused, we like others more, and we want to share our good fortune even with strangers" (43). You might note here that correlations (happiness with optimism, and happiness with altruism) quickly translate into causalities in which happiness becomes its own cause: happiness causes us to be less self-focused, more optimistic, which in turn causes us to be happier, which means we cause more happiness for others, and so on.

Not only does happiness become an individual responsibility, a redescription of life as a project, but it also becomes an instrument, as a means to an end, as well as an end. We make ourselves happy, as an acquisition of capital that allows us to be or to do this or that, or even to get this or that. Such a means-based model of happiness is at odds with classical conceptions such as Aristotle's work, which I will discuss in chapter 1, where happiness is "the end of all ends." Positive psychology involves the instrumentalization of happiness as a technique. Happiness becomes a means to an end, as well as the end of the means.[13]

Happiness becomes, then, a way of maximizing your potential of getting what you want, as well as being what you want to get. Unsurprisingly, positive psychology often uses economic language to describe happiness as a good. Heady and Wearing, for example, describe the "relatively stable personal characteristics" which account for some people being generally happier than others, which they call "stocks," including social background, personality, and social networks (1991: 49). Happiness gets you more in the bank; happiness depends on other forms of capital (background, personality, networks) as well as acquiring or accumulating capital for the individual subject.

One of the most recent proponents of positive psychology is Alan Carr, whose work also crosses the border between popular and academic readerships. Carr also describes the project of positive psychology in terms of the twin objectives of understanding and facilitating happiness and subjective well-being (2004: 1). Positive emotions "like pleasure or contentment tell us something good is happening" (12). He argues that happy and unhappy people "have distinctive personality profiles" (16). A happiness profile would be the profile of the kind of person who is most likely to be happy, as we can also see in the following classic description:

> happy persons are more likely to be found in the economically prosperous countries, whose freedom and democracy are held in respect and the political scene is stable. The happy are more likely to be found in majority groups than among minorities and more often at the top of the ladder than at the bottom. They are typically married and get on well with families and friends. In respect of their personal characteristics, the happy appear relatively healthy,

both physically and mentally. They are active and openminded. They feel they are in control of their lives. Their aspirations concern social and moral matters rather than money making. In matters of politics, the happy tend to the conservative side of middle. (Veenhoven 1991: 16)

The face of happiness, at least in this description, looks rather like the face of privilege. Rather than assuming happiness is simply found in "happy persons," we can consider how claims to happiness make certain forms of personhood valuable. Attributions of happiness might be how social norms and ideals become affective, as if relative proximity to those norms and ideals creates happiness. Lauren Berlant has called such a fantasy of happiness a "stupid" form of optimism: "the faith that adjustment to certain forms or practices of living and thinking will secure one's happiness" (2002: 75).

For Carr happiness profiles are also profiles of social forms as well as individual persons: he suggests that certain types of families "promote the experience of flow" by optimal levels of clarity, centering, choice, and challenge (62). If certain ways of living promote happiness, then to promote happiness would be to promote those ways of living. Thus happiness promotion becomes very quickly the promotion of certain types of families. The idea of "flow" to describe the relationship between happy persons and happy worlds is powerful. Deriving primarily from the work of Mihály Csíkszentmihályi, flow describes the experience of an individual engaged with the world, or involved with the world, where the world is not encountered as alien, as an obstacle or resistance. "The best moments in our lives" Csíkszentmihályi suggests, "are not the passive, receptive, relaxing times — although such experiences can also be enjoyable, if we have worked hard to attain them. The best moments usually occur when a person's body or mind is stretched to its limits in a voluntary effort to accomplish something difficult and worthwhile" (1992: 3). He argues that "in the long run optimal experiences add up to a sense of mastery — or perhaps better, a sense of *participation* in determining the content of life — that comes as close to what is usually meant by happiness as anything else we can conceivably imagine." (4)

When the subjects are not "in flow" they encounter the world as resistant, as blocking rather than enabling an action. Unhappy subjects hence feel alienated from the world as they experience the world as alien. I suspect that Csíkszentmihályi can teach us a great deal about the phenomenology of happiness as an intimacy of body and world. What if to flow into the world is not simply understood as a psychological attribute? What if the world "houses" some bodies more than others, such that some bodies do not experience that world as resistant? We might need to rewrite happiness by considering how it feels to be stressed by the very forms of life that enable some bodies to flow into space. Perhaps the experiences of not following, of being stressed, of not being extended by the spaces in which we reside, can teach us more about happiness.

Unhappy Archives

I will not respond to the new science of happiness by simply appealing for a return to classical ideas of happiness as *eudaimonia*, as living a good, meaningful, or virtuous life. Examples of such arguments are evident in work by Richard Schoch (2006) and Terry Eagleton (2007: 140–48). Schoch argues in *The Secrets of Happiness* that we have become "Deaf to the wisdom of the ages" and that "we deny ourselves the chance of finding a happiness that is meaningful" (1). He suggests that "we've settled, nowadays for a much weaker, much thinner, happiness," which he describes as "mere enjoyment of pleasure" (1). Critiques of the happiness industry that call for a return to classical concepts of virtue not only sustain the association between happiness and the good but also suggest that some forms of happiness are better than others. This distinction between a strong and weak conception of happiness is clearly a moral distinction: some forms of happiness are read as worth more than other forms of happiness, because they require more time, thought, and labor. Noticeably, within classical models, the forms of happiness that are higher are linked to the mind, and those that are lower are linked to the body. In Schoch's description a "weaker, thinner" happiness is linked to "mere enjoyment of pleasure." Hierarchies of happiness may correspond to social hierarchies that are already given.

If higher forms of happiness are what you get for being a certain kind of being, then the being of happiness would certainly be recognizable as bourgeois. We could even say that expressions of horror about contemporary cultures of happiness involve a class horror that happiness is too easy, too accessible, and too fast. We just have to remember that the model of the good life within classical Greek philosophy was based on an exclusive concept of life: only some had the life that enabled one to achieve a good life, a life that involved self-ownership, material security, and leisure time. For Aristotle the happiest life is the life devoted to "contemplative speculation," as a form of life that would only be available to some and not others (1998: 193).[14] The classical concept of the good life relied on a political economy: some people have to work to give others the time to pursue the good life, the time, as it were, to flourish.[15] Arguably, such a political economy is essential rather than incidental to the actualization of the possibility of living the virtuous life.

Ideas of happiness involve social as well as moral distinctions insofar as they rest on ideas of who is worthy as well as capable of being happy "in the right way." I suspect that an attachment to happiness as a lost object involves not simply a form of mourning but also an anxiety that the wrong people can be happy, and even a desire for happiness to be returned to the right people (the people with the time and privilege for philosophy, perhaps). To consider happiness as a form of world making is to consider how happiness makes the world cohere around, as it were, the right people. It is no accident that philosophers tend to find happiness in the life of the philosopher or that thinkers tend to find happiness in the thinking of thought. Where we find happiness teaches us what we value rather than simply what is of value. Happiness not only becomes what is valued but allows other values to acquire their value. When happiness is assumed to be a self-evident good, then it becomes evidence of the good.

This book proceeds by suspending belief that happiness is a good thing. In this mode of suspension, we can consider not only what makes happiness good but how happiness *participates* in making things good. I have taken it as given that happiness involves good feeling, even though I would challenge some of the models of good feeling offered in the science of happiness. This is not to reduce happiness to good feeling. The association between happiness with good feeling is a modern one, as Darrin M. McMahon (2006) shows us in his monumental history of happiness. We have inherited this association such that it is hard to think about happiness without thinking about feeling. My task is to think about *how* feelings make some things and not others good.

In considering happiness in this way, my book can be situated within the feminist cultural studies of emotion and affect (Berlant 2000, Sedgwick 2003, Cvetkovich 2003, Brennan 2004, Probyn 2005, Ngai 2005, Munt 2007, Love 2007, Woodward 2009). If much of this work takes "bad feelings" as the starting point[16]—shame, hate, fear, disgust, anger, and so on—then this book starts at a different point, with good feeling, although I do not assume that the distinction between good feeling and bad feeling will hold (and, as we will see, it does not). Developing the arguments I made in *The Cultural Politics of Emotion* (2004), I explore how feelings are attributed to objects, such that some things and not others become happiness and unhappiness causes. Feelings do not then simply reside within subjects and then move outward toward objects. Feelings are how objects create impressions in shared spaces of dwelling. Building on my approach in *Queer Phenomenology* (2006), I explore how we are directed by the promise of happiness, as the promise that happiness is what follows if we do this or that. The promise of happiness is what makes certain objects proximate, affecting how the world gathers around us.

In order to consider how happiness makes things good, I track the word *happiness*, asking what histories are evoked by the mobility of this word. I follow the word *happiness* around.[17] I notice what it is up to, where it goes, who or what it gets associated with. If I am following the word *happiness*, then I go where it goes. I thus do not go where the word *happiness* does not go. The risk of using this method is that I could give the word *happiness* too much power in order to challenge the power happiness can give. My method does have this limitation: if my aim is to describe what kind of world takes shape when happiness provides a horizon, then I will not be exploring worlds that take shape under different horizons. In my view, there is such a general emphasis on happiness as the point of human existence that we need to ask what follows from this point. We will also need other kinds of critical and creative writing that offer thick descriptions of the kinds of worlds that might take shape when happiness does not provide a horizon for experience.

In describing my method in these terms, it should be clear that I am not producing a new concept of happiness. Claire Colebrook following Gilles Deleuze differentiates a philosophical concept from an everyday concept. Rather helpfully for my purposes she uses the concept of happiness to make her point. As she describes: "Our day-to-day usage of concepts works like shorthand or habit; we use concepts so that we *do not* have to think" (2002: 15). A philosophical concept of happiness, she suggests, "would not refer to this or that instance of happiness: it would *enact or create* a new possibility or thought of happiness" (17).[18] Philosophy brackets the everyday or ordinary and thinks with extreme forms, such as found in modern art. This book in contrast explores the everyday habits of happiness and considers how such habits involve ways of thinking about the world that shape how the world coheres. I want to attend to how happiness is spoken, lived, practiced; happiness, for me, is what it does.

This does not mean I bracket philosophy. After all, the history of philosophy could be described as a history of happiness. Happiness could even be described as the one philosophical teleology that has not been called into question within philosophy. François Jullien argues persuasively that philosophy's submission to the idea that happiness is the goal of human existence is the point at which "its inventiveness is nowhere to be found" (2007: 104).[19] I would abbreviate the status of happiness in philosophy in the following way: happiness is *what we want, whatever it is*. Disagreement seems restricted to the content of this "whatever," which is perhaps how happiness retains its role in philosophy as the placeholder of human desire. I think of philosophy here not only as a body of texts that describe themselves as inheritors of philosophy, and that engage with philosophical histories, but also as a "happiness archive": a set of ideas, thoughts, narratives, images, impressions about what is happiness. Happiness appears within ethical and political philosophy, philosophy that aims to describe the good life.[20] Happiness also appears in the philosophy of mind. In this book I draw in particular on the empiricist account of the passions offered by John Locke.

To speak of philosophy as a happiness archive is not to say that happiness can simply be found in philosophy or that happiness exhausts the project of philosophy, as its only horizon of thought. And it is not to say that all philosophy rests on the conviction that happiness is necessarily good. We can find philosophers who challenge this conviction; a countertradition has much to teach us about happiness, whether in the dark pessimism of writers such as Alfred Schopenhauer or in the claims that we should be morally indifferent to happiness that we find in the formalist ethics of Immanuel Kant. Other philosophers write themselves as being against specific traditions of happiness — for instance, utilitarianism — by placing their hope not in unhappiness, or indifference to happiness, but in other ways of thinking about happiness. One can think of Nietzsche's affirmation of the happiness of the over-man, which he opposes to the happiness of serfs in such terms. And if we think of Freudian and Lacanian psychoanalysis as philosophy, or if we read their psychoanalysis as offering a psychoanalysis of the happiness of the philosopher-subject, then we learn so much about the emptiness of the promise of happiness, as an emptiness that haunts the subject in the very restlessness of its desire.[21]

To read for the habits of happiness thus involves reading philosophy. How do I read philosophy? We could contrast my method with Darrin M. McMahon's *Happiness: A History*, a book that gives us so many threads to unravel. He begins with the question "How to write a history of something so elusive, so intangible—of this 'thing' that is not a thing, this hope, this yearning, this dream?" (2006: xi). This is a good question with which to begin. We can also ask: what does it mean to think of happiness as having a history? How or why would we write such a history? Who or what would belong in this history? McMahon's history of happiness is premised on the belief that thinking about happiness means thinking about how different ideas of happiness have been conceptualized over time. He calls his history of happiness an "intellectual history" (xiv).

It is useful to note that Darrin McMahon describes himself as being for "methodological pluralism" (xv), suggesting that his history is one history of happiness that should exist alongside others: "there are infinite histories of happiness to be written" (xiii). He implies that such histories would be told from more specific viewing points as "histories not only of the struggles and pursuits of the peasants, slaves, and apostates mentioned by Freud—but of early-modern women and late-modern aristocrats, nineteenth-century bourgeois and twentieth century-workers, conservatives and radicals, consumers and crusaders, immigrants and natives, gentiles and Jews" (xiii). Different histories, we might imagine, unfold from the struggles of such groups.

The Promise of Happiness does not supplement McMahon's history with a history told from a specific viewing point, as a particular history within a general history. I want to think about how the intellectual history of happiness—as a history of an idea—can be challenged by considering what gets erased if we take a general viewing point, where to see what is erased would change the view you see from this point. In other words, this general history of happiness could itself be considered rather particular. Just note how women appear or don't appear in McMahon's intellectual history. In the index, we have one reference to women, which turns out to be a reference to John Stuart Mill's *The Subjection of Women*. Even the category of "women" refers us back to a male genealogy, to philosophy as white male European inheritance. Treating happiness as an intellectual history amounts to becoming indifferent to how differences matter within that history, troubling the very form of its coherence.

Unhappiness remains the unthought in much philosophical literature, as well as in happiness studies.[22] Its neglect can partly be explained by the assumed transparency of the "un": the presumption that unhappiness is simply not, not happy, defined only by the lack of happiness, as the absence of its presence. I aim to give a history to unhappiness.[23] The history of the word *unhappy* might teach us about the unhappiness of the history of happiness. In its earliest uses, unhappy meant "causing misfortune or trouble." Only later, did it come to mean "miserable in lot or circumstances" or "wretched in mind." The word *wretched* also has a suggestive genealogy, coming from *wretch*, referring to a stranger, exile, or banished person. The wretch is not only the one driven out of his or her native country but is also defined as one who is "sunk in deep distress, sorrow, misfortune, or poverty," "a miserable, unhappy, or unfortunate person," "a poor or hapless being," and even "a vile, sorry, or despicable person."[24] Can we rewrite the history of happiness from the point of view of the wretch? If we listen to those who are cast as wretched, perhaps their wretchedness would no longer belong to them. The sorrow of the stranger might give us a different angle on happiness not because it teaches us what it is like or must be like to be a stranger, but because it might estrange us from the very happiness of the familiar.

I thus offer an alternative history of happiness not simply by offering different readings of its intellectual history but by considering those who are banished from it, or who enter this history only as troublemakers, dissenters, killers of joy. In the first chapter of the book, I draw on the intellectual history of happiness as a resource to consider how happiness is attributed to objects. My aim is not to offer an account of different philosophies of happiness but to develop my own approach to how happiness makes some things and not others seem promising. What I call "unhappy archives" emerge from feminist (chapter 2), queer (chapter 3), and antiracist histories (chapter 4), as well as in socialist and revolutionary modes of political engagement (chapter 5). The first three of these chapters take the negativity of a political figure as their organizing trope: the feminist killjoy, unhappy queer, and melancholic migrant. These figures have their own political histories, which are unfinished, leaky, and shared. The figure of the angry black woman, for instance, must appear and does appear in the chapters on feminist killjoys and melancholic migrants. There are risks in organizing a book around figures, as if the intelligibility of the figure preserves the coherence of a history. Chapter 5 is framed differently, taking "the future" as its opening question, and considers the significance of what I call "happiness dystopias" for the imagining of alternative futures. I could have taken the figure of the "raging revolutionary" as my title, but didn't. That figure seems to gather too much, thus saying too little.

I call the archives that I draw on in these chapters "unhappy archives." It is not simply a question of finding unhappiness in such archives. Rather, these archives take shape through the circulation of cultural objects that articulate unhappiness with the history of happiness. An unhappy archive is one assembled around the struggle against happiness. We have inherited already so much from authors who have challenged the very appeal of happiness—and yet these authors are never or rarely cited by the literatures of happiness. These archives do not simply supplement philosophy and its happiness archive. They challenge it. My aim is to follow the weave of unhappiness, as a kind of unraveling of happiness, and the threads of its appeal.

Of course, I still had to find my objects, make choices, include some things, and exclude others. I have thus assembled my own archives out of the unhappy archives we have inherited. In the chapter on feminist killjoys, almost all the books I cite I first encountered in women's writing courses in the late 1980s—books that stayed with me, in part as they showed so powerfully the sadness implicit in becoming conscious of gender as loss. Others texts I read more recently and had been moved by them, noticing how happiness and unhappiness were doing things. *The Well of Loneliness* is such an example, a book I engaged with in *Queer Phenomenology*, commenting then on its thematization of heterosexuality as unthinking happiness (2006: 105). Still other books were books I happened to be reading at the time of writing this book, which gave me a new angle on what I was thinking. Andrea Levy's work is one example of such a happening (I was so struck by how well she describes the jolting experience of becoming conscious of racism), and Nancy Garden's *Annie on My Mind* is another, with its demonstration of how parents express a fear of unhappiness in response to the queer child. Uncannily (or so it felt at the time), I was reading that book on the plane to Vancouver in 2006 to deliver my first paper drawn from my happiness research. Some of my experiences as a reader and viewer shaped my desire to write about happiness—seeing *Bend It Like Beckham* at the cinema in 2002 was one of the experiences that made me want to write about happiness (it was the happy image of reconciliation the film offers in its ending that captured my interest).

Other examples I found through talking to people in formal events such as seminars and conferences, as well as informally. Someone suggested I read *Our Sister Killjoy* after I gave a talk at Kent University. In chapter 5, I discuss *The Joy Makers*: I was lucky enough to be given the book by the author, James Gunn, who was in the audience when I gave a paper on happiness at Kansas University in 2007. Reading *The Joy Makers* led me to reread *Brave New World* and to consider its political demand for "the right to be unhappy." The generosity of strangers is behind so many of these arrivals. Of course, I cannot give you the story of the arrival of every object. But it matters, how we assemble things, how we put things together. Our archives are assembled out of encounters, taking form as a memory trace of where we have been.

Every writer is first a reader, and what we read matters. I think of myself primarily as a reader of feminist, queer, and antiracist books — these books form the intellectual and political horizon of this book. I would describe these books as my philosophy books in the sense that they are the books that have helped me to think about how happiness participates in the creation of social form. But my archive does not just include books or films. If you follow the word *happiness* you end up everywhere! So my archive is also my world, my life-world, my past as well as present, where the word *happiness* has echoed so powerfully.

One of the speech acts that always fascinated me is "I just want you to be happy," which I remember being said to me an awful lot when I was growing up. Writing this book has given me a chance to wonder more about what it means to express "just want" for the happiness of another. But this is just one kind of happiness speech act. There are many! Others you will encounter in this book include "I'm happy if you are happy," "I cannot bear you to be unhappy," "I want to make you happy," "I want to see you being happy," and "I want to be the cause of the happiness that is inside you." How often we speak of happiness! If my task is to follow the words, then I aim to describe what kind of world takes shape when it is given that the happiness of which we speak is good.

The question "what does happiness do?" is inseparable from the question of how happiness and unhappiness are distributed over time and in space. To track the history of happiness is to track the history of its distribution. Happiness gets distributed in all sorts of complicated ways. Certainly to be a good subject is to be perceived as a happiness-cause, as making others happy. To be bad is thus to be a killjoy. This book is an attempt to give the killjoy back her voice and to speak from recognition of how it feels to inhabit that place. I thus draw on my own experiences of being called a killjoy in describing the sociability of happiness. So many of the discussions I have had about this research have involved "swapping killjoy stories." I remember one time at a conference table when we were discussing being killjoys at the family table. The conference was organized by the Australian Critical Race and Whiteness Studies Association in 2007, and it was the first time I had been to a conference in Australia as a person of color from Australia where I felt at home. I now think of spaces created by such conferences as providing new kinds of tables, perhaps tables that give support to those who are unseated by the tables of happiness.

I know that I risk overemphasizing the problems with happiness by presenting happiness as a problem. It is a risk I am willing to take. If this book kills joy, then it does what it says we should do. To kill joy, as many of the texts I cite in the following pages teach us, is to open a life, to make room for life, to make room for possibility, for chance. My aim in this book is to make room.

CHAPTER ONE

Happy Objects

I MIGHT SAY "YOU MAKE ME HAPPY." Or I might be moved by something in such a way that when I think of happiness I think of that thing. Even if happiness is imagined as a feeling state, or a form of consciousness that evaluates a life situation we have achieved over time (Veenhoven 1984: 22–23), happiness also turns us toward objects. We turn toward objects at the very point of "making." To be "made happy" by this or that is to recognize that happiness starts from somewhere other than the subject who may use the word to describe a situation.

In this chapter, I want to think about how objects become happy, as if happiness is what follows proximity to an object. Happiness involves affect (to be happy is to be affected by something), intentionality (to be happy is to be happy about something), and evaluation or judgment (to be happy about something makes something good). If happiness creates its objects, then such objects are passed around, accumulating positive affective value as social goods.[1] In particular, this chapter will consider the family as a happy object, as being what good feelings are directed toward, as well as providing a shared horizon of experience.

Affect, Objects, Intentionality

I do not begin by assuming there is something called happiness that stands apart or has autonomy, as if it corresponds to an object in the world. I begin instead with the messiness of the experiential, the unfolding of bodies into worlds, and what I call "the drama of contingency," how we are touched by what comes near. It is useful to note that the etymology of happiness relates precisely to the question of contingency: it is from the Middle English word *hap* suggesting chance. The word *happy* originally meant having "good 'hap' or fortune," to be lucky or fortunate. This meaning may now seem archaic: we may be used to thinking of happiness as an effect of what you do, as a reward for hard work, rather than being "simply" what happens to you. Thus Mihály Csíkszentmihályi argues that "happiness is not something that happens. It is not the result of good fortune or random choice. It is not something that money can buy or power command. It does not depend on outside events, but, rather on how we interpret them. Happiness, in fact, is a condition that must be prepared for, cultivated and defended privately by each person" (1992: 2). Such a way of understanding happiness could be read as a defense against its contingency. I want to return to the original meaning of happiness as it refocuses our attention on the "worldly" question of happenings.

What is the relation between the "what" in "what happens" and what makes us happy? Empiricism provides us with a useful way of addressing this question, given its concern with "what's what." Take the work of the seventeenth-century empiricist philosopher John Locke. He argues that what is good is what is "*apt to cause or increase pleasure, or diminish pain in us*" ([1690] 1997: 216). We judge something to be good or bad according to how it affects us, whether it gives us a pleasure or pain. Locke uses the example of a man who loves grapes. Locke suggests that "when a man declares in autumn, when he is eating them, or in spring, when there are none, that he *loves* grapes, it is no more, but that the taste of grapes delights him" (216). When something causes pleasure or delight, it is good for us. For Locke, happiness is a form of pleasure: "the greatest happiness consists in the having those things which produce the greatest pleasure" (247). Happy objects could be described simply as those objects that affect us in the best way.

Happiness thus puts us into intimate contact with things. We can be happily affected in the present of an encounter; you are affected positively by something, even if that something does not present itself as an object of consciousness. To be happily affected can survive the coming and going of objects. Locke is after all describing the "seasonal" nature of enjoyment. When grapes are out of season, you might recall that you find them delightful; you might look forward to when they will be in season, which means that grapes would sustain their place as a happy object in the event of their absence. However, this does not mean that the objects one recalls as being happy always stay in place. Locke observes, "Let an alteration of health or constitution destroy the delight of their taste, and then he can be said to *love* grapes no longer" (216–17). Bodily transformations might also transform what is experienced as delightful. If our bodies change over time, then the world around us will create different impressions.

It is not that good things cause pleasure, but that the experience of pleasure is how some things becomes good for us over time.[2] Locke's argument here is consistent with the models of passion in Descartes and affect in Spinoza: despite key differences in how they theorize the mind-body relationship, these philosophers all show us how objects acquire value through contact with bodies. For Spinoza, "We call a thing good which contributes to the preservation of our being, and we call a thing evil if it is an obstacle to the preservation of our being: that is to say, a thing is called by us good or evil as it increases or diminishes, helps or restrains, our power of action" ([1677] 2001: 170). If an object affects us in a good way with joy, then it is good for us.[3] Descartes argues that objects do not excite diverse passions because they are diverse but because of the diverse ways they may harm and help us ([1649] 1989: 51). Whether something harms or helps us is matter of how we are affected by it. As Susan James suggests, "The evaluations of good and harm contained in passions directed to objects outside the mind are therefore not in the world, waiting to be read" (1997: 103).

To be affected by something is to evaluate that thing. Evaluations are expressed in how bodies turn toward things. A phenomenology of happiness might explore how we attend to those things we find delightful.[4] As Edmund Husserl describes in the second volume of *Ideas*, "Within the joy we are 'intentionally' (with feeling intensions) turned toward the joy-Object as such in

've 'interest'" ([1950] 1989: 14). Some things, you might say,
.ition. To give value to things is to shape what is near us, gener-
.usserl might call "our near sphere" or "core sphere" ([1946] 2002:
.s a sphere of practical action. This sphere is "a sphere of things that I
.each with my kinestheses and which I can experience in an optimal form
.rough touching, seeing etc." (149).

Happiness might play a crucial role in shaping our near sphere, the world that takes shape around us, as a world of familiar things. Objects that give us pleasure take up residence within our bodily horizon. We come to have our likes, which might even establish *what we are like*. The bodily horizon could be redescribed as a horizon of likes. To have "our likes" means certain things are gathered around us. Of course, we do encounter new things. To be more or less open to new things is to be more or less open to the incorporation of things into our near sphere. Incorporation may be conditional on liking what we en- counter. Those things we do not like we move away from. Awayness might help establish the edges of our horizon; in rejecting the proximity of certain objects, we define the places that we know we do not wish to go, the things we do not wish to have, touch, taste, hear, feel, see, those things we do not want to keep within reach.

To be affected "in a good way" thus involves an orientation toward something as being good. Orientations register the proximity of objects, as well as shape what is proximate to the body. Happiness can be described as *intentional* in the phenomenological sense (directed toward objects), as well as being *affective* (having contact with objects). To bring these arguments together, we might say that happiness is an orientation toward the objects we come into contact with. We move toward and away from objects through how we are affected by them. After all, note the doubling of positive affect in Locke's example: we *love* the grapes, if they taste *delightful*. To say we love what tastes delightful is not to say that delight causes our love but that the experience of delight involves a loving orientation toward the object, just as the experience of love registers what is delightful.

To describe happiness as intentional does not mean there is always a simple correspondence between objects and feelings. Robin Barrow is right to argue that happiness does not "have an object" the way that some other emotions do (1980: 89; see also Perry 1967: 71). Let's stay with Locke's example of the man who loves grapes. Grapes acquire meaning for us, as something we can consume, grapes can be tasted and "have" a taste, even though we cannot know whether my grape taste is the same as yours. The pleasure evoked by the grapes is the pleasure of eating the grapes. But pleasures are not only directed toward objects that can be tasted, that come into a sensuous proximity with the flesh of the body, as a meeting of flesh. As I have already suggested, we can recall the pleasure of grapes as a memory; we can simply think about the grapes, as a thought that is also a feeling, even when we do not have the possibility of eating the grapes. We can just recall pleasure to experience pleasure, even if these pleasures do not involve exactly the same sensation, even if the impressions of memory are not quite as lively.[5] Pleasure creates an object, even when the object of pleasure appears before us. The creativity of feeling does not require the absence of an object.

We are moved by things. In being moved, we make things. An object can be affective by virtue of its own location (the object might be *here*, which is *where* I experience this or that affect) and the timing of its appearance (the object might be *now*, which is *when* I experience this or that affect). To experience an object as being affective or sensational is to be directed not only toward an object but to what is around that object, which includes what is behind the object, the conditions of its arrival. What is around an object can become happy: if one receives something delightful in a certain place, then the place itself is invested with happiness, as being "what" good feeling is directed toward. Or if you are given something by someone whom you love, then the object itself acquires more affective value: seeing it makes you think of the other who gave you the gift. If something is close to a happy object, then it can become happy by association.

Happiness can generate objects through proximity. Happiness is not simply about objects, or directed toward objects that are given to consciousness. We have probably all experienced what I would call "unattributed happiness." You feel happy, not quite knowing why, and the feeling can be catchy, as a kind of brimming over that exceeds what you encounter. It is not that the feeling floats freely; in feeling happy, you direct the feeling to what is close by, smiling, for instance, at a person who passes you by.[6] The feeling can also lift or elevate a proximate object, making it happy, which is not to say that the feeling will survive an encounter with anything. It has always interested me that when we become conscious of feeling happy (when the feeling becomes an object of thought), happiness can often recede or become anxious. Happiness can arrive in a moment and be lost by virtue of its recognition.[7] Happiness as a feeling appears very precarious, easily displaced not only by other feelings but even by happiness itself, by the how of its arrival.

I suggest that happiness involves a specific kind of intentionality, which I would describe as "end oriented." It is not just that we can be happy *about* something, as a feeling in the present, but some things become happy *for us*, if we imagine they will bring happiness *to us*. Happiness is often described as "what" we aim for, as an endpoint, or even an end-in-itself. Classically, happiness has been considered as an ends rather than as a means.[8] In *Nicomachean Ethics*, Aristotle describes happiness as the Chief Good, as "that which all things aim at" (1998: 1). Happiness is what we "choose always for its own sake" (8). Anthony Kenny describes how, for Aristotle, happiness "is not just an end, but a perfect end" (1993: 16). The perfect end is the end of all ends, the good that is good always for its own sake.

We don't have to agree with the argument that happiness is the perfect end to understand the implications of what it means for happiness to be thought in these terms. If happiness is the end of all ends, then other things (including other goods) become means to happiness.[9] As Aristotle describes, we choose other things "with a view to happiness, conceiving that through their instrumentality we shall be happy" (8). Aristotle is not referring here to material things or physical objects but is differentiating between different kinds of goods, between instrumental goods and independent goods (6). So honor, pleasure, or intellect we choose "with a view to happiness" as being instrumental to happiness, and the realization of the possibility of living a good or virtuous life.

If we think of instrumental goods as objects of happiness, important consequences follow.[10] Things become good, or acquire their value as goods, insofar as they point toward happiness. Objects become "happiness means." Or we could say they become happiness pointers, as if to follow their point would be to find happiness. If objects provide a means for making us happy, then in directing ourselves toward this or that object, we are aiming somewhere else: toward a happiness that is presumed to follow. The temporality of this following does matter. Happiness is what would come after. Given this, happiness is directed toward certain objects, which point toward that which is not yet present. When we follow things, we aim for happiness, as if happiness is what you get if you reach certain points.

Promises

The biography of a person is intimately bound up with objects. We could say that our biographies are biographies of likes and dislikes. Locke argues that human diversity means that our "*happiness* was placed in different things" ([1690] 1997: 246). Freedom becomes the freedom to be made happy by different things.[11] If we are made happy by different things, then we are affected by different things differently.

Are we simply made happy by different things? To think of happiness as involving an end-oriented intentionality is to suggest that happiness is already associated with some things more than others. We arrive at some things *because* they point us toward happiness, as a means to this end. How do we know what points happily? The very possibility of being pointed toward happiness suggests that objects are associated with affects before they are even encountered. An object can point toward happiness without necessarily having affected us in a good way.

It is possible that the evocation of an object can be pleasurable even if we have not yet experienced an object as pleasing: this is the power after all of the human imagination as well as the social world to bestow things that have yet to be encountered with an affective life. Things might have an affective life as a result of being given or bestowed with affect, as gifts that may have been forgotten. An object might even be given insofar as it is assumed to have an affective quality, for example, as if to give somebody x is to give them happiness.

We might assume that the relationship between an object and feeling involves causality: as if the object causes the feeling. A happy object would be one that causes our happiness. In *The Will to Power*, Nietzsche suggests that the attribution of causality is retrospective ([1901] 1968: 294–95).[12] I might assume, then, that the experience of pain is caused by the nail that is lying near my foot. But I only notice the nail given that I experience an affect. The object of feeling lags behind the feeling. The lag is not simply temporal but involves active forms of mediation. We search for the object: or as Nietzsche describes "a reason is sought in persons, experiences, etc. for why one feels this way or that" (354). The very tendency to attribute an affect to an object depends upon "closeness of association" where such forms of closeness are already given. We apprehend an object as the cause of an affect (the nail becomes known as a pain-cause, which is not the only way we might apprehend the nail). The proximity of an encounter might be what survives an encounter. In other words, the proximity between an affect and object is preserved through habit.

We can loosen the bond between the object and the affect by recognizing the form of their bond. The object is not simply what causes the feeling, even if we attribute the object as its cause. The object is understood retrospectively as the cause of the feeling. Having understood it in this way, I can just apprehend the nail and I will experience a pain affect, given that the association between the object and the affect has been given. The object becomes a feeling-cause. Once an object is a feeling-cause, it can cause feeling, so that when we feel the feeling we expect to feel, we are affirmed.[13] The retrospective causality of affect that Nietzsche describes quickly converts into what we could call an *anticipatory causality*. We can even anticipate an affect without being retrospective insofar as objects might acquire the value of proximities that are not derived from our own experience. For example, with fear-causes, a child might be told not to go near an object in advance of its arrival. Some things more than others are encountered as "to-be-feared" in the event of proximity, which is exactly how we can understood the anticipatory logic of the discourse of stranger danger (see Ahmed 2000).

We can also anticipate that an object will cause happiness in advance of its arrival; the object enters our near sphere with a positive affective value already in place. The proximity between an object and feeling coheres in how that object is given. Objects can become "happiness-causes" before we even encounter them.[14] We are directed toward objects that are already anticipated to cause happiness. In other words, the judgment that some things are good not only precedes our encounter with things but directs us toward those things.

So rather than say that what is good is what is apt to cause pleasure, we could say that what is apt to cause pleasure is already judged to be good. This argument is different from Locke's account of loving grapes because they taste delightful: I am suggesting that the judgment about certain objects as being "happy" is already made, before they are even encountered. Certain objects are attributed as the cause of happiness, which means they already circulate as social goods before we "happen" upon them, which is why we might happen upon them in the first place.

We anticipate that happiness will follow proximity to this or that object. Anticipations of what an object gives us are also expectations of what we should be given. How is it that we come to expect so much? After all, expectations can make things seem disappointing. If we arrive at objects with an expectation of how we will be affected by them, this affects how they affect us, even in the moment they fail to live up to our expectations. Happiness is an expectation of what follows, where the expectation differentiates between things, whether or not they exist as objects in the present. For example, the child might be asked to imagine happiness by imagining certain events in the future, such as the wedding day, the "happiest day of your life."

The very expectation of happiness gives us a specific image of the future. This is why happiness provides the emotional setting for disappointment, even if happiness is not given: we just have to expect happiness from "this or that" for "this and that" to be experienceable as objects of disappointment. Our expectations come from somewhere. To think the genealogy of expectation is to think about promises and how they point us somewhere, which is "the where" from which we expect so much. We could say that happiness is promised through proximity to certain objects. Objects would refer not only to physical or material things but also to anything that we imagine might lead us to happiness, including objects in the sense of values, practice, styles, as well as aspirations. Doing x as well as having x might be what promises us happiness. The promise of happiness takes this form: if you have this or have that, or if you do this or do that, then happiness is what follows. In *Twilight of the Idols*, Nietzsche interprets what I am calling the promise of happiness as the basic formula of religion and morality: "Do this and this, refrain from this and this — and you will be happy!" ([1889] 1990: 58).

The promising nature of happiness suggests happiness lies ahead of us, at least if we do the right thing.[15] To promise after all is to make the future into an object, into something that can be declared in advance of its arrival. Hannah Arendt describes how: "Promises are the uniquely human way of ordering the future, making it predictable and reliable to the extent that this is humanly possible" (1972: 92). Think of the promise as a situation, and of what do we think. We think of a promise made by someone to someone that might take the form "I promise to." A promise can be a declaration of will, that the person who promises will do something or not do something. The promise is an assurance, a positive declaration intended to give confidence and trust that an expectation will be met. John Austin in *How to Do Things with Words* describes speech acts that successfully bring about an action as happy performatives. For the promise to be happy would require good intentions: the one who prom- ises must intend to keep the promise, such that the structure of intent is the condition of possibility for the promise to promise ([1962] 1975: 40).[16] For a promise to be happy might also depend upon certain conditions being in place that would allow the person to keep it. A promise can be happy in a situation in which what we will happens, where what we will is willed for another, even when that other is my own self conceived as the recipient of my promise. The promise is also an expression of desire; for something to be promising is an indication of something favorable to come. So in receiving what you have been promised, something good has happened to you, where the happening fulfils an expectation of what should have come to you given that the promise has been promised. Promises ground our expectations of what is to come.

This imagined situation does not exhaust the lived horizon of the promise. In other words, promising is not always a speech act, or something someone gives to someone. The speech act "I promise you" slides into "the promise of," where the promise is an impression of something, as being what would be given by being given that thing. The promising thing (which is an idea of something as being promising) might be proximate to the loved other who says, "I promise to" or "I promise you that." So if someone I love promises me something, that thing can embody the promise of love. The slide between the "I promise to" and "the promise of" is how promises are distributed, or shared. The promise of happiness is what makes some things promising, as if to share in things is to share in happiness. When something promises happiness, we have an idea of that thing as being promising. In receiving that something, we imagine the good things that will follow.

Or we could say that if we desire happiness, then we follow its promise. Lauren Berlant suggests thinking of objects as a "cluster of promises" is an- other way of thinking about the object of desire (2008a: 33). Do objects clus- ter around the promise of happiness? We desire x because x is desirable. The desirability of x is that it promises us happiness. Importantly, desire is already double. We desire x, and we desire x because we desire y, where y is happiness. Even if we desire different things we would have in common the desire for happiness: as John Locke describes, "Though all men's desires tend to happi- ness, yet they are not moved by the same object" ([1690] 1997: 247). Happi- ness as a word thus gathers different objects together. Happiness becomes a container for the diversity of such objects. We could speculate that happiness by giving permission to want in diverse ways also contains diversity within specific forms. Happiness by providing a container in which we can deposit our wants might also contain those wants.

If happiness is what we desire, then happiness involves being intimate with what is not happy, or simply with what is not. This is why for Locke the causation of delight (the happy object) is no simple matter. If happiness is what we desire, then happiness involves what Locke calls uneasiness. We experience uneasiness in "the absence of anything, whose present enjoyment carries the idea of delight" (217). His argument is not simply that happiness makes us uneasy. He suggests that something does not become good for us "until our desire . . . makes us uneasy in the want of it" (234). Given this, for Locke, uneasiness is what drives human action: it is what accounts for the push and pull of human feeling. So even though Locke argues that happiness is what we want or aim for, as the end point of human action, he actually suggests that uneasiness is more compelling: "a little burning felt pushes us more powerfully than greater pleasures in prospect draw or allure" (234).[17]

Psychoanalysis of course has taught us about this intimacy between desire and anxiety; the orientation toward the good becomes a form of pressure in a world in which the good cannot exhaust the realm of possibility. Freud argued in *Civilization and its Discontents* that happiness "is quite incapable of being realized; all the institutions of the universe are opposed to it" ([1930] 2004: 16). However we understand this opposition to happiness, we could say the contingency of happiness is also what makes it difficult to achieve. Happiness cannot eliminate the hap of what happens. Happiness means living with the contingency of this world, even when we aim to make happiness necessary.

Desire is both what promises us something, what gives us energy, and also what is lacking, even in the very moment of its apparent realization.[18] There can be nothing more terrifying than getting what you want, because it is at this moment that you face what you want. For Slavoj Žižek this terror would be because you don't "really" want what you want; he argues that happiness is "inherently hypocritical" or a form of self-deception (2002: 60). I would say that getting what you want can be terrifying because what you want is not simply "ready" as an object; this lack of readiness is what makes the desired object so desirable. Not getting what you want allows you to preserve the happiness of "the what" as fantasy, as if once we are ready, we can have it.

The obstacle to desire hence performs a psychic function in preserving the fantasy that getting what you want would make you happy. Lacan's analysis of courtly love demonstrates the fantasy-preserving character of obstacles. As he describes it, courtly love "is an altogether refined way of making up for the absence of sexual relation by pretending that it is we who put up an obstacle to it" (1982: 141). Courtly love puts an obstacle in place of love, which preserves the fantasy that we would have love if only the obstacle did not get in the way. Likewise, the very obstacle to happiness is what allows happiness to be sustained as the promise of the good life: as if happiness is what we would have, if that thing did not get in the way. The obstacle could be redescribed as the unhappy object; by being the thing that gets in the way, we imagine happiness as being what will happen "on the way." The obstacle can also be a missing thing. As Jonathan Lear suggests, "People tend to fantasise that if they just had this missing thing, it would make them happy" (2000: 23), such that "happiness is that—*whatever it is*—which makes life desirable and lacking in nothing" (27; emphasis added).

Indeed, the very promise of happiness may acquire its force by not being given by the objects that are attributed as happiness-causes.[19] The happy object circulates even in the absence of happiness by filling a certain gap; we anticipate that the happy object will cause happiness, such that it becomes a prop that sustains the fantasy that happiness is what would follow if only we could have "it." The happy object, in other words, is a gap-filler. The promise of the object is always in this specific sense ahead of us; to follow happiness is often narrated as following a path (it is no accident that we speak of "the path of happiness"), such that if we follow the path we imagine we will reach its point.

Happiness becomes a question of following rather than finding. If the pursuit of happiness is augmented as a constitutional right, then happiness becomes "whatever" is pursued and hence achieves its affectivity by not being given or found. The promise of happiness is the promise that the lines we follow will get us there, where the "there" acquires its value by not being "here." This is why happiness is crucial to the energy or "forward direction" of narrative.[20] Happiness may be preserved as a social promise only through its postponement: so we imagine that the happiness we were promised will eventually come to us, or to those who follow us. Happiness is what makes waiting for something both endurable and desirable—the longer you wait, the more you are promised in return, the greater your expectation of a return.

A happy object accumulates positive value even in situations of unhappiness: we can live with disappointment by imagining the promise of happiness will be given to those who follow us.[21] Parents can live with the failure of happiness to deliver its promise by placing their hope for happiness in their children. Happiness can involve a gesture of deferral, as a deferral that is imagined simultaneously as a sacrifice and gift: for some, the happiness that is given up becomes what they give. To be given happiness is thus to stay proximate to the scene of giving up.

Good Habits

Objects not only embody good feeling; they come to embody the good life. How is the good life imagined through the proximity of objects? Locke evokes good feeling through the sensation of taste. As he describes: "For as pleasant tastes depend not on the things themselves, but their agreeability to this or that palate, wherein there is great variety; so the greatest happiness consists in the having those things which produce the greatest pleasure" ([1690] 1997: 247). Locke locates difference in the mouth. We have different tastes insofar as we have different palates.

We can see here that the apparent chanciness of happiness—the hap of what happens—can be qualified.[22] It is not that we just find happy objects anywhere. After all, taste is not simply a matter of chance (whether you or I might happen to like this or that) but is acquired over time. As Pierre Bourdieu showed in his monumental *Distinction*, taste is a very specific bodily orientation that is shaped by what is already decided to be good or a higher good. Taste or "manifested preferences" are "the practical affirmation of an inevitable difference" such that "aesthetic intolerance can be terribly violent. Aversion to different lifestyles is perhaps one of the strongest barriers between the classes" ([1979] 1986: 56).

So we learn to differentiate between higher and lower objects by learning to discern what tastes good and what is disgusting: delight and disgust are social as well as bodily orientations. When people say, "How can you like that!" they make their judgment against another by refusing to like what another likes,

by suggesting that the object in which another invests his or her happiness
is unworthy. This affective differentiation is the basis of an essentially moral
economy in which moral distinctions of worth are also social distinctions of
value, as Beverley Skeggs (2004) has shown us. What "tastes good" to us can
reveal whether we have "good taste."

To become oriented means to be directed toward specific objects that are
already attributed as being tasteful, *as enjoyable to those with good taste*. I have
suggested that the objects we encounter are not neutral: they enter our near
sphere with an affective value already in place, which means they are already
invested with positive and negative value. Bodies also do not arrive in neutral: the acquisition of tendencies is also the acquisition of orientations toward
some things and not others as being good. If we do not simply find happy objects anywhere, we also do not simply inhabit the right kind of body. We acquire habits, as forms of good taste that differentiate between objects in terms
of their affective as well as moral value. We have to work on the body such that
the body's immediate reactions, how we sense the world and make sense of the
world, take us in the "right" direction.

The distinction between good and bad taste, or even the distinction between
having and not having taste, is in part secured through the status of the object.
So to have good taste would be directed toward things that are already attributed as being good. But having good habits is not simply about the kinds of
objects you enjoy; it is also about the nature of your relationship to objects.
Take Bourdieu's critique of Kantian aesthetics. Bourdieu argues that for Kant
simple forms of pleasure are "reduced to a pleasure of the senses" in the "taste
of the tongue, palate and the throat." The lower senses are lower because they
depend on the body, and an object is lower if it "insists on being enjoyed"
([1979] 1986: 489). Pure taste is thus directed in the right way toward things
that allow the subject to be free from any involvement with an object. Pure
taste becomes disinterested. To have good habits is to be oriented in the right
way toward the right objects (not to insist on being proximate to objects that
insist on enjoyment), and which would allow a fantasy of transcendence from
the bodily domain to be sustained. To work on the body such that you have the
right reactions allows the body to disappear from view.

Bourdieu's "vulgar critique" of Kantian aesthetics is to redescribe the aesthetics of pure taste as the "occupational ideology of those who like to call
themselves 'creators'" (491). The aesthetics of pure taste transforms an ide-

ology into a creation. Norbert Elias usefully describes the formation of good habits as "the civilisation of the affects" ([1939] 1969: 166). The civil body acquires its civility by the "restraint of affect-charged impulses" (210). Civilized happiness belongs to the bourgeoisie whose freedom is self-narrated as freedom from impulse or inclination.[23]

Consider the film *Educating Rita* (1983, dir. Lewis Gilbert). This is a film about education as self-transformation. Susan, a working-class girl, becomes Rita (she takes the name from Rita Mae Brown, author of the book *Rubyfruit Jungle*, which I discuss in chapter 3), through a process of being educated in literature. The narrative dramatizes how becoming civil is not simply about learning to read the right books or learning to appreciate the right objects but is about developing a different relationship to those objects. So in the first instance Rita learns by *switching affections*, by learning to appreciate some things, or to appreciate the difference between pulp fiction and literature. But by the end she becomes free from any such affection. She says, "You think you did nothing for me. You think I ended up with a whole lot of quotes and empty phrases. Well, all right. I did. But that wasn't your doing. I was too hungry for it all. I didn't question anything. I wanted it all too much so I wouldn't let it be questioned. Told you I was stupid." Her hunger for knowledge about x becomes symptomatic of her failure to transcend the working-class habitus that makes becoming educated desirable in the first place.

For Rita to become educated requires that she become free from hunger for things, from insistence on and in enjoyment. Having become free, Rita can now choose, with the capacity for choice being organized through tropes of indifference: "I might go to France. I might go to London. I might just stay here and carry on with my studies. I might even stay here and have a baby. I don't know. I will make a decision. I will choose." Becoming civil converts the language of "must" to the language of "might" and eventually to the language of will and choice. We end up with a fantasy of a moral and middle-class subject as the one who is without habit, who will and can choose insofar as they are imagined as free from inclination.

Happiness becomes a moral injunction, as a will to will, through the disappearance of its habit. A good habit appears and thus disappears as freedom. Or we could say that freedom becomes a habit. In thinking of the habits of happiness it is useful to note how Locke withdraws from the relativist implications of his model of the diversity of happy object choices. He suggests that while we are free to find happiness in our own way, the paths of happiness will take us toward a higher good: "for that being intended for a state of happiness, it must certainly be agreeable to everyone's wish and desire: could we supposed their relishes as different there, as they are here, yet the manna in Heaven will suit everyone's palate" (253). So although we might find different things pleasing, we will be directed "in the right way" by happiness, as that which finds its realization in the universal delight of the manna in heaven. Even if happiness can be found in different things, happiness should still take us in the right direction. So for Locke "men may and should correct their palates" (255). The concept of correctible tastes suggests that happiness is about learning to be affected by objects in the right way. The very possibility that we can affect our affections by action, or through will or reason, becomes the basis of an ethical imperative.

It is useful to return to Aristotle given the emphasis he places on habit or habituation in his ethics. As many scholars have pointed out, for Aristotle happiness cannot be reduced to good feeling or what Deal W. Hudson calls "well feeling" (1996: xii): rather, happiness or *eudaimonia* refers to "the good life" or the virtuous life, which is a life-long project or achievement. Aristotle suggests that it is a point of "pretty general agreement" that "living well" and "doing well" are the same as "being happy" (1998: 3). Happiness relies on activities that generate "good character" and hence on what is called habituation, "the result of the repeated doing of acts which have a similar or common quality" (Smith 1998: ix). The good life is the life that is lived in the right way, by doing the right things, over and over again.

However, feelings do have a crucial role in Aristotle's model of habituation. For the good man will not only have the right habits but his feelings will also be directed in the right way: "a man is not a good man at all who feels no pleasure in noble actions; just as no one would call that man just who does not feel pleasure in acting justly" (11–12). To be good one must feel the right way, or as Julia Annas describes in her *Morality and Happiness*, the virtuous agent "will act rightly and will have the right amount of appropriate feeling, where this will be a moderate amount" (1993: 61).[24] The virtuous agent will not only feel pleasure and pain where appropriate, in relation to the right objects, but will also experience the right amount of such feeling, where the right amount is the "mean," which means not too much or too little. Being good becomes then about how one feels feelings: "to feel them when we ought on what occasions, toward whom, and why, and as, we should do, is the mean, or in the other words, the best state, and this is the property of virtue" (Aristotle 1998: 27).[25] Aristotle's portrait of the good man, who has moral character, is hence a portrait of a sentient man whose pleasures are "just right," as we can see in the following description:

> the man of Perfected Self-Mastery is in the mean with respect to these objects: that is to say, he neither takes pleasure in the things which delight the vicious man, and in fact rather dislikes them, nor at all in improper objects; nor to any great degree in any object of the class; nor is he pained at their absence; nor does he desire them; or, if he does, only in moderation, and neither more than he ought, nor at improper times, and so forth; but such things as are conducive to health and good condition of body, being also pleasant, these he will grasp at in moderation and as he ought to do, and also such other pleasant things as do not hinder these objects, and are not unseemly or disproportionate to his means; because he that should grasp at such would be liking such pleasures more than is proper; but the man of Perfected Self-Mastery is not of this character, but regulates his desires by the dictates of right reason. (54)

A happy life, a good life, hence involves the regulation of desire. It is not simply that we desire happiness but that happiness is imagined as what you get in return for desiring well. Good subjects will not experience pleasure from the wrong objects (they will be hurt by them or indifferent to them) and will only experience a certain amount of pleasure from the right objects. We learn to experience some things as pleasure—as being good—where the experience itself becomes the truth of the object ("it is good") as well as the subject ("we are good"). It is not only that the association between objects and affects is preserved through habit; we also acquire good tastes through habit. When history becomes second nature, the affect seems obvious or even literal, as if it follows directly from what has already been given. We assume that we experience delight because "it" is delightful.

The literalism of affect slides into the literalism of the moral economy: we assume something feels good because it is good. We are good if it feels good. In other words, when we are affected in a good way by what is attributed as being good, we become the good ones, the virtuous and happy ones. Happiness allows us to line up with things in the right way. As Jacques Lacan suggests in

Ethics: "Moral experience as such, that is to say, the reference to sanctions, puts man in a certain relation to his own action that concerns not only an articulated law, but also a direction, a trajectory, in a word, a good that he appeals to, thereby engendering an ideal of conduct" ([1986] 1992: 3). Happiness directs you toward the good, while creating the impression that the good is what gives you direction.

Sociable Happiness

If we learn from the promissory nature of happiness, we learn that happiness is about how some things are made into goods, before we happen upon them. To be directed toward such good things is to be directed in the right way. It is important that we share this direction with others. The fan club or hobby group makes explicit what is implicit in social life: *that we tend to like those who like the things we like*. This is why the social bond is always sensational. If the same objects make us happy—or if we invest in the same objects as if they make us happy—then we would be directed or oriented in the same way. To be affected in a good way by objects that are already evaluated as good is a way of belonging to an affective community. We align ourselves with others by investing in the same objects as the cause of happiness.

The role of affect as a shared orientation is clear in classical philosophy. For instance, Socrates in Plato's *Republic* asks, "Isn't it the sharing of feelings of pleasure and distress which binds a community together—when (in so far as it is feasible) the whole citizen body feels more or less the same pleasure or distress at the same gains and losses" (1998: 176). We do not have to assume such feelings are what we have in common. Rather, the social bond is binding insofar as feelings are deposited in the same object, which may then accumulate value as happy or unhappy objects: a group may come together by articulating love for the same things, and hate for the same things, even if that love and hate is not simply felt by all those who identify with the group.

The more happy objects circulate, the more they accumulate affective value, as signs of the good life. But what happens when happy objects circulate? How do happy objects sustain their promise in the absence of happiness being given? Consider that the word *promise* derives from the Latin verb *promittere*, suggesting "to let go or send forth, to put forth" as well as "to promise, guarantee, or predict." The promise of happiness might be what sends happiness forth. When objects are promising, they are sent out or sent forth; *to promise can mean to pass around a promise.*

Is happiness sent forth? Does the promise of happiness mean that happiness is passed around? If we were to say that the promise of happiness means that happiness is sent forth, we might also suggest that happiness is contagious. David Hume's approach to moral emotions rests on a contagious model of happiness.[26] He suggests that "others enter into the same humour, and catch the sentiment, by a contagion or natural sympathy" and that cheerfulness is the most communicative of emotions: "the flame spreads through the whole circle; and the most sullenly and remorse are often caught by it" ([1748] 1975: 250–51; see also Blackman 2008). A number of scholars have recently taken up the idea of affects as contagious, drawing in particular on the work of the psychologist of affect Silvan Tomkins (Gibbs 2001; Brennan 2004; Sedgwick 2003; Probyn 2005). As Anna Gibbs describes: "Bodies can catch feelings as easily as catch fire: affect leaps from one body to another, evoking tenderness, inciting shame, igniting rage, exciting fear—in short, communicable affect can inflame nerves and muscles in a conflagration of every conceivable kind of passion" (2001: 1).

Thinking of affects as contagious does help us to challenge what I have called an "inside out" model of affect (Ahmed 2004: 9), by showing how we are affected by what is around us. However, the concept of affective contagion does tend to treat affect as something that moves smoothly from body to body, sustaining integrity in being passed around. When Sedgwick argues that shame is contagious, for example, she suggests that proximity to someone's shame generates shame (2003: 36–38). The implication of such arguments is that affects are sustained in being passed around: shame creates shame in others, and happiness creates happiness in others, and so on.[27] I wonder whether the concept of affective contagion might underestimate the extent to which affects are contingent (involving the "hap" of a happening): to be affected by another does not mean that an affect simply passes or "leaps" from one body to another. The affect becomes an object *only given the contingency of how we are affected.* We might be affected differently by what gets passed around.

If contagion can be described as a "natural sympathy," to use David Hume's term quoted earlier, then to be sympathetic would be *to return feeling with like feeling.*[28] To be sympathetic would be to *feel like.* If the model of contagion describes the body-to-body process of being affected in terms of the passing of like feeling, then it also generates an idea of social feeling as feeling like. And yet, social feeling does not give feeling a definite content. So what is feeling like actually like?

We can take the example of atmosphere. We might describe an "atmosphere" as a feeling of what is around, which might be affective in its murkiness or fuzziness, as a surrounding influence which does not quite generate its own form. At the same time, in describing an atmosphere, *we give this influence some form*. We might say the atmosphere was tense, which would mean that the body that arrives into the room will "pick up" tension and become tense, as a way of being influenced. When feelings become atmospheric, we can catch the feeling simply by walking into a room, from a crowd or the collective body, or from being proximate to another. Returning to happiness, we would say that to sympathize with another's happiness would be to feel happiness. For happiness to be atmospheric you would be affected happily by walking into a room in which happiness has already been given in return. You would be "lifted up" by inhabiting what has been shared, a sensation of well feeling or good feeling, however murky.

But do we pick up feelings in quite this way? Consider the opening sentence of Teresa Brennan's book *The Transmission of Affect*: "Is there anyone who has not, at least once, walked into a room and 'felt the atmosphere'?" (2004: 1). Brennan writes very beautifully about how the atmosphere "gets into the individual," using what I have called an "outside in" model, also very much part of the intellectual history of crowd psychology and the sociology of emotion (Ahmed 2004: 9). However, later in the introduction she makes an observation that involves a different model.[29] Brennan suggests that "if I feel anxiety when I enter the room, then that will influence what I perceive or receive by way of an 'impression' (a word that means what it says)" (6). I agree. Anxiety is sticky: rather like Velcro, it tends to pick up whatever comes near. Or we could say that anxiety gives us a certain kind of angle on what comes near. Anxiety is, of course, one feeling state among others. If bodies do not arrive in neutral, if we are always in some way or another moody, then what we will receive as an impression will depend on our affective situation. This second argument suggests the atmosphere is not simply "out there" before it gets "in": how we arrive, how we enter this room or that room, will affect what impressions we receive. To receive is to act. To receive an impression is to make an impression.

So we may walk into the room and "feel the atmosphere," but what we may feel depends on the angle of our arrival. Or we might say that the atmosphere is already angled; it is always felt from a specific point. The pedagogic encounter is full of angles. How many times have I read students as interested or bored, such that the atmosphere seemed one of interest or boredom (and even felt myself to be interesting or boring), only to find students recall the event quite differently! Having read the atmosphere in a certain way, one can become tense: which in turn affects what happens, how things move along. The moods we arrive with do affect what happens: which is not to say we always keep our moods. Sometimes I arrive heavy with anxiety, and everything that happens makes me feel more anxious, while at other times things happen which ease the anxiety, making the space itself seem light and energetic. We do not know in advance what will happen given this contingency, given the hap of what happens; we do not know "exactly" what makes things happen in this way and that. Situations are affective given the gap between the impressions we have of others and the impressions we make on others, all of which are lively.

Think too of experiences of alienation. I have suggested that happiness is attributed to certain objects that circulate as social goods. When we feel pleasure from such objects, we are aligned; we are facing the right way. We become alienated—out of line with an affective community—when we do not experience pleasure from proximity to objects that are attributed as being good. The gap between the affective value of an object and how we experience an object can involve a range of affects, which are directed by the modes of explanation we offer to fill this gap.

We might feel disappointed. Disappointment can be experienced as a gap between an ideal and an experience that demands action. We can return to the example of the wedding day: the "happiest day of your life." What does it mean for such a day to be anticipated as being the happiest day when the day is actually happening? We might say that the day happens because of this anticipation of happiness. But however the day happens, when it does happen, happiness must follow. As Arlie Russell Hochschild explores in her classic book *The Managed Heart*, if the bride is not happy on the wedding day and even feels "depressed and upset," then she is experiencing an "inappropriate affect" ([1983] 2003: 59) or is being affected inappropriately.[30] You have to save the day by feeling right: "sensing a gap between the ideal feeling and the actual feeling she tolerated, the bride prompts herself to 'be happy'" (61).

The capacity to "save the day" depends on the bride being able to make herself be affected in the right way or at least being able to persuade others that she is being affected in the right way. When it can be said that "the bride looked happy," then the expectation of happiness has become the happiness of expectation. To correct our feelings is to become disaffected from a former affection: the bride makes herself happy by stopping herself being miserable. Of course we learn from this example that it is possible not to inhabit fully one's own happiness, or even to be alienated from one's happiness, if the former affection remains lively, or if one is made uneasy by the labor of making yourself feel a certain way. Uneasiness might persist in the very feeling of being happy, as a feeling of unease *with* the happiness you are in.

The experience of a gap between the promise of happiness and how you are affected by objects that promise happiness does not always lead to corrections that close this gap. Disappointment can also involve an anxious narrative of self-doubt (why am I not made happy by this, what is wrong with me?), or a narrative of rage, where the object that is supposed to make us happy is attributed as the cause of disappointment. Your rage might be directed against the object that fails to deliver its promise, or it might spill out toward those who promised you happiness through the elevation of some things as good. Anger can fill the gap between the promise of a feeling and the feeling of a feeling. We become strangers, or affect aliens, in such moments.[31]

We can also feel alienated by forms of happiness that we think are inappropriate. Take the example of laughter in the cinema. How many times have I sunk desperately into my chair when that laughter has been expressed at points I find far from amusing! We do not always notice when others sink. One can feel unjustly interpellated in such occasions: the gestures of discomfort and alienation do not register; they do not affect the collective impression made by the laughter. To an outsider, it might simply appear that the audience found the film funny, and that the laughter was contagious, affecting everybody.

The example reminds us that even when "a crowd" is experienced as if it has "a mind of its own," this does not mean that those in the crowd experience the crowd in the same way. Turning to Gustave Le Bon's classic account of crowd psychology, it is interesting that he stresses the importance of direction: "When defining crowds, we said that one of their general characteristics was an excessive suggestibility, and we have shown to what an extent suggestions are contagious in every human agglomeration; a fact which explains the rapid turning of the sentiments of a crowd in a definite direction" ([1895] 2002: 14; see also Blackman and Walkerdine 2001). Note that Le Bon does not suggest here that sentiments simply spread; rather what spreads are "suggestions" that in turn direct sentiments in a certain way. We have already seen how sentiment involves directionality, or a way of being directed. What is striking in this model is the presumption that the crowd both preexists this shared direction (the crowd turns) and is an effect of that direction (the turning of the crowd is how sentiments cohere).

And yet, experiences of being in a crowd do not necessarily mean that we are all directed in the same way. Early work in media studies shows that experiences of being in a crowd often involve a sense of not participating in a shared event, for example, of not being able to "see" whatever is in the direction the crowd faces (Lang and Lang 1969). The crowd may appear with a mind of its own only from the point of view of being outside the crowd, watching "it" in the unfolding of an event or spectacle. Alien bodies who do share the affective direction simply disappear from such a viewing point. We cannot even assume that those who appear directed "in the right way" feel the same way about the direction they are facing.

Good and bad feelings can be generative, even if they do not simply spread. When people feel bad, they can certainly bring other people down. They might complain, worry, and convey anxiety or hurt, or express pessimism about the future. The expressions can be repeated by others, as a form of return, which will affect what impressions we have of that space. Expressing bad feeling can even become habitual in certain times and places, as a way of belonging to an affective community. The use of complaint as a form of social bonding would be a case in point. Good feelings are also affective. A person who is "in a good mood" can bring others up. Smiling, laughing, expressing optimism about what is possible will affect others. It is not that you necessarily catch the feeling but that the experience of being with and around a person in a good mood gives a certain lightness, humor, and energy to shared spaces, which can make those spaces into happy objects, what we direct good feelings toward.

Then again, good feelings do not simply generate good feeling. We can be asked to smile in order to occupy certain spaces as a form of emotion work (Hochschild [1983] 2003). In such cases, happiness becomes a technology of self-production, which can intensify bad feelings by keeping them on hold. Or, if someone feels bad and encounters somebody being cheerful, it can feel like a pressure and can even be painful: as if that person is trying to "jolly you up." Happy moods are precarious, even when they are generative. Sometimes what you encounter cannot extend the good feeling; then you lose the good feeling and you are "brought down." Such moments of loss are quickly converted into anger: you become angry as the object not only hurts but has taken your good feelings away.[32] Happiness is precarious and even perverted because it does not reside within objects or subjects (as a form of positive residence) but is a matter of how things make an impression.

So when happy objects are passed around it is not necessarily the feeling that passes. To share objects, or have a share in objects, might mean simply that you *share an orientation toward those objects as being good*. What passes is the promise of the feeling, which means that feelings lag behind the objects that are assumed to contain them.[33] Objects become saturated with affects as sites of personal and social tension. The passing of happy objects may generate forms of antagonism even when we share an orientation toward those objects as being good.

What passes through the passing of happy objects remains an open and empirical question. After all, passing can be used to convey not only processes of sending over or transmitting but also "the process or fact of changing from one state to another."[34] Like the game Chinese whispers, perhaps what passes between proximate bodies might be affective because it deviates and even perverts what is "sent out."[35] Indeed, returning to Le Bon, if it is suggestion rather than sentiment that spreads, then "what happens" involves "spreading the word." If words mutate as they are passed around—as we know they do in gossip and rumor as well as suggestion—then to spread is to pervert.[36] What interests me is how affects involve perversion and what I would describe as conversion points.

I am not suggesting here that affects simply get converted as they pass around: for instance, in the conversion from good to bad feeling, or from excitement to anxiety, and so on—though such conversions do happen. Rather, I want to suggest that objects become affective as points of conversion. Good and bad feelings accumulate "around" objects, such that those objects become sticky. Objects become ambivalent in the conversion between negative and positive feeling states: "happy objects" can become "unhappy" over time, in the contingency of what happens, which is not to say that their happiness no longer persists as an impression, available as memory.[37] We do not know in advance what forms such affective conversions take. One of my key questions in this book is how such conversions happen, and "who" or "what" gets seen as converting bad feeling into good feeling and good into bad. We can think of narrative as a form of affective conversion. Through narrative, the promise of happiness is located as well as distributed. To make a simple point: some bodies more than others will bear the promise of happiness.

Happy Families

I have suggested that happiness involves a way of being aligned with others, of facing the right way. The points of alignment become points of happiness. The family, for example, is a happy object, one that binds and is binding. We hear the term "happy families" and we register the connection of these words in the familiarity of their affective resonance.[38] Happy families: a card game, a title of a children's book, a government discourse; a promise, a hope, a dream, an aspiration. The happy family is both a myth of happiness, of where and how happiness takes place, and a powerful legislative device, a way of distributing time, energy, and resources. The family is also an inheritance. To inherit the family can be to acquire an orientation toward some things and not others as the cause of happiness. In other words, it is not just that groups cohere around happy objects; we are asked to reproduce what we inherit by being affected in the right way by the right things.

The happy family is both an object (something that affects us, something we are directed toward) and circulates through objects. The family photograph album might be one such object: the picture of the family as happy is one way in which the family is produced as a happy object. That these objects are on display, that they make visible a fantasy of a good life, depends on returning such a direction with a "yes," or even with gestures of love, or witnessing these objects as one's own field of preferred intimacy. To preserve the family you must preserve certain things. Simone de Beauvoir describes how: "The ideal of happiness has always taken material form in the house . . . Within its walls the family is established as a discrete cell or a unit group and maintains its identity as generations come and go; the past, preserved in the form of furniture and ancestral portraits, gives promise of a secure future" ([1949] 1997: 467). The promise of the family is preserved through the inheritance of objects, which allow the family to be assembled.

To inherit the family is to inherit the demand to reproduce its form. The family also becomes a pressure point, as being necessary for a good or happy life, which in turn is how we achieve a certain orientation toward something and not others as good. One novel that most powerfully captures the pressure to reproduce what you inherit is Laurie Colwin's *Family Happiness* ([1982] 1990), a book that can be considered part of an unhappy feminist archive that I discuss more fully in the next chapter. We begin with Polly, a happy housewife, who is also a good daughter and a good mother. In the first instance, Polly feels "fortunate": she has a good husband (Henry), good children (Pete and Dee-Dee), as well as a loving and attentive mother (Wendy) (11). Her family is held together by shared values and by a shared orientation toward family itself: "Polly and Henry were so right for each other, so unified in their feelings about life, family, and children" (13). Marriage here becomes about reproducing the family as a social form: "The kind of marriage Polly knew was based on family, on the creation of family, on keeping family together, on family events, circumstances, occasions, celebrations" (194). The point of the family is to keep family the point.

The family becomes a happy object through the work that must be done to keep it together. Being together means having a place at the table, or we could say it means being occupied in the same way: "Nothing had deviated on the Solo-Miller Sunday breakfast table for so long as anyone can remember. They are in the dining-room with extra leaves in the table" (19). The table is itself a happy object, insofar as it secures the very form of the family over time. The table is what we could call a kinship object (Ahmed 2006: 81), which gives form to the family as a social gathering, as the tangible thing over which the family gathers. The table is happy when it secures this point.

This orientation toward the family is what makes certain objects proximate (tables, photographs, and other objects that secure family intimacy), as the objects through which the family itself become given. This does not mean that to be oriented toward the family means inhabiting the same place. After all, as we know from Locke, pleasures can be idiosyncratic: even if we learn good habits,

people do not like the same things. Those who I am like can find things delightful that I do not like. The word *idiosyncratic* suggests a "peculiarity of constitution or temperament." Families may give one a sense of being "on the same
side" or having "a place at the table" through the conversion of idiosyncratic
difference into a happy object: love "happily" means knowing the peculiarity
of a loved other's likes and dislikes. The creation of small differences can be
binding. In other words, we can achieve a field of preferred intimacy through
becoming intimate with different likes. Love becomes an intimacy with what
the other likes (rather than simply liking what the other likes), and is given on
condition that such likes do not take us outside a shared horizon. Happiness
creates its own horizon.

The family involve knowledge of the peculiar, or the transformation of the
peculiar into habit and ritual. So you make coffee for the family, and you know
"just" how much sugar to put in this cup and that. Failure to know this "just"
is often felt as a failure to care. Even if we do not experience the same objects
as being pleasurable, sharing the family means sharing happy objects, both in
the sense of sharing knowledge of happy objects (of what makes others happy)
and also in the sense of distributing the objects in the right way. In *Family Happiness*, the distribution of happy objects is described as a family ritual: "It was
not necessary to consult menus. Everyone always had the same thing. A plate
of steamed vegetables with green mayonnaise was brought for Andreya; Polly
and Wendy had the salmon; Henry, Jr. the tournedos; and Henry Demarest the
special" (181). The family reproduces itself through this affective distribution
between things.

By living this life, Polly is living the life not only that her parents expected
her to live but a life they have already lived: "she and Henry set about repli-
cating the comfort and success of their parents' lives. Polly had never been so
happy" (65). For Polly, happiness is what follows following her parents' lives.
This following is presented as a duty, as a way of being good: "No one had ever
asked Polly to be excellent, or to do excellent things. Rather, she had been
encouraged in that direction by Wendy [her mother] and now everyone was
used to her" (170). To be encouraging is often thought of as a generous, as a
way of energizing somebody, of enabling them to be capable. To encourage can
be to give courage. But to encourage can also be forceful. Being encouraged
can be a way of being directed toward somebody else's wants. The generosity

of encouragement can hide the force of being directed somewhere. And once you are there, you can get stuck there. I think we know this.

Consider the word *influence*, which can be defined as "the exertion of action of which the operation is unseen or insensible (or perceptible only in its effects), by one person or thing upon another." To be influenced is to be directed in one way or another, where we cannot quite see the point of pressure. With prohibitions, we can usually notice the pressure point, the harshness of being brought up against what you are not. There is no doubt about the power of the "no words," the "don't do that" or "no that's wrong" that might be articulated in anticipation of the deviation of the child's desire (those "just in case" no's that almost want the act of deviation to acquire a sense of retrospective justice) as well as in response to deviation. We can hear that "no" in part as it asks us to stop doing something. It might be harder to hear the "yes words"—the "yes," or the "yes that's good," or the "yes that's a good way to be"—because the words seem to "go along" with or affirm what we are already doing.[39] To think about happiness is to think about the role of affirmation. To affirm can mean to state or assert positively, as well as to establish, confirm, or ratify. To be affirmed is to be given positive encouragement, which might be what confirms a certain order of things or creates order out of things.

We are affirmed by happiness: we go along and get along by doing what we do, and doing it well. Happiness means here living a certain kind of life, one that reaches certain points, and which, in reaching these points, creates happiness for others. The family is after all "where" the child is cultivated, where the child learns the right habits, which, in turn, render some objects as happy for the child. In *Family Happiness*, the children "were being brought up under the old order, which required that parents inspire all manners of good habits in their children" (11). If parenting is about orienting the children in the right way, then children must place their hopes for happiness in the same things. The family becomes a happy object if we share this orientation.

Happiness involves here the comfort of repetition, of following lines that have already been given in advance. For Polly, this path is described as the straight path (199). Happiness involves the labor of staying on the right path. When Polly deviates, the world falls apart: she loses "her place in her marriage, her place in her family, her place in herself" (78). By not being oriented toward the "family table," she becomes disoriented, losing her place in the world. When Polly deviates from the path of making others happy, she disturbs everything; she even causes disturbance. She herself is even disturbed at this point. She becomes an affect alien. The affect alien is the one who converts good feelings into bad, who as it were "kills" the joy of the family.[40] The following three chapters of this book will explore happy families from the point of view of those who are alienated from its promise: feminist killjoys, unhappy queers, and melancholic migrants.

In 1960, the problem that has no name burst like a boil through the image of the happy American housewife. In the television commercials the pretty housewives still beamed over their foaming dishpans . . . But the actual unhappiness of the American housewife was suddenly being reported . . ., although almost everybody who talked about it found some superficial reason to dismiss it.   BETTY FRIEDAN

CHAPTER TWO

Feminist Killjoys

BETTY FRIEDAN IN *The Feminine Mystique* identifies a problem that has no name by evoking what lies behind the image of the happy American housewife (1965: 19–20). What lies behind this image bursts through, like a boil, expos- ing an infection underneath her beaming smile. Friedan proceeds by exposing the limits of this public fantasy of happiness. The happy housewife is a fantasy figure that erases the signs of labor under the sign of happiness. The claim that women are happy and that this happiness is behind the work they do functions to justify gendered forms of labor, not as a product of nature, law, or duty, but as an expression of a collective wish and desire. How better to justify an unequal distribution of labor than to say that such labor makes people happy? How better to secure consent to unpaid or poorly paid labor than to describe such consent as the origin of good feeling?

And yet, who or what do we see in this image of the happy housewife? She is, as Friedan points out, a fantasy. Even as fantasy, however, she evokes the embodied situation of some women more than others. After all, many women at this time were not housewives: for some women to work at home would be an aspiration rather than situation. bell hooks in *Feminist Theory* points to this exclusivity of the happy housewife, even when understood as fantasy:

"When Friedan wrote *The Feminine Mystique*, more than one-third of all women were in the workforce. Although many women longed to be housewives, only women with leisure time and money could actually shape their identities on the model of the feminine mystique" (2000: 2). Friedan's solution to the unhappiness of housewives — that they should be liberated from the house — has consequences for those women who could not shape their identities around the feminine mystique. As hooks points out, "She did not discuss who would be called in to take care of the children and maintain the home if more women like herself were freed from their house labor and given equal access with white men to the professions" (1–2). While the fantasy of the happy housewife conceals the signs of domestic labor under the sign of happiness, the fantasy of the housewife becoming happy through being liberated from the home might also conceal the labor of other women, who might be required to take over "the foaming dishpans."

When we track this figure of the happy housewife, we need to think of what the figure does, and how that figure works to secure not just ideas of happiness but ideas of who is entitled to happiness. White liberal feminists such as Betty Friedan taught us that proximity to the fantasy of the good life does not mean proximity to happiness. Sheila Rowbotham describes how "in the writing of the early years there is a struggle to assert a separate identity and challenge the house as a fantasy of happiness" (1989: 3). Black feminists such as bell hooks teach us that some women — black and working-class women — are not even entitled to be proximate to the fantasy, though they may be instrumental in enabling others to approximate its form. We can consider not so much how happiness as such is distributed (this would forget what was important about the second-wave critique of the unhappiness concealed by the figure of the happy housewife) but the distribution of *relative proximity to ideas of happiness*. Or we might speculate that what is unequally distributed is the feeling that you have what should make you happy, a distribution of the promise of a feeling, or the feeling of a promise, rather than the distribution of happiness, as such.

Have images of happy housewives been replaced by rather more desperate ones? While there is a diversification of affects tied to the figure of the happy housewife, which gives her a more complex affective life, it does not necessarily dislodge the happiness that is presumed to reside in "what" she does, even in descriptions of relative unhappiness. Unhappiness can function as a sign of frustration, of being "held back" or "held up" from doing what makes her happy. Explanations of relative unhappiness can function to restore the power of an image of the good life in the form of nostalgia or regret for what has been lost.

The happy housewife retains its force as a place holder for women's desires and could even be said to be making a return. Take the following passage from Darla Shine's *Happy Housewives*: "Being home in a warm, comfy house floating around in your pajamas and furry slippers whiles sipping coffee as your babies play on the floor and your hubby works hard to pay for it all is not desperation. Grow up! Shut up! Count your blessings!" (2005: 15). Shine conjures for the reader a very specific image of what makes housewives happy. In conjuring this image — of leisure, comfort, and ease — she calls for us to return to a certain kind of life, as if this was the kind of life that women gave up in embracing feminism: her fantasy of the happy housewife is as much a white bourgeois fantasy of the past, a nostalgia for a past that was never possible as a present for most women, let alone being available in the present. Shine argues that women have become invested in "being desperate" and have been betrayed by the feminist movement that has "dropped the ball for women at home" (19). Alluding to the program *Desperate Housewives* as an example of what women do *not* want, Shine encourages us to adopt a new image: "I want mothers everywhere to dismiss this horrible image of desperation and come together to promote the image of the happy housewife" (6). This new image comes with a commitment to specific values: "respect; pride; confidence; passion; friendship; a clean beautiful home; and, most importantly, a close relationship with your children" (2). While mothering is a crucial element here in this manual for happiness, so too is marriage, as an institution described in terms of heterosexual intimacy: Shine suggests that "you will never be a happy housewife if you're not intimate with your husband" (53).

Shine's book is unexceptional. On the Internet, we witness a new generation of bloggers who take on this identity of "the happy housewife." These bloggers use the opportunity of the public space generated by new technologies to make public their claim of happiness. This claim is also an insistence on the error of feminism and on the importance of instructing women on how to be happy; happiness is being good at being a housewife, as well as what follows being good. Such blogs typically include recipes, tips on doing housework, thoughts on mothering, as well as belief statements that register the happy housewife as an important social role and duty that must be defended, as if the speech act ("I am a happy housewife") is itself a rebellion against a social orthodoxy. The image of the happy housewife is repeated and accumulates affective power in the very narration of her as a minority subject who has to reclaim something that has been taken from her. This affective power not only presses against feminist claims that behind the image of the happy housewife was an unspoken collective unhappiness but also involves a counterclaim that happiness is not so much what the housewife has but what she does: *her duty is to generate happiness by the very act of embracing this image.*

In this political context, it is not surprising that research in happiness studies has "shown" that traditional housewives are happier than their working counterparts, as the American journalist Meghan O'Rourke explores in her aptly named article "Desperate Feminist Wives" (2006). By implication, it is feminism that gives women the desires that have made them unhappy. This chapter will offer a different way of understanding the relationship between feminism and unhappiness. I begin by reflecting on how happiness was used historically as an argument for sustaining a gendered division of labor, taking as a starting point the work of the philosopher Jean-Jacques Rousseau on education. My argument challenges Lesley Johnson and Justine Lloyd's claim that the happy housewife was a feminist myth—what they call "a myth of a myth"—through which the feminist subject could generate the housewife as "the other" (2004: 2). I suggest that the happy housewife has a very long genealogy, and that she emerges as a figure at least in part as a response to feminist claims.

By providing a genealogy of the happy housewife, we can reflect on the political landscape in which the figures of the unhappy housewife and the feminist killjoy emerge. My suggestion is that we can reread the negativity of such figures in terms of the challenge they offer to the assumption that happiness follows relative proximity to a social ideal. I focus not only on the affective power of these figures but also on feminist consciousness as a form of unhappiness, suggesting that earlier feminist languages of "consciousness-raising" and even "false consciousness" may be useful in an exploration of the limitations of happiness as a horizon of experience.

Happiness, Education, and Women

In the previous chapter, I argued that happiness functions as a promise that directs you toward certain objects, as if they provide you with the necessary ingredients for a good life. Happiness involves a form of orientation: the very hope for happiness means we get directed in specific ways, as happiness is assumed to follow from some life choices and not others.

If happiness is an affective form of orientation, then happiness is crucial to education, which can be considered an orientation device. The child—who we might recall is considered by John Locke as a blank slate—is the site of potential. What happens to the child will shape what the child can become; the child's presumed emptiness becomes an imperative to shape its becoming. Education becomes about directing such potentiality; about steering the child in the right direction. Or to use a metaphor from horticulture, education is about cultivation, whereby, through tending the soil, you encourage the plants to grow in some ways rather than others. To educate is to orient, which is why education plays a central role in debates about happiness. Nel Noddings describes how "happiness should be an aim of education, and a good education should contribute significantly to personal and collective happiness" (2003: 1).[1]

Since classical times, the role of education as a form of orientation has been explicit. In *Republic* education is described as "the art of orientation" (1998: 245). Education should "devise the simplest and most effective methods of *turning minds around*. It shouldn't be the art of implanting sight in the organ, but should proceed on the understanding that the organ already has the capacity, but is improperly aligned and isn't facing the right way" (245–46; emphasis added). Education provides a way of getting the would-be subject to face the right way such that they can receive the right impressions. Education involves being directed not only by being turned around but by being turned "the right way" round. To turn minds around is an educational imperative only given the presumption that the would-be subject is improperly aligned.

The promise of happiness involves being "turned around." We can see how happiness involves turning in Rousseau's *Émile* ([1762] 1993), a book which has been described as "haunted" by Plato: Rousseau himself considered *Republic* "the most beautiful book on education that had yet been written" (Strong

2002: 135).[2] *Émile* is told in the first person, by a narrator whose duty is to instruct a young orphan named Émile, in order that he can take up his place in the world. Education for Émile is about becoming a good man. Within this book, happiness plays a crucial role: the good man does not seek happiness but achieves happiness as a consequence of virtue. This book had considerable influence on European thought and became a key reference point within feminist debates.[3] Rousseau offers a model of what a good education would do for his Émile, but also for Émile's would-be wife Sophy, whom he introduces in the fifth book. Rousseau's argument was that women and men should be educated in different ways that enabled them to fulfill their specific duties as gendered beings.

In this book, education for Sophy is about what she must become in order to be a good wife for Émile. Happiness provides a script for her becoming. As Rousseau explains, the aim for woman is "to be pleasing in his sight, to win his respect and love, to train him in childhood, to tend him in manhood, to councel and console, to make his life pleasant and happy, these are the duties of women for all time, and this is what she should be taught while she is young. The further we depart from this principle, the further we shall be from our goal, and all our precepts will fail to secure her happiness or our own" ([1762] 1993: 393). Any deviation from gender roles defined in terms of women being trained to make men happy is a deviation from the happiness of all.

For Rousseau the good woman has a duty to keep the family together, to preserve the integrity of its form. Rousseau asks us to "imagine a virtuous and charming wife, adorned with such accomplishments and devoting them to her husband's amusement; will she not add to his happiness? When he leaves his office worn out with the day's work, will she not prevent him seeking recreation elsewhere? Have we not all beheld happy families gathered together, each contributing to the general amusement?" (404). Subjects do not participate equally in the "general amusement." Women must learn to make men happy in order to keep families together, in order to prevent recreation from taking place elsewhere. It is women's duty to keep happiness in house.

The good woman is good in part because of what she judges to be good, and hence how she aligns her happiness with the happiness of others. The good woman is made happy by what is good. As Rousseau describes: "She loves virtue because there is nothing fairer in itself, she loves it because it is a woman's glory and because a virtuous woman is little lower than the angels;

she loves virtue as the only road to real happiness, because she sees nothing but poverty, neglect, unhappiness, shame, and disgrace in the life of a bad woman; she loves virtue because it is dear to her revered father, and to her tender and worthy mother; they are not content to be happy in their own virtue, they desire hers; and she finds her chief happiness in the hope of just making them happy" (431). The complexity of this statement should not be underestimated. She loves virtue as it is the road to happiness; unhappiness and disgrace follow from being bad. The good woman wants to be happy and hence wants what is good. The good woman also loves what is good because this is what is loved by her parents. The parents desire not only what is good; they desire their daughter to be good. The daughter is good to give them what they desire. For her to be happy, she must be good, as being good is what makes them happy, and she can only be happy if they are happy.

Statements on the conditionality of happiness—how one person's happiness is made conditional upon another's—ensure that happiness is directive: happiness becomes what is given by being given as a shared orientation toward what is good. It might seem that what I am calling "conditional happiness" involves a relationship of care and reciprocity: as if to say, I will not have a share in a happiness that cannot be shared. And yet, the terms of conditionality are unequal.[4] If certain people come first—we might say those who are already in place (such as parents, hosts, or citizens)—then their happiness comes first. For those who are positioned as coming after, *happiness means following somebody else's goods*.

The concept of conditional happiness allows me to develop my argument about the sociality of happiness. I suggested in the previous chapter that we might have a social bond if the same objects make us happy. I am suggesting here that happiness itself can become the shared object. Or to be more precise, if one person's happiness is made conditional on another person's happiness, such that the other person's happiness comes first, then *the other person's happiness becomes a shared object*. Max Scheler's differentiation between communities of feeling and fellow-feeling might help explain the significance of this argument. In communities of feeling, we share feelings because we share the same object of feeling (so we might feel sorrow at the loss of someone whom we both love; our sorrow would be directed toward an object that is shared). Fellow-feeling would be when I feel sorrow about your grief although I do not share your object of grief: "all fellow-feeling involves *intentional reference* of the feeling of joy or sorrow to the other person's experience" (Scheler [1913] 2008: 13). In this case, your grief is what grieves me; your grief is the object of my grief. I would speculate that in everyday life these different forms of shared feeling can be confused because the object of feeling is sometimes but not always exterior to the feeling that is shared.

Say I am happy about your happiness. Your happiness is with x. If I share x, then your happiness and my happiness is not only shared but can accumulate through being returned. Or I can simply disregard x: if my happiness is directed "just" toward your happiness, and you are happy about x, the exteriority of x can disappear or cease to matter (although it can reappear). Alternatively, because I experience happiness in your happiness, I could wish that our feeling of fellowship in happiness amounts to being happy about the same things (a community of happiness), such that x becomes shared as a happiness wish. Of course, if the object that makes you happy is my happiness wish, then this would be precarious basis for sharing something (as wishing to be happy about x can also be an admission that one is not simply happy about x). In cases where I am also affected by x, and I do not share your happiness with x, I might become uneasy and ambivalent, as I am made happy by your happiness but I am not made happy by what makes you happy. The exteriority of x would then announce itself as a point of crisis: I want your happiness to be what makes me happy, but I am reminded that even if my happiness is conditional on yours, your happiness is conditional on x and I am not happy with x. In such occasions, conditional happiness would require that I take up what makes you happy *as* what makes me happy, which may involve compromising my own idea of happiness (so I will go along with x in order to make you happy even if x does not "really" make me happy).[5] In order to preserve the happiness of all, we might even conceal from ourselves our unhappiness with x, or try to persuade ourselves that x matters less than the happiness of the other who is made happy by x.[6]

We have a hint of the rather uneasy dynamics of conditional happiness in *Émile*. For Sophy, wanting to make her parents happy commits her in a certain direction, regardless of what she might or might not want. If she can only be happy if they are happy, then she must do what makes them happy. In one episode, the father speaks to the daughter about becoming a woman: "You are a big girl now, Sophy, you will soon be a woman. We want you to be happy, for our sakes as well as yours, for our happiness depends on yours. A good girl finds her own happiness in the happiness of a good man" (434). Sophy's father offers a happiness commandment: it is for the sake of her own happiness and the happiness of her parents that she *must* find happiness in the right place, which is in the happiness of a good man. So it is not simply that groups cohere by taking up the same objects as the causes of happiness; some subjects are required to take up the happiness causes of others. In this case, for the daughter not to go along with the parents' desire for her marriage would not only cause her parents unhappiness but would threaten the very reproduction of social form. The daughter has a duty to reproduce the form of the family, which means *taking up the cause of parental happiness as her own.*

In this case, Sophy "happily" does what her parents want her to do. We might imagine that she wishes to be made happy by the same things and receives some comfort by the realization of a happiness wish. Of course, we do not "really" know if Sophy gets what she wants. The book can give us a happy ending by *not* giving us an account of Sophie's desires beyond the articulation of a wish to make her parents happy. The narrator declares triumphantly: "At last I see the happy day approaching, the happiest day of Émile's life and my own; I see the crown of my labours, I begin to appreciate their results. The noble pair are united till death do part; heart and lips confirm no empty vows; they are man and wife" (526–27). The happy ending involves not simply the alignment of desire but the willingness of the daughter to align her desire with the parental desire for happiness.

Happiness is how the given becomes given. In *Émile* happiness is linked to nature: as being what follows naturally from how things are, or how things are if they are allowed to flourish. As Rousseau explains: "I kept to the path of nature, until she should show me the path of happiness. And lo! their paths were the same, and without knowing it this was the path I trod" (487). Happiness becomes what follows nature's paths. Deviations from nature become deviations from the common good. For women to be educated to be anything other than wives for men would hence take them away from nature, and from what can promise happiness.

It should be no surprise that Rousseau's treatment of Sophy was a crucial object of feminist critique. Mary Wollstonecraft in her *Vindication of the Rights of Women* spoke out against Rousseau's vision of what makes women happy.[7] She comments wryly about his treatment of Sophy: "I have probably had an opportunity of observing more girls in their infancy than J. J. Rousseau" ([1792]

1975: 43). The political plea of *Vindication* is against the right of men to decide what happiness means for women. As Wollstonecraft argues: "Consider, I address you as a legislator, whether, when men contend for their freedom, and to be allowed to judge for themselves respecting their own happiness, it be not inconsistent and unjust to subjugate women, even though you firmly believe that you are acting in the manner best calculated to promote their happiness?" (5). The struggle over happiness forms the political horizon in which feminist claims are made. My argument is simple: we inherit this horizon.

Troublemakers

We learn from this history how happiness is used as a technology or instrument, which allows the reorientation of individual desire toward a common good.[8] We also learn from rereading books like *Émile* how happiness is not simply used to secure social relations instrumentally but works as an idea or aspiration within everyday life, shaping the very terms through which individuals share their world with others, creating "scripts" for how to live well.

We can think of gendered scripts as "happiness scripts" providing a set of instructions for what women and men must do in order to be happy, whereby happiness is what follows being natural or good. Going along with happiness scripts is how we get along: to get along is to be willing and able to express happiness in proximity to the right things. The child thus has a happiness duty. A duty can function as a debt, a way of returning what is owed. In the previous chapter, I spoke of happiness as involving the logic of deferral: the parents defer their hope for happiness to the next generation in order to avoid giving up on the idea of happiness as a response to disappointment (you can keep your belief in happiness while being disappointed as long as you can place your hopes for happiness in another). The obligation of the child to be happy is a repaying of what the child owes, of what is due to the parents given what they have given up. The duty of the child is to make the parents happy and to perform this duty happily by being happy or by showing signs of being happy in the right way.

Going along with this duty can mean simply approximating the signs of being happy—passing as happy—in order to keep things in the right place. Feminist genealogies can be described as genealogies of women who not only do not place their hopes for happiness in the right things but who speak out about their unhappiness with the very obligation to be made happy by such things. The history of feminism is thus a history of making trouble,[9] a history of women who refuse to become Sophy, by refusing to follow other people's goods, or by refusing to make others happy.

The female troublemaker might be trouble because she gets in the way of the happiness of others. Judith Butler shows how the figure of the trouble-maker exposes the intimacy of rebellion and punishment within the law. As she argues in her preface to *Gender Trouble*: "To make trouble was, within the reigning discourse of my childhood, something one should never do precisely because that would get one *in* trouble. The rebellion and its reprimand seemed to be caught up in the same terms, a phenomenon that gave rise to my first critical insight into the subtle ruse of power: The prevailing law threatened one with trouble, even put one in trouble, all to keep one out of trouble" (1990: vii). Happiness might be what keeps you out of trouble only by evoking the unhappiness of getting into trouble. We can consider how nineteenth century bildungsroman novels by women writers offered a rebellion against *Émile* in the narrativization of the limitations of moral education for girls and its narrow precepts of happiness. Such novels are all about the intimacy of trouble and happiness.

Take, for example, George Eliot's *The Mill on the Floss*, which is told from the point of view of Maggie Tulliver.[10] The early stages of the novel depict Maggie's childhood, the difficulty of her relationship with her brother Tom, and her per-petual fear of disappointing her parents. The novel contrasts Tom and Maggie in terms of how they are judged by their parents: "Tom never did the same sort of foolish things as Maggie, having a wonderful instinctive discernment of what would turn to his advantage or disadvantage; and so it happened that though he was much more wilful and inflexible than Maggie, his mother hardly ever called him naughty" ([1860] 1965: 73). Various incidents occur that con-tribute to Maggie's reputation as a troublemaker: when she lets Tom's dogs die (37); when she cuts her dark hair (73); when she knocks over Tom's building blocks (96); and when she pushes their cousin Lucy into the water (111–12).

The novel shows us how trouble does not simply reside within individu-als but involves ways of reading situations of conflict and struggle. Reading such situations involves locating the cause of trouble, which is another way of talking about conversion points: the troublemaker is the one who violates the fragile conditions of peace. If in all these instances Maggie is attributed as the cause of trouble, then what does not get noticed is the violence that makes her act in the way that she does, as the violence of provocation that hovers in the background. Even when Tom is told off, it is Maggie who is the reference point in situations of trouble. Mrs. Tulliver says to Tom: "'Then go and fetch her in this minute, you naughty boy. And how could you think o' going to pond and taking your sister where there was dirt. You know she'll do mischief if there's mischief to be done.' It was Mrs. Tulliver's way, if she blamed Tom, to refer his misdemeanor, somehow or other, to Maggie" (114). Maggie gets into trouble because she is already read as being trouble before anything happens.

Maggie gets into trouble for speaking: to speak is already a form of defiance if you are supposed to recede into the background. She speaks out when something happens that she perceives to be wrong. The crisis of the novel is when her father loses the mill, threatening his ability to look after his family. Maggie is shocked by the lack off sympathy and care they receive from their extended family. Maggie speaks back out of a sense of care for her parents: "Maggie, having hurled her defiance at aunts and uncles in this way, stood still, with her large dark eyes glaring at them as if she was ready to await all consequences. . . . 'You haven't seen the end o' your trouble wi' that child, Bessy,' said Mrs Pullet; 'she's beyond everything for boldness and unthankfulness. Its dreadful. I might ha' let alone paying for her schooling, for she's worse nor ever'" (229). Girls who speak out are bold and thankless. It is important that Maggie is compelled to speak from a sense of injustice. Already we can witness the relationship between consciousness of injustice and being attributed as the cause of unhappiness.

The novel relates Maggie's tendency to get into trouble with her desire, will, and imagination, with her love of new words that bring with them the promise of unfamiliar worlds. For instance, she loves Latin because "she delighted in new words" (159). For Maggie "these mysterious sentences, snatched from an unknown context—like strange horns of beasts and leaves of unknown plants, brought from some far-off region—gave boundless scope to her imagination and were all the more fascinating because they were in a peculiar tongue of their own, which she could learn to interpret" (159–60). The association between imagination and trouble is powerful. It teaches us how the happiness duty for women is about the narrowing of horizons, about giving up an interest in what lies beyond the familiar.

Returning to *Émile*, it is interesting that the danger of unhappiness is associated precisely with women having too much curiosity. At one point in the
narrative, Sophy gets misdirected. Her imagination and desires are activated
by reading too many books, leading to her becoming an "unhappy girl, overwhelmed with her secret grief" (439–40). If Sophy were to become too imagi-
native, we would not get our happy ending, premised on Sophy being given to
Émile. The narrator says in response to the threat of such an unhappy ending,
"Let us give Émile his Sophy; let us restore this sweet girl to life and provide
her with a less vivid imagination and a happier fate" (441).[11] Being restored
to life is here being returned to the straight and narrow. Imagination is what
makes women look beyond the script of happiness to a different fate. Having
made Sophy sweet and unimaginative, the book can end happily.

Feminist readers might want to challenge this association between unhappiness and female imagination, which in the moral economy of happiness, makes
female imagination a bad thing. But if we do not operate in this economy —
that is, if we do not assume that happiness is what is good — then we can read
the link between female imagination and unhappiness differently. We might
explore how imagination is what allows women to be liberated from happiness
and the narrowness of its horizons. We might want the girls to read the books
that enable them to be overwhelmed with grief.

It is Sophy's imagination that threatens to get in the way of her happiness,
and thus of the happiness of all. Imagination is what allows girls to question
the wisdom they have received and to ask whether what is good for all is necessarily good for them. We could describe one episode of *The Mill on the Floss*
as Maggie becoming Sophy (or becoming the Sophy that Sophy must be in
order to fulfil her narrative function). Maggie has an epiphany: the answer
to her troubles is to become happy and good: "it flashed through her like the
suddenly apprehended solution of a problem, that all the miseries of her young
life had come from fixing her heart on her own pleasure as if that were the
central necessity of the universe" (306). From the point of view of the parents, their daughter has become good because she has submitted to their will:
"Her mother felt the change in her with a sort of puzzled wonder that Maggie
should be 'growing up so good'; it was amazing that this once 'contrairy' child
was becoming so submissive, so backward to assert her own will" (309). To
be good as a girl is to give up having a will of one's own. The mother can thus

love the daughter who is becoming like furniture, who can support the family by staying in the background: "The mother was getting fond of her tall, brown girl, the only bit of furniture now in which she could bestow her anxiety and pride" (309).

It is as if Maggie has chosen between happiness and life, by giving up life for happiness: "'I've been a great deal happier,' she said at last timidly, 'since I have given up thinking about what is easy and pleasant, and being discontented because I couldn't have my own will. Our life is determined for us — and it makes the mind very free when we give up wishing and only think of bearing what is laid upon us and doing what is given us to do'" (317). Happiness is associated here with the renunciation of desire.[12] It is her friend Philip whom Maggie is addressing at this point. It is Philip who refuses to allow Maggie to give up her life for happiness in this way. He says impatiently: "'But I can't give up wishing . . . It seems to me that we can never give up longing and wishing while we are thoroughly alive'" (317).

It is Philip who loves Maggie for her aliveness, who gives her books that rekindle her sense of interest and curiosity about the world. He gives her one book that she cannot finish as she reads in this book the injustice of happiness, which is given to some and not others, those deemed worthy of love. "'I didn't finish the book,' said Maggie. 'As soon as I came to the blond-haired young girl reading in the park, I shut it up and determined to read no further. I foresaw that that light-complexioned girl would win away all the love from Corinne and make her miserable. I'm determined to read no more books where the blond-haired women carry away all the happiness. I should begin to have a prejudice against them. If you could give me some story, now, where the dark woman triumphs, it would restore the balance. I want to avenge Rebecca, and Flora MacIvor, and Minna, and all the rest of the dark unhappy ones'" (348–49). Exercising a racialized vocabulary, Maggie exposes how darkness becomes a form of unhappiness, as lacking the qualities deemed necessary for being given a happy ending.[13] Maggie gives up on giving up her life for happiness by speaking out against the injustice of happiness and how it is given to some and not others.

The novel relies on contrasting the cousins Lucy and Maggie in terms of their capacity to be happy and dutiful. Maggie admits her unhappiness to Lucy: "One gets a bad habit of being unhappy" (389). For Lucy, being happy is a way of not being trouble; she cannot live with the reality of getting into trouble: as she says, "I've always been happy. I don't know whether I could bear much trouble" (389). Happiness involves a way of avoiding what one cannot bear.

The climactic moment of the novel comes when Stephen, who is betrothed to Lucy, announces his desire for Maggie, who is swept away by it. She almost goes along with him but realizes that she cannot: "Many things are difficult and dark to me, but I see one thing quite clearly: that I must not, cannot, seek my own happiness by sacrificing others" (471). Maggie chooses duty as if without duty there would be only the inclination of the moment. As a good Kantian subject, she says: "If the past is not to bind us, where can duty lie? We should have no law but the inclination of the moment" (499), to which Stephen replies, "But it weighs nothing with you that you are robbing me of *my* happiness" (500–501).[14] By choosing duty, Maggie does not avoid causing unhappiness. She must pay for her moment of transgression. Having deviated from the path of happiness, she has fulfilled her destiny as trouble. As she says in one letter: "Oh God, is there any happiness in love that could make me forget *their* pain" (528). Death as a result of a natural disaster (a flood) thus liberates Maggie from the unhappy consequences of causing trouble, of deviating from the paths of happiness. The injustice of her loss of life is how the novel speaks against happiness, which itself is narrated as the renunciation of life, imagination, and desire.

Even if books like *The Mill on the Floss* seem to punish their heroines for their transgressions, they also evoke the injustice of happiness, showing what and whom happiness gives up. In giving up on those who seem to give up on happiness, happiness acquires its coherence. We could describe happiness quite simply as a convention, such that to deviate from the paths of happiness is to challenge convention. What is a convention? The word *convention* comes from the verb "to convene." To convene is to gather, to assemble, or to meet up. A convention is a point around which we gather. To follow a convention is to gather in the right way, to be assembled. Feminism gives time and space to women's desires that are not assembled around the reproduction of the family form. Feminists must thus be willing to cause disturbance. Feminists might even have to be willful. A subject would be described as willful at the point that her will does not coincide with that of others, those whose will is reified as the general or social will.[15]

The figure of the female troublemaker thus shares the same horizon with the figure of the feminist killjoy. Both figures are intelligible if they are read through the lens of the history of happiness. Feminists might kill joy simply by not finding the objects that promise happiness to be quite so promising. The word *feminism* is thus saturated with unhappiness. Feminists by declaring themselves as feminists are already read as destroying something that is thought of by others not only as being good but as the cause of happiness. The feminist killjoy "spoils" the happiness of others; she is a spoilsport because she refuses to convene, to assemble, or to meet up over happiness.

In the thick sociality of everyday spaces, feminists are thus attributed as the origin of bad feeling, as the ones who ruin the atmosphere, which is how the atmosphere might be imagined (retrospectively) as shared. In order to get along, you have to participate in certain forms of solidarity: you have to laugh at the right points. Feminists are typically represented as grumpy and humorless, often as a way of protecting the right to certain forms of social bonding or of holding onto whatever is perceived to be under threat.[16] Feminists don't even have to say anything to be read as killing joy. A feminist colleague says to me that she just has to open her mouth in meetings to witness eyes rolling as if to say "oh here she goes."

My experience of being a feminist has taught me much about rolling eyes. This is why when people say the bad feeling is coming from this person or that person, I am never convinced. My skepticism comes from childhood experiences of being a feminist daughter in a relatively conventional family, always at odds with the performance of good feeling in the family, always assumed to be bringing others down, for example, by pointing out sexism in other people's talk. Say we are seated at the dinner table. Around this table, the family gathers, having polite conversations, where only certain things can be brought up. Someone says something that you consider problematic. You respond, carefully, perhaps. You might be speaking quietly; or you might be getting "wound up," recognizing with frustration that you are being wound up by someone who is winding you up. The violence of what was said or the violence of provocation goes unnoticed. However she speaks, the feminist is usually the one who is viewed as "causing the argument," who is disturbing the fragility of peace.

Let's take this figure of the feminist killjoy seriously. Does the feminist kill other people's joy by pointing out moments of sexism? Or does she expose the bad feelings that get hidden, displaced, or negated under public signs of joy?

Does bad feeling enter the room when somebody expresses anger about things, or could anger be the moment when the bad feelings that circulate through objects get brought to the surface in a certain way? Feminist subjects might bring others down not only by talking about unhappy topics such as sexism but by exposing how happiness is sustained by erasing the very signs of not getting along. Feminists do kill joy in a certain sense: they disturb the very fantasy that happiness can be found in certain places. To kill a fantasy can still kill a feeling. It is not just that feminists might not be happily affected by the objects that are supposed to cause happiness but that their failure to be happy is read as sabotaging the happiness of others.

We can consider the relationship between the negativity of the figure of the feminist killjoy and how certain bodies are "encountered" as being negative. Marilyn Frye argues that oppression involves the requirement that you show signs of being happy with the situation in which you find yourself. As she puts it, "It is often a requirement upon oppressed people that we smile and be cheerful. If we comply, we signify our docility and our acquiescence in our situation" (1983: 2). To be oppressed requires you to show signs of happiness, as signs of being or having been adjusted. As a result, for Frye, "anything but the sunniest countenance exposes us to being perceived as mean, bitter, angry or dangerous" (2). If an oppressed person does not smile or show signs of being happy, then he or she is read as being negative: as angry, hostile, unhappy, and so on. Happiness becomes the expected "default position" for those who are oppressed, such that it comes to define the sphere of neutrality. You are either happy: or you are not.

To be recognized as a feminist is to be assigned to a difficult category and a category of difficulty. You are "already read" as "not easy to get along with" when you name yourself as a feminist. You have to show that you are not diffi-cult through displaying signs of good will and happiness. Frye alludes to such experiences when she observes that "this means, at the very least, that we may be found to be 'difficult' or unpleasant to work with, which is enough to cost one one's livelihood" (2–3). We can also witness an investment in feminist unhappiness (the myth that feminists kill joy because they are joyless). There is a desire to believe that women become feminists *because* they are unhappy, perhaps as a displacement of their envy for those who have achieved the hap-piness they have failed to achieve.[17] This desire functions as a defense of hap-piness against feminist critique. This is not to say that feminists might not be unhappy; we might be unhappy after all with this representation of feminism as caused by unhappiness. My point here would be that feminists are read as being unhappy, such that situations of conflict, violence, and power are read as *about* the unhappiness of feminists, rather than being what feminists are unhappy *about*.

Of course, within feminism, some bodies more than others can be attributed as the cause of unhappiness. We can place the figure of the feminist killjoy alongside the figure of the angry black woman,[18] explored so well by writers such as Audre Lorde (1984) and bell hooks (2000). The angry black woman can be described as a killjoy; she may even kill feminist joy, for example, by pointing out forms of racism within feminist politics. She might not even have to make any such point to kill joy. You can be affectively alien because you are affected in the wrong way by the right things. Or you can be affectively alien because you affect others in the wrong way: your proximity gets in the way of other people's enjoyment of the right things, functioning as an unwanted reminder of histories that are disturbing, that disturb an atmosphere. Listen to the following description from bell hooks: "A group of white feminist activists who do not know one another may be present at a meeting to discuss feminist theory. They may feel they are bonded on the basis of shared womanhood, but the atmosphere will noticeably change when a woman of color enters the room. The white women will become tense, no longer relaxed, no longer cele-bratory" (56).

It is not just that feelings are "in tension" but that the tension is located somewhere: in being felt by some bodies, it is attributed as caused by another body, who thus comes to be felt as apart from the group, as getting in the way of its organic enjoyment and solidarity. The body of color is attributed as the cause of becoming tense, which is also the loss of a shared atmosphere (or we could say that sharing the experience of loss is how the atmosphere is shared). As a feminist of color you do not even have to say anything to cause tension. The mere proximity of some bodies involves an affective conversion. To get along you have to go along with things which might mean for some not even being able to enter the room. We learn from this example how histories are condensed in the very intangibility of an atmosphere, or in the tangibility of the bodies that seem to get in the way. Perhaps atmospheres are shared if there is an agreement in where we locate the points of tension.

To speak out of anger as a woman of color is to confirm your position as the cause of tension; your anger is what threatens the social bond. As Audre Lorde describes: "When women of Color speak out of the anger that laces so many of our contacts with white women, we are often told that we are 'creating a mood of helplessness,' 'preventing white women from getting past guilt,' or 'standing in the way of trusting communication and action'" (1984: 131). The exposure of violence becomes the origin of violence. The woman of color must let go of her anger for the white woman to move on.

The figure of the angry black woman is also a fantasy figure that produces its own effects. Reasonable thoughtful arguments are dismissed as anger (which of course empties anger of its own reason), which makes you angry, such that your response becomes read as the confirmation of evidence that you are not only angry but also unreasonable! To make this point in another way, the anger of feminists of color is attributed. So you might be angry *about* how racism and sexism diminish life choices for women of color. Your anger is a judgment that something is wrong. But in being heard as angry, your speech is read as motivated by anger. Your anger is read as unattributed, as if you are against x because you are angry rather than being angry because you are against x. You become angry at the injustice of being heard as motivated by anger, which makes it harder to separate yourself from the object of your anger. You become entangled with what you are angry about because you are angry about how they have entangled you in your anger. In becoming angry about that entanglement, you confirm their commitment to your anger as the truth "behind" your speech, which is what blocks your anger, stops it from getting through. You are blocked by not getting through.

Some bodies become blockage points, points where smooth communication stops. Consider Ama Ata Aidoo's wonderful prose poem *Our Sister Killjoy*, where the narrator Sissie, as a black woman, has to work to sustain the comfort of others. On a plane, a white hostess invites her to sit at the back with "her friends," two black people she does not know. She is about to say that she does not know them, and hesitates: "But to have refused to join them would have created an awkward situation, wouldn't it? Considering too that apart from the air hostess's obviously civilized upbringing, she had been trained to see to the comfort of all her passengers" (1977: 10).

Power speaks here in this moment of hesitation. Do you go along with it? What does it mean not to go along with it? To create awkwardness is to be read as being awkward. Maintaining public comfort requires that certain bodies "go along with it." To refuse to go along with it, to refuse the place in which you are placed, is to be seen as trouble, as causing discomfort for others. There is a political struggle about how we attribute good and bad feelings, which hesitates around the apparently simple question of who introduces what feelings to whom. Feelings can get stuck to certain bodies in the very way we describe spaces, situations, dramas. And bodies can get stuck depending on what feelings they get associated with.

Consciousness and Unhappiness

To be against forms of power and violence that are concealed under signs of happiness does not necessarily mean becoming unhappy, even if it does mean refusing to go along with things by showing signs of getting along. It is striking that Shulamith Firestone's "dream action" for the women's liberation movement is "a smile boycott, at which declaration, all women would instantly abandon their 'pleasing' smiles, henceforth only smiling when something pleased *them*" (1970: 90). To refuse the promise of happiness is to refuse the demand that you show signs of happiness. For Firestone, this means a shift of orientation; it means changing one's bodily habits: "In my own case, I had to train myself out of the phony smile, which is like a nervous tic on every teenage girl. And this meant that I smiled rarely, for in truth, when it came down to real smiling, I had less to smile about" (90). To refuse to keep smiling for Firestone is not a refusal of joy or any of those good feelings that are not distributed along accepted paths of happiness. If anything, the false smile sustains the very psychic and political condition of unhappiness. The feminist who does not smile when she is not happy wants a more exciting life. Indeed, as Firestone argues: "Eroticism is *exciting*. No-one wants to get rid of it. Life would be a drab and routine affair without at least that spark. That's just the point. *Why has all joy and excitement been concentrated, driven into one narrow difficult-to-find alley of human experience, and all the rest laid waste?*" (155; second emphasis added). Feminism involves challenging the very "pressure" of happiness, the way it restricts the possibilities for finding excitement, of being excited.

This is not to say that feminism makes women happy. It is simply that feminism by refusing to go along with public displays of happiness can participate in the widening of horizons in which it is possible to find things. Feminism does not guarantee what we will find through this expansion of bodily horizons. It simply opens up the places where we can look. The fact that any such opening is read as a sign of hostility, or of killing other people's joy, tells us something. The public investment in happiness is an investment in a very particular and narrow model of the good; being happy requires a commitment to find what Firestone brilliantly describes as a "narrow difficult-to-find alley" of human experience.

I have explored how feminism is represented as causing unhappiness and as caused by unhappiness. Rather than disregarding the possibility of a link between feminism and unhappiness, I want to consider another way of thinking about it. We could describe consciousness raising as raising consciousness of unhappiness. As Gayle Greene argues, "For though education raised women's expectations, it *also made many of them unhappy*, creating ambitions that were frustrated by the rigid domestic ideology that urged them back into the home" (1991: 9; emphasis added). Indeed, you have to experience limitations *as* limitations; the act of noticing limitations can actually make life seem more rather than less limited. If the world does not allow you to embrace the possibilities that are opened up by education, then you become even more aware of the injustice of such limitations. Opening up the world, or expanding one's horizons, can thus mean becoming more conscious of just how much there is to be unhappy about. Unhappiness might also provide an affective way of sustaining our attention on the cause of unhappiness. You would be unhappy *with* the causes of unhappiness. Consciousness-raising does not turn unhappy housewives into happy feminists, even though sometimes we might wish that this were the case!

Feminism involves political consciousness of what women are asked to give up for happiness. Indeed, in even becoming conscious of happiness as loss, feminists have already refused to give up desire, imagination, and curiosity for happiness. There can be sadness simply in the realization of what one has given up. Feminist archives are thus full of housewives becoming conscious of unhappiness as a mood that seems to surround them: think of Virginia Woolf's *Mrs. Dalloway*. The feeling is certainly around, almost as a thickness in the air. We sense the unhappiness seeping through the tasks of the everyday. There she is, about to get flowers, enjoying her walk in London. During that walk, she disappears: "But often now this body she wore (she stopped to look at a Dutch picture), this body, with all its capacities, seemed nothing—nothing at all. She had the oddest sense of being herself invisible; unseen; unknown; there being no more marrying, no more having children now, but only this astonishing and rather solemn progress with the rest of them, up Bond street, this being Mrs. Dalloway; not even Clarissa anymore; this being Mrs. Richard Dalloway" ([1925] 1953: 14).

Becoming Mrs. Dalloway is itself a form of disappearance: to follow the paths of life (marriage, reproduction) is to feel that what is before you is a kind of solemn progress, as if you are living somebody else's life, simply going the same way others are going. It is as if you have left the point of life behind you, as if your life is going through motions that were already in motion before you even arrived. As I argued in *Queer Phenomenology* (2006), for a life to count as a good life, it must take on the direction promised as a social good, which means imagining one's futurity in terms of reaching certain points along a life course. If happiness is what allows us to reach certain points, it is not necessarily how you feel when you get there. For Mrs. Dalloway, to reach these points is to disappear. The point of reaching these points seems to be a certain disappearance, a loss of possibility, a certain failure to make use of the body's capacities, to find out what it is that her body can do.[19] To become conscious of possibility can involve mourning for its loss.

For Clarissa this rather uncanny sensation of becoming Mrs. Dalloway as a loss of possibility, as an unbecoming, or becoming "nothing at all" does not enter her consciousness in the form of sadness *about* something.[20] The sadness of the book—and it is a sad book—is not one expressed as a point of view. Instead, each sentence of the book takes thoughts and feelings as if they are objects in a shared world: the streets of London, the very oddness of the occasion of passing others by, a feeling of that oddness. Sometimes it can feel like a coincidence, how one coincides with others. To say "it is just a coincidence" can create the impression that the absence of a causal relation between events is the absence of any connection. But feeling a coincidence might mean recognizing that to fall in the same time and place as others, to happen with others or to happen upon others, is a kind of connection. As Clarissa goes out with her task in mind (she has to buy her flowers for her party), she walks into a world with others. You might be in your world (with your own tasks, your own recollections) and yet you share the world of the street, if only for a moment, a fleeting moment, a moment that flees. Things appear as modes of attention: the plane above that writes letters in the sky, the plane that is seen by those who pass each other by. Questions unfold as shared questions: What letter is that? What word is that? "'What are they looking at?' said Clarissa Dalloway" (42). It is as if the mere direction of a glance is enough to create a shared world. Although each brings to the street a certain kind of moodiness, a preoccupation with this or with that, the street itself can become moody, when an object grabs attention, like the plane that creates words in the sky above, although for each person who looks up, what is seen might be quite different.

If unhappiness becomes a collective impression, then it too is made up of fragments that only loosely attach to points of view. In particular, the proximity between Mrs. Dalloway and the character Septimus is what allows unhappiness to be shared even if it is not passed between them; two characters who do not know each other, though they pass each other, but whose worlds are connected by the very jolt of unhappiness. We have the immanence of the shock of how one person's suffering can have an effect on the life world of another. Septimus suffers from shell shock; and we feel his feelings with him, the panic and sadness as the horror of war intrudes as memory. His suffering brings the past into the time of the present, the long time of war, its persistence on the skin as aftermath, its refusal of an after. To those who observe him from a distance, those who share the street on this day, he appears as a madman, at the edge of respectable sociality, a spectacle. To encounter him on the street, you would not know the story behind his suffering. To be near to suffering does not necessarily bring suffering near.

Clarissa and Septimus, as characters who do not meet, thus achieve an odd intimacy: the not-just-private suffering of the housewife and the not-quite-public suffering of the returned soldier are interwoven. Importantly, their sadness is proximate but not contagious. They do not catch sadness from each other; their sadness is what keeps alive histories that are not shared, that cannot be shared, as they pass by on the street. And yet something is shared, perhaps those very things that cannot simply be revealed. Clarissa, thinking of her "odd affinities" with strangers "she had never spoken to," sits on the bus and wonders whether the "unseen part of us" might provide a point of attachment to others and might even be how we survive through others, "perhaps — perhaps" (231–32).

It is Septimus's wife, Rezia, whose musings reflect most directly on the difficulty of experiencing emotions that are simply revealed to proximate others. Rezia is so anxious to reveal her own unhappiness that she "almost felt sometimes that she must stop people in the street, if they looked like good, kind, kind people just to say to them 'I am unhappy'" (125). She is conscious of how her feelings and Septimus's feelings cannot simply be revealed to passers by: "was there, after all, anything to draw attention to them, anything to make a passer-by suspect here is a young man who carries in him the greatest message in the world, and is, moreover, the happiest man in the world, and the most miserable?" (126). To inhabit a feeling world does not create a world out of feeling.

Much of the novel is about an event that will happen. For Mrs. Dalloway is planning a party. To some feminist readers, the preoccupation with the party makes the book disappointing. Simone de Beauvoir reads Mrs. Dalloway's enjoyment of parties as a sign that she is trying to turn her "prison into glory," as if as a hostess she can be "the bestower of happiness and gaiety" ([1949] 1997: 554). For de Beauvoir, the gift of the party turns quickly into duty; such that Mrs. Dalloway, "who loved these triumphs, these semblances," still "felt their hollowness" (555). For Kate Millett, Mrs. Dalloway is a rather disappointing figure; she exposes Woolf's failure to turn her own unhappiness into a politics: "Virginia glorified two housewives, Mrs. Dalloway and Mrs. Ramsey, recorded the suicidal misery of Rhoda in *The Waves* without ever explaining its causes" (1970: 37). We might say that it is because Mrs. Dalloway is planning a party that we do not have much revealed about her unhappiness, other than the sadness of recalling lost intimacies with Peter and with Sally, who both turn up, unexpectedly during her day, in a way, it is implied, that does not just happen but bears some relation to Mrs. Dalloway's own thoughts: "all day she had been thinking of Bourton, of Peter, of Sally" (280). Such lost intimacies become lost possibilities, hints of a life she might have lived, if things had not turned out the way they did.

If Mrs. Dalloway is distracted from the causes of unhappiness by the party (and we can have some sympathy with the necessity of distractions), the party is also the event in which unhappiness comes to life. For Mrs. Dalloway, her party is life; it is how she can make things happen; it a gift, a happening (185). What happens? That this question is a question is a preservation of the gift. And something does happen. For it is in the party that Septimus's life "touches" Mrs. Dalloway most directly. It touches her through death. Lady Bradshaw says to her: "'Just as we were starting, my husband was called up on the telephone, a very sad case. A young man (that is what Sir William is telling Mr. Dalloway) had killed himself. He had been in the army.' Oh! Thought Clarissa, in the middle of my party, here's death, she thought" (279). In the middle of the party, words accumulate as a narrative, telling the story of a death. A young man kills himself, and the death itself (and not just the narrating of the death) takes place in the middle of the party, in the middle of the life of the party. The soul of the party is death. The reader has already read about this death; we have witnessed it. Now, we witness the ripples of this death; how it acquires a life of its own, how it takes place somewhere in the middle. For Mrs. Dalloway, this death becomes something to imagine, to bring to life by thought:

> What business had the Bradshaws to talk of death at her party? A young man had killed himself. And they talked of it at her party—the Bradshaws, talked of death. He had killed himself—but how? Always her body went through it first, when she was told, suddenly, of an accident; her dress flamed, her body burnt. He had thrown himself from a window. Up had flashed the ground; through him, blundering, bruising, went the rusty spikes. There he lay with a thud, thud, thud in his brain, and then a suffocation of blackness. So she saw it. But why had he done it? And the Bradshaws talked of it at her party!
>
> She had once thrown a shilling into the Serpentine, never anything more. But he had flung it away. They went on living (she would have to go back; the rooms were still crowded; people kept on coming). They (all day she has been thinking of Bourton, of Peter, of Sally), they would grow old. A thing there was that mattered; a thing, wreathed about with chatter, defaced, obscured in her own life, let drop every day in corruption, lies, chatter. This he had preserved. Death was defiance. Death was an attempt to communicate; people feeling the impossibility of reaching the centre which, mystically, evaded them; closeness drew apart; rapture faded; one was alone. There was an embrace in death. (280–81)

Septimus's death becomes a question that takes Mrs. Dalloway away from the party; she attends to his death, wonders about it; she becomes a retrospective witness even though she was not and could not have been there. The shudder: the sounds of it; the thud, thud, thud of it; the ground that flashes; the rusty spikes. His death becomes material, becomes fleshy through her thoughts. His death announces not only that sadness can be unbearable but that we don't have to bear it, that you can fling it away. And in this moment, when death intervenes in the life of the party, life becomes chatter, becomes what goes on, "they went on living," what comes and goes, "people kept on coming." Death comes to embody the suffering that persists when life becomes chatter.

What is striking about Mrs. Dalloway is how suffering has to enter her consciousness from the edges, through the arrival of another, another who is an intruder, who has not been invited to the party. It is the suffering of an intruder that exposes the emptiness of life's chatter. Suffering enters not as self-consciousness—as a consciousness of one's own suffering—but as a heightening of consciousness, a world-consciousness in which the suffering of those who do not belong is allowed to disturb an atmosphere. Even when unhappiness is a familiar feeling, it can arrive like a stranger, to disturb the familiar or to reveal what is disturbing in the familiar.

The arrival of suffering from the edges of social consciousness might teach us about the difficulty of becoming conscious of suffering or teach us about our own resistances to recognizing those seemingly "little" uneasy feelings of loss or dissatisfaction as unhappiness with one's life. The party might expose the need to keep busy, to keep going in the face of one's disappearance. So much sadness revealed in the very need to be busy. So much grief expressed in the need not to be overwhelmed by grief. It is hard labor just to recognize sadness and disappointment, when you are living a life that is meant to be happy but just isn't, which is meant to be full, but feels empty. It is difficult to give up an idea of one's life, when one has lived a life according to that idea. To recognize loss can mean to be willing to experience an intensification of the sadness that hopefulness postpones.[21]

To inherit feminism can mean to inherit sadness. There is sadness in becoming conscious not only of gender as the restriction of possibility, but also of how this restriction is not necessary. After all, we have inherited the book Mrs. Dalloway; we have passed the book around, and the book itself has passed into other cultural forms.[22] Take the film The Hours (2002, dir. Stephen Daldry), based on Michael's Cunningham's novel The Hours (1998), which takes its title from Woolf's original title for Mrs. Dalloway. The Hours places three generations of women alongside each other and follows their life on a single day: we have a fictionalized account of a day in the life of Virginia Woolf (Nicole Kidman); of Laura Brown (Julianne Moore), an unhappy housewife living in the 1950s as she bakes a cake and reads Mrs. Dalloway; and of Clarissa Vaughan (Meryl Streep), who is organizing a party like Mrs. Dalloway, this time for her former lover and friend Richard (Ed Harris), who is dying of AIDS.

Mrs. Dalloway the novel is inherited by *The Hours* in multiple ways; we inherit the lost name of the book, the book itself. *The Hours* also mimics the book: following its orientation, its directionality in time, by depicting a whole life in a single day. The film attends closely to gestures which bind each generation to the figure of Mrs. Dalloway: Clarissa, for instance, begins her day by saying she will get the flowers for the party. The gestures or tasks of the everyday become forms of inheritance.

I want to focus in particular on Laura Brown, the unhappy 1950s housewife. She is reading *Mrs. Dalloway*, and we hear the voice of Virginia Woolf as she has been evoked by the film, and the voice travels over time, as a trace of a history that is not gone, of a past that lingers. Laura longs to read the book. She caresses the book; she wants to stay in bed with it; she wants to keep reading, to read more and more. Her desire for the book is also her desire not to be in her life, to be suspended from its time and rhythms: she wants to spend time with the book to avoid spending time with her husband and child.

It is a day, one day. It is her husband's birthday; but Laura wants to say in bed with the book; we imagine that she wants to be in bed with Virginia. Later, when her husband has gone, her friend Kitty arrives and asks her about the book. Laura talks of Mrs. Dalloway, as if she was co-present, as if she shares the same space, the same world. She says of Mrs. Dalloway, "Because she is confident everyone thinks she is fine. But she isn't." To be confident is to convince the world of a happiness that does exist; it is to pass as happy with what does exist. You work to support the belief that everything is fine — when it isn't. The story of *Mrs. Dalloway* becomes Laura's description of her own present, what surrounds her, her life world. She identifies with Mrs. Dalloway through suffering, by sharing her grief, as a grief that is not revealed, as if to say: like you, I am not fine, like you, my life is about maintaining the appearance of being fine, an appearance which is also a disappearance.

What happens when domestic bliss does not create bliss? Laura tries to bake a cake. She cracks an egg. The cracking of the egg becomes a thematic gesture throughout the film, connecting the domestic labor of women over time. To bake a cake ought to be a happy endeavor, a labor of love. Instead, the film reveals a sense of oppression that lingers in the very act of breaking the eggs. If, as I suggested in the last chapter, happiness creates its own horizon, as a horizon of likes, then it is possible to be surrounded by likes that are not your own, and by promises that haunt you in their emptiness. Not only do such objects not cause your happiness but they may remind you of your failure to be made happy; they embody a feeling of disappointment. The bowl in which you crack the eggs waits for you. You can feel the pressure of its wait. The empty bowl feels like an accusation. Feminist archives are full of scenes of domesticity in which domestic objects, happy objects, become alien, even menacing.

In one very poignant scene in *The Hours*, when Laura's family gathers around the table, having their own party with the cake she has finally baked, the prom-ise of happiness is evoked. Her husband is telling their child the story of how they met. He says: "I used to think about bringing her to this house. To a life, pretty much like this. And it was the thought of the happiness, the thought of this woman, the thought of this life, that's what kept me going. I had an idea about our happiness." As he speaks, tears well in Laura's eyes. Her sadness is with his idea of happiness, with what keeps him going, and the world it creates for her. Laura explains to Clarissa at the end of the film how she came to leave her husband and child: "It would be wonderful to say that you regretted it; it would be easy. But what does it mean? What does it mean to regret when you had no choice? It is what you can bear. There it is. No one is going to forgive me. It was death. I choose life." A life premised on "an idea about our happi-ness," for Laura, would be unbearable. Such happiness would be death. She does not leave this life for happiness. She leaves this happiness for life.

We might say, why not leave his happiness for another kind of happiness, a happiness that could be called her own? Couldn't we understand the creativity of feminism, its potentiality for generating new horizons, as giving us alter-native ideas of happiness? Perhaps what is revealed in Laura's sadness is how happiness is saturated by its own history becoming too hard to separate from an idea, from an idea her husband has for her. For Laura, to leave happiness is to leave everything behind her; it is to cause unhappiness for those who are left behind, an unhappiness which is inherited by her child, who, we learn by the end of the film, is Richard. And it is Clarissa who in *The Hours* cares for Richard and attends to his unhappiness, who has to pick up the pieces of the happiness that Laura has shattered. Clarissa: who ends up (like Mrs. Dallo-way) organizing a party for her friend, worrying (like Mrs. Dalloway) that her parties are trivial. Clarissa (like Mrs. Dalloway) tries desperately not to be sad; to use the happy occasion of the party, its celebration of Richard's award of the Carrouthers Prize for poetry, to stop herself thinking about the sadness of his imminent death; to avoid being overwhelmed by grief.

The film might in its dramatization of the unhappiness caused by Laura, the woman who cannot bear the idea of happiness, withdraw its sympathy from her plight. I think it does. Perhaps we can learn from this withdrawal of sympathy. If the one who leaves happiness must cause unhappiness to those who are left behind, then she must refuse to be sympathetic: she must not return feeling with like feeling (happiness with happiness, love with love) if she is to escape from the very obligation to return. In other words, to give up happiness is to become unsympathetic. That Laura's act is only narratable as extreme, even as violence, as the cause of suffering that cannot be repaired, shows us just how hard it can be to give up on the idea of happiness because that idea is also bound up with the impulse to care for the happiness of others. There are, I think we know, many who stay in situations of unhappiness out of fear of causing unhappiness, out of fear of losing sympathy, of becoming unsympathetic.

It is hard to leave happiness for life. There is always a gap between becoming conscious of what is lost by living according to an idea of happiness and being able to leave happiness for life, a gap where things happen, where lives are lived and lives are lost. Not only is there sadness in recognizing gender as the loss of possibility but there is also the sadness of realizing that recognizing such loss does not necessarily make things possible.[23] After all, Clarissa in *The Hours* spends her time, as does Clarissa in *Mrs. Dalloway*, caring for the happiness of Richard: it is her relationship with Sally that suffers, which does not have her attention.[24] Perhaps the film teaches us that Clarissa's unhappiness is both her inheritance from Mrs. Dalloway and her failure to inherit from Laura, from Laura's act of rebellion, rather than being what she catches from Richard, as the child Laura left behind.[25] In the end it is Clarissa's daughter who is sympathetic toward Laura. We learn from this intergenerational sympathy: perhaps it takes more than one generation to reproduce a feminist inheritance, where we can acquire sympathy (maybe a sympathy for affect aliens or an alien sympathy) toward those whose acts are publicly remembered without sympathy, as causing unhappiness to others.

To leave happiness for life is to become alive to possibility. The concept of feminism as "becoming alive" was crucial to second wave feminism even in the mode of its critique of the happy housewife, which seems at one level to deposit feminist hope in happiness. In *The Feminine Mystique*, for instance, Friedan recognizes that some women may be happy as housewives — by saying this, she also implies that making women happy is not the point of feminism.

As she argues, "Surely there are many women in America who are happy at the moment as housewives, and some whose abilities are fully used in the house-wife role. But happiness is not the same thing as the aliveness of being fully used" (1965: 223–24). The concept of aliveness is held up as an alternative social value to happiness. Indeed, Friedan argues that women who can fit the image of the happy housewife are the ones who are more likely to adjust to this role and who then give up — without any conscious act of sacrifice — other opportunities for "finding yourself" (310). Behind this argument is a critique of the concept of adjustment, how happiness demands adjusting your body to a world that has already taken shape. If we take the shape of what is given (which depends on being able to take this shape), we experience the comfort of being given the right shape. As Charlotte Perkins Gilman argued, "Comfort and happiness are very likely a matter of prolonged adjustment. *We like what we are used to*" ([1903] 2002: 8; emphasis added). What lies behind this adjustment is the loss of other possible ways of living, a loss that must remain unmourned if you are to stay well-adjusted. To even recognize such loss is to mourn, which is why it can be easier to avoid recognition. Feminist subjects in refusing to be well-adjusted not only mourn the losses but in mourning open up other possibilities for living, as openings that we inherit over generations.

Consciousness and Racism

Our feminist archive teaches us about unhappiness and what it can do. Feminism involves a sociality of unhappiness not only by generating talk about the collective nature of suffering that is concealed and reproduced by the figure of the happy housewife (which is perhaps how we could consider consciousness-raising) but also through passing books around. To inherit unhappiness through the circulation of books is not necessarily to inherit the same thing. It is not simply that feminism coheres around the inheritance of books such as *Mrs. Dalloway*, which offer alternative forms of consciousness of the world in their narration of gender as loss. After all, if we were to assume feminist consciousness took the form of consciousness of gender as the restriction of possibility, then we would be excluding other kinds of political consciousness from our idea of feminism. Black feminists have had a lot to say, after all, about happiness as a political myth that does things, writing not from the point of view of those who should be happy because they have what promises happiness but instead of those who are already imagined as being unhappy, as lacking the very qualities and attributes that would make a life good.

Consider Toni Morrison's *The Bluest Eye*, which offers us a very different account of unhappiness than that found in the unhappy housewife novels, though it also critiques the idea of the happy family. *The Bluest Eye* begins its critique of the happy family by sentencing it to death: "Here is the house. It is green and white. It has a red door. It is very pretty. Here is the family. Mother, Father, Dick and Jane live in the green-and-white house. They are very happy" ([1970] 1979: 1). By taking the punctuation out of the sentence until it becomes "hereisthehouseitis" (2), the picture-book story becomes nonsense, becomes gabble. To disturb the promise of happiness, which has become literalized, such that happiness is "in house" requires disturbing the very technologies through which we make sense.

The novel tells the story of a family that deviates from the social ideal, that cannot be the "they are very happy" of the picture book. This family is not white, not middle class, where "being not" means being unhappy. Unhappiness becomes a kind of want. In this novel, the family is narrated as wanting, as lacking the qualities or attributes that would make for a good or happy life. Most powerfully, the novel describes the discourses of happiness in terms of the conflation of whiteness with beauty and virtue: the happy ones are blue eyed, the blue-eyed ones are beautiful ones, the beautiful ones are the good ones, the good ones are the happy ones. The "not family," the Breedloves are the ugly ones, as if their ugliness is a curse: "You looked at them and wondered why they were so ugly; you looked closely and you could not find the source" (28). For some, deviation from the happiness scripts is itself an inheritance; you inherit unhappiness by not being the blue-eyed ones, as if "the master had said, 'you are Ugly people'" (28). The evocation of the master is the evocation of the history of slavery. Unhappiness becomes an inheritance of the violence of history.

The story of the novel is the story of what happens to the Breedloves, violence, despair, and misery being what follows being not. The novel offers us different narrators, beginning with the sisters Claudia and Frieda, before switching to the Breedloves: the mother Pauline, the father Cholly, and their daughter Pecola. In a way, the novel is the story of the unhappiness inherited by Pecola, who is raped by her father and who loses her child, an unwanted black baby conceived through violence, in a miscarriage. We first witness Pecola's unhappiness in the opening passage written from the point of view of Claudia: "*So deeply concerned were we with the health and the safe delivery of Pecola's baby we could think of nothing but our own magic: if we planted the seeds, and said the right words over them, they would blossom and everything would be all right. It was a long time before my sister and I admitted to ourselves that no green was going to spring from our seeds. Once we knew, our guilt was relieved only by fights and mutual accusations over who was to blame. For years I thought my sister was right: it was my fault. I had planted them too far down in the earth. It never occurred to either of us that the earth might have been unyielding*" (3). I have described happiness as a technology of cultivation; of cultivating subjects "in the right way" so they will flourish. What is so powerful in this description is how much the failure to flourish is not the failure of care or orientation but the failure of the earth to yield. For some, the earth is unyielding, unable to provide the soil in which life can flourish. The unyielding earth provides the grounds of whiteness, as the restriction of life possibility, as giving life to some and not others.

Our first narrator, Claudia, learns to notice that this earth might be unyielding. Claudia expresses rage at the world that asks her to love in a certain way: "It had begun with Christmas and the gift of dolls. The big, the special, the loving gift was always a big, blue-eyed Baby Doll. From the clucking sounds of adults I knew that the doll represented what they thought was my fondest wish. . . . which were supposed to bring me great pleasure, succeeded in doing quite the opposite. . . . Traced the turned-up nose, poked the glassy-blue eyes, twisted the yellow hair. I could not love it. But I could examine it to see what it was that all the world said was lovable. . . . I destroyed white baby dolls" (13–15). By not experiencing pleasure in the right way, toward the right things, she must destroy things, transferring her hatred and rage from white baby dolls to white baby girls. To hate what is loved is to recognize your alienation from the beloved.[26]

In contrast, Pecola, in wanting happiness, wants what is attributed as the cause of happiness: the bluest eyes. For Pecola: "Long hours she sat looking in the mirror, trying to discover the secret of the ugliness, the ugliness that made her ignored or despised at school, by teachers and classmates alike. . . . It had occurred to Pecola some time ago that if her eyes, those eyes that held the pictures, and knew the sights—if those eyes of hers were different, that is to say, beautiful, she herself would be different" (34). In the following paragraph we return to the picture-book family: "*Pretty eyes. Pretty blue eyes. Big blue pretty eyes. Run, Jip, run. Jip runs. Alice runs. Alice has blue eyes. Jerry has blue eyes. Jerry runs. Alice runs. They run with their blue eyes. Four blue eyes*" (34). The desire for blue eyes is the desire not to be not white; the double negative does not amount to a positive.

This is a bleak novel, bleak as it shows us that the consequences of unhappiness can be more unhappiness.[27] To be conscious of unhappiness is to be conscious of being "not," or of being "un," as lacking the qualities or attributes of happiness. To be not happy is to be not in the eyes of others, in the world of whiteness, which is the world as it coheres around white bodies. Consciousness of "being not" involves self-estrangement: you recognize yourself as the stranger. Note that consciousness is already worldly if you are the one whose arrival disturbs an atmosphere. To recognize yourself as the stranger is to become conscious of the violence directed toward you. Audre Lorde dramatizes how becoming conscious of being a stranger involves a retrospective renaming of apparently random events as racism:

> Tensions on the street were high, as they always are in racially mixed zones of transition. As a very little girl, I remember shrinking from a particular sound, a hoarsely sharp, guttural rasp, because it often meant a nasty glob of grey spittle upon my coat or shoe an instant later. My mother wiped it off with the little pieces of newspaper she always carried in her purse. Sometimes she fussed about low-class people who had no better sense nor manners than to spit into the wind no matter where they went, impressing upon me that this humiliation was totally random. It never occurred to me to doubt her. It was not until years later once in conversation I said to her: "Have you noticed people don't spit into the wind so much the way they used to?" And the look on my mother's face told me that I had blundered into one of those secret places of pain that must never be spoken of again. But it was so typical of my mother when I was young that if she couldn't stop white people spitting on her children because they were Black, she would insist it was something else. (1982: 17–18)

An event happens. And it happens again. The violence is directed from the white body to the black child, who receives that violence by shrinking, shrinking away from its sound. But the mother cannot bear to speak of racism and creates an impression that the violence is random. Racism is a pain that is hard to bear. Consciousness of racism becomes retrospective, and the question of its timing does matter. You learn not to see racism as a way of bearing the pain. To see racism, you have to un-see the world as you learned to see it, the world that covers unhappiness, by covering over its cause. You have to be willing to venture into secret places of pain.

Some forms of "taking cover" from pain—from not naming the causes of pain in the hope that it will go away—are to protect those we love from being hurt, or even to protect ourselves from hurt, or are at least meant as a form of protection. If happiness does provide a way of "taking cover," it is not always offered to protect us from hurt. It can also work to conceal the causes of hurt or to make others *the cause of their own hurt*. In *The Cancer Journals*, Audre Lorde offers a powerful critique of the politics of happiness. She writes as a black lesbian feminist who is experiencing breast cancer: Lorde never refuses the power of "writing as" nor assumes it can abbreviate an experience. Faced with medical discourse that attributes cancer to unhappiness and survival or coping to being happy or optimistic, she suggests: "Looking on the bright side of things is a euphemism used for obscuring certain realities of life, the open consideration of which might prove threatening or dangerous to the status quo" (1997: 76). To obscure or to take cover by looking on the bright side is to avoid what might threaten the world as it is. Lorde moves from this observation to a wider critique of happiness as an obscurant: "Let us seek 'joy' rather than real food and clean air and a saner future on a liveable earth! As if happiness alone can protect us from the results of profit-madness" (76). Lorde suggests that the very idea that our first responsibility is for our own happiness must be resisted by political struggle, which means resisting the idea that our own resistance is a failure to be responsible for happiness: "Was I really fighting the spread of radiation, racism, woman-slaughter, chemical invasion of our food, pollution of our environment, the abuse and psychic destruction of our young, merely to avoid dealing with my first and greatest responsibility to be happy?" (77).[28] I think Audre Lorde has given us the answer to her question.

We can now see how you can retrieve a model of false consciousness in critiquing claims to happiness. You would not be saying "you are wrong, you are not happy, you just think you are as you have a false belief." Rather you would be saying there is something false about our consciousness of the world; we learn not to be conscious, not to see what happens right in front of us. Happiness provides as it were a cover, a way of covering over what resists or is resistant to a view of the world, or a worldview, as harmonious. It is not that an individual person suffers from false consciousness but that we inherit a certain false consciousness when we learn to see and not to see things in a certain way.[29]

Becoming conscious — refusing to take cover — is a form of political struggle. I have been thinking about the labor of becoming conscious of racism and what that does to how we inhabit and know the world. It is hard labor, for sure. I am speaking to a black feminist colleague about racism. We are just talking, recognizing each other, as you do, in how we recognize racism in those everyday encounters you have with people who can't handle it, the idea of it. That's what they always say, she says to me, that you always reduce everything to racism. Racism becomes your paranoia. Of course, it's a way of saying that racism doesn't really exist in the way you say it does. It is as if we had to invent racism to explain our own feeling of exclusion, as if racism provides us with a way of not being responsible for the places we cannot go. It is a form of racism to say that racism does not exist. We know this.

But I am thinking more about paranoia, and the good reasons for bad feelings. I guess the problem is that I do feel paranoid even if I know that this paranoia is reasonable. I do have a kind of paranoid anxiety about things that do and could happen. I am never sure, when x happens, whether x is about racism or is a result of racism. I am never sure. And because I am never sure, then x is lived as possibly about racism, as being what explains how you inhabit the world you do. Racism creates paranoia, that's what racism does. Whiteness is reproduced both by the fantasy of paranoia (it doesn't "really" exist) and by the effect of the fantasy of paranoia, which is to make us paranoid. Our feelings become its truth. And when we scream the truth, we are the sore points. Some people describe the struggle against racism as hitting your head against a brick wall. The wall keeps its place, so it is you that gets sore.

One of the best literary descriptions of how consciousness of racism puts you in a different world is offered in Andrea Levy's *Fruit of the Lemon* (1999). The novel tells the story of Faith Jackson, a black British girl whose parents migrated to England from Jamaica. She is getting along with her life, doing her own thing. She moves out of home, into a share house with her white friends. Her parents let her go: "'Ah Faith, what can we do with you? You just go your own sweet way,' my parents had decided a long time before. 'Your own sweet way'" (19). I will return to this idea of the children of immigrant families being allowed to go on their "own sweet way" in chapter 4. What follows here is a powerful description of a girl experiencing blackness, as something that jolts her consciousness and puts her into a different world.

Again, there is an event. Something happens. Faith and her flatmate Simon witness a violent attack on a black woman. He runs after the attackers, and they are caught. Events are what catch you out and catch you up. We witness the event through Faith's eyes: "A black woman was standing in the doorway of a bookshop. She looked composed, although she had a startled stare—like she's just won the pools and couldn't quite believe it. But sliding slowly down one side of her face were several strings of blood—thick, bright, red blood. I stood in front of her and asked, 'Are you all right?' and felt stupid when she collapsed onto the ground" (150). They return to tell the story of the event.

The story creates a certain kind of drama, in which Simon becomes not simply witness or participant but also the savior, the hero, and even the victim. The housemates gather around him as if this has happened to him, as if what made the event an event was how it affected him: "Simon's hands shook as he lifted his cigarette to his mouth—he couldn't hold it steady. Marion put her hand over his hand to support it. 'I think you're in shock.' Sweet tea is what you need,' she said looking closely into Simon's face. 'Mick, put the kettle on'" (156). Faith watches the black woman disappear as they gather around him. She interrupts the gathering. "I interrupted the story twice. 'She was a black woman,' I said. Simon had just called her the woman who worked there. Twice I had to tell them this woman was black like me. And both times Simon and Mick had looked at me and nodded" (156). Faith identifies with the black woman who has been hurt; she says she was black, she says she was *black like me*. The point of political identification rests on this recognition of another's hurt.

But they keep going with their story, as if her blackness was just a detail that can be passed over. They fuss over Simon: giggling, full of the drama of an event. And then Faith can't bear it anymore. She can't bear the violence of the event, as a violence that acquires its force by being directed against a black woman, to be passed over: "But then I tipped my cup of tea slowly over the table. 'Will you all just shut up. Just fucking shut up. Its not funny!' And there was complete silence as they stopped and stared at me I left the house" (158). To speak of racism, to name racism, to be conscious of racism, puts Faith in a different world, a world where blackness cannot be passed over. The black woman shouts to be heard. And in shouting, the black woman is the one who becomes the origin of bad feeling. So it is she who must leave. Although she returns, she has been undone. She cannot look at her friends; she cannot bear her own reflection in the mirror, as if what the mirror reflects back to her, her black face, is something she can now see and thus can no longer bear. How can one be disturbed by one's own arrival? The familiar is that which recedes to those who inhabit it. To become estranged from the familiar is thus to have it revealed to you. The familiar is disclosed in the revelation of your estrangement. You learn to see yourself as you are seen by those who can inhabit the familiar, because they can recede into its form as Frantz Fanon demonstrated so powerfully in *Black Skin, White Masks* ([1952] 1986).

What follows is a story of Faith going home, as a home that she has never been to, going back to where her parents are from, back to Jamaica. In a way the plot of this novel is simple, as if going home, discovering your roots, can be the solution. It can be read that way—but that's not how I would read it. Consciousness of racism becomes consciousness of being out of place in a world oriented around whiteness. For Faith, finding her place means learning of her parents' arrival, which means learning about where they are from, her own coming into being, an inheritance of displacement. This is not a story of her becoming happy. But it is a story of becoming black as an act of resistance to being passed over, where becoming black means restoring family connections, of hearing family stories. White feminist consciousness novels tend to involve freedom-from-family and its narrow scripts of duty and obligation. Black feminist consciousness novels may involve freedom-to-family, as family is what is lost through unfolding histories of displacement and dispossession.

Feminist consciousness can thus be thought of as consciousness of the violence and power that are concealed under the languages of civility and love, rather than simply consciousness of gender as a site of restriction of possibility. We learn from this so much, too much. We learn to see what is concealed by signs of happiness. You can cause unhappiness merely by noticing something. And if it can cause unhappiness simply to notice something, you realize that the world you are in is not the world you thought you were in. Feminism becomes a kind of estrangement from the world and thus involves moments of self-estrangement. Our feminist archive is an archive of unhappiness even though the threads of unhappiness do not weave our stories together.

In calling for us to recognize how feminist politics involves killing joy, I am also asking us to turn back, to return to feminist histories, as a history of those who have struggled against happiness. I am thus uncertain what it means to call for a more affirmative feminism in our present time.[30] Rosi Braidotti has suggested that the focus on negativity has become a problem within feminism. She offers a rather bleak reading of bleakness: "I actively yearn for a more joyful and empowering concept of desire and for a political economy that foregrounds positivity, not gloom" (2002: 57). The call for affirmation *rather* than negativity in her work involves an explicit turn to happiness. As she argues: "I consider happiness a political issue, as are well-being, self-confidence and a sense of empowerment. These are fundamentally ethical concerns. . . . The feminist movement has played the historical role of placing these items at the centre of the social and political agenda: happiness as a fundamental human right and hence a political question" (2006a: 230). My desire is to revitalize the feminist critique of happiness as a human right and as the appropriate language for politics.

To revitalize the critique of happiness is to be willing to be proximate to unhappiness. I have suggested that feminist consciousness involves consciousness of unhappiness that might even increase our unhappiness, or at least create this impression. Happiness can work to cover over unhappiness, in part by covering over its causes, such that to refuse to take cover can allow unhappiness to emerge. This process of consciousness raising involves not simply becoming conscious of unhappiness but also achieving (with others) better ways of understanding unhappiness. We can recognize that unhappiness is structured, and that what happens to us might be connected in some way to what happens to others. We can recognize not only that we are not the cause of the unhappiness that has been attributed to us but also the effects of being attributed *as* the cause. We can talk about being angry black women or feminist killjoys; we can claim those figures back; we can talk about those conversations we have had at dinner tables or in seminars or meetings; we can laugh in recognition of the familiarity of inhabiting that place. There is solidarity in recognizing our alienation from happiness, even if we do not inhabit the same place (as we do not). There can even be joy in killing joy. And kill joy, we must and we do.

"You might have a good story there," Dick said, "but . . . you cannot make homosexuality attractive. No happy ending. . . ." In other words, my heroine has to decide she's not really queer. . . . "That's it. And the one she's involved with is sick or crazy." VIN PACKER

CHAPTER THREE

Unhappy Queers

IN THIS EXCHANGE Vin Packer, author of the first bestselling lesbian pulp novel *Spring Fire*, first published in 1952, and her publisher come to an agreement. The novel will be published, but only on condition that it does not have a happy ending, as such an ending would "make homosexuality attractive" ([1952] 2004: vi). Queer fiction in this period could not give happiness to its characters *as* queers; such a gift would be readable as making queers appear "good": as the "promotion" of the social value of queer lives, or an attempt to influence readers to become queer.[1]

Somewhat ironically, then, the unhappy ending becomes a political gift: it provides a means through which queer fiction could be published.[2] If the unhappy ending was an effect of censorship, it also provided a means for overcoming censorship. In her introduction to the new issue of *Spring Fire* published in 2004, Vin Packer does express regret for the compromise of its ending. But she also describes how although it "may have satisfied the post office inspections, the homosexual audience would not have believed it for a minute. But they also wouldn't care that much, because more important was the fact there was a new book about us" (vii). The unhappy ending satisfies the censors while also enabling the gay and lesbian audience to be satisfied; we are not obliged to "believe" in the unhappy ending by taking it literally, as "evidence" that lesbians and gays must turn straight, die, or go mad. What mattered was the existence of "a new book about us."

We can see that reading unhappy endings in queer archives is a complicated matter. A literal reading suggests that the very distinction between happy and unhappy endings "works" to secure a moral distinction between good and bad lives. When we read this unhappy queer archive (which is not the only queer archive) we must resist this literalism, which means an active disbelief in the necessary alignment of the happy with the good, or even in the moral transparency of the good itself. Rather than reading unhappy endings as a sign of the withholding of moral approval for queer lives, we must consider how unhappiness circulates within and around this archive, and *what it allows us to do*.

My aim in this chapter is to consider unhappy queers as a crucial aspect of queer genealogy. As Heather Love has argued, "We need a genealogy of queer affect that does not overlook the negative, shameful and difficult feelings that have been so central to queer existence in the last century" (2007: 127). Scholars such as Eve Kosofsky Sedgwick (2003), Elspeth Probyn (2005), and Sally Munt (2007) have offered us powerful defenses of the potentialities of shame for queer politics. I will consider what it might mean to affirm unhappiness, or at least not to overlook it. Unhappiness might appear as feelings that reside within individual characters — from tormented narrators to grief-stricken lovers — or moods that linger without direction, aim, or purpose, which are only loosely attached to points of view, as we saw in *Mrs. Dalloway* in the previous chapter. Unhappiness might involve feelings that get directed in a certain way, and even give the narrative its direction. We can ask how queer fiction attributes and locates unhappiness and how queer fiction might offer different explanation of queer unhappiness rather than simply investing its hope in alternative images of happy queers.

In exploring a queer politics of unhappiness I turn to the classic novel *The Well of Loneliness*. Lisa Walker has argued that "*The Well*'s status as *the* lesbian novel is inseparable from its reputation as *the most depressing* lesbian novel ever written" (2001: 21). *The Well* has even been described as a "narrative of damnation," which gives "the homosexual, particularly the lesbian, riddling images of pity, self-pity and of terror" (Stimpson 1988: 101). The book has been criticized for making its readers feel sad and wretched, perhaps even causing queer unhappiness. I would not dismiss such criticisms: they are part of our shared archive. Indeed, the very expression of unhappiness *about* unhappiness is what makes this archive work; the threads of negative affect weave together a shared inheritance. We can, of course, inherit unhappiness differently. I will read novels such as *The Well of Loneliness* as part of a genealogy of unhappy queers, including within that genealogy a film that seems to be predicated on the social hope of happy queers, *If These Walls Could Talk 2*. I will also, in reflecting on the novels *Rubyfruit Jungle* and *Babyji*, consider how being happily queer might involve a different orientation to the causes of unhappiness.

Just Happiness

I have suggested that promise of happiness directs us toward certain objects, as being necessary for a good life. The good life, in other words, is imagined through the proximity of objects. There is no doubt that the affective repertoire of happiness gives us images of a certain kind of life, a life that has certain things and does certain things. There is no doubt that it is hard to separate images of the good life from the historic privileging of heterosexual conduct, as expressed in romantic love and coupledom, as well as in the idealization of domestic privacy. Lauren Berlant describes so well the "foggy fantasy of happiness" within zones of privacy (2000: 36). In sentimental spaces, or spaces of sentiment, the constitutional rights of those whose love takes certain recognizable forms are secured, where security is what gives both comfort and warmth. The bliss in domestic bliss takes us somewhere, for sure.

There is also no doubt that heterosexual happiness is overrepresented in public culture, often through an anxious repetition of threats and obstacles to its proper achievement. Heterosexual love becomes about the possibility of a happy ending; about what life is aimed toward, as being what gives life direction or purpose, or as what drives a story. It is difficult to separate out narrative as such from the reproduction of happy heterosexuality. As Julie Abraham points out, the "desire of literature" rests not only on "the fiction of desire" but on the "fiction of heterosexual desire" (1996: 3).

In the previous chapter I reflected on happiness scripts as gendered scripts and how following such scripts is what orients subjects toward heterosexuality: for girls, you must become a woman by finding your happiness in the happiness of "a good man." Happiness scripts could be thought of as straightening devices, ways of aligning bodies with what is already lined up. The points that accumulate as lines can be performatives: a point on a line can be a demand to stay in line. To deviate from the line is to be threatened with unhappiness. The unhappiness of the deviant has a powerful function as a perverse promise (if you do this, you will get that!), as a promise that is simultaneously a threat (so don't do that!). Happiness scripts are powerful even when we fail or refuse to follow them, even when desires deviate from their lines. In this way, the scripts speak a certain truth: deviation can involve unhappiness. Happiness scripts encourage us to avoid the unhappy consequences of deviation by making those consequences explicit. The "whole world," it might seem, depends on subjects being directed in the right way, toward the right kind of things. To deviate is always to risk a world even if you don't always lose the world you risk. Queer and feminist histories are the histories of those who are willing to risk the consequences of deviation.

Happiness is not just how subjects speak of their own desires but also what they want to give and receive from others. Happiness involves reciprocal forms of aspiration (I am happy for you, I want you to be happy, I am happy if you are happy) and also forms of coercion that are exercised and concealed by the very language of reciprocity, such that one person's happiness is made conditional not only on another person's happiness but on that person's willingness to be made happy by the same things.

We do things when we speak of happiness, when we put happiness into words. Let's take the statement *I am happy if you are happy*. Such a statement can be attributed, as a way of sharing an evaluation of an object. I could be saying I am happy about this if you are happy about this. The statement does not require an object to mediate between the "I" and the "you": the "you" can be the object, can be what my happiness is dependent upon. The statement might translate as: *I will only be happy if you are*. If I can only be happy when you are happy, then I would be unhappy if you were unhappy. *I will be unhappy if you are*. If I was happy and you were unhappy, then I would no longer be happy. *Your unhappiness would threaten my happiness*. If my happiness is dependent upon your happiness, then you have the power to determine my happiness. You might thus feel obliged to conceal your unhappiness in order to protect my happiness. *You have a duty to be happy for me*.

I am not saying that such speech acts always translate in quite this way. But we can note the swiftness of conversion between desire and duty; the very desire for the happiness of others can be the point at which others are bound to be happy for us. If to love another is to want that person's happiness, then love might be experienced as the duty to be happy for another.[3] We can examine the relationship between happiness and love more closely. Robert Heinlen defines love as "a condition in which the happiness of another person is essential to your own" (cited in Lucas 2006: 74).[4] Gottfried Leibniz also offers a definition of love in which happiness is integral: "love is to be disposed to take pleasure in the perfection, well-being or happiness of the object of one's love" ([1765] 1981: 163).[5] In the previous chapter, I explored some of the consequences of what I called conditional happiness. We can now consider more closely what it means for happiness to be a condition of love.

We might want the happiness of the other, or want to give the other happiness, or want to be the cause of the other's happiness. We might want all of these things at once. What follows from such wants? It is interesting that wanting the happiness of the loved other often hesitates with the signifier "just." "I just want you to be happy." What does it mean to want "just" happiness? What does it mean for a parent to say this to a child? The "just" might reveal something: as if wanting happiness is not to want other things that might demand more from the child. In a way, the desire for the child's happiness seems to offer a certain kind of freedom, as if to say: "I don't want you to be this, or to do that; I just want you to be or to do 'whatever' makes you happy." You could say that the "whatever" seems to release us from the obligation of the "what." The desire for the child's happiness seems to offer the freedom of a certain indifference to the content of a decision.[6]

Let's take the psychic drama of the queer child. You could say that the queer child is an unhappy object for many parents. In some parental responses to the child coming out, this unhappiness is not so much expressed as being unhappy about the child being queer, but as *being unhappy about the child being unhappy*.[7] In the classic book on lesbian and gay liberation, *No Turning Back*, one of the typical parental responses to the child coming out is "I just want you to be happy, dear, and it's such an unhappy life" (1983: 17). Queer fiction is full of such speech acts in which the parents express their fear that the queer child is destined to have an unhappy life.[8] Let's take the following exchange from the lesbian novel *Annie on My Mind* (1982) by Nancy Garden.

"Lisa," my father said, "I told you I'd support you and I will. And right now I can see we're all too upset to discuss this very much more, so in a minute or two I'm going to take you and your mother and me out to lunch. But honey, I know it's not fashionable to say this, but—well, maybe it's just that I love your mother so much and you and Chad so much that I have to say to you I've never thought gay people can be very happy—no children for one thing, no real family life. Honey, you are probably going to be a damn good architect—but I want you to be happy in other ways, too, as your mother is, to have a husband and children. I know you can do both. . . ." *I am happy*, I tried to tell him with my eyes. *I'm happy with Annie; she and my work are all I'll ever need; she's happy, too—we both were until this happened.* (191)

This speech act functions powerfully. The parent makes an act of identification with an imagined future of necessary and inevitable unhappiness. Such an identification through grief about what the child will lose reminds us that the queer life is already constructed as an unhappy life, as a life without the "things" that make you happy, or as a life that is depressed as it lacks certain things: "a husband, children." To love is here to want the child not to give up on such things; you want the child to have happiness by not giving up on these things. The desire for the child's happiness is thus far from indifferent. The speech act "I just want you to be happy" is directive at the very point of its imagined indifference.

For the daughter, it is only the eyes that can speak; and they try to tell an alternative story about happiness and unhappiness. In her response, she claims happiness, for sure. She is happy "*with* Annie," which is to say, she is happy with *this* relationship and *this* life that it will commit her to. The power of the unspoken response is lodged in the use of the word *until*: we were happy "until" this happened, where the "until" marks the moment that the father speaks his disapproval. The unhappy queer is here the queer who is judged to be unhappy: the judgment of unhappiness creates unhappiness, in the very performance of the failure to recognize the social viability of queer relationships, in its failure to recognize queer love. The father's speech act creates the very affective state of unhappiness that is imagined to be the inevitable consequence of the daughter's decision. When "this" happens, unhappiness does follow.

The social struggle within families often involves a struggle over the causes of unhappiness. The father is unhappy as he thinks the daughter will be unhappy if she is queer. The daughter is unhappy as the father is unhappy with her being queer. The father witnesses the daughter's unhappiness as a sign of the truth of his position: that she will be unhappy because she is queer. Even the happy queer might become unhappy at this point. And clearly the family can only be maintained as a happy object, as being what is anticipated to cause happiness, by making the unhappiness of the queer child its point.

The speech act "I just want you to be happy" can also be used as a form of tolerance or acceptance in coming out stories. A contrasting example to *Annie on My Mind* was presented in Dana's story of coming out to her parents in the first and second series of *The L Word*. In the first instance, Dana's mother, Sharon Fairbanks, can't handle the very idea of it and tries to convince her daughter to be straight.[9] But eventually, when her daughter and her partner Tonya speak of their love, she is more accepting. She says: "I can see that you've found love. It doesn't matter what form it takes as long as it makes you happy."

It is always paradoxical to say something does not matter: if you have to say something does not matter, it usually implies that it does. You might offer recognition on condition that the one that you recognize will ensure that the difference that matters becomes a difference that does not matter. Queer love might be recognized on condition that such love is recognizable as love, whereby love is itself conditional on happiness. As I have already established, some things more than others are attributed as happiness-causes. In this occasion, the couple are asking for parental blessing of their marriage: a straight way of doing queer love, perhaps. If queers have to the approximate signs of happiness in order to be recognized, then they might have to minimize signs of queerness.[10]

There are of course good reasons for telling stories about queer happiness, in response to and as a response to the very presumption that a queer life is necessarily and inevitably an unhappy life.[11] We just have to hear the violence of Michael's tragic comment, "Show me a happy homosexual and I'll show you a gay corpse," from Matt Crowley's play *The Boys in the Band* (1968) to be reminded of these reasons (cited by Sanderson 1999: 141–42). And yet, at the same time, and perhaps even for the same reasons, we can see why telling stories about queer unhappiness might matter. It might be the pain of not being recognized. It might be the conditions of recognition. It might even be the work required to counter the perception of your life as being unhappy: the very pressure to be happy in order to show that you are not unhappy can create unhappiness for sure.

Causing Unhappiness

To arrive into the world is to inherit the world that you arrive into. The family is a point of inheritance, shaping what is proximate to the child (see Ahmed 2006). The queer child fails to inherit the family by reproducing its line. This failure is affective; you become an unhappiness-cause. As I pointed out in my introduction to this book, "unhappiness" was first used to describe those who cause misfortune or trouble rather than those who feel sad or wretched. We can learn from the swiftness of the translation between causing unhappiness and being described as being unhappy. We must learn.

You can become unhappy *because* you are attributed as the cause of unhappiness. Freud's reading of the case of homosexuality in one of his female patients dramatizes this point. What is striking about the case is that the woman who provides it is presented as "happy" with her sexuality: "she did not try to deceive me by saying that she felt any urgent need to be freed from her homosexuality" (Freud [1920] 1955: 153). On the contrary, as Freud himself puts it, "she could not conceive of any other way of being in love" (153). The homosexual woman does express a therapeutic desire to Freud: not the desire to redirect her sexual orientation but the desire not to be the cause of parental unhappiness. She is made unhappy by their unhappiness with her sexual orientation.

Sarah Schulman's novel *Empathy* begins with an epitaph from Freud's case. In this novel, Anna goes to see a therapist and says: "Now, I happen to be a happy person, Doc, I like *my* life the way it is" ([1992] 2006: 52). Anna is not unhappy with her life being the way that is it. She is not unhappy wanting women as a woman. Instead she says that it is "ideas about structures" that make her unhappy. The Doc's conclusion is that she is suffering from empathy (52). To be empathetic is to suffer: it is to be made unhappy by other people's unhappiness. It is not necessarily that you catch their feeling but that you have to live with their unhappiness with your life choices ("ideas about structures"). Such unhappiness is directed toward those who do not live according to the right ideas. They are unhappy with you for not being what they want you to be.

You can be made unhappy by not being what the other wants you to be, even if you don't want to be what the other wants you to be.

It is hard when your very arrival into the world becomes the cause of unhappiness. We could take any number of sad queer books and they would show us this. Let's take Radclyffe Hall's *The Well of Loneliness*. The novel tells the story of Stephen Gordon, who is described throughout as an invert, whose life hurtles toward the "tragic and miserable ending" that seems to be the only available plot for inversion (Hall [1928] 1982: 411).[12] Throughout the novel, Stephen has a series of tragic and doomed love affairs, ending with her relationship with Mary Lewellyn, described as "the child, the friend, the belovèd" (303). The novel does not give us a happy ending, and this seems partly its point: Stephen gives up Mary as a way of relieving her from the burden of their love. Stephen imagines saying to Mary: "I am one of those whom God marked on the forehead. Like Cain, I am marked and blemished. If you come to me, Mary, the world will abhor you, will persecute you, will call you unclean. Our love may be faithful even unto death and beyond—yet the world will call it unclean" (303).

A key turning point in the novel is when Stephen and Mary arrive at Alec's bar, a space in which the "miserable army" of the inverted and perverted reside. Stephen is approached by Adolphe Blanc, a "gentle and learned Jew." He says to her: "In this little room, tonight, every night, there is so much misery, so much despair, that the walls seem almost too narrow to contain it. . . . Yet outside there are happy people who sleep the sleep of the so-called just and righteous. When they wake it will be to persecute those who, through no fault of their own, have been set apart from the day of their birth, deprived of all sympathy, all understanding. They are thoughtless, these happy people who sleep" (395). In this extraordinary passage, Adolphe Blanc, a marginal character in the book, who arrives "through the crowd" at Alec's bar, speaks what I would be tempted to describe as the truth of the novel: the happiness of the straight world is a form of injustice. Heterosexual happiness is narrated as a social wrong, as based on the unthinking exclusion of those whose difference is already narrated as deprivation. Happiness for some involves persecution for others: it is not simply that this happiness produces a social wrong; it might even depend upon it. The unhappiness of the deviant performs a claim for justice.

Every sad book has its moments, moments where it is all "too much," when a body, a life, a world becomes unbearable. Thinking about bearable and unbearable lives might offer a different angle on Judith Butler's (2004) concept of livable and unlivable lives. A bearable life is a life that can hold up, which can keep its shape or direction, in the face of what it is asked to endure. To bear can also then be a capacity; a bearable life is a life that we can bear. A bearable life suggests that the conditions of liveability involve a relationship to suffering, to "what" a life must endure. A bearable life is a life where what must be endured does not threaten that life, in either the bare facts of its existence or in the sense of its aim, direction, or purpose. A bearable life is a life that in being endured can keep its bearings. The unbearable life is a life which cannot be tolerated or endured, help up, held onto. The unbearable life "breaks" or "shatters" under the "too much" of what is being borne. You might note here that the conditions of bearability relate not only to the object (what someone is asked to bear, though it includes this what), nor do they relate only to the subject (who is doing the bearing, though it includes this who). What makes for an unbearable life takes place *somewhere* between the subject and the world that throws "things" up; sometimes, something becomes "too much" to bear, where the "too much" is experienced as the breaking of a long history of involvement or the endurance that sustains suffering insofar as it is borne. When "it" is too much, things break, you reach a breaking point.

At one point, Stephen and Mary are rejected by a woman who had befriended them to protect her own reputation and the reputation of her daughter. She sends them a letter announcing that she has been forced "to break off our friendship" and asks them not to come to her house for Christmas as had been planned (374). In other words, to protect her family happiness she has to reject proximity to those who might "stain" her reputation, those who already attributed as unhappiness-causes, as being or embodying the unhappiness they are assumed to cause. They are no longer welcome at the family table; they cannot share the celebration.

We can see from this example how the very idea of contagion can be evoked in the self-regulation of feeling worlds.[13] You might refuse proximity to somebody out of fear that you will be infected by unhappiness, or you might seek proximity to somebody out of hope that you will be infected by happiness. An affective geography of happiness takes shape.[14] Unhappiness is pushed to the margins, which means certain bodies are pushed to the margins, in order that the unhappiness that is assumed to reside within these bodies does not threaten the happiness that has been given.

To be rejected in order to preserve happiness can mean that you experience the feelings that are attributed to you. The pain of this rejection is the breaking point of the novel: "Then it seemed to Stephen that all the pain that had so far been thrust upon her by existence, was as nothing to the unendurable pain which she must now bear to hear that sobbing, to see Mary thus wounded, and utterly crushed, thus shamed and humbled for the sake of their love, thus bereft of all dignity and protection" (375). Stephen cannot bear the unhappiness that she witnesses on the face of the beloved. It is because the world is unhappy with queer love that queers become unhappy, because queer love is an unhappiness-cause for the others whom they love, who share their place of residence. It is not that queers feel sad or wretched right from the beginning. Queer unhappiness does not provide us with a beginning. Certain subjects might appear as sad or wretched, or might even become sad or wretched, because they are perceived as lacking what causes happiness, and as causing unhappiness in their lack.

We can see why it is difficult to give happiness to queers *as* queers when accounting for such a world. What kind of ending can be written? I would argue that the novel offers us two endings. The first ending depicts the experience of Jamie and Barbara, who are presented as "like" Stephen and Mary: an invert and her beloved. Their ending provides one possible ending for unhappy queers: "Then all in a moment the floodgates gave way and she wept and she wept like a creature demented. Bewailing the life of hardship and exile that had sapped Barbara's strength and weakened her spirit; bewailing the cruel dispensation of fate that had forced them to leave their home in the Highlands; bewailing the terrible thing that is death to those who, still loving, must look upon it. Yet all the exquisite pain of this parting seemed as nothing to an anguish that was far more subtle: 'I can't mourn her without bringing shame on her name—I can't go back home now and mourn her,' wailed Jamie" (407). Barbara's death is narrated as an effect of a life of hardship that is the lot of the inverted. A life of hardship and exile saps your strength, weakens your spirit; it is a life that kills you slowly, day by day. In a scene that has been echoed so much in our unhappy queer archive, the pain of experiencing the death of a beloved is intensified by the impossibility of mourning. So familiar, too familiar: the familiarity of a scene of suffering should not stop us from describing the suffering of the scene. Jamie cannot return home with Barbara; she cannot grieve for her beloved, at home, without causing more unhappiness. The nonrecognition of the lives and loves of the inverted finds its most torturous expression in this inability to mourn the death of one's beloved. In despair at Barbara's death, and then at the impossibility of mourning her death, Jamie commits suicide: "Stephen would again and again go over the last heart-rending days with Barbara and Jamie, railing against the outrageous justice that had led to their tragic and miserable ending. She would clench her hands in a kind of fury. How long was this persecution to continue?" (411). For Stephen, witnessing this "tragic and miserable" ending is about witnessing the personal costs of injustice. It also involves witnessing a potential ending for her and Mary: that they too will not bear either the life or death that their love will bring.

We can read this "tragic and miserable ending" as the first narrative ending in the novel, as an ending that demands to be rewritten. The scene evokes an earlier encounter with Adolphe in Alec's bar, when Stephen says: "When one comes to a place like this, one feels horribly sad and humiliated. One feels that the odds are too heavily against any real success, any real achievement. Where so many have failed who can hope to succeed? *Perhaps this is the end*" (395; emphasis added). Adolphe replies: "You are wrong, very wrong—*this is only the beginning*. Many die, many kill their bodies and souls, but they cannot kill the justice of God, even they cannot kill the eternal spirit. From their very degradation that spirit will rise up to demand of the world compassion and justice" (396; emphasis added). The second ending of the novel offers a flawed but brave attempt to write an alternative ending to this first one, to find an ending that is not only "miserable and tragic" (though it *must be* and *will be* that) but one that in its very depiction of misery can also offer a new beginning.

In the second ending, Stephen gives Mary up, by appearing to give Mary to Martin. For some readers this ending shows that the novel does not place its own hopes for happiness within lesbianism. Jay Prosser, for instance, argues "that Stephen gives up Mary to Martin Hallam in spite of Mary's devotion to her indicates that the invert functions not as a figure for lesbianism—a lure or a construct—but precisely as its refusal. Through her passing over Mary (both passing over her and passing her over to Martin), Stephen affirms her identification with the heterosexual man" (1998: 166). I want to read what is being affirmed by Stephen's gesture quite differently. Does Stephen give Mary to Martin, as Prosser suggests? I want to suggest that an alternative gift economy is at stake. Take the following passage: "Never before had she seen so clearly all that was lacking to Mary Llewellyn, all that would pass from her faltering grasp, perhaps never to return, with the passing of Martin — children, a home that the world would respect, ties of affection that the world would hold sacred, the blessèd security and the peace of being released from the world's persecution. And suddenly Martin appeared to Stephen as a creature endowed with incalculable bounty, having in his hands all those priceless gifts which she, love's mendicant, could never offer. *Only one gift she could offer to love, to Mary, and that was the gift of Martin*" (438–39; emphasis added). Stephen does not give Mary to Martin. *She gives Martin to Mary.* She gives Martin to Mary as a way of giving Mary access to a happiness that she cannot give. This gift signals not a failure to love but a form of love: it is because the world is unhappy with their love that Stephen cannot be the cause of Mary's happiness.

We can see the problems with the idea that love is to cause or to want to cause happiness for a queer politics, given a world in which queerness is read as wretched. A queer lover might not be able to cause happiness for her beloved if her beloved cannot bear being rejected by the straight world. We could of course point to a counterhistory of queers who have caused other queers to be happy through their love, even if the world has not been happy with such love. But I do wonder whether a queer definition of love might want to separate love from happiness, given how happiness tends to come with rather straight conditions. I thus offer Simone Weil's definition of love as a queer definition: "Love on the part of someone who is happy is the wish to share the suffering of the beloved who is unhappy. Love on the part of someone who is unhappy is to be filled with joy by the mere knowledge that his beloved is happy without sharing in this happiness or even wishing to do so" ([1952] 2002: 63). Queer love might involve happiness only by insisting that such happiness is *not* what is shared.

Stephen might not insist on sharing Mary's happiness, but it is her desire for Mary's happiness that leads to the awkward gift of Martin. We do not know, in the novel, whether Mary receives this gift: we are not given an ending for Mary, as Clare Hemmings suggests (2001: 194). Perhaps the point is that Mary's happiness cannot be told, as Mary's "real story has yet to be told," as Esther Newton describes so well (2000: 188).[15] If anything, for Mary, Stephen's gesture is lived as a death: "A mist closing down, a thick black mist. Someone pushing the girl away, without speaking. Mary's queer voice coming out of the gloom, muffled by the folds of that thick black mist, only a word here and there getting through: "'All my life I've given . . . you've killed . . . I loved you . . . Cruel, oh cruel! You're unspeakably cruel . . .' Then the sound of the rough and pitiful sobbing" (445). Martin does arrive at this moment, but it is only because Stephen has put him there. Beyond the frame of the ending, Mary could yet refuse Stephen's gift. The violence in Stephen's gesture might be how it misrecognizes the unbearability that drives it, by locating that unbearability within Mary. It is Stephen who cannot bear witnessing the pain and unhappiness of persecution on the face of her beloved. It is "too much" for Stephen, not Mary. Or we could say that if the novel locates that violence and misery within the walls of inversion, rather than within the body of the inverted, then the "too much" becomes, if anything, a common ground.

Perhaps the injustice of the ending is the presumption that Mary's happiness depends on being given up. Or does the ending give up on happiness by giving Mary up? This alternative ending does not convert unhappiness into happiness but does something else with unhappiness. In her grief for Barbara and Jamie, Stephen redescribes shame not as the affective situation of inhabiting the wrong body, as she expressed in an earlier stage of the novel, but as the failure to identify with, or declare solidarity with, those who share the unhappiness of one's situation in the world: "As for those who were ashamed to declare themselves, lying low for the sake of peaceful existence, she utterly despised such of them as had brains; they were traitors to themselves and their fellows, she insisted" (413). What is shameful is the very act of hiding underneath happy heterosexuality for the "sake of a peaceful existence," as it refuses to recognize the bond of shared affliction.

In the moment Stephen gives up on happiness, she feels a bond of unhappiness with those who share the signs of inversion. Stephen hears the suffering voices of other inverts and they call her by name: "'Stephen, Stephen!' The quick, the dead, and the yet unborn—all calling her, softly at first, then louder. Aye, and those lost and terrible brothers from Alec's, they were here, and they were also calling: 'Stephen! Stephen, speak with your God and ask Him why He has left us forsaken!' She could see their marred and reproachful faces with the haunted, melancholy eyes of the invert—eyes that had looked too long on a world that lacked all pity and understanding" (446). Her unhappiness offers a queer kinship: you share not simply unhappiness but the unhappy consequences of being the cause of social and familial unhappiness. The return to Alec's bar, this recognition of the eyes of the inverted as a form of speech, is what allows Stephen not to give up her life (as Jamie did earlier) but to give her life to the miserable army:

> Rockets of pain, burning rockets of pain—*their pain, her pain*, all welded together into one consuming agony. Rockets of pain that shot up and burst, dropping scorching tears of fire on the spirit—*her pain, their pain* . . . all the misery at Alec's. And the press and the clamour of those countless others—they fought, they trampled, they were getting her under. *In their madness to become articulate through her*, they were tearing her to pieces, getting her under. They were everywhere now, cutting off her retreat; neither bolts nor bars would avail to save her. The walls fell down and crumbled before them; at the cry of their suffering *the walls fell and crumbled*: "We are coming, Stephen—we are still coming on, and our name is legion—you dare not disown us!" She raised her arms, trying to ward them off, but they closed in and in: "You dare not disown us!" They possessed her. *Her barren womb became fruitful*—it ached with its fearful and sterile burden. It ached with the fierce yet helpless children who would clamour in vain for their right to salvation. (447; emphasis added)

This is quite an extraordinary passage—with clear religious undertones, as Sally Munt (2001: 200) has argued of the book in general. What is striking for me is the switch between "her pain, their pain" and "their pain, her pain"; the passage weaves the stories of pain together. She comes to embody this pain, to speak it, to articulate it.[16] At this moment, the moment when she seems most on her own, she is also most connected to others. And at this very moment, this moment of madness, "the walls fell down." This is an image of revolution: the walls that contain the misery are brought down; an un-housing that is not only a call for arms but a disturbance in the very grounds for happiness, insofar as the happy folk, those who sleep, those who do not think to think, depend on misery being kept underground. Indeed, the moment of revolution is a new form of reproduction, a reproduction of another kind of life form, a queer life form, perhaps. Queer unhappiness offers a rather deviant form of fertility.

The alternative ending in this novel turns misery and unhappiness into revolution: Stephen refuses what she sees as the only end point for her and Mary in this world not simply by giving Mary up but by revolting against the world. It is the promise of revolution—of coming to arms through misery—that animates the unhappy ending of this novel. Not only does the novel explain the unhappiness of its ending as an effect of the violence of the happiness that resides within the straight world but it locates the promise of happiness for queers in revolution against the structures — the walls — that keep that world in place.

The Well of Loneliness teaches us about unhappy queer histories: "the sad old queens and long-suffering dykes who haunt the historical record" (Love 2007: 32). The novel can also help us describe the present. We can contrast The Well of Loneliness with the film Lost and Delirious (2001), directed by Léa Pool, and based (very loosely) on Susan Swan's novel The Wives of Bath (1993). This is a moody, sad, and awkward film that hurtles its way toward a seemingly inevitable tragic ending, which it seems no one or nothing can change; as with The Well of Loneliness, the linking of queer fates with "fatality" seems partly the point. This film is based in a girl's boarding school in Canada and follows a passionate love affair between two girls, Paulie (Piper Perabo) and Tori (Jessica Paré). We witness their love through Mouse (Mischa Barton), who arrives at the school after the death of her mother and who shares a room with Paulie and Tori. The film presents itself from the start as a story of the "lost girls": when Mouse becomes friends with Paulie and Tori, Paulie says: "Now you're one of the lost girls. Welcome to the club."

One of the most striking scenes in the film occurs when the three girls write imaginary letters to their mothers: Paulie to the mother she does not know, who gave her up for adoption; Mouse to her dead mother, whose face she struggles to recall; and Tori to her living and ever-present mother. In the scene, each girl witnesses the impossibility of sharing happiness with her mother; in turn, each weeps for the other girls' stories of loss and betrayal. The most painful letter, the one that somehow prefigures the unhappiness of the ending of the film is the one written by Tori, the only one of the girls who can be close to her mother. She writes: "Dear Mummy, I hate you for multiple reasons, the most recent one being because you went on and on about my teeth at Easter in front of all your gross friends. You want me to be like your perfect junior league girl, and grow up to do charity balls and be the concubine for some banker, like you. But the truth of it is I am like addicted to you like chocolate. I always want to be around you. I'm some like stupid little puppy and you keep like kicking my teeth in with your words and your tone. Sometimes, I wish you were dead." This powerful, ambivalent, and passionate expression of attachment cuts through the film. It is a shocking address, as reflected by the shock on Paulie's and Mouse's faces. The daughter who cannot be what her mother wants her to be, who cannot be like her mother, who cannot even stand what her mother is like, cannot bear to give up on her and the possibility of being with her. This desire to be with the mother who wants her to be who she cannot be is a kind of death wish.

The climactic moment of the film comes when Tori's sister finds Tori and Paulie in bed together. For Tori, "being seen" with Paulie threatens to break her world apart; it is "too much." When Paulie tries to comfort her, Tori says: "She'll go hysterical. She'll go straight to Mum and Dad." What follows is the beginning of the ending. To protect her capacity to cause her mother happiness, Tori must prove she is "really" straight, and thus she has to give up Paulie. When her sister asks whether she is sure she is not a lesbian, Tori replies: "Ali, I love guys. I am boy crazy, if anything." She turns straight by talking straight—bonding with her sister through boy talk—a turning toward the straight world lived as a turning away from a queer object. For Tori, "turning straight" is melancholic in the way described by Judith Butler in *The Psychic Life of Power* (1997). Turning straight means turning away from a queer object choice, which registers as grief before the grief can be covered over. She desperately and rather badly performs heterosexuality as a defense against becoming queer and as a way of not being undone by the loss of this becoming. To do straightness is not to be undone by giving up queer love.[17]

For Tori, to be in a relationship with Paulie would cause her own unhappiness because it would cause her mother's unhappiness. If Tori can only be happy if her mother is happy (if she must, to return to my discussion in the previous chapter, become Sophy), then she must give up Paulie. So yes, being queer, for Tori, would be unbearable. It would mean losing the very possibility of familial love, of being the cause of family happiness and whatever it promises to bring. She says later to Mouse: "You don't know my parents. They are super, super straight. My mother would never speak to me again. *I couldn't deal with losing them.* I love Paulie. You know I do. There's this life I am *supposed* to live. *There is a dream my mother and father have for me.* And even though it is killing me, I cannot be with Paulie ever, not ever, ever again." Tori has two endings in sight, both of which are kinds of death: she loves Paulie and loses her family and gives up the life she is "supposed" to live, the life her parents dreamt for her; or she gives up Paulie, even though "it is killing." She gives up

Paulie, rather than giving up this life, even though she loves Paulie: she cannot bear the thought of not living the life her parents have imagined for her. For Tori to be queer is to risk her place in history, her home, siblings, parents, her life as it has been imagined by herself or by others, even if the content of that life is not what she wishes for.

For Paulie, losing Tori is a certain death. Much of the rest of the film charts her descent into an alienated, desperate, passionate rage at the world that takes her love away, narrated by Mouse as a descent into "darkness" and "madness." She befriends a vulture, a bird of prey. In the tragic ending, we watch as Paulie, with her vulture, jumps off the roof of the school, as if to "fly away." It is at this moment that her descent becomes an ascent. Our eyes do not follow her down; she does not go down. The camera pans up, showing only an ascent; she and the bird rise above the heads of the teachers and schoolgirls who look upon the scene with a passive horror and disbelief.

In ending with her death, the film ends with flight: we don't reach an end-point — and that's at least partly the point. Paulie does not "fly away" on her own but with her friend, a wild injured bird that she saved: "We will fly away from here," she says, "we will fly away from here together." While this together-ness may seem far from the promise of a queer community, perhaps it is more promising than we realize.[18] In this ending, Paulie becomes the bird, or the bird becomes Paulie, the open sky above the school signifying both the promise of another world and the wretched emptiness of the one they leave behind. In both *The Well of Loneliness* and *Lost and Delirious*, the unhappy ending does not just end there; we do not end with unhappiness as such. The depiction of the costs of happy heterosexuality involves the work of social critique: a collective rebellion against this very script, or at least a flight from the violence of its demand.

Reading *The Well of Loneliness* and *Lost and Delirious* together, an early-twentieth-century novel with a twenty-first-century film, is plausible. The fact that it is plausible tells us about the politics of unhappy endings as an enduring sign of how unbearable it can still be to live in this world, this world of "happy folk," as queers. We can see too the importance of embracing the unhappy queer, rather than simply placing our hopes in an alternative figure of the happy queer. The unhappy queer is unhappy with the world that reads queers as unhappy. The risk of promoting the happy queer is that the unhappiness of this world could disappear from view. *We must stay unhappy with this world.*

Some of the responses to the *Lost and Delirious* teach us about the risks of promoting queer happiness. Some critics suggested that this film was dated. Cynthia Fuchs, for example, even describes it as "time-warped."[19] The implication of such a description is that queers can now come out, be accepted, and be happy. Those of us committed to a queer life know that forms of recognition are either precariously conditional, you have to be the right kind of queer by depositing your hope for happiness in the right places (even with perverse desire you can have straight aspirations), or it is simply not given. Not only is recognition not given but it is often not given in places that are not noticeable to those who do not need to be recognized, which helps sustain the illusion that it is given (which means that if you say that it has not been given, you are read as paranoid). Indeed, the illusion that same-sex object choices have become accepted and acceptable (for example, that civil partnerships would mean queer civility) both conceals the ongoing realities of discrimination, non-recognition, and violence and requires that we approximate the straight signs of civility. So yes, we must stay unhappy with this world.

The recognition of queers can be narrated as the hope or promise of becoming acceptable, where in *being* acceptable you must *become* acceptable to a world that has already decided what *is* acceptable. Recognition becomes a gift given from the straight world to queers, which conceals queer labor and struggle (see Schulman 1998: 102), the life worlds generated by queer activism. It is as if such recognition is a form of straight hospitality, which in turn positions happy queers as guests in other people's homes, reliant on their continuing good will. In such a world you are asked to be grateful for the bits and pieces that you are given. To be a guest is to experience a moral obligation to be on your best behavior, such that to refuse to fulfil this obligation would threaten your right to coexistence. The happy queer, who has good manners, who is seated at the table in the right way, might be a strategic form of occupying an uncivil world. But strategic occupations can keep things in place. Or we can stay in place through the effort of an occupation. Queer activisms create "a place at the table" in the hope that the table will not keep its place (Ahmed 2006: 174). A revolution of unhappiness might require an unhousing; it would require not legitimating more relationships, more houses, even more tables but delegitimating the world that "houses" some bodies and not others. The political energy of unhappy queers might depend on not being in house.

Happy Queers

Of course, to describe a queer archive as an unhappy queer archive is not to reduce that archive to unhappiness. To narrate unhappiness can be affirmative; it
can gesture toward another world, even if we are not given a vision of the world
as it might exist after the walls of misery are brought down. I want to consider
If these Walls Could Talk 2 (2000) as a film involving a narrative conversion from
unhappiness, death, and loss to happiness, hope, and life. Does happiness for
queers involve a revolution in the organization of sexuality, desire, and the
body, or does it simply make queers part of the same world, the world of "happy
folk," even if we have to work to get there?

The story, however, is not simply about progress toward queer happiness.
The film is in fact three short films, each with a different director and cast;
each film involves a story about a different generation, moving "forward"
through time: from 1961 (dir. Jane Anderson) to 1972 (dir. Martha Coolidge) to
2000 (dir. Anne Heche). What the generations share, what provides as it were
the common ground, is the house. The walls, if they could talk, would tell the
story. Indeed, reflecting back on *The Well of Loneliness*, we might note the significance of "the walls" as a motif: the walls create spaces; they mark the edge
between what is inside and out. The walls contain things by holding up; they
bear the weight of residence. In *The Well*, the walls contain misery, and the
revolution of the ending involves bringing them down. In this film, the walls
are container devices, but "what" they contain depends on the passing of time,
shaped by the comings and goings of different bodies. Inside the house, we are
occupied. Things happen.

The action of the *If These Walls Could Talk 2* certainly largely takes place
inside the house. However, what links the three films that make up the larger
film is footage of feminist and lesbian and gay demonstrations: while the
drama of each of the sections take place within private spaces, or in the semi-
public space of queer bars, what holds the film together is the public space of
activism: the streets. In the opening sequence, these different temporalities,
embodied as generations, are placed alongside each, as frames. On the left
side, we have the happy housewife (see chapter 2). In the middle, we have a
picture of activism: a demonstration in the streets. On the right side, we have
an image of a happy queer family. Feminist and queer activisms are the mediat-

ing point, as "what" must take place to get from happy heterosexuality (which as we know creates unhappiness conditions for queers) to queer happiness. Activism is imagined as converting unhappy queers into happy ones.[20] The use of archives within the film is powerful: we are given a history of queer happiness as a history that comes alive in the weave of the film: a history not only of suffering but of struggle, of labor, of getting together, and of love. But how is queer happiness imagined once we get there? What does it mean to move from unhappy to happy queers through this temporal and spatial sequencing? In my reading, I will focus on the relation between the first and final film, asking how happiness and unhappiness is distributed within and between them.

The first film tells the story of a lesbian couple, Edith (Vanessa Redgrave) and Abby (Marian Seldes), and what happens when Abby dies. In one of the opening scenes, Abby, a bird lover, climbs a tree to tend to the birds in the birdhouse while Edith is in the kitchen. The film begins with the quietness of their intimacy, with the everyday domesticity of their shared world. Everything is shattered when Abby slips and falls. What follows is perhaps one of the most moving accounts of unrecognized grief I have seen. It recalls the trauma of *The Well of Loneliness*, when Jamie cannot mourn for her beloved. In much of this film, the camera hesitates on Edith's face, which is both expressionless and expressive, as if what she endures is too much to be spoken, or as if to speak would be to fail to recognize its force. Indeed, the film explores the significance of attachments that are secretive, that don't "come out," and how loss itself becomes a secret, an existential pain that must be borne alone, must be kept apart, even from the witnessing "eye" of the camera. Edith's eyes "well up," but she does not speak about her grief, other than to speak of Abby and of the kind of life she lived.

In the scene after the fall, we are in the hospital waiting room. Edith is waiting. Another woman arrives, visibly upset, and says: "They just took my husband in, he had a heart attack." Edith comforts her. The comfort is not returned: when Edith explains why she is there—"my friend fell off a tree, we think she had a stroke"—the woman's response is to ask "is your husband still alive?" When Edith replies, "I never had a husband," the woman says, "That's lucky, because you won't have the heartbreak of losing one." Heterosexuality becomes a form of having in this articulation of loss. The history of heterosexuality, we might even say, is the history of broken hearts, or even just the history of hearts. To be recognized as having a heart is to be recognized as having the potential to be broken.[21] With such recognition, comes care, comfort, support. Without recognition, even one's grief cannot be supported or held by the kindness of another.

And so Edith waits. The temporality of this wait feels like a shudder; as each moment passes, as we wait with her, the mood of the film becoming unbearably sad, as it lingers over her loss by lingering. When she asks the hospital staff to see Abby they say "only family are allowed." She is excluded from the sphere of "intimates": she is a nonrelative, or nonfamily. The nurse asks: "Is she any relation of yours, madam?" Edith replies, "I'm a friend, a very good friend." They respond only with another question: "Does she have any family?" The friend disappears in the weight of the address. The recognition of family ties, as the only ties that are binding, means Abby dies alone; it means Edith waits all night, alone. There relationship is hidden under the sign of friendship, while friendship itself is produced as a lesser tie, a tie that is not binding, that does not endure in matters of life and death. The power of the distinction between friends and family is legislative, as if only family counts, as if other relationships are not real, or are simply not. When queer grief is not recognized, because queer relationships are not recognized, then you become "nonrelatives," you become unrelated, you become not. You are alone in your grief. You are left waiting.

The remainder of this short film depicts the arrival of Abby's nephew Ted (Paul Giamatti), his wife Alice (Elizabeth Perkins), and daughter Maggie (Marley McLean) for the funeral. Before they arrive, Edith removes traces of hers and Abby's relationship from the house, including photographs from the wall, which exposing lighter spaces underneath, as traces of their absence. The house is figured as a zone of intimacy; their love literally occupies the walls, keeping them busy. The house is not represented as property but as a space in which they have extended themselves: mementos, cards, photographs; queer intimacy leaves an impression on the walls. They are happy objects that Edith takes down; objects that embody their love, that create their own horizon. These objects betray their secret. If queers can surround themselves with objects that embody their happiness, in a world that does not bear queer deviations, this happiness will be precarious, even dangerous. If their happiness creates a horizon, it is not one that can be shared with others. The removal of signs of queer intimacy empties the house, re-creating the house as a vacant space, as if the walls too must wait.

When Abby's "family" arrives—her nephew Ted, his wife Alice, and their child Maggie—the house is transformed from a zone of queer intimacy into property. The house was in Abby's name. There is no will. The objects, the house itself, become "theirs." When they arrive, they treat the house as theirs, as if Edith is the guest. So when Edith says that both Abby and she paid the mortgage, Ted replies, "I have no problem with you staying here. Maybe we can work out some sort of rental situation." Staying becomes a question of receiving Ted's hospitality: he has the power to give and to take the house away. Indeed, the objects that embody the happy intimacy of Abby and Edith are taken away, in part by being transformed into property, as something that *can be* taken: The question "what was Aunt Abby's?" is a way of asking "what is ours?"

The drama of this situation unfolds through the objects; they embody Edith's life and her life with Abby. But for Abby's relatives, they are hers, as objects that are owned and inheritable. In particular, Abby's porcelain birds, her most loved and precious objects, become the site of contestation over family values and the value of family. Alice says to Edith, "They are beautiful," and when Alice picks one up, Edith replies, "I gave her that one, it's a lovely gift." In the following exchange between Edith and Alice we have a partial recognition of loss—which, in underdescribing that loss, works to annul the force of recognition. "It must be very sad for you to lose such a good friend." To which Edith replies, inadequately "Yes it is." At this moment, Edith's face is blank, her eyes glistening; she withholds. The affirmative response, the "Yes it is," becomes a disavowal of the loss, a way of keeping the truth of the loss a secret.

It is at this moment that Edith is undone. For having said yes to *this*, Alice says, "I think you should have something of hers to remember her by. I would really like for you to pick one of these birds to have as a keepsake." These objects which signify her love for Abby and Abby's love are taken away in the very gesture of being returned: they are turned into a gift, a keepsake, as if she must be grateful for this return. The birds become integrated into the family as possessions: "You know they really are part of the family . . . Maggie would want them someday." The objects Abby loved most, which were part of her, become kinship objects for Ted's family. The objects become family relatives, what can be inherited, passed down the family line, reassembled to give the family its form. It is this loss, the loss of what her lover loved, the loss of what caused her lover's happiness, that is "too much."

When Edith breaks down, it is the child Maggie who bears witness and who recognizes her suffering. Maggie offers Edith a handkerchief—Abby's handkerchief—and says she can have it. Edith responds: "Little girl, it is not for you to say what I can and cannot have. It is not for your parents to tell you what you can take." In response, Maggie says, "I am sorry." It is a moment; it is a moment of sympathy, perhaps even an alien sympathy as I described in the previous chapter, however small and fragile. Having received sympathy, Edith speaks for the first time about Abby and her kindness and how she "couldn't bear to see anything suffer," and of the birds she looked after, those birds that fell out of their nests. The birds become queer kinship objects, objects that embody a different promise: the promise to care for those who are homeless, who do not have the safety and protection of walls. Edith, in telling this story to Maggie, offers her another kind of inheritance. Maggie, having heard about her aunt, finds a starling's egg on the ground, which she gives to Edith, and which Edith later returns to the birdhouse. This circulation of gifts is more promising. When they leave, Edith and the girl shake hands, as if in the midst of suffering, new connections can be made, creating the grounds to alleviate the suffering that must be endured, or what endures as suffering.

This short film shows us the pain that follows from the failure of recognition. Indeed, the unhappiness of this film reminds us that the desire for recognition is not necessarily about having access to a good life. It is not even necessarily an aspiration for something: rather it is comes from the experience of what is unbearable, what cannot be endured. The desire for a bearable life is a desire for a life where suffering does not mean that you lose your bearings, where you become unhoused. If the pain in *The Well of Loneliness* involves an imagined future of revolution as a project of unhousing, this film begins with the house, showing how queer inhabitance of the house is precarious, how queers can be unhoused (not willingly in acts of revolution but against their will), and the unhappiness of any such unhousing.

The final short film in *If These Walls Could Talk 2* tells the story of another lesbian couple, Fran (Sharon Stone) and Kal (Ellen DeGeneres). They are very much "in the house." The plot is simple: they want to have a family; to conceive a child. The narrative is humorous and playful—they have to choose a sperm donor, and there are obstacles, bumps, and confusions on the way. The soundtrack is upbeat and uplifting, including songs like "Women Doing It for Themselves" and "Celebration."

This short film moves us from the desire for a bearable life to a desire for a good life, taking us from death to life, from nonrecognition to recognition, from unhappy queers to happy ones. What is the social promise of the happy queer? What does the happy queer do? What occupies her attention? In two scenes in the film, Fran and Kal gaze longingly at children in the playground. The film is organized by their desire not only for children but also to be with other mothers in the playground, which is overdetermined as a ground of happiness. It is the desire "to be there," to be in and on the grounds of the world of "happy folk." In other words, queer reproductive desire is already framed as a desire not only to be a family but to be like other families, to have what they have.

The desire is very much for a respectable kind of reproductivity. In one scene, Fran and Kal are deciding which sperm to choose, which is represented as a consumer choice organized around the desire for a respectable donor: they are looking for "good sperm," which is measurable through the provision of a family history of the donor. Queer desire for family is directed here toward the very desire to reproduce good family lines.

As they discuss which sperm to pick, Fran suggests, "Maybe we should think about having an ethnic baby. Ethnic babies are so beautiful," to which Kal replies forcefully, "I'd like it to look a little like me." Whiteness works powerfully here: both as a desire for the ethnic other (they are "so beautiful") and the desire to be the same: to look alike would be for the child to look white. They want to be a family; to look like a family would be to look alike, which would be to look white. This desire is not just about the desire to be a family alongside others; the desire is to be recognized as a family by taking its form as one's own. Happiness seems to involve here a narrative of assimilation in the specific sense of becoming like. I considered earlier how if recognition for queers is made conditional on happiness, then they might have to minimize signs of queerness. One could also ask whether queer happiness involves an increasing proximity to social forms that are already attributed as happiness-causes (the family, marriage, class mobility, whiteness), which of course suggests that promoting queer happiness might involve promoting social forms in which other queers will not be able to participate.

In this film, there are two moments where unhappy language is used, that is, language that evokes a sense of injury or injustice. The first relates to Fran and Kal's anger at not being able to get pregnant without a man. They have a conversation about who hates more the fact that they can not get pregnant together: "When I fell in love with you, I decided I never wanted another man in my life or in my bedroom at least. And now in order to get pregnant I have to have another man or at least a part of the man in the bedroom and *it is not fair* so I hate it more." Here, social exclusion is reduced to exclusion from the world of straight reproduction: it is not fair that women cannot get each other pregnant. The second moment is when they contemplate the life their child will have. Fran asks, "Do you think it's selfish to want to bring a child into this world? I mean aside from all the craziness and violence, it's our child, it's gonna get teased and it's gonna have to defend us." Kal replies, "Maybe, but kids get teased. All kids get teased. That's just part of childhood isn't it? And hopefully by the time our child is old enough to know what discrimination is, the world will have changed a bit."

Fran and Kal imagine the future by imagining their child as being in the future. The possibility of injury is displaced into the future, which becomes a promise, as if the future itself is what will overcome injury or any other signs of hurt. In this exchange, discrimination is both recognized as possible, as part of the present, and imagined as ordinary (as a form of teasing, which could be thought of as not very discriminating, insofar as teasing can roam across all kinds of difference), and also something that maybe or even will be overcome in the future. In other words, the disturbing thought of discrimination is not allowed to interrupt queer happiness. The happy queer is a form of social hope, a sign of "how far we have come" or hope for a world where discrimination has been overcome. The risk of this hope is that it reimagines the world *as if* there is no discrimination: and as if in bearing new life, the world itself will become bearable in the time of the arrival of new life. When they imagine the future, they imagine the child as being not only the product of their love but a witness to their love: "Honey, come on, all I want to do is love you. Loving you and loving our kid and having our kid witness this love . . . it's all from love, how can that be wrong?" Queer love offers its own promise of happiness.

The ending of the film is happy: they get pregnant. They dance around the bathroom; the promise of the child becomes the promise of happiness. We end with this promise, this promise of a new life, and with what seems the rather ordinary fertility of queer happiness. Of course, this ordinary fertility involves work: you don't "just" get pregnant; it involves not only using the technologies of artificial insemination but also the active negotiation of what it means to create a family. The family is a decision (in its original sense of a crisis) rather than a point on a line. Queers have to "make babies" in a very specific kind of way.

So what is being reproduced here in this happy image of queer reproduction? After all, even if queer happiness makes babies, the conditions of arrival for those babies are not entirely ordinary: the baby itself inherits points of deviation, as a way of dwelling in the world. If the queer family is promising, then what it promises is a dwelling space, where (at least some) signs of deviation are not excluded from what already resides at home. This final film in *If These Walls Could Talk 2* could be read as imagining queer happiness as approximating the family form, as having access to those "things" that accumulate as family possessions. Or it could be read as creating a different kind of happiness, where the promise of happiness is not located as a point on a straight line, which, by staying with the family, might yet make the familiar walls of the house, the walls that secure dwelling, seem rather strange.

The film shows the activism that is required to get from unrecognized grief to recognizable happiness. Our question becomes: can we sustain the struggle for recognition, the struggle to make the world bearable for queers, without approximating the very forms of happy heterosexuality? What kinds of alternative kinship stories are possible, which are not organized by the desire for reproduction, or the desire to be like other families, or by the promise of happiness as "being like"? Do happy queer endings have to annul the political force and energy of the unhappy queer?

The disappointment of this film—that the pain can lead just to "this"—should not stop us from thinking with it. For even if the image of Ellen and Sharon dancing together does not make us happy, this film allows us to place the queer desire for happiness, whatever its form, within a longer genealogy of negative queer affect and activism. The film does end perhaps with a rather bleak vision of happy homonormativity.[22] And yet the film might allow us to question our own perception of homonormativity as simply or only a sign of assimilation: after all, it is the struggle to have a bearable life that might get us here. In other words, if we do not read the film as a narrative of progress, as if the point is to arrive at the endpoint, then positive and negative feelings can gather, creating an "archive of feelings," to use Ann Cvetkovich's (2003) description.

Happily Queer

It might be that queers are rewarded with happiness in return for approximating signs of straightness. Or it might be that it is hard to hope for happiness
without the hope directing us toward certain points along a life course, even if
some of these points seem to take us off course. And yet, queer archives are also
full of more perverse desires, of bodies that desire "in the wrong way" and are
willing to give up access to the good life to follow their desire. Queers can be affectively alien by placing their hopes for happiness in the wrong objects, as well
as being made unhappy by the conventional routes of happiness, an unhappiness which might be an effect of how your happiness makes others unhappy.
I want to focus in this section on queer happiness in "bad object choices" in
order to offer some reflection on how being happily queer (rather than being a
happy queer) does not necessarily promote an image of happiness that borrows
from the conventional repertoire of images. As Elizabeth Freeman suggests,
we might be able to glimpse in our archives "historically specific forms of pleasure" that have not been "subsumed into institutional forms" (2005: 66). To
be happily queer might mean being happy to be the cause of unhappiness (at
least in the sense that one agrees to be the cause of unhappiness, even if one
is not made happy by causing unhappiness), as well as to be happy with where
we get to if we go beyond the straight lines of happiness scripts.

To think more about being happily queer I want to begin with a reflection
on Rita Mae Brown's novel *Rubyfruit Jungle*, first published in 1973, which tells
the story of Molly Bolt. One of the first lesbian books I read, it is for me a very
happy object. I loved it, in part because I loved Molly, for her fierceness, her defiance, her willingness to get into trouble. Molly Bolt participates in the genealogy of female troublemakers I describe in the chapter 2, alongside Maggie
Tulliver in George Eliot's *The Mill on the Floss*.

Judith Butler (1990) has helped teach us about gender trouble and how we
trouble gender when we do not follow conventional routes that separate identification from desire (being a girl means wanting a boy, being a boy means
wanting a girl). In chapter 2, I suggested that we can think of trouble as an
affective politics; acts of deviation mean getting in trouble but also troubling
conventional ideas of what it means to have a good life that puts things into
certain places. To cause trouble has effects. The troublemaker will be punished

and will be put back in her place. Books such as *Rubyfruit Jungle* are powerful as they narrate *the refusal to be put back into place*. In the opening sequence of events, Molly does indeed get into trouble: a real entrepreneur, she earns money by getting the school kids to pay to see Brockhurst Detwiler's uncircumcised penis. When she is scolded furiously by her mother, Carrie, she thinks to herself: "So what, so what I'm a bastard. I don't care. She's trying to scare me. She's always trying to throw some fear in me. The hell with her and the hell with anyone else if it makes a difference to them" (1973: 8). Molly embodies the energy or vitality of the subject who is defiant, who is willing and able to defy authority, who will not be brought down by others.

The novel depicts numerous attempts to turn Molly around, to bring her wayward desires back into line. One girl, Cheryl Spiegelglass, says to Molly: "You'll see. You think you can do what boys do but you're going to be a nurse, no two ways about it. It doesn't matter about brains, brains don't count. What counts is whether you're a boy or a girl" (31). Molly's response is violent: "I hauled off and belted her one. Shirley Temple Spiegelglass wasn't gonna tell me I couldn't be a doctor, nor nobody else" (31). Molly's rage evokes Claudia's rage in *The Bluest Eye*, which was also directed against Shirley Temple as iconic of good white bourgeois femininity.[23] For Molly, being told what she cannot do because she is a girl generates not submission, obedience, or fear of unhappiness but further acts of rebellion. Rage against the good white girls is what makes Molly, like Claudia, affectively alien.

To be trouble is to put certain norms of conduct or aspirations to conduct into trouble. In one instance, Molly is in conflict with her mother: "The whole crew got Carrie's version of my sins and I couldn't open my mouth in self-defense. I guess she thought she'd shame me in front of all of them, but I stared at her with real pride as I marched into the bedroom. She wasn't going to beat me down, no how. Let 'em all get mad at me, I wasn't giving her a goddamned inch, not one" (39). To be shamed before you can defend yourself does not mean to experience shame. This moment of queer pride is a refusal to be shamed by witnessing the other as being ashamed of you.

Molly is a girl who wants girls, and the story of the book is a story of her wanting girls and getting the girls she wants. As she says in response to the question of how many women she has slept with: "Hundreds. I'm irresistible" (200). *Rubyfruit Jungle* offers us a story of a queer girl who refuses to give up her desires, even if they take her outside the parameters of happiness, even though they get her into trouble.

The queer who is happily queer still encounters the world that is unhappy with queer love, but refuses to be made unhappy by that encounter. I have argued that the risk of promoting happy queers is that the unhappiness of this world can disappear from view. To be happily queer can also recognize that unhappiness; indeed to be happily queer can be to recognize the unhappiness that is concealed by the promotion of happy normativity. Molly, our irresistible heroine, teaches us this. When she is called into the dean's office at the University of Florida after her lesbian behavior had been reported, she is asked by the dean about her problem with girls:

> "Dean Marne, I don't have any problems relating to girls and I'm in love with my roommate. She makes me happy."
>
> Her scraggly red eyebrows with the brown pencil glaring through shot up. "Is this relationship with Faye Raider of an, uh—intimate nature?"
>
> "We fuck, if that's what you're after."
>
> I think her womb collapsed on that one. Sputtering, she pressed forward. "Don't you find that somewhat of an aberration? Doesn't this disturb you, my dear? After all, it's not normal."
>
> "I know it's not normal for people in this world to be happy, and I'm happy." (127)

Rather than being disturbed by being found disturbing, Molly performs the ultimate act of defiance by claiming her happiness as abnormal. To be happily queer is to explore the unhappiness of what gets counted as normal. It is as if queers, by doing what they want, expose the unhappiness of having to sacrifice personal desires, in the perversity of their twists and turns, for the happiness of others.[24]

Despite all her charm and her rather infectious enthusiasm for queer life worlds, it is not that Molly's experiences are happy ones, in the sense of being able to make and get her way. Indeed, throughout, her experiences involve discrimination, violence, and rejection from would be-lovers who cannot bear the consequences of following queer desire past the forms of recognition of the straight world. She is simply not defeated by these experiences. Of course, we need to take care to avoid turning characters such as Molly into good object lessons: as if we could create a moral imperative from the example of her fictional life. And yet, reading about characters who are happily queer in the face of a world that is unhappy with queer lives and loves can be energizing, can give us hope. Even the ending of the novel is not happy. Molly does not receive any offers to work in the film industry other than ones that make a spectacle of her difference: a "famous man" wants her to "consider dressing as a hermaphrodite for his next film" (245). So when one of her classmates goes "right into CBS," she is told they are "full up" (245). Molly is forced to learn from what is not opened up to her: "No, I wasn't surprised, but it still brought me down. I kept hoping against hope that I'd be the bright exception, the talented token that smashed sex and class barriers. Hurrah for her. After all, I was the best in my class, didn't that count for something?" (245).

And yet the novel does not end with this moment of being brought down. It ends instead with Molly making wishes: "Damn, I wished the world would let me be myself. But I knew better on all counts. I wish I could make my films. That wish I can work for. One way or another I'll make those movies and I don't feel like having to fight until I'm fifty. But if it does take that long then watch out world because I'm going to be the hottest fifty-year-old this side of the Mississippi" (246). Molly recognizes that some of her aspirations might not be attainable simply by the fact of wishing for them. But she can work for what she wishes—and she can wish for what she works. Not only that: she recognizes that if such wishes might not be given or granted, she can still wish for something, which is to endure, even to endure happily, as a queer.

It is thus possible to give an account of being happily queer that does not conceal signs of struggle. Another, more recent novel narrated by a happily queer subject is *Babyji* by Abha Dawesar (2005). Set in India, this novel is written from the point of view of Anamika Sharma, a smart, spirited, and sexy teenager who seduces three women: an older divorcée she names India, a servant girl called Rani, and her school friend Sheela. As a character, Anamika is very appealing. Everyone desires her, wants something from her, such that the reader is encouraged to desire her too as well as to identify with her desire. There is a lot of desire in this book.

We do not notice happiness used as a requirement that Anamika gives up her desires. Instead, the first use of happiness as a speech act is of a rather queer nature: "'I want to make you happy,' I said as I was leaving. 'You do make me happy,' India said. 'No, I don't mean that way. I mean in bed'" (31). Anamika separates her own desire to make her lover happy from "that way," from the ordinary way, perhaps, that you might want to make another happy, by wanting to give her access to a good life. Instead, Anamika wants to make India happy in bed, to be the cause of her pleasure. This restriction of the desire for the other's happiness to being happy in bed is important—it refuses to give happiness the power to secure a specific image of what would count as a good life.

Babyji is certainly about the perverse potential of pleasure. This is not to say that Anamika does not have to rebel or does not get into trouble. The trouble centers on the relationship between the father and queer daughter and again turns on the axis of happiness. Anamika says to her father: "You like tea, and I like coffee. I want to be a physicist, and Vidur wants to join the army. I don't want to get married, and mom did. How can the same formula make us all happy?" To which he replies: "What do you mean you don't want to get married?" (177). Anamika recognizes what I've called the idiosyncratic nature of happy object choices: different people are made happy by different things; we have a diversity of likes and dislikes, and includes marriage as one happy object choice among others. The inclusion of marriage as something that you might or might not like is picked up by the father, turning queer desire into a question that interrupts the flow of the conversation.

The exchange shows us how object choices are not equivalent, how some choices such as marrying or not marrying are not simply presentable as idiosyncratic likes or dislikes, as they take us beyond the horizon of intimacy, in which those likes can gather as a shared form. Although the novel might seem to articulate a queer liberalism, whereby the queer subject is free to be happy in her own way, it evokes the limits of that liberalism by showing how the conflation of marriage with the good life is maintained as the response to queer deviation. While queers might go beyond marriage, it does not follow that you will be promised happiness in return. Although we can live without the promise of happiness, and we can do so "happily," we live with the consequences of being an unhappiness-cause for others, which is why the process of coming out and being out is an ongoing site of possibility and struggle.

Babyji ends with a discussion between Anamika and a school official about scholarships and colleges in the United States. It is a moment, perhaps, when quite conventional aspirations for a good life are expressed in Anamika's own confidence in her future: being exceptional and having an exceptional life is associated with education and travel. But the conversation reveals other kinds of desire: "'I kept some college materials for you. I think you're the best candidate from Delhi who has walked through the door this year,' she said, pointing to her office door. 'Thanks,' I said. 'There are others with the same grades, but you have the best extracurriculars.' I smiled sheepishly. I could suddenly think of no extracurriculars except Sheela and India and Rani. I felt hot in the face" (354). I think what is striking about this passage is how the queer moment is what gets in the way of the conversation: the sheepish body, the body that heats up, is one that recollects past queer experiences that are not exactly what the official had in mind. At one level, the novel's investment in the freedom to be happy for queers corresponds with conventional class desires for upward mobility, in which the good life is associated with getting up and getting out. But at another level, queerness is what gets in the way, allowing the body to intrude with another kind of desire. Such desires might even queer our aspirations.

We need to think more about the relationship between the queer struggle for a bearable life and aspirational hopes for a good life. Maybe the point is that is it hard to struggle without aspirations, and aspirations are hard to have without giving them some form. We could remember that the Latin root of the word *aspiration* means "to breathe." I think the struggle for a bearable life is the struggle for queers to have space to breathe. Having space to breathe, or being able to breathe freely, as Mari Ruti describes (2006: 19), is an aspiration. With breath comes imagination. With breath comes possibility. If queer politics is about freedom, it might simply mean the freedom to breathe.

Multicultural communities tend to be less trusting and less happy . . . people frankly, when there are other pressures, like to live in a comfort zone which is defined by racial sameness . . . people feel happy if they are with people like themselves.   TREVOR PHILLIPS, chair, Commission of Equalities and Human Rights, UK, 2006

CHAPTER FOUR

Melancholic Migrants

TREVOR PHILLIPS SUGGESTS that the problem with multiculturalism is that it makes people unhappy. Or we could say that he turns multiculturalism into a problem by attributing it as the cause of unhappiness: as if when we are "in" multiculturalism, we are "out" of our comfort zone. Phillips made these comments in the third episode of the BBC program *The Happiness Formula* that aired in the United Kingdom in 2006.[1] The episode argues that the social project "to make people happier" means to "make societies more cohesive" or to "put glue back into communities." Happiness is imagined as social glue, as being what sticks people together. The mission to put glue back into communities not only suggests that communities lack such glue but also that they once had it. The program offers as its idea of happiness an image of a world in which people are less physically and socially mobile: for example, it describes a small French village, where people stay put over generations, as being the happiest possible way of living together. This nostalgic vision of a world of "staying put" involves nostalgia for whiteness, for a community of white people happily living with other white people. The nostalgic vision of whiteness is at once an image of racial likeness or sameness. In mourning the loss of such a world, migration enters the narrative as an unhappiness cause, as what forces people who are "unalike" to live together.

Given that multiculturalism is being perceived as causing unhappiness, it is unsurprising that *multiculturalism* itself has become an unhappy term. The preface to the *Good Race Relations* guide published by the Commission for Racial Equality in the UK suggests that "multiculturalism no longer provides the right answer to the complex nature of today's race relations. Integration based on shared values and loyalties is the only way forward."[2] The heading of the preface to this document reads "Integration is not a dream: it is a matter of survival." To say something is a matter of survival is usually to announce survival as that which is under threat. Multiculturalism is presented as a threat to national survival. Multiculturalism has even been declared dead.[3]

It does not follow that multiculturalism no longer participates in the national ideal. This BBC program, for example, does not simply give up on multiculturalism but suggests that we have an obligation to make multiculturalism happier, premised on the model of "building bridges."[4] Trevor Phillips evokes unhappy instances of community conflict or violence between communities by claiming that "*this* is exactly what happens when people who look very different, and think they are very different, never touch and interact." The "this" stands in for unhappy instances of violence, such that they are evoked without being named (from personal distrust to conflict between communities and international terrorism). Unhappiness is read as caused not simply by diversity but by the failure of people who embody such diversity to "touch and interact." Phillips recommends that communities integrate by sharing "an activity" such as football "that takes us out of our ethnicity and connects us with people of different ethnicities if only for a few hours a week." If we do this, he says, "then I think we can crack the problem."

The shift from unhappy to happy multiculturalism involves the demand for interaction. Happiness is projected into the future: when we have "cracked the problem" through interaction, we can be happy with diversity. That football becomes a technique for generating happy multiculturalism is no accident.[5] The fantasy of football presented here is that it can transcend ethnicity. Football provides a national ground, when it gives ground to happiness. Multiculturalism might become happy when it involves loyalty to what has already been established as a national ideal. Happiness is thus promised in return for loyalty to the nation, where loyalty is defined in terms of playing its game.

In this chapter, I explore the relationship between histories of empire and the promise of happiness, with specific reference to the British Asian experience. I begin by considering how, in the nineteenth century, the imperial mission was legitimated through the utilitarian injunction of maximizing happiness, and how empire is remembered as a history of happiness. I then explore how the figure of the melancholic migrant emerges, attending to the conversion points between unhappy racism and multicultural happiness in two British Asian films: *Bend It Like Beckham* and *East Is East*. Finally, by reflecting on narratives written from the point of view of second-generation daughters, I consider the relationship between migration, experiences of racism, and "alien affects."

Utilitarianism and Empire

Utilitarianism involves the ethical injunction to maximize happiness, as "the greatest happiness of the greatest number." Friedrich Nietzsche's devastating critique of utilitarianism offers a critique of this "greatest number" as a form of nation building: "In the end, they all want *English* morality to be recognized as authoritative, inasmuch as mankind, or the 'general utility' or 'the happiness of the greatest number,' —no! the happiness of *England*, will be best served thereby. They would like, by all means, to convince themselves that the striving after *English* happiness, I mean after *comfort* and *fashion* . . . is at the same time the true path of virtue" ([1886] 1997: 96). The very shift in this paragraph from English morality to the happiness of England to English happiness works powerfully to suggest that the maxim "the happiness of the greatest number" allows the conflation of moral and national character. For Nietzsche, the injunction to maximize happiness involves the universalization of English morality. Utilitarian happiness, as the happiness of the greatest number, provides a technology for promoting Englishness.

Utilitarian happiness is certainly interested. After all, utilitarian thinkers played a key role in the defense of the British Empire. This is not to say that utilitarianism provided a singular justification of empire. As H. S. Jones points out, there were a "diversity of utilitarian approaches to the question of empire" (2005: 82).[6] Utilitarian thinkers including Jeremy Bentham, James Mill, Henry Sidgwick, and John Stuart Mill drew on the discourse of maximizing happiness in support of the imperial mission, though they did so in distinct ways (see

Schultz and Varouxakis 2005). Utilitarianism offered a way of "weighing up," of considering the relative costs and benefits of empire. James Mill, for example, argued that the costs of empire outweigh the benefits for the colonizer (Jones 2005: 182).[7] Utilitarian justifications for empire rested primarily on its benefits for the colonized and were largely premised on an economic rationale: for empire to fulfill the greatest happiness principle, the benefits of empire for the colonized must exceed the costs for the colonizer. James Mill argued that the empire fulfils the greatest happiness principle in exactly these terms.

Utilitarian justifications of empire were crucial not only to colonial governance but also to commercial interests. As is well known but perhaps less well understood, both James Mill and his son John Stuart Mill were involved in the East India Company.[8] In an article published in the *Monthly Review*, John Bruce, a historiographer for the East India Company, drew on the vocabularies offered by utilitarianism to justify the "formation of a European — British — population in India," which he acknowledged might be "the object of dread" for the British at home (1813: 29). He argued that the population of India would benefit by being ruled by a class of "philanthropic men" in the following way: "The pace of civilisation would be quickened beyond all examples. The courts, the knowledge, and the manners of Europe would be brought to their doors, and forced by an irresistible moral pressure on their acceptance. *The happiness of the human race would thus be prodigiously augmented*" (30; emphasis added).[9] Empire is justified in terms of the augmentation of human happiness. If colonial rule becomes (to evoke Kipling's famous poem) "the white man's burden," then this burden is understood as a duty to promote "the happiness of the human race." This duty is narrated through the language of philanthropy: the love of the people becomes the will to augment happiness. Philanthropy is what is given to alleviate others from suffering or the impoverishment of an existence. The will to augment happiness is at once a mission to relieve others from suffering. This philanthropic gift is also a sacrifice: given that the colonies were widely perceived as costing more than they earned, the augmentation of happiness was often presented as a relative cost to the happiness of the colonizers.

This gift of happiness is imagined here in terms of civility. Human happiness is increased through the courts (law/justice), knowledge (reason), and manners (culture, habits). Civilization is imagined first as what is brought to "their doors" and second as an irresistible moral pressure. In the first image, the civilizer would be the guest who awaits the opening of the door. The second, in contrast, uses the language of force. The civilizer may remain a guest but demands entry, as an entry that cannot be refused. Empire becomes a gift that cannot be refused, a forced gift. If the empire is understood as giving happiness, then perhaps happiness names the force of this gift.

The civilizing mission can be redescribed as a happiness mission. For happiness to become a mission, the colonized other must first be deemed unhappy. The imperial archive can be considered as an archive of unhappiness. Colonial knowledges constitute the other as not only an object of knowledge, a truth to be discovered, but as being unhappy, as lacking the qualities or attributes required for a happier state of existence.[10] James Mill's own *History of British India* is a crucial text within this unhappy colonial archive, given how it constitutes the misery of native culture as justification of colonial rule.[11]

For Mill happiness provides a way of measuring civility. He argues that "exactly in proportion as *Utility* is the object of any pursuit, may we regard a nation as civilized. Exactly in proportion as its ingenuity is wasted on contemptible or mischievous objects, though it may be, in itself, an ingenuity of no ordinary kind, the nation may safely be dominated as barbarous" ([1818] 1997: 105). The happiness of imperial culture is guaranteed as a happiness formula: in making happiness our end, we can impose our end. We can impose our end on those without happiness as their end: barbarism is named simply as the deviation from the end of happiness. Returning to Nietzsche's critique of utilitarian happiness as the universalization of English morality, we might conclude that his critique finds its object: the end of happiness defined by utilitarianism corresponds with the end of colonial governance. The point of happiness might be the point of such correspondence. Colonial rule is justified as a duty to make others live according to the happiness end.

History of British India is a highly strategic deployment of history: demonstrating the unhappiness of un-British India was a way of defending the happiness of the colonial end. In the first volume of this series, Mill justifies himself as an authority on India in a rather unconventional way: he describes himself as an expert witness on India *because* he has not been there. Mill argues that to go somewhere is to be "swayed" by one's impressions in such a way that judgment would become possible ([1818] 1997: xxiii). He suggests that the very orientation toward pleasure means that sensations are an unreliable source of knowledge: "The well-known pleasure which a man finds, in meeting, at every step, with proofs that he is in the right, inspiring an eagerness to look out for that source of satisfaction; and secondly, the well-known aversion which a man usually has, to meet with proofs that he is in the wrong, yielding a temptation, commonly obeyed, to overlook such disagreeable objects" (xxv). Mill suggests that if you look for what is in agreement with judgments you have already made, you experience pleasure in finding agreement. Mill likens the desire for agreement with primitive forms of fetishism: "Prior to experience and instruction, there is a propensity in the imagination to endow with life whatever we behold in motion; or in general, whatever appears to be the cause of any event. A child beats the inanimate object by which it has been hurt, and caresses that by which it has been gratified. The sun, which is the cause of the day, the savage regards as a benevolent deity" (230). For Mill the child and the native are alike insofar as they invest objects with magical properties: this tendency to see the object that causes pleasure as being good becomes a sign of being uneducated or immature. The impartial witness—the civilized man—stands back and looks for the true causes of action in the world.

It may seem that such an account of the fetishism of sensory involvement is far removed from our analysis of happiness and empire. But it is not. After all, Mill evokes the failure of natives to stand back from objects of pleasure as a symptom of their immaturity: the writing of the book itself hence becomes an object lesson in happiness, a way of appreciating things without being swayed by things. Although utilitarianism is often presumed to be orientated toward pleasure and unable to differentiate pleasure from happiness as a higher form of good,[12] we can see that a hierarchy is already in place that relies upon this distinction: happiness stands back and can judge what is good from a distance, while pleasure is to proximate to the object, mistaking the cause of pleasure for the good. For Mill, the natives are mistaken, swayed by their inclinations, immersed in the object that gives pleasure: like children, they are assumed to be in need of redirection.

Mill locates fetishism in the body of the child and the native, creating the impression that his book does not invest happiness within certain objects. And yet, what follows in this volume is an argument about what is distasteful—we could even say bad or disgusting—about Indian and Hindi culture; they become bad objects for Mill, just as his happiness becomes the cause of the good. According to Mill, the natives not only experience pleasure from the wrong things in the wrong way but they are also "rude." The repetition of this adjective has an odd effect for the contemporary reader: we now call people rude if they said something offensive. In this early usage, rude becomes a sign of a lack of good manners, as well as a lower morality: "No people, how rude and ignorant so-ever, who have been so far advanced as to leave us memorials of their thoughts in writing, have ever drawn a more gross and disgusting picture of the universe, than what is presented in the writings of the Hindus" (267). Mill is disgusted by what he perceives as disgusting, as if his own way of being affected by something discloses the truth of that thing. Rudeness becomes a character or quality of culture, as well as a sign of the primitive, of that which must be overcome; indeed implicit in the urgency of this description is a fantasy of overcoming rudeness in the very description of something *as* rude.

The question of manners is linked to the question of gender: "The condition of the women is one of the most remarkable circumstances in the manners of nations. Among rude people, the women are generally degraded; among civilized people they are exalted. In the barbarian, the passion of sex is a brutal impulse, which infuses no tenderness; and his undisciplined nature leads him to abuse his power over every other creature that is weaker than himself. The history of uncultivated nations uniformly represents the women as in a state of abject slavery, from which they slowly emerge as civilization advances" (309). Empire becomes a moral and pedagogic project of improving manners, a project of cultivation, described in familiar terms of the emergence of women from a state of "abject slavery." In relation to India, James Mill argues that "nothing can exceed the habitual contempt which the Hindus entertain towards their women" (311). The "habitual contempt" is what women must be liberated from. The investment in the abjection of colonized women can serve to justify empire as the liberation of women from abjection. Gayatri Spivak's description of this investment as "white men saving brown women from brown men" remains extraordinary for its precision (1988: 297).

Empire is justified as *liberation from abjection*. To be liberated from abjection is to be liberated from suffering even if it causes suffering. So although in volume 9 Mill does recognize that colonialism involves suffering for the natives, he argues that the good that colonialism brings for India outweighs any such suffering: "For, although the country has suffered, and must ever suffer, many and great disadvantages from the substitution of strangers for its own functionaries, its own chiefs, its own sovereigns, it has been, in some degree, compensated for their loss, by exemption from the fatal consequences of native mis-rule—by protection against external enemies—by the perpetuation of internal tranquillity—by the growth of trade—the increase of cultivation— and the progressive introduction of the arts and sciences, the intelligence and civilisation of Europe" (396). Precolonial self-rule is here constructed as a death wish. Becoming cultivated and civilized, understood as becoming European, is presented as both a compensation for past loss and the avoidance of future misery.

The utilitarian focus on empire as an agent of relative happiness (as causing more happiness than suffering) also meant an investment in what Eric Stokes calls very aptly "secular evangelicism": the "transposition of evangelicalism to wholly secular objects" (1959: 308). Utilitarians and evangelicalists believed in the liberal policy of assimilation: a policy that challenged some of the ideologies of colonial governance insofar as it was premised on the belief that the natives could be converted. Stokes suggests that both utilitarianism and evangelicalism rest on a narrative of conversion: "Resulting in a complete transformation of the personality, the process of conversion, of 'justification and sanctification,' consisting in the soul turning in upon itself, and stripping itself of the clothing of habit smothering its awareness" (29). For utilitarians, conversion was a liberation of the individual; they sought "to liberate the individual from the slavery of custom" (54). The word *custom* shares the same root as the word *habit*. Yet the word *custom* also suggests bad habits. To have bad manners is to be held back by custom, where custom evokes what is customary. Good habits are differentiated from what is "merely" habitual.

Colonialism is justified as necessary not only to increase human happiness but to teach the natives how to be happy. They must learn "good habits" by unlearning what is custom or customary. The general end of happiness translates into the particular end of the individual: the creation of "individuals" becomes the purpose of colonial education or training. To become happy in these terms requires the individual be liberated from custom, to become an end-in-itself. As I suggested in chapter 2, happiness involves being "redirected," or turned around. *To turn others into individuals is to turn them around, by turning them toward the norms, values and practices of the colonizer.*

As James Mill's own writings on education make clear, happiness plays a key role in this redirection. Mill describes "the end of education" as rendering "the individual, as much as possible, an instrument of happiness" (1828: 12). He argues that the earliest sensations have the most profound effects and that "education, then, or the care of forming the habits, ought to commence as much as possible, with the period of sensation itself" (32). It is because the child is most impressionable that an impression must be made upon the child. Mill concludes that "the business of skilful education is, so to arrange the circumstances by which the child is surrounded, that the impressions made upon him shall be in the order most conducive to this happy result" (35). If, for Mill, the natives are like children, then they are impressionable and must learn to receive the right impressions. Education is an arrangement of circumstances in such a way that happiness is the result.

The colonial project is thus imagined as a form of moral training or habituation. As Achille Mbembe describes, "The coloniser might inculcate habits in the colonized, treat him/her violently if need be, speak to him/her as a child, reprimand or congratulate him/her" (2001: 27). The education of the native became a matter of morality, of teaching the natives the path to happiness *as* the path to civilisation: "raising the native to where he/she can contemplate the recovery of his/her rights requires moral education" (35). To become educated is to acquire the capacity to discover one's rights: you cease to be an alien if you recover your inalienable rights as the right to pursue happiness (which is also to lose the right not to pursue happiness or not to make this idea of happiness your end).

The discovery of rights through moral education is how the native becomes a subject with certain manners, habits, and inclinations. Colonial education in teaching the natives "good habits" creates a new "class of persons" described famously by Thomas Babington Macaulay in his "Minute on Indian Education" as "Indian in blood and colour, but English in taste, in opinions, in morals, and in intellect" ([1835] 2003: 237). Becoming an individual thus means becoming English. In this becoming, the colonized other also becomes, as Homi Bhabha (2004) has shown so powerfully, drawing on an astute reading of this passage from Macaulay, the "mimic man." The utilitarian promotion of happiness involves technologies of mimicry: the imperative to make the colonial elite "like us" in matters of taste, opinions, morals, and intellect. In mimicking the colonizer, the other becomes happy not in the sense of feeling happy but in the sense of acquiring good habits, which might involve an affective disposition: you learn to be affected in the right way by the right things. Becoming "like" the colonizer is still to inhabit a body that is markedly different from that of the colonizer. As Bhabha shows, mimicry produces a hybrid subject: *almost the same but not quite, almost the same, but not white* (1994: 122, 128). One wonders whether the happiness formula for the colonized rests also on the hesitation of the almost: *almost happy, but not quite; almost happy, but not white.*

Happiness thus becomes a justification of empire not only in the sense of giving support to the existence of the colonies but also as being what is assumed to be augmented through empire. We might expect that this history of happiness has become a rather unhappy history: that shame about the colonial past, and the violence of this past, might have involved a withdrawal of commitment from utilitarian logics. And yet I would argue that contemporary race politics in the UK involves not only a direct inheritance of this history but a social obligation to remember the history of empire *as* a history of happiness.

This memory of empire as happiness has even become a form of nation building. To be a national subject might involve expressing happiness *about* imperial history. In such expressions, imperialism is remembered "happily," as an agent of relative happiness. One speech by Trevor Phillips, "We Need a Highway Code for a Multi-Ethnic Society" (2005), evokes the history of imperialism in such terms: "And we can look at our own history to show that the British people are not by nature bigots. We created something called the empire where we mixed and mingled with people very different from those of these islands."[13] Empire here become proof that British are "not bigots" but are able to "mix and mingle" with others. Indeed, empire itself becomes a sign of a British tendency toward happy diversity; toward mixing, loving, and cohabiting with others.

In the context of the "crisis of multiculturalism" discussed in my opening comments of this chapter, the social obligation to be happy *about* imperial history accrues an affective force. However, this obligation is not simply neutral; it falls unequally on subjects, depending on their own relation to this history. Migrants are increasingly subject to what I am calling the happiness duty, in a way that is continuous with the happiness duty of the natives in the colonial mission. If in the nineteenth century the natives must become (more) British in order to be recognized as subjects of empire, in a contemporary context, it is migrants who must become (more) British in order to be recognized as citizens of the nation. Citizenship now requires a test: we might speculate that this test is a happiness test.

The Home Office has produced a guide for migrants upon which citizenship tests are based, *Life in the United Kingdom: A Journey to Citizenship* (2005b). What can be learned from this book? Interestingly, the idea of Britishness is

MELANCHOLIC MIGRANTS 131

explicitly linked to diversity: becoming British is about positively embracing diversity, where diversity itself becomes a national attribute: "We want British citizenship to embrace positively the diversity of background, culture and faiths that living in modern Britain involves" (3). The nation is imagined as happily diverse, or as being happy with its diversity.[14]

Diversity also becomes a way of remembering empire. I have noted how the history of the British Empire is evoked happily as a sign of good character. In *Life in the United Kingdom* the imperial past is mentioned on few occasions and in all of these is represented in positive terms.[15] Take the following passage:

> for many indigenous peoples in Africa, the Indian subcontinent, and else-where, the British empire often brought more regular, acceptable and im-partial systems of law and order than many had experienced under their own rulers, or under alien rulers other than European. The spread of the English language helped unite disparate tribal areas that gradually came to see themselves as nations. Public health, peace, and access to education can mean more to ordinary people than precisely who are their rulers. One legacy of empire was that when nationalism grew most of those who first claimed self-government did so in terms resting heavily on European, on specifically British, ideals of liberty and representative government. (32)

The British Empire is evoked as bringing good things to indigenous peoples of the world—law, unity, self-government, liberty, and so on. Indeed, the language of empire is that of a gift: through empire, others were given forms of nationhood that rested on European and specifically British ideals. It is important to remember that this passage appears in the book upon which citizenship texts for migrants are based. To become British is to accept empire as the gift of happiness, which might involve an implicit injunction to forget or not to remember the violence of colonial rule. The book then comments specifically on British rule in India:

> Transitions and transplantations seldom work exactly as intended and are often resented, but India is an interesting example of a national identity gradually emerging amid political institutions that are clearly mutations from the homeland of the imperial era. Indigenous fears that Christianity would replace Moslem and Hindu beliefs were plainly exaggerated, and often the British administrators on the ground, concerned primarily with civil order

and often fascinated by and learned in the ways of local traditions, were not helpful to evangelical missionaries. To some degree the English tolerance of different national cultures in the United Kingdom itself may have influenced the character of their imperial rule in India. (32)

Modern India is described as inheriting the political institutions of England as well as mutating those institutions into its own forms. The investment is clear: the British Empire is evoked to show that the British administrators were "good rulers" who, unlike "evangelical missionaries," were fascinated by and responsive to local traditions. The good rulers become in turn a sign of the quality of national character and national culture ("English tolerance").

Happiness can thus involve a project of social description: to see happily is not to see violence, asymmetry, or force. When we are asked to recall the empire as a happy history we are employing *the same terms* in which empire was justified in history. To employ happy terms does not mean, of course, that happy feelings are simply generated. Paul Gilroy has argued that British nation is suffering from a postcolonial melancholia, an inability to "mourn its lost empire" (2004: 111), such that Britain needs to recognize "the horrors" of imperial history (108). Perhaps what we are witnessing is a failure to recognize that there is something to be mourned, a disbelief in the very existence of damage or that empire was damaging. Such failures are reproduced through the happiness injunction: the social obligation to remember the colonial history as the history of happiness involves an adjustment to history as the history of adjustment. To become well adjusted is to be adjusted to colonial history. In other words, the British nation has been rather good at defending itself against shame. It does so in part by the retrospective fantasy that such shame has become compulsory, such that national happiness and pride are expressed as if they are minoritized feelings.[16]

If happiness provides a powerful technology for social description, it creates an impression that there is nothing to be mourned. I will discuss later the distinction between melancholia and mourning. It is useful to note that Freud's description of mourning as "commonly the reaction to the loss of a beloved person, or an abstraction taking the place of the person, such as fatherland, freedom, an ideal, and so on" ([1917] 2005: 203). The British Empire was a historical reality, but it was also an ideal; indeed the ideal of empire participates in its justification as a moral project. The ideal of empire is *retained* by being rerouted through the moral understanding of empire as the gift of happiness. We need to understand the consequences of this retention.

Freedom to Be Happy

Understanding the role of happiness in imperial history gives us a lens through which to consider the relationship between happiness, nationhood, and citizenship. In the British context, it is not the case that "the pursuit of happiness" is enshrined as a right as it is in the United States, in the form of the Declaration of Independence (1776). And yet, I have suggested that happiness is still used as a technology of citizenship, as a way of binding migrants to a national ideal. To be bound *to* happiness is to be bound *by* what has already been established as good. We need of course an approach that can account for how such goods are established in the first place. In chapter 2, I introduced the concept of "conditional happiness," where one person's happiness is made conditional upon another's. I suggested that the terms of conditionality are unequal: for those who "come first," their happiness "comes first," which is how some acquire the right to define the conditions of happiness for others. Citizenship provides a technology for deciding whose happiness comes first. What is at stake in citizenship is the differentiation between those who *are* and who are *not yet* citizens (what I call "would-be citizens"), where the "not yet" is offered as promise of what is to come. If the promise of citizenship is offered as a promise of happiness, then you have to demonstrate that you are a worthy recipient of its promise.

What does it mean to be worthy of happiness? How is happiness promised in return for becoming British? To explore such questions, I offer a reading of the film *Bend It Like Beckham* (2002, dir. Gurinder Chadha). The film was promoted as a "delightful feel-good comedy" and presents a very happy picture of British multiculturalism. Happiness plays a crucial role within the film's narrative. Indeed, the primary conflict or obstacle in the film is resolved through a speech act, addressed from father to daughter, that takes the approximate form of "I just want you to be happy." In chapter 3 I discussed some of the paradoxes of this speech act, focusing on how the desire for just happiness appears to give the other a certain freedom and yet directs the other toward what is already agreed to be the cause of happiness.

Before we can consider the role of the happiness speech act in *Bend It Like Beckham*, we need to describe the conflict of the film, or the obstacle to the happy ending. The film can be described as about the generational conflict within a migrant Indian family in England. Jess, the daughter (Parminder Nagra), is good at football. Her idea of happiness would be to bend it like Beckham, which requires that she bends the rules about what Indian girls can do. The generational conflict between parents and daughter is also represented as a conflict between the demands of cultures: as Jess says, "Anyone can cook Alo Gobi, but who can bend the ball like Beckham?" This contrast immediately sets up "cooking Alo Gobi" as commonplace and customary, against an alternative world of celebrity, individualism, and talent.

As I argued in the previous section, the customary is associated with what is merely habitual rather than being understood as a form of creative action. Although the film seems to embody the idea of "the culture clash," where the migrant is caught between two cultures, it does not simply represent the two cultures as "cultures" in quite the same way. If anything, the migrant culture appears as culture, as something given or possessed, through being contrasted with the individualism of the West, where you are free to do and to be "whoever" you want to be, understood as the freedom to be happy. Recall here Stokes's description of secular evangelicalism as "the liberation of the individual from custom." The struggle of the film could thus be described as a struggle between individual desire and custom, between freedom and duty, and between happiness and loyalty.[17]

The story of an individual who wants to "bend it like Beckham" is certainly a story of a desire that conflicts with family convention. At one level, it seems to be about the desires of the football-loving daughter, and how such desires are in tension with the desire of the family to reproduce its form. In reading the story in terms of Jess's desire, we could put the question of cultural difference to one side. We could read the story as about the rebellion of the daughter and an attempt to give validation to her rescripting of what it means to have a good life. We might cheer for Jess, as she "scores" and finds happiness somewhere other than where she is expected to find it. We would be happy about her freedom and her refusal of the demand to be a good girl, or even a happy housewife.[18] We might applaud this film as showing the happiness that can follow leaving your parent's expectations behind and following less well-trodden paths. Yet such a reading would fall short. It would not offer a reading of the "where" the happiness of this image of freedom takes us.

Cultural differences are associated with different affects: we have a contrast between the open space of the football pitch, where there is movement, sound, and laughter, and the domestic interiors of Jess's home, full of restrictions, demands, and conflict. In other words, these two worlds are not given the same affective value. The happiness promised by football is of course over-determined. The desire to be like Beckham has a narrative function in the film. In the opening humorous shots, presented as Jess's fantasy (she stares at a poster of Beckham before the scene unfolds), Jess takes up a place beside Beckham on the football ground and is the one who scores the goal. Football signifies not only the national game but also the opportunity for new identi-fications, where you can embody hope for the nation by filling up an empty place alongside its national hero. By implication, the world of football promises freedom, allowing you not only to be happy but to become a happy object, by bringing happiness to others, who cheer as you score. The inclusion of Jess in the national game might be framed as Jess's fantasy, but it also functions as a national fantasy about football, as the "playing field" which offers signs of di-versity, where "whoever" scores will be cheered.

In her other world, Jess experiences frustration, pain, and anxiety. The shots are all of domestic interiors: of dark and cramped spaces, where Jess has to do this or that. Indeed, in her Indian home, she is the object of parental shame. Her mother, Mrs. Bhamra (Shaheen Khan), says, "I don't want shame on the family. That's it, no more football." For Jess, this means playing football in secret: what makes her happy becomes a sign of shame, while her shame be-comes an obstacle to happiness. In this secretive life she forms new bonds and intimacies: first with Jules (Keira Knightley), who gets her on the girl's team, and then with Joe (Jonathan Rhys Meyers), her football coach, with whom she falls in love. This other world, the world of freedom promised by football, puts her in intimate contact with a white girl and a white man. Freedom takes form as proximity to whiteness.

For Jess, the dilemma is: how can she be in both worlds at once? The climatic moment of the film comes as the final of the football tournament coincides with her sister Pinky's (Archie Panjabi) wedding. Jess must go to Pinky's wed-ding, which means not going to the football match. Unhappiness shows how

Jess is "out of place" in the wedding. She is unhappy, as she is not where she wants to be. Jess's friend Tony (Ameet Chana) intervenes and suggests she should leave the wedding and play in the game. Jess replies, "I can't. Look how happy they are, Tony. I don't want to ruin it for them." In this moment, Jess accepts her own unhappiness by identifying with the happiness of her parents: she puts her own desire for happiness to one side. But her father, Mr. Bhamra (Anupam Kher), overhears and says: "Pinky is so happy and you look like you have come to your father's funeral. If this is the only way I am going to see you smiling on your sister's wedding day then go now. But when you come back, I want to see you happy." The father is not happy with her being unhappy even though she wants him to be happy. He lets her go because he wants to see her happy. He cannot be indifferent to her unhappiness: later he says to his wife, "Maybe you could handle her long face, I could not."

At one level, this desire for the daughter's happiness involves a form of indifference to "where" she goes. From the point of view of the film, the desire for happiness is far from indifferent: indeed, the film works partly by "directing" the apparent indifference of this gift of freedom. After all, this is the moment in which the father switches from a desire that is out of line with the happy ending of the film (not wanting Jess to play) to being in line (letting her go) Importantly, the happy ending is about the coincidence of happy objects. The daughters are happy (they are living the life they wish to lead), the parents are happy (as their daughters are happy), and we are happy (as they are happy). Good feeling involves these "points" of alignment. We could say positive affect sutures the film, resolving the generational and cultural split: as soon as Jess is allowed to join the football game, the two worlds come together in a shared moment of enjoyment. While the happy objects are different from the point of view of the daughters (football, marriage), they allow us to arrive at the same point.

The explicit politics of this film is that the daughters should be free to find happiness in their own way. As the father says, "Two daughters made happy on one day, what else could a father ask for." And yet, the film does not give equal value to the objects in which the daughters' good feelings come to reside. Jess's happiness is contrasted to that of her sister Pinky, who is ridiculed throughout the film as not only wanting less but as being less in the direction of her want. Pinky asks Jess why she does not want "this." Jess does not say that she wants something different; she says she wants something "more." That word *more* lingers and frames the ending of the film, which gives us flashes of an imagined future (pregnancy for Pinky, photos of Jess on her sport's team, her love for Joe, and her friendship with Jules). During the sequence of shots as Jess gets ready to join the football final, the camera pans up to show an airplane. Airplanes are everywhere in this film, as they often are in diasporic films. I would argue that they matter here as technologies of flight, signifying what goes up and away. Happiness is promised by what goes "up and away."

The "up and away" does not signal a line of connection to the world they have left behind but a way of leaving a world behind. In an earlier scene, the song "Moving on Up" is playing, as Jess and Jules run toward us. They overtake two Indian women wearing *shalva kamises*, leaving those women lagging behind. I suggest that the spatial promise of the "up and away" is narrated as moving on, as leaving Indian culture behind, even though Jess as a character articulates a fierce loyalty to her family and culture. Your customs are what would leave you "lagging behind." The desire to play football, to join the national game, is read as moving up by leaving your culture of origin behind you. Through the juxtaposition of the daughter's happy objects, the film suggests that *this desire gives a better return.*

The freedom to be happy is thus directive: it involves an act of identification in Jacques Lacan's sense of "the transformation that takes place in the subject" when assuming an image (2006: 1–2). The freedom to be happy is premised on not only the freedom *from* family or tradition but also the freedom *to* identify with the nation as the bearer of the promise of happiness. To identify with the nation, you become an individual: you acquire the body of an individual, a body that can move out and move up. This is how happiness becomes a forward motion: almost like a propeller, happiness is imagined as what allows subjects to embrace futurity, to leave the past behind them, where pastness is associated with custom and the customary. In other words, in becoming an individual, you acquire a sense of freedom: you acquire capacities, energies, and projects. In turn these capacities, energies and projects become a sign of the good of your freedom. To become an individual is to assume an image: becoming free to be happy turns the body in a certain direction.

In reading the "directed" nature of narratives of freedom, we need to consider how the film relates to wider discourses of the public good. The film locates the "pressure point" in the migrant family, who pressure Jess to live a life she does not want to live. And yet, migrants are under increasing pressure to integrate, where integration is the key term for the promotion of multicultural happiness. Although integration is not defined as "leaving your culture behind" (at least not officially), it is unevenly distributed, as a demand that new or would-be citizens "embrace" a common culture that is already given. The migrant daughter who identifies with the national game is thus already an ideal. The daughter who deviates from family convention becomes a sign of the happiness of integration. The unconventional daughter of the migrant family might even provide a conventional form of social hope.

Melancholia and Conversion

The happiness of this film is partly that it imagines that multiculturalism can deliver its social promise by extending freedom to migrants on the condition that they embrace its game. If happiness is promised on condition, then unhappiness would be the cost of not meeting this condition. Although *Bend It Like Beckham* presents a happy picture of British multiculturalism, it does evoke the cost of unhappiness. The background of the film—we might say what is behind the film—is the risk or danger of melancholia. I use *melancholia* quite deliberately here: the risk evoked by the film is not simply feeling bad or bad feeling but getting stuck in bad feeling, or bad feeling as a way of being stuck. If the film is about happiness for migrant subjects, then those subjects must first get over their suffering; they must become unstuck. Freedom to be happy involves, at least for some, the moral and emotional labor of becoming unstuck. This is not to say that the bad feeling is the background feeling of the film: there is little that intrudes upon its happy affectivity; the upbeat soundtrack keeps you feeling up. The risk of melancholia is made present through what is spoken in terms of the father's own past experiences of racism, as experiences that took place before the time frame of the film.

Before we can explore this conversion between melancholia and happiness, I need to explain what I mean by melancholia. The classic point of reference is Freud's essay on "Mourning and Melancholia" ([1917] 2005). In this essay, Freud describes mourning as the relatively healthy process of grieving for a lost object: the aim of this grief is to let go of the object, or to let the object go. The subject "moves on" and is free to form new attachments, which in turn mean a kind of return to life, or a way of staying alive: "just as mourning impels the ego to renounce the object by declaring its death, and offers the ego the reward of staying alive, each individual battle of ambivalence loosens the fixation of the libido upon the object, by devaluing, disparaging, and, so to speak, even killing it" (217).

The distinction between mourning and melancholia can easily be translated into ethical imperatives: "to let go" becomes a healthy relation to loss, and "to hold on" becomes a form of pathology. In his later work Freud does challenge any sharp distinction between melancholia and mourning and considers the incorporation of loss as part of the ordinary process of the forming of the ego ([1923] 1960: 23–24; see also Butler 1997). Yet the distinction between good and bad ways of dealing with the lost object survives at the level of cultural diagnosis. The melancholic may appear *as a figure* insofar as we recognize the melancholic as the one who "holds onto" an object that has been lost, who does not let go, or get over loss by getting over it.

The crucial question for me is the status of the object itself, the "it" that we do or do not get over. In Freud's essay, whatever grief aims for, one thing is not in question: that we are speaking of a loss in history, a loss that is real, or given in or to history, even if what is lost can be uncertain or abstract. Just take the case of the death of a beloved. Someone has died. Usually, for death to be an event, this someone would be known to you, loved by you.[19] Mourning would involve at least two deaths: if someone has died, that person must be declared dead for the death to be real. We do not necessarily experience more than one death. Time is not orderly in hard times. The second death would be the first death for the mourner. The object must be recognized as dead for death to become real. As David L. Eng and Shinhee Han argue, the recognition of death is what makes the object dead; we could even say that recognition of death kills the object for the subject, as a killing again (2003: 365).

If the second death is the first death, if death requires somebody to declare death, then can the declaration be false? It is possible to mourn on the basis of a misapprehension that somebody is dead. Such a possibility can be exercised as a form of hope. That is, the mourner might secretly hope for confirmation that the death is a misapprehension, as a form of hope that will postpone the recognition of the death. But this uneasy psychic dynamic is not what I want to consider here. I want to consider what it means to recognize loss when the loss does not take the form of the loss of someone. As I have already mentioned, for Freud, mourning is "the reaction to the loss of a beloved person, or an abstraction *taking the place* of the person, such as fatherland, freedom, an ideal and so on." ([1917] 2005: 203; emphasis added). If the loss of an abstraction is a displacement, the loss of the beloved might remain the real loss in this model. Or we might say that the loss of the beloved is the real loss insofar as the beloved is the primary object of love (the love of an ideal is already imagined as the displacement of a love for a person, for example, when subjects give their love to the fatherland, then the fatherland has taken the place of the father). I do not want to assume that the love or loss of an idea or ideal is simply a displacement of a more primary love or loss in quite this way. I would argue that the loss of an abstraction *borrows its certainty as loss* by being imagined as a displacement of the loss of a beloved.

When we consider the love of an abstract idea, it is clear that it is possible to mourn what is lost without knowing for certain whether we have lost what is mourned. Freud himself argues that "reality-testing has revealed that the beloved object no longer exists, and demands that the libido as a whole sever its bonds with that object" (204). Of course, to be invested in the belief that "reality-testing" is actually "testing reality" would not be to follow the lesson of psychoanalysis, which asks us to listen to reality as psychically unstable, as not easily separable from the direction of a wish. The severing of the bonds with an object could itself be a wish, a wish that the object is gone, that we can declare its death. After all, the desire for the death of the loved other is the classic scene of ambivalence described by Freud, as the kernel of what makes the social bond binding in the first place, in the form of an irreparable guilt for wanting such a death. The melancholic is hence a subject not only of loss but of desire, where the desire can be for the loss of what is desired.

We can begin to register the significance of such thoughts when we recall that for Freud the melancholic is never sure what has been lost, even when the loss is itself affectively registered on and by the body. What is lost is withdrawn from consciousness. This does not mean that the feeling of loss is unconscious but rather than we can be unconscious of what is lost even when we feel we have lost it. The object of loss for melancholics is missing; they do not know what they are missing.

But if we judge others to be melancholic, do we know what they are missing? Or does melancholia become a judgment against others by the very idea that they are missing something when they speak of their loss? Rather than assuming others are melancholic because they have failed to let go of an object that has been lost, I want to consider melancholia as a way of reading or diagnosing others as having "lost something," and as failing to let go of what has been lost. To read others as melancholic would be to read their attachments as death-wishes, as attachments to things that are already dead. To diagnose melancholia would become a way of declaring that their love objects are dead. Others would be judged as melancholic because they have failed to give up on objects that we have declared dead *on their behalf*. The diagnosis of melancholia would thus involve an ethical injunction or moral duty: the other must let go by declaring the objects that we declare dead as being dead in the way that we declare.

We can learn here about the affective forms of shared grief. Membership in an affective community can require not only that you share an orientation toward certain objects as being good, what I have called simply happy objects, but also that you recognize the same objects as being lost. So if an affective community is produced by sharing objects of loss, which means letting objects go in the right way, then the melancholics would be affect aliens in how they love: their love becomes a failure to get over loss, which keeps them facing the wrong way. The melancholics are thus the ones who must be redirected, or turned around.

Melancholia gives a direction to feeling. For Freud, melancholia involves self-hurt — the lost object is introjected by the ego such that aggressivity toward the lost object is turned back on the self: "Melancholia is mentally characterised by a profoundly painful depression, a loss of interest in the outside world, the loss of the ability to love, the inhibition of any kind of performance and a reduction in the sense of self expressed in self-recrimination and self-directed insults, intensifying into the delusory expectation of punishment" (204). The melancholic subjects expect to be hurt and are unable to love, to form new attachments. As Freud put it, "The complex of melancholia behaves like an open wound, drawing investment energies to itself from all sides" (212). If the melancholics' open wound draws investment, it also drains energy. To stay sore is to be drained of energy. We might even suggest that the figure of the melancholic provides "us" with a wound; by providing a sore point, the melancholic might allow us to keep what is sore at that point. This is how the melancholic migrant *comes to figure*: if the migrant is a sore point, then soreness can be attributed to the migrant.[20]

We can return to *Bend It Like Beckham*. Although this film seems to be about the promise of happiness, I believe that injury and bad feeling play an important narrative function in the film. I am interested in how bad feelings are converted into good feelings. What are the conversion points in this film? We can focus here on two speeches made by Jess's father. The first occurs early on in the film, and the second at the end:

> When I was a teenager in Nairobi, I was the best fast bowler in our school. Our team even won the East African cup. But when I came to this country, nothing. And these bloody gora in the club house made fun of my turban and sent me off packing. . . . She will only end up disappointed like me.

> When those bloody English cricket players threw me out of their club like a dog, I never complained. On the contrary, I vowed that I would never play again. Who suffered? Me. But I don't want Jess to suffer. I don't want her to make the same mistakes her father made, accepting life, accepting situations. I want her to fight. And I want her to win.

In the first speech, the father says she *should not play* in order not to suffer like him. In the second, he says she *should play* in order not to suffer like him. The desire implicit in both speech acts is the avoidance of the daughter's suffering, which is expressed in terms of the desire that she does not repeat his own. The second speech suggests that the refusal to play a national game is the "truth" behind the migrant's suffering: you suffer because you do not play the game, where not playing is read as self-exclusion. For Jess to be happy, her father lets her be included, narrated as a form of letting go. By implication, not only is he letting her go; he is also letting go of his own suffering, the unhappiness caused by accepting racism, as the "point" of his exclusion. I suggest that the father is represented in the first speech as melancholic: as refusing to let go of his suffering, as incorporating the very object of own loss. His refusal to let Jess go is readable as a symptom of melancholia: as a stubborn attachment to his own injury. As he says: "Who suffered? Me."

The figure of the melancholic migrant appears as the one who refuses to participate in the national game. Suffering becomes a way of holding on to a lost object. We can certainly see how the father's idea of himself, or his ideal self, is threatened by the experience of racism ("I was the best fast bowler in our school"). Racism becomes an explanation for the failure to live up to an ideal ("when I came to this country, nothing"). The melancholic migrant appears as a figure in this translation from experience to explanation. Racism as an explanation of migrant suffering (they "made fun of my turban and sent me off packing") functions to preserve an attachment to the very scene of suffering. Bad feeling thus originates with the migrant who won't let go of racism as a script that explains suffering.

Let's consider the significance of the turban. We could say that the turban is what keeps an attachment to culture, to religion, to the homeland. The turban is what the migrant should give up in order to embrace the national ideal. Or at least, if the migrant wants to keep the turban (the nation after all can incorporate some forms of difference), then he must convert the turban into a happy object that can coexist with other objects, such as the flag. The melancholic migrant fails to make this conversion. He holds on not simply to difference, to what keeps him apart, but also to the unhappiness of difference as an historical itinerary. In other words, he is hurt by the very memory of being teased about the turban, which ties the turban to a history of racism. The object of love is converted into a memory of racism which allows the object to be retained.[21]

Consciousness of racism becomes somewhat counterintuitively readable as a form of melancholia. This point is counterintuitive because melancholia is usually associated with unconscious processes, and with what cannot be revealed to consciousness. If consciousness of racism is framed as melancholic, it becomes a kind of false consciousness, in the sense that it is imagined as a way of not becoming conscious of what has been lost, and thus a way of holding on to what has gone. I would even say that racism becomes readable as what the melancholic migrant is attached *to*, as an attachment to injury that allows migrants to justify their refusal to participate in the national game ("the gora in their club house"). By implication, it is the repetition of the narrative of injury which causes injury: the migrants exclude themselves if they insist on reading their exclusion *as* a sign of the ongoing nature of racism.[22] The narrative implicit in the resolution of the father's trauma is not that migrants "invented racism" to explain their loss but that they preserve its power to govern social life by not getting over it. The moral task is thus "to get over it," as if when you are over it, it is gone.

In other words, the task is to put racism behind you. Jess is the one who *takes up this task*. The father's experience of being excluded from the national game is repeated in Jess's own encounter with racism on the football pitch (she is called a "Paki"), which leaves to the injustice of her being sent off. Jess's anger and hurt do not stick. She lets go of her suffering. How does she let go? When she says to Joe, "You don't know what it feels like," he replies, "Of course I know how it feels like, I'm Irish." It is this act of identification with suffering that brings Jess back into the national game (as if to say, "We all suffer, it is not just you.").[23] The film suggests that whether racism hurts depends upon individual choice and capacity: we can let go of racism as something that happens, a capacity that is attributed to skill (if you are good enough, you will get by, or even do well), as well as the proximate gift of empathy, where the hurt of racism is reimagined as a common ground.

It is important to note that the melancholic migrant's fixation with injury is read as an obstacle not only to his own happiness but also to the happiness of the generation to come, and even to national happiness. This figure may even quickly convert in the national imaginary to the "could-be-terrorist" (Ahmed 2004). His anger, pain, misery (all understood as forms of bad faith insofar as they won't let go of something that is presumed to have gone) becomes "our terror." To avoid such a terrifying end point, the duty of the migrant is to attach to a different happier object, one that can bring good fortune, such as the national game. The film ends with the fortune of this reattachment. Jess goes to America to take up her dream of becoming a professional football player, a land which makes the pursuit of happiness an originary goal.

The love between Jess and Joe offers another point of reattachment. Heterosexuality becomes itself a form of happy return promising to overcome injury. It is worth noting here that the director of the film, Gurinder Chadha, originally planned to have Jess and Jules falling in love. This decision to drop the lesbian plot was, of course, to make the film more marketable.[24] We can see here the importance of "appeal" as a form of capital, and how happiness can function as a moral economy, a way of making what *is* good into things that can circulate *as* goods. In *Bend It Like Beckham*, the heterosexual script involves proximity to queer. Not only does the film play with the possibility of female rebellion as lesbianism (girls with short hair who wear sports bras are presented as "could-be" lesbians rather than as "being" lesbians); it also involves the use of a queer male character, Tony, in which an alternative set of desires is deposited. Gayatri Gopinath suggests that the film "ultimately reassures viewers that football-loving girls are indeed properly heterosexual by once again using the gay male figure as the 'real' queer character in the film" (2005: 129). Indeed, we could argue that the narrative of bending the rules of femininity involves a straightening device: you can bend only insofar as you return to the straight line, which provides as it were our end point. So girls playing football leads to the male football coach. Narratives of rebellion can involve deviations from the straight line if they return us to this point.

Heterosexuality also promises to overcome the injury or damage of racism. The acceptance of interracial heterosexual love is a conventional narrative of reconciliation, as if love can overcome past antagonism and create what I would call hybrid familiality: *white with color, white with another*.[25] Such fantasies of proximity as premised on the following belief: if only we could be closer, we would be as one.[26] Proximity becomes a promise: the happiness of the film is the promise of "the one," as if giving love to the white man as the national subject, or the ideal subject of the nation, would allow us to have a share in this promise.

The final scene is a cricket scene: the first of the film. As we know, cricket is an unhappy object in the film, associated with the unhappiness of racism. Jess's father is batting. Joe, in the foreground, is bowling. Joe smiles as he approaches us. He turns around, bowls, and gets the father out. In a playful scene, Joe then "celebrates" and his body gesture mimics that of a plane, in a classic football gesture. As I have suggested, planes are happy objects in the film, associated with flight, with moving up and away. By mimicking the plane, Joe becomes the agent that converts bad feeling (unhappy racism) into good feeling (multicultural happiness). It is the white man who enables the father to let go of his injury about racism and to play cricket again. It is the white man who brings the melancholic migrant back into the national fold. *His body is our conversion point.*

We can contrast *Bend It Like Beckham* with *East Is East* (1999, dir. Damien O'Donnell), which does not convert melancholia to happiness in quite the same way. The film's failure to offer an affective conversion (even though it was also marketed as a feel-good comedy) might be explained by its own preoccupation with the figure of the Muslim father, who is perhaps not quite so easy to reconcile into a happy image of multiculturalism. Indeed, the contrast between these films helps us to extend our understanding of how melancholia is located in certain attachments, which become death wishes, and the relation between such attachments and consciousness of racism.

In *East Is East* the father's desire is for his children to be good Muslims, primarily figured as the desire to arrange marriages for them. This desire is presented as more violent and desperate than in *Bend It Like Beckham*. It figures as a kind of damage to his five children, who have diverse relationships with him and with Britain: the tomboy daughter, the good Muslim, the homosexual (who is pronounced dead by the father when he refuses marriage), the Casanova, and the peacemaker, who alone of the children wants everyone to be happy.

The film does not "feel good" partly given the care of its presentation of the impossibility and violence of the father's desire. Even in scenes which one suspects are meant to be humorous (the father tries to marry his sons off to two "ugly sisters"), we witness the father's desire for his children to be good Muslims as the cause of their misery, as well as his own. The film represents the traumatic consequences of the necessary failure of his identity project: his children cannot want what would allow the father to be what he wants to be. At the end of the film, the father says in defeat: "I'm trying to show you a good place to live. English people will never accept you. In Islam, everyone is equal. No black man, no white man. Just Muslims." The desire for them to be Muslim is associated with his consciousness of racism. This is a complicated association. One reading of the father's speech act would be to say that racism itself becomes a defense mechanism, a way of refusing to embrace the happy diversity promised by living in Britain. This very act of pointing to England as unaccepting of difference becomes a symptom of the violence of his retention of Islam as a love object. Investments in Islam become sublimations of aggressiveness or ways of projecting aggressiveness onto the host nation.

The violence of the father exceeds the frame of reconciliation: in one traumatic scene toward the end of the film, he beats the son who identifies with him as the good Muslim. His violence becomes a self-directed violence, a form of self-harm. Such an internalization of aggression is at once a redirection of aggressiveness by the Muslim subject. To be Muslim is to be the cause of your own violence. When he beats his son, his wife intervenes and says to him: "I'm not going to stand by and watch you crush them one by one because of your pig-blooded ignorance." His violence erupts at this point, and he physically attacks her: "You called me a pig, you bitch." That his violence is a response to a speech act that is offensive to Muslims does matter. His violence becomes readable as taking offense. In a wider context, the offendability of Muslims has been understood as what threatens our freedom of speech as well as our happiness.[27] To take offense is to cause hurt by being hurt. The migrant who is caught up and invested in his own hurt becomes the origin of social and sexual violence.[28]

The father's desire to be a good Muslim (by insisting that his children be good Muslims) is thus presented as melancholic; he fails to recognize that his own attachment is to an object that has gone, which is a failure rehearsed as a "crushing" violence in which everyone gets hurt. Not only does he fail to let go of an object that has already been lost but this failure to let go is what blocks his children's freedom to be happy. The father is represented as uninterested in the children's happiness. His wife says to him: "No, you should be ashamed, George. You are not interested in these kids being happy. You just want to prove to them what a great man you are. Because you are ashamed of me, George, and you are ashamed of our kids." The melancholic migrant is ashamed of his family for not being what he wants them to be. When one of his sons says to him, "Are you happy now, Dad? Is this what you wanted?" he says in response, "I only want to help you son. I don't want to hurt you." The statement "I don't want to hurt you" contrasts with the father's speech in *Bend It Like Beckham*, which is expressed in the terms "I don't what you to be hurt." Here, hurt is explicitly framed as what the father has done to the children by his inability to desire their happiness at the cost of his own. Even his concern with their hurt becomes a self-concern, a concern with what he has done ("hurt you") rather than what has been done to the child ("be hurt").

Happiness can only be projected into the future in this film: we imagine the children as having the freedom to do whatever makes them happy once the father's will has been crushed. One reconciliation fantasy is present in the film, even if it is not quite premised on the father's conversion. The wife and mother, the white woman, defends her husband and is loyal to him despite his violence: "That bastard you are talking about is my husband. And whatever you think of him he is still your father. So if I hear another foul-mouthed word out of any of you, I will have you." She returns to him, which allows him to return. The final conversation of the film is the gentle and easy language of intimacy: "Do you want a cup of tea?" she asks, and he replies, "I will have half a cup." This exchange returns us to interracial intimacy as the grounds for reconciliation, a return that turns upon a signifier of Englishness tied closely to political economies of empire, and the circulation and consumption of tea (Chatterjee 2001). The quiet intimacy of the family provides a horizon in which likes can gather as a shared form. In this instance, it is the white woman who brings the melancholic migrant back into the national fold. Her capacity to forgive is represented as caring for his happiness (even in the face of his own indifference to happiness). By caring for his happiness and for the happiness of the family, she enables them to share a horizon. *Her body is our conversion point.*

In both films racism comes up most obviously *in* the father's memory of an unresolved pain, and *as* what is perceived by the father as an obstacle to migrant participation in national happiness. The melancholic migrant is thus a rather ghostly figure, haunting contemporary culture as a kind of unnecessary and hurtful remainder of racism. We can understand the spectrality of this figure if we consider how histories of empire have been narrated in terms of happiness. The migrant who remembers other, more painful aspects of such histories threatens to expose too much. The task of politics becomes one of conversion: if racism is preserved *only* in migrants' memory and consciousness, then racism would "go away" if only they would let it go away, if only they too would declare it gone. To turn away from such histories is thus to turn toward happiness and toward others who care for your happiness, who allow you to share in their happiness. This is why even the quiet murmur of family intimacy can offer a fantasy of reconciliation, a fantasy that we can forget about racism, and that we can put such histories of hurt behind us.

Alien Affects

My readings of these films explore a national desire for the second generation to desire in a way that refuses family convention—a desire that takes form as the freedom to be happy in your own way. In films such as *Bend It like Beckham* and *East Is East*, the investment in good or bad migrants is distributed in generational terms: the second-generation children are the ones who desire their own happiness. The nation must intervene to protect the second generation from the first, those who have failed to let go of their past attachments and who hence can only suffer and transmit their suffering, which easily gets turned into terror and rage.[29] The nation becomes the good family who can give the children the freedom to be happy in their own way. However, in framing these films in terms of national desire, I have not considered the desires of the second generation. Writing myself as a second-generation daughter of a mixed-race family, with a Pakistani Muslim father and an English Christian mother, it must be registered as curious that I could read the unconventional migrant daughter purely as a good object for the nation.[30] She seems rather vacated of any place by being read as in place.

What about the desires of the daughters? In this section, I consider the work of two writers, Meera Syal and Yasmin Hai, who in their memoirs of early childhood experiences have given a language to the desires of the daughters of parents who migrated from India or Pakistan in the 1950s and 1960s, and who in so doing allow us to explore the ambivalence of such desires, which do not get directed either simply toward or away from family. Their books teach us about what Shirley Tate has described very well as "the hybridity of the everyday" (2005: 7).

Anita and Me, Meera Syal's first book, is a semiautographical novel about of a girl called Meena, the daughter of the only Punjabi family in the mining village of Tollington. In the cover description of the book, Meena's wants are foregrounded: "She wants fish fingers and chips, not just chapati and dhal; she wants an English Christmas, not just the usual interminable Punjabi festivities—but more than anything, more than mini-skirts and the freedom to watch *Opportunity Knocks*, Meena wants to roam the backyards of working-class Tollington with feisty Anita Rutter and her gang." These wants are not presented as simply in opposition: she wants *not just* chapatis and dhal *but also* fish and chips. So we are talking about a choice here: a choice between just chapatis and dhal, or chapatis and dhal *and* fish and chips. By implication, what her parents want for her is just chapatis and dhal. The happiness fantasy implicit in this expression of desire is *for more that just that*, where "just that" becomes defined in terms of the culture of origin.

It is important to recognize here that growing up is usually narrated as generational conflict: the child wants what the parents do not want for the child. Stories of happy families are presented as the reconciliation of want: either the child comes to see the wisdom of the parents and aligns her want with what the parents want for her, or the parents come to see the wisdom of the child and align their wants for the child with what the child wants; alternatively (and usually) some sort of compromise is formed. A compromise is happy insofar as it is a compromise in what is wanted.[31] In representations of the migrant family, the conflict between generational want is overdetermined, such that the parents' wants are associated with the culture of origin (where you are from), and the child's want is associated with the culture of destination (where you are at).[32] But once we enter the text, we learn that things are not quite so simple.

Meena is a troublemaker in the best sense, and *Anita and Me* could certainly be read as part of our genealogy of female troublemaking fiction that I have explored throughout this book. Her self-identification as trouble is what drives her friendship with Anita, as if their points of deviation are what makes them kin: "And Anita never looked at me the way my adopted female cousins did; there was never fear or censure or recoil in those green, cool eyes, only the recognition of a kindred spirit, another mad bad girl trapped inside a super-ficially obedient body. In fact, sometimes when I looked into her eyes, all I could see and cling to was my own questioning reflection" ([1996] 2004: 150). Meena's self-identification as "a mad bad girl" involves a kinship with rebellion, a kinship of alien affect, a refusal to want the right things. Once, when she is in trouble for lying, her mother says, "There's rice and dhal inside. Go and wash your hands." Meena replies, "I don't want that . . . that stuff! I want fish fingers! Fried! And chips! *Why can't I eat what I want to eat?*" (60; emphasis added). In the context of the narrative, Meena's expression of want for fish fingers is a form of disobedience, perhaps even a way of revenging herself against her parents by wanting something other than what they want her to want.

Generational and cultural differences—articulated as differences of taste—can be powerfully mobilized within situation of conflict. It is not that such differences necessarily cause conflict; rather, they "come up" in the timing of conflict, in the heat of its moment, almost as something that you can do something with.[33] Meena says she wants *this* and not *that* in return for being told off for lying, for being found wanting. Her desire to do what she wants, which I have discussed in this book as the freedom to do whatever makes you happy, certainly seem to direct her toward Englishness and away from India. And yet, if wanting fish fingers is a response to being found wanting, we can ask: what is it really that she wants?

We learn from *Anita and Me* that individual want is not the beginning of the story. How do you know what you want? The opacity of desire can be pedagogic. Doing what she wants does not mean for Meena becoming happy. Happiness enters the explicit terms of the novel as being something she has lost, and it does so via the father. The father evokes time and time again how Meena "used to be such a happy girl." Of course, the evocation of the lost happy child can be described as a parental cliché: parents often evoke happiness nostalgically when they are faced with the moodiness of the child becoming teenager. Her father keeps asking her what is wrong: "Papa cleared his throat and took in a deep breath of air, 'Meena, is there something worrying you?' I shook my head . . . Papa continued, 'You were always so . . . happy. You talked to me. Why have you stopped?'" (147). Meena feels "wrong-footed and bewildered" in response (147). To be presented with your unhappiness is to become disoriented. Her father says to her later, "I do not like what you have become, Meena. . . . I have watched you change, from a sweet happy girl into some rude, sulky monster" (249). There is no doubt that the investment here is not only in the daughter's happiness but also in her being good; to become sulky is to lose your place within the family or to acquire a place as the cause of family unhappiness, as the one who "gets in the way" of its enjoyment.

We do not need to assume that the father is right or wrong to describe the daughter in this way. What interests me is the relation between description of the child as wanting and perceptions of happiness. In *Bend It Like Beckham*, Jess is unhappy because she is not doing what she wants, even though she wants to make her parents happy. She becomes happy when she is allowed to do what she wants to do, which requires that her father let go of his own suffering, which gets in the way of his happiness as well as hers. In *Anita and Me*, the daughter is also presented because unhappy as she is not allowed to do what she wants. But when she does get what she wants, she does not become happy. The father, by perceiving her unhappiness, catches her mood in some way.

By reflecting on Meena's feelings, the book gives us an itinerary of her desire. It is not simply that she desires happiness but that she desires what she desires because she is not happy. So it is not that she wants what she wants because she wants it. We learn about the curious nature of want when she speaks of wanting whiteness, which is also about not wanting the body she has: "I had never wanted to be anyone else except myself only older and famous. But now, for some reason, I wanted to shed my body like a snake slithering out of its skin and emerge reborn, pink and unrecognisable. I began avoiding mirrors, I refused to put on Indian suits my mother laid out for me on the bed when guests were due for dinner, I hid in the house when Auntie Shaila bade loud farewells in Punjabi to my parents from the front garden, I took to walking several paces behind or in front of my parents when we went on a shopping trip, checking my reflection in shop windows, bitterly disappointed it was still there" (146). Meena wants to be white, or to be closer to whiteness, because she cannot bear her own reflection in the mirror. The desire for whiteness is lived as the desire to be at a distance from her family, who can reflect only her failure to be white. She wants not simply to be friends with Anita but to be Anita, to be white like Anita.

Rather than locating happiness in what follows increasing proximity to whiteness, the book suggests that the desire for proximity to whiteness is a form of unhappiness, with a feeling of being out of place, of being not quite at home, of not being able to share in the happiness of others. When celebrating *Diwali*, for instance, Meena waits for others to mark the occasion: "I had hung around the yard all morning with what I hoped was a general expression of celebration. Everyone's indifference had stunned me and I now understood why my parents made an effort to mark Jesus' birthday" (92). Wanting to celebrate Christmas is partly about wanting to celebrate what others celebrate, to share in happy objects. Wanting to celebrate what others celebrate is also an effect of others not recognizing your celebration, of how others are indifferent to your happiness. The desire to participate in English culture hence is not simply a form of assimilation, wanting to be like, but rather wanting to participate in a shared community of wants. *Anita and Me* reflects constantly on the difficulty of belonging to a world that takes its points of happiness from lines you do not follow.

In one of the novel's crucial incidents, a gang of Meena's friends turns against an Indian man. "Sam interrupted, a sly grin curling the corners of his mouth. 'You don't do nothing but talk, Uncle. And give everything away to some darkies we've never met. We don't give a toss for anybody else. This is our patch. Not some wogs' handout.' I felt as if I had been punched in the stomach. My legs felt watery and a hot panic softened my insides to mush" (193). The shock of this incident is the shock of realizing that the world you are in is not available to you, that you do not belong in the world that you imagined would give you happiness in return for being a certain way. Of course, Sam is not talking to Meena, even if she is one of "them." Later he says, "When I said them . . . I never meant you, Meena! It was all the others, not you!" (313). Meena replies, "I *am* the others, Sam. You did mean me" (314). The power of this statement, "I am the others," is the power of an identification, of recognizing yourself in the insult directed toward another even when you are not recognized as one of the others. In seeing yourself as the other who is insulted, you affirm your allegiance with others *as* others.

The turning point in the novel is the arrival of Meena's grandmother from India. In the first place, Meena feels ambivalent: "Usually, mama and papa were the most polite and careful neighbours, always shushing me if I made too much noise down the entries, always careful to keep windows closed during papa's musical evenings. But tonight, I noticed disapprovingly, they were as noisy and hysterical as anyone else. I had never seen the Elders so expansive and unconcerned, and knew that this somehow had something to do with Nanima" (204). But getting to her grandmother is what allows Meena to recognize her family history as not simply behind her. She gains a context for the stories of the places she has not been: "But gradually I got used to Nanima's world, a world made up of old and bitter family feuds. . . . They all put mama's rickshaw story and papa's unexploded bomb tale into some kind of context for me; my parents' near brushes with death were not one-off happenings, they were simply two more incidents in a country that seemed full to bursting with excitement, drama and passion, history in the making, and for the first time I desperately wanted to visit India and claim some of that magic as mine" (210–11).

The recognition of the significance of the family and country that has been left behind involves recognition of what has been lost. The recognition of loss does not involve the pathos of realizing that something has gone that cannot be retrieved but rather the excitement of recognizing what can be retrieved, of what is still possible, even if it is not available at present. The daughter begins to recover a sense of what she might be missing. This is not to say that migration does not mean losing things but rather that to lose something can also mean to gain a potential to find something (not just for the subject who migrates but for those who inherit her displacement and arrival), even if what you find will not be the same things that have been lost.[34]

The novel ends with Meena sending a letter to Anita, indicating that she will be going to grammar school, an ending that echoes Babyji in the last chapter; "getting into school" signifies the promise of new forms of mobility and freedom. In a way, what Meena leaves behind is not only the idea that she could be Anita (that she could be white like her) but also the white working-class lifeworld, which is narrated primarily in terms of violence and racism. Moving up for Meena is certainly coded in terms of bourgeois aspirations for a better life, as if class mobility is how you can leave racism behind. If Bend It Like Beckham is structured by a fantasy that individual talent can mean being unaffected by racism, in *Anita and Me* the fantasy is that migrants can transcend racism by leaving working-class culture behind them.[35]

We can compare *Anita and Me* to Yasmin Hai's more recent memoir *The Making of Mr Hai's Daughter: Becoming British* (2008). What is so important about this memoir is that it is written from the point of view of the daughter whose father wants her to assimilate, to become British (though as a desire it was not without ambivalence). The book thus joins earlier accounts of migrant experience such as Hanif Kureishi's novella *My Son the Fanatic* ([1994] 2008) in challenging the standard "directionality" of integration discourse, which rests on the perception of first-generation migrants as inherently unwilling to integrate (such that integration is narrated as something that must be forced, or reimagined, as a form of second-generation resistance).[36] Migrant memoirs and fiction give texture and complexity to the migrant experience, to the different ways in which hope, fear, anxiety, longing, and desire shape the decisions to leave one's country as well as the experiences of arriving and becoming familiar with a new country.

Yasmin begins her memoir with a reflection on her father's account of his migration experience, and how much it was driven by the desire for happiness. Her father is rather unconventional, a political dissident, a communist. This detail matters: one of the myths of integration discourse is that first-generation migrants are always conventional, that migrants assemble around culture, turning culture into a fetish, in the fear that they are losing it. Yasmin imagines, "I would have thought that giving up such an illustrious and dangerous political career back home for a mundane life in cold and damp England would have been upsetting. And though, for the sake of a good story, my father liked to pretend this was the case, it wasn't true. He was very happy to come here. Very happy indeed" (8). Migration can involve its own promise of happiness; you can be happy to migrate, to give up where you are for where you are going.

Yasmin's experience of growing up contrasts with Jess's and Meena's: her father wants her to be a good English girl, not a good Pakistani girl. To be a good English girl means that she is shamed out of proximity to her culture of origin. In one scene, she eats with her hands, as her mother does. Her (white English) aunt asks, "Are you a Paki?" Yasmin is distressed: "I shake my head. My face is burning, and my head starting to swirl. From the corner of my eyes, I can see my father shaking his head in despair. The word doesn't offend him one bit. I can see he even agrees with her" (52). She is shamed into assimilation, taking on the insult as a sign of the failure to be in the right way. They have to turn her into an English girl, with good manners. So her mother cuts her hair: "When my mother held the mirror up, I saw a perfect little bob, just like Milly-Molly-Mandy, the English heroine of the book I was reading. I looked like a proper English girl" (54). Becoming English is having the right image reflected back into the mirror.

Eventually Yasmin is told to stop speaking Urdu. "My mother carries on speaking to us in Urdu, but we children only speak to her in English" (60). Not speaking Urdu is experienced as a loss, primarily because her mother does not speak English. Yasmin realizes that "after dropping Urdu, she became lost to me for ever" (61). Rather than integration being a way of recognizing loss, the very desire for integration is what makes something lost. Yasmin in losing Urdu loses her mother and her point of connection to a history that is not simply or only behind her.

The father believes that happiness is what follows becoming English (in the right way), where becoming English is to become cultured. As a desire it is not without ambivalence: it sets limits on the kind of English he wants his daughter to become, which means that some forms of English culture remain prohibited. So, for instance, Yasmin's father won't let her watch *Top of the Pops*. "'But Dad,' I wanted to say, 'all my friends watch it.' But what was the point of objecting? He would never be convinced. Still, my father's attitude baffled me. Hadn't he always told us that being *modern* was good?" (77). Later he won't let her see the film *Grease*, which he describes as "Western low-brow rubbish." Yasmin suggests that her father differentiates Western (bad) from modern (good) but what seems crucial is the separation of lowbrow from highbrow. Becoming English is related to an ethical imperative to become English in a highbrow way.

This "becoming" is not smooth or easy. The story is full of ambivalence, described in terms of being happy and sad in becoming English: "I didn't know whether to be happy or sad about how English I was" (76). The very failure to be given happiness in return for becoming British, is narrated as the impossibility of being what you are asked to become. Yasmin goes to a nondenominational school, a secular school. Secularity becomes a cultural ideal insofar as it is imagined as neutral. When they sit for assembly, Yasmin is shocked that they sing the Lord's Prayer and stumbles over the words: "My father might have tried to educate me about Christianity to stop me from feeling alienated, but the more I became acquainted with Christian England, the more I began to realise that there were some things about England and the way that the English lived that I would never be part of. It was as if I lived in a parallel world" (68). Proximity to whiteness creates a point of alienation.

The use of the term "parallel worlds" evokes in the British context the spectre of segregation, in which the communities that do not mix and mingle are framed as minority communities in ways that do not even have to be made explicit: "we cannot claim to be a truly multicultural society if the various communities live, as Cantle puts it, parallel lives that do not touch at any point."[37] Parallel lines are not created by migrants who refuse to integrate but by the ways in which the imagined neutral and open spaces take certain bodies as the norm. To live in a parallel would is to be unable to follow the lines of that world that are not even visible as lines. Invisible lines could be described as life forms. To be affectively alien is to be unable to inhabit such forms.

Yasmin does want what her father wants; she wants to be like the other girls, to pass into the school community, to be English like them. But she cannot have what they have; she cannot be what she wants. In one incident, she and another British Asian girl, Lulu, have a fight about who eats more English food. Lula calls Yasmin a curry-lover, and Yasmin pours orange juice over her (86– 87). Yasmin is the one that gets into trouble, and she becomes troubled, which she experiences as uneasiness, as the loss of the capacity to be happy: "School life soon returned to normal. *I should have been happy but I wasn't.* Something had changed. It wasn't that I had been exposed for being less English than Lulu. For some reason I didn't care about that anymore. It was just from then on, whatever I did or wherever I went, I knew how out of place I was. It wasn't that I hadn't noticed it before. But before I'd believe that with a bit of knowledge and a bit of wiliness I could make myself belong anywhere. Now, I no longer believed that" (89; emphasis added).

To be alienated from happiness is to recognize not only that you are the one who is out of place but also that you cannot make yourself be in place, that you cannot make yourself belong "anywhere." Such recognition involves an alienation from the abstract potentiality of the individual, premised on the belief that you can do or be whatever you want to do or be. Without that self-belief, happiness seems to recede from "where" one is, as if within the loss of the "whatever" is also the loss of a "wherever." We are reminded that the freedom to be happy, even as fantasy, might evoke "somewhere," as a where that only some can be. Being who Yasmin is, where she is, means being estranged from this "whatever" of happiness.

The memoir offers an account of the good migrant daughter (who is good for the nation because she wants to be English) becoming unhappy with English-ness, coming to experience its promise of happiness as empty. In witnessing the emptiness of the promise, Yasmin becomes angry. The unconventional daughter of the migrant family can thus lose her proximity to national hope: "Despite our good jobs in television, our lively social lives, something about living in Britain troubled us, and we both knew that race had a large role to play in our angst. . . . We were always flying off the handle about issues of race and identity, unable to take comfort in the racially tolerant environment that we were constantly being told we lived in. Our anger was also the dynamic that helped feed our creative passions, but sometimes it just felt all-consuming" (267). Tolerance offers its own promise of happiness: as if the world is open to you, as if you can do what you want in the world that you are in. Your ex-perience of living in the world exposes this openness as a fantasy. Anger fills the gap between the promise and what happens. Sometimes that anger can be creative, sometimes not.

And of course, events happen. We follow Yasmin as she responds to what happens: September 11, 2001, the war on terror, the U.S.–led invasion of Af-ghanistan. To be responsive you are not necessarily responding to the same thing. "'I can't believe it', I said to Jay, surprised by the extent of support for the invasion. It was the first time in my memory that I felt so frighteningly out of line with the public mood. It's not where I wanted to be" (287). The child who wants to be British becomes the adult who knows the promise is empty: "Ever since 9/11 I had anguished over the Muslim part of my identity. But I now real-ised my Britishness was just as troublesome. I had always been proud of being British, but the way politicians and the media were now forcing their phoney definitions down our throats—superficially evoking the principle of the En-lightenment on the way—left me feeling less British that I ever had felt in my entire life" (329). Yasmin describes so well how it feels to be alienated through how you are affected by the world. Here, to be an affect alien is to experience alien affects—to be out of line with the public mood, not to feel the way others feel in response to an event.

The book is also a form of mourning for Yasmin's father, the good migrant who wants what the nation wants him to want, to integrate, to live and die by its dream. She returns to his grave. She writes of his desire. She writes of the failure of that dream: "My father never understood why, in the England I had grown up in—complete with Union Jacks, swamping speeches by Thatcher, Paki beatings and later calls for loyalty test—embracing my 'other' self was so important. And wasn't it the case that being close to my cultural heritage also allowed me to reconnect with my mother after my father's death. I had lost one parent, I couldn't bear losing another" (332–33). We are shown the ethical importance of holding on to a memory as a way of keeping a connection to what and who survives in the present. The memoir helps us to realize that the figure of the melancholic migrant as it is exercised in the contemporary politics of race is missing something. It is the very desire to assimilate, to let the past go, which returns to haunt the nation. It is the migrant who wants to integrate who may bear witness to the emptiness of the promise of happiness.[38]

And yet, integration remains a national ideal, a way of imagining national happiness. Migrants as would-be citizens are thus increasingly bound by the happiness duty not to speak about racism in the present, not to speak of the unhappiness of colonial histories, or of attachments that cannot be reconciled into the colorful diversity of the multicultural nation. The happiness duty for migrants means telling a certain story about your arrival as good, or the good of your arrival. The happiness duty is a positive duty to speak of what is good but can also be thought of as a negative duty not to speak of what is not good, not to speak from or out of unhappiness. It is if you should let go of the pain of racism by *letting go of racism as a way of understanding that pain*. It is as if you have a duty not to be hurt by the violence directed toward you, not even to notice it, to let it pass by, as if it passes you by. To speak out of consciousness of such histories, and with consciousness of racism, is to become an affect alien. Affect aliens can do things with alien affects, and do things we must.

At the same time, there is something rather hopeful about my critique of the happiness duty. I have suggested that affective communities take shape by a shared orientation toward certain things as being good. The experience of migration makes explicit how we always occupy more than one community; if the possibility that we occupy more than one community is structural, then even one community involves the experience of more than one. For those of us conscious of being attached to more than one, it might seem that you can be caught out, that you want things that are opposed to each other. The classic test that poses "more than one" forms of allegiance as an opposition is the cricket test, which is also a citizenship test, and a happiness test: who would you support if the English team was playing the nation from which you came? This test gives you a choice and presumes that your happiness choice reveals your true identity, a coming-out story of sorts. If England winning makes me happy, then I would be English. If the other team winning makes me happy, then I would be other, not English.

We could say in response to such identity tests that being made happy by the wrong thing (say being happy if the Pakistani cricket team beats England) does not mean supporting England *in other ways*, does not mean not loving England *in other ways*. To think about culture through the lens of migration might even help us think differently about happiness and identity. If migration is recognized as part of the unfolding history of culture, rather than something that happens to culture, then culture becomes what unfolds over time. If culture is what unfolds, then to share something would not depend on being directed in the same way. We might build a looser sense of being together, where we would not be required to place our hopes for happiness in the same things.

Of course, such a looser model of national belonging can easily be described in terms of liberal multiculturalism, which would permit idiosyncratic differences at a national level. We must do more than diversify happy object choices. After all, the political struggle over national belonging exists because some happy objects are seen as overly compromising, as giving up on the very idea of who or what is the national subject. Some happy objects—one might think of the turban or burqa—become the cause of national unhappiness not simply because they cannot exist alongside the happy objects of the nation but because they are saturated by unhappy histories, as histories of empire that are erased under the sign of happiness. Objects become unhappy when they embody the persistence of histories that cannot be wished away by happiness. To recognize unhappiness would be to explore how the diversification of happiness does not and cannot eliminate antagonism from political memory, which is at once the present of national time. We would recognize the impossibility of putting certain histories behind us; these histories persist, and we must persist in declaring our unhappiness with their persistence.

The wise man, knowing how to enjoy achieved results without having constantly to replace them with others, finds in them an attachment to life in the hour of difficulty. But the man who has always pinned all his hopes on the future and lived with his eyes fixed upon it, has nothing in the past as a comfort against the present's afflictions, for the past was nothing to him but a series of hastily experienced stages. What blinded him to himself was his expectation always to find further on the happiness he had so far missed. Now he is stopped in his tracks; from now on nothing remains behind or ahead of him to fix his gaze upon.   ÉMILE DURKHEIM

CHAPTER FIVE

Happy Futures

TO PIN HOPES ON THE FUTURE is to imagine happiness as what lies ahead of us. For Durkheim an attachment to the future would mean to be missing something, unable to experience the past or the present as something other than hasty, as something we have to get through, rush through, in order to be somewhere else. When happiness is before us, we might even be stopped on our tracks. I have also focused throughout this book on the futurity of happiness, how happiness offers us a promise, which we glimpse in the unfolding of the present. The desire for happiness sends happy objects forth, creating lines and pathways in their trail, as if we might find happiness by following these paths.

It does not follow that we can simply collapse happiness with the future or into the future. The future after all can be imagined in ways that are far from happy: if we feel we have lost the possibility of happiness, if we feel we have lost hope that we might find happiness somewhere along the way, then the future will embody that loss of possibility. So too happiness can be imagined as past, as being what we once had, as being what we have lost in arriving somewhere, or even what we have given up so others can get somewhere. Nostalgic and promissory forms of happiness belong under the same horizon, insofar as they imagine happiness as being somewhere other than where we are in the present. And when happiness is present, it can recede, becoming anxious, becoming the thing that we could lose in the unfolding of time. When happiness is present, we can become defensive, such that we retreat with fear from anything or anyone that threatens to take our happiness away.

But can we simply give up our attachment to thinking about happier futures or the future of happiness? Queer theorists have been the most vocal in refusing to affirm the future, refusing to embrace the future in a politics of affirmation. Lee Edelman, in his provocatively titled *No Future: Queer Theory and the Death Drive*, writes: "Rather than rejecting, with liberal discourse, this ascription of negativity to queer, we might, as I argue, do better to consider accepting and even embracing it. Not in the hope of forging thereby some more perfect social order—such a hope, after all, would only reproduce the constraining mandate of futurism, just as any order would equally occasion the negativity of the queer—but rather to refuse the insistence of hope itself as affirmation, which is always an affirmation of an order whose refusal will register as unthinkable, irresponsible, inhumane" (2004: 4). For Edelman, queer theory must be hopeless, must have "no future," which means saying no to the future.[1] To affirm an order might be to define and regulate what is thinkable in advance of thought.

In response to Edelman's polemic, I want to take seriously the question of whether all forms of political hope, all forms of optimism as well as utopianism, all dreams of "some more perfect order," can be described as performing the logic of futurism, which in turn would require negativity to be located in those who cannot inherit this future. And yet Edelman is still affirming something in the act of refusing affirmation. I find something rather optimistic and hopeful about Edelman's polemic, where hope rests on the possibility opened up by inhabiting the negative. Michael D. Snediker has suggested that the queer embrace of negativity might be "optimistically motivated" (2009: 15). Snediker argues for a "queer optimism," which would not be an optimism of an ordinary sort. For Snediker, "Queer optimism cannot guarantee what such a happiness would look like, how such happiness would feel. And while it does not promise a road to an Emerald City, *Queer Optimism* avails a new terrain of critical enquiry, which seems a felicity in its own right" (30). Happiness becomes interesting for queer optimists. Snediker argues that rather than presuming the normativity of happiness, we could imagine happiness as "theoretically mobilizable, as conceptually difficult." He asks, "What if happiness weren't merely, self-reflexively happy, but interesting?" (30).

I agree: happiness is interesting. The more I follow the word *happiness* around, the more it captures my interest. We can still recognize the significance of queer pessimism as an alien affect: a queer politics which refuses to organize its hope for happiness around the figure of the child or other tropes for reproductivity and survival is already alienated from the present. Queer pessimism matters as a pessimism *about* a certain kind of optimism, as a refusal to be optimistic about "the right things" in the right kind of way.[2] Certain forms of political negativity are read as stubbornness or as a way of being stuck. We learned about this dynamic from the figure of the melancholic migrant who is read as holding on to something that has already gone in the very act of noticing racism as going on and ongoing. Indeed the very act of recognizing injustice in the present is read as a theft of optimism, a killing of joy, a failure to move on or to put certain histories behind us. Queer pessimism becomes interesting as an alien affect, although to become pessimistic as a matter of principle is to risk being optimistic about pessimism itself.

Snediker is right to point out that queer affirmations of negativity are not simply negative. To embrace the negative or to say yes to a no cannot be described as a purely negative gesture. To affirm negation is still an affirmation, which could reinstitute a certain yes as the proper signifier of queer politics, even as a yes to what's not (see Ahmed 2006: 175). I am tempted to call this move "being for being against." My response to the affirmation of negation would not be to affirm or negate affirmation in return but to ask for a different orientation to what is being or not being affirmed. Rather than affirming positive or negative affects, my task throughout this book has been to read how positive and negative affects are distributed and how this distribution is pedagogic—we learn about affect by reading about the how of its distribution. In this chapter, I want to think about the redistribution of affect that is possible in the achievement of what we can call "revolutionary consciousnesses" and how this redistribution takes time and animates our relationship to time. Forms of political consciousness must be achieved, as György Lukács taught us in *History and Class Consciousness* (1971). It is important not to individuate such an achievement but to recognize the role of collective labor in the process of becoming conscious of class, race, and gendered forms of oppression, which involves a necessary estrangement from the present.

We can explore the strange and perverse mixtures of hope and despair, opti-mism and pessimism within forms of politics that take as a starting point a critique of the world as it is, and a belief that the world can be different. I will do so by offering a consideration of dystopian forms, including what I call happiness dystopias. Why dystopia? Why not utopia, which seems to rest as a form more explicitly on visions of happy futures? Of course, utopias cannot be reduced to happy futures. As Jean Baudrillard argues, "Utopia does not write itself into the future. It is always, from right now, what the order of the day is missing" ([2001] 2006: 62). Fredric Jameson agrees, suggesting that utopias do not present us with happy images of an after-this-life: "This is why it is a mistake to approach Utopias with positive expectations, as though they offered visions of happy worlds" (2005: 12). The utopian form is a testimony to the possibility of an alternative and involves hope in the very mode of its negative critique. Indeed, Jameson argues that "the Utopian form itself is the answer to the universal ideological conviction that no alternative is possible" (232). The utopian form might not make the alternative possible, but it aims to make impossible the belief that there is no alternative.

Jameson's most powerful argument is about the need to reorientate our af-fective relation to the future. He argues that "we need to develop an anxiety about losing the future" (233). In this chapter, I offer readings of dystopian forms insofar as they take as a starting point the possibility that the future might be something we have already lost—this is not a vision only of an un-happy future but the possibility of no future at all, where no future is not con-ceived as unhappiness (which would be predicated on the survival of a subject) but no hap, no chance, no possibility. I want to think about what it means for happiness to depend on there being a future, as a dependence that enables a certain anxiety about the possibility of its loss. I offer a rereading of some classic expressions of pessimism and optimism in philosophy (Schopenhauer and Leibniz), alongside an analysis of affective orientations toward the future in the film *Children of Men* (2006, dir. Alfonso Cuarón), based on the novel by P. D. James (1993). The film is premised on the belief that we are not anxious enough about losing the future, showing us not only that a future can be lost but also that we will lose the future if we don't think of the future as something that can be lost. I want to think with this film, in order to think more about how political struggle might struggle with the future, as a struggle over happi-ness, in the recognition that the future might be a time of loss.

The film's dystopic vision is of global infertility: no future means no children. It seems to rest, as does James's novel, which Lee Edelman rightly critiques, on reproductive futurism, by placing its hope for redemption in the remarkability of the birth of a child.[3] I want to suggest that if we read the film purely in these terms we will be missing something about its rather awkward temporalities. This film is certainly an event in which the future unfolds as a question in the present. When released on DVD, it included a number of interviews with prominent academics, including Slavoj Žižek and Saskia Sassen, who focus in their commentaries on the contemporary politics of despair, hope, utopia, and fear, with specific reference to the politics of immigration, security, and environmental catastrophe. In the film, the hero, a habitual pessimist, is Theo (Clive Owen); his life is awful and he does not care about anything, embodying the very affective situation of a world without a future. But Theo gets drawn into caring for something; he is the subject of an appeal by his former wife Julian (Julianne Moore), a member of the revolutionary group the Fishes. They have discovered that a refugee girl named Kee (Clare-Hope Ashitey) is pregnant, and Theo has to get her to a boat called *Tomorrow*, so that she can join a utopian project, the Human Project. The story of the film is the story of their journey. The nightmare in the film is predicated on an explicitly political vision of an unjust present: a world where foreigners and refugees are considered and treated as aliens, and where the pollution of the environment involves the treatment of others as pollutants. I want to offer a reading of the film in order to explore the role of despair and hope in the struggle for a "tomorrow," and what it means to be fighting for the future when "today" seems so hopeless.

Alienation and Revolutionary Consciousness

I have written in this book about "affect aliens": affect aliens are those who are alienated by virtue of how they are affected by the world or how they affect others in the world. How does alienation relate to the possibility of revolutionary consciousness? Can we even speak of revolutionary consciousness today? Of course, it is a much-repeated assertion that history itself has made the very concept of a political revolution impossible: the failure of communism to deliver its promise of an alternative future has been read as evidence of the impossibility of any other future but global capitalism. But that's too easy: there is

too much evidence of the failure of global capitalism to deliver its own promise of the good life to the populations of the world for it to become evidence
of the impossibility of alternatives. We learn much from how the very idea
of alternatives to global capitalism comes across as silliness.[4] David Graeber
argues in his phenomenological anthropology of anarchism that "faced with
anything that remotely resembles creative, nonalienated experience, it tends
to look as ridiculous as a deodorant commercial during a time of national disaster" (2007: 410). The silly or ridiculous nature of alternatives teaches us not
about the nature of those alternatives but about just how threatening it can be
to imagine alternatives to a system that survives by grounding itself in inevi-
tability.

It is important to say here that consciousness does not simply turn people
into revolutionaries—such a statement would constitute a form of idealism,
refuting the urgency of a Marxist inheritance. What I want to describe is how a
failure of consciousness, a false consciousness about the world, is what blocks
other possible worlds, as a blockage that makes possibles impossible, such that
possibles are lost before they can be lived, experienced, or imagined. It is important to note here that false consciousness was not a term used by Marx. As
Joseph McCarney points out, the first written reference to "false consciousness" appears in a letter from Engels: "Ideology is a process accomplished by
the so-called thinker consciously, it is true, but with a false consciousness.
The real motive forces impelling him remain unknown to him; otherwise it
simply would not be an ideological process. Hence he imagines false or seem-
ing motive forces" (cited in McCarney 2005: n.p.). In this reference, false consciousness is used to describe the impossibility of the bourgeoisie knowing
their own motives, knowing the coincidence between their beliefs and their
interests. Conscious beliefs are ideology; they support interests through the
withdrawal of the interested nature of such beliefs from consciousness. We
might assume that the idea of "false consciousness" depends upon false/true
dichotomies that are no longer viable—such an assumption is so pervasive that
the very phrase "false consciousness" seems at best dated. But as I suggested
in chapter 2, there are grounds for revitalizing this concept given that we do
not have to assume that consciousness is what belongs to an individual subject.
Consciousness might be about how the social is arranged through the sharing
of deceptions that precede the arrival of subjects. As Lukács describes so well,
"The veil drawn over the nature of bourgeois society is indispensable to the

bourgeois itself" (1971: 66). The veil may participate in the reproduction of the social order by covering over the reproduction of the order.

The key might not be so much the distinction between truth and falsity but the role of falsity in the reproduction of the truth. In other words, consciousness is false because it fails to coincide with itself, which is what allows a certain order to be reproduced, defining the horizon of intelligibility or truth. Reproduction might depend then on the failure to recognize the failure of coincidence. To become conscious of the order is not to coincide with oneself in the sense of acquiring true consciousness or consciousness of the truth. The revolutionary might simply witness the failure of coincidence; the veil is not unveiled to reveal the truth; the veil is revealed, which is a revelation that must be partial and flawed.[5]

The recognition of the failure of coincidence is another way of talking about becoming conscious of the falsity of consciousness, and of the interested nature of social belief. How are such forms of recognition linked to alienation? Let's turn to Marx's early work on alienation. Marx following Hegel makes labor key to an understanding of human practice. Dirk J. Struik describes in his introduction to *The Economic and Philosophical Manuscripts of 1844* how the labor process is that "process of concrete, living man in creating his existence in daily practice, where he breathes and eats and loves and suffers" (1964: 41). The human being is sensuous and worldly; human needs require interaction with the environment, such that the environment provides more than a dwelling space (food to eat, air to breathe) as well as interaction with others, with whom we can create an existence. Man as an "objective, sensuous being is therefore a *suffering* being—and because he feels what he suffers, a *passionate* being. Passion is the essential force of man energetically bent on its object" (Marx [1844] 1964: 182).

Workers are estranged from what they make, giving their energy to the object of labor, which is then taken away, becoming commodity: "the worker puts his life into the object; but now his life no longer belongs to him, but to the object" (106). For Marx, this process of alienation, where workers become alienated from themselves, is described as simultaneously "the loss of an object" and a "bondage to it" (106). In other words, the worker is bound to a lost object: capitalism as such might rest on melancholia. The worker "does not feel content but unhappy" (110). Marx describes the worker as a form of "*living* capital" and therefore "a capital *with needs*" (120). To be living capital is described as a form of "misfortune" (120). The appropriation of labor makes the worker suffer; the more the worker works, the more the worker produces, the more the worker suffers. Alienation is both an alienation from the products of one's labor—a kind of self-estrangement—and a feeling-structure, a form of suffering that shapes how the worker inhabits the world. Workers suffer from the loss of connection to themselves given that the world they have created is an extension of themselves, an extension that is appropriated.

Consciousness of alienation involves both recognition of suffering and recognition of what produces that suffering. To become conscious of alienation is to become conscious of how one's being has been stolen. It is not simply to become alienated from the world but to become conscious of how alienation is already, as it were, in the world. One becomes alienated from one's alienation. We can describe this "double alienation" by considering anticolonial forms of revolutionary consciousness. Let's turn to Frantz Fanon's classic *The Wretched of the Earth* ([1961] 2001). Fanon describes how it is that natives take up their arms and revolt against the colonizer, which means revolting against the colonizer's world. How is such action possible? For Fanon, natives can only revolt through consciousness: natives must first become conscious of the colonizer's world as an alien world before they can take arms. But this does not mean becoming conscious of the colonizers as alien beings, or as foreigners or impostors. Rather it means "seeing through" the native's own alienation, which has been managed as a perception into an unrecognizable truth: "Thus the native discovers that his life, his breath, his beating heart and the same as those of the settler. He finds out that the settler's skin is not of any more value than a native's skin; and it must be said this discovery *shakes the world in a very necessary manner*" (35; emphasis added). The native's alienation is an alienation from the alienation that guaranteed acceptance of a subordinate place. The world "shakes." The native recognizes in this second alienation that he is not the alien he thought he was, and this consciousness returns him to the very recognition of his living body as no more or no less alive than the body of the colonizer. He recognizes that his life has been stolen, and he recognizes the theft of life by turning to life. The body that breathes refuses to be made alien; this, as a result, demands and requires action against those who stole his life.

If, as I discussed in the last chapter, colonial occupation is justified through a utilitarian discourse of happiness, then the native is alienated not only from life but from the good life. The violence of the native *responds to this very appeal to the good*: "But it so happens that when the native hears a speech about Western culture he pulls out his knife — or at least he makes sure it is within reach" (33). The native hears the violence of the words "Western culture" as a form of violence that is softened under the veil of kindness and responds to this violence *in kind*. The violence of revolution requires violence against not only those who occupy but also the very values and manners that domesticated otherness as relative proximity. To undo the violence of such a history the native must expose the violence and channel himself against it: "But let us return to that atmosphere of violence, that violence which is just under the skin. We have seen that in its process towards maturity many leads are attached to it, to control it and show it the way out. Yet in spite of the metamorphoses which the colonial regime imposes upon it in the way or tribal of regional quarrels, that violence makes its way forward, and the native identifies his enemy and *recognizes all his misfortunes*, throwing all the exacerbated might of his hate and anger into this new channel" (55–56; emphasis added). The wretched of the earth expose the wretchedness of the earth. The wretches direct their anger and hatred toward the world that deems them wretched. The recognition of the wretched is revolutionary. It involves recognition that wretchedness is not an inevitable consequence of being in a certain way but is an effect of the occupation and violence of the colonizer. Misfortune and unhappiness are caused. To recognize suffering — to recognize that one has been *made an alien*, which also means recognizing that one is not that which one has been made — is here to recognize its cause. To recognize suffering by recognizing the cause of suffering is thus part of the revolutionary cause. False consciousness is that which sustains an affective situation (the workers and the natives suffer) but misrecognizes the cause, such that the misrecognition allows the cause to "cause" suffering.

It is no accident that revolutionary consciousness means feeling at odds with the world, or feeling that the world is odd. You become estranged from the world as it has been given: the world of good habits and manners, which promises your comfort in return for obedience and good will. As a structure of feeling, alienation is an intense burning presence; it is a feeling that takes place before others, from whom one is alienated, and can feel like a weight that both holds you down and keeps you apart. You shift, drop your head, sweat, feel edgy and uncertain. Everything presses against you; you feel against the world and the world feels against you. You are no longer well adjusted: you cannot adjust to the world. The revolutionary is an affect alien in this specific sense. You do not flow; you are stressed; you experience the world as a form of resistance in coming to resist a world.

As I discussed in the introduction to this book, in positive psychology, the flow experience is the optimum positive psychic reality. For the stressed subject, your being is "out" as you are out of time. As Charlotte Bloch describes, "Common features of the descriptions of stress experiences were the contesting of our being in time, an expression of reality as resistance, an experience of other people as barriers, contesting of the taken-for-granted experience of the embodied self" (2002: 107). So while "flow connotes qualities of effortlessness and fluidity," Bloch suggests that "stress connotes qualities as strain and resistance" (101). If we think of revolution and affect, we might notice that flow and stress are distributed and redistributable: you can be stressed by a world in which you flowed, which you experienced as compliant and easy, by the very act of noticing that world as a world. Indeed, revolutionary consciousness might be possible only as a willingness to be stressed, to let the present get under your skin. To revolt is an "out-of-skin" experience.

If revolutionary action requires a will to be stressed, then it also entails a refusal of what Herbert Marcuse calls "a *happy consciousness* which facilitates acceptance of the misdeeds of this society" ([1964] 2002: 79). Of course, it is important that we do not produce a heroic model of the unhappy revolutionary whose suffering is a gift to the world. You can be unhappy as a way of doing nothing; unhappiness as a belief can be a way of holding on to the present by roaming across objects with a certain indifference (you are unhappy with everything, which anticipates any one thing, so that are unhappy with something before anything happens).[6] I want to turn here to the film *Children of Men*, which does offer us an image of revolutionaries, the Fishes, who are presented as irrational subjects "fixated" on a certain truth. In the film, the revolutionaries whose motto is "The Fishes are at war with the government until they recognize equal rights for every immigrant in Britain" are shown as committing acts of "senseless violence," even though their cause seems just. It is as if what they are fighting for has become the fight itself, which means the fight makes them against what they are for.

There is a lot to say about this. On the one hand, we might question the stereotype of the activist as a terrorist: as the one who has fixed on violence, where violence has become its own cause. And yet, on the other hand, we can recognize in the depiction of the violence of revolution a certain truth: the violence of revolting "repeats" the violence which is its cause. The conservatism of this film might be the extent to which this repetition is assumed necessarily to be the loss of a cause.

The figure of the raging revolutionary or angry activist teaches us something: those who fight for alternative futures are seen as committing acts of senseless violence, *which stops any hearing of the ways in which revolution makes sense*. Indeed, we might consider the very politics of who or what gets seen as the origin of violence: the revolutionaries expose violence, but the violence they expose is not recognized as violence: structural violence is violence that is veiled. As Raymond Williams argues in *Modern Tragedy*, "The essential point is that violence and disorder are institutions as well as acts. When a revolutionary change has been lived through we can usually see this quite clearly. The old institutions, now dead, take on their real quality as systematic violence and disorder; in that quality, the source of the revolutionary action is seen" (2006: 91; see also Arendt [1961] 1973: 35).[7] If the exposure of violence is read as the origin of violence, then the violence that is exposed is not revealed.

The film does offer us an alternative model of a revolutionary, who is described as having a "lost cause" or as having lost his cause. The revolutionary who has lost his cause is not really a revolutionary.[8] This is our hero, Theo, who is presented as a "has-been activist" and who is disaffected, cynical, sad, depressed, and numb. That bad feeling becomes a kind of non- or no-feeling or even not-feeling tells us something: bad feeling hovers, holds, weighs, until what is felt is a kind of nothing at all.

We could describe Theo as the affect alien in the film. The first sound we hear in the opening sequence is the generic voice of the BBC presenter, giving us the news of the day. The stories could almost be today's stories: "The Muslim community demands an end to the army's occupation of mosques." "The Homeland Treaty is ratified. After eight years, British borders will remain closed. The deportation of illegal immigrants will continue." And then, the lead story: "Good morning, our lead story. The world was stunned today by the death of baby Diago, the youngest person on the planet." The death of an individual person is the lead story, individual grief taking precedence over collective grievance. In the opening sequence, we are in a cafe. A group of people are all staring mournfully upward toward a video screen, and we hear the crying and gasping sounds of grief. The group coheres through sharing a direction: their grief at a lost object, the loss of the world's youngest person, symbolizing the loss of the future as a shared loss. Theo comes through the crowd and does not look up to watch the screen. He orders a coffee and walks out.

Theo is alienated from the group, refusing to share in the grief toward the lost object, as an object that also functions as a symptom and reminder of lost fertility, the real cause of human grief. Later he goes to work. We see an open-plan office: each worker sits in front of a screen. We recall Marx at this point: the alienation of the worker is so well expressed in the antisociality of the open-plan office, where each worker is a cut off from other workers, a violence that is sustained by the illusion of sharing space. They are watching the story of Diago's death unfold on their individual screens, as if what is being shared is the same thing. The news report intones how "throughout his life, Diago was a tragic reminder of the infertility that humanity has endured and its effects upon the world we now live in." Theo gets up at this point and goes to his boss, saying, "I seem to be more affected by baby Diago's death than I realize," as a way of getting out, using affection as a form of self-narration. He leaves and goes to visit his friend Jasper. Theo is alienated from the shared expression of grief. As he says to Jasper, "That was even worse. Everyone crying. Baby Diago — come on, the guy was a wanker."

To be an affect alien does not mean you necessarily respond to the same events with a different affect (to be made unhappy by other people's happiness). Rather an affect alien might experience the same affect but in relation to different objects, which are judged by others as "the wrong objects." Theo shares the bad feeling that hovers around the film in the harsh edges of its dystopic vision. But Theo's unhappiness is not directed in the right way, toward Diago and the failure of the human race to reproduce. He just feels like shit. As he says to Jasper (Michael Caine): "Same as every other day. Woke up. Felt like shit. Went to work. Felt like shit." Theo has an unattributed grief, a grief about anything and everything, a general sense of despair about the possibility of living a life other than the life that just goes on. The film looks for the cause of his despair, which in turn is what causes the action to unfold.

In this conversation, Theo and Jasper are speaking of the "Human Project." The Human Project begins as a rumor of some alternative future, a community that will sustain the human race. Theo is a disbeliever. Jasper is making a joke. Theo responds: "The Human Project. Why do people believe this crap . . . even if they discovered the cure for infertility. Doesn't matter. Too late. The world went to shit. You know what. It was too late before the infertility thing happened, for fuck's sake." Not only is it "too late," but it "was too late" before it even happened. For Theo, this means there was nothing that could have been done, as well as there being nothing to do. There *was* nothing to do when it *is* too late. The "too late" provides both a critique of hopefulness and a retrospective disbelief that anything could have been done, a suggestion that there was never any hope to hope.

Theo is an affect alien, even at this point. For Jasper is making a joke: "I was just trying to tell a joke, mate." Theo responds: "All right, sorry, go on." The scene shows the affective knot of the outburst: that moment when negative affect spills out, directed toward who or what is proximate. You direct that which has hovered around; you snap. Just the words "Human Project" incite this reaction, this anger and outrage disturb the flow of a conversation. For the unhappy subject, the very promise of something other than the cause of unhappiness is outrageous. For those in despair, the possibility of an alternative is not only outrageous but hurtful: it hurts by threatening to take away the hurt, or it trivializes hurt as a feeling that could simply "go away."

The energy of the film is about redirecting Theo's misery into a purpose, which does not necessarily make Theo suffer less but turns him toward other possible worlds. In the following sections, I want to explore how optimism and hope participate in this turning. I do not want to argue that optimism and hope are always good things or necessary tools for revolutionaries. To be turned is not always about being turned *into* action but can be about how one is turned *by* the actions of others.

Optimism and Pessimism

To become revolutionary would seem to require a belief in the possibility of revolution. To become revolutionary would also seem to require a belief that a revolution is necessary. In other words, you would agree that what exists is something against which we should revolt. The revolutionary might have pessimism about the present but optimism about the future. This does not mean that revolutionary action depends upon subjects acquiring the right kind of orientations toward the present or the future.

It is commonplace to think of optimism and pessimism as forms of psychological disposition, as involving different outlooks or perspectives on the same thing. You can have optimistic or pessimistic tendencies. You can tend or not tend to look at things from "the bright side." The classic expression of optimism/pessimism as a question of sides is posited in the question "Is the glass half full or half empty?" This is a question of perception, of how we perceive the glass in terms of its emptiness and fullness. We could say of course that *a priori* the glass is both half full and half empty (being half full makes it half empty and being half empty makes it half full—this statement would be true by virtue of the meaning of the word *half*). Optimists and pessimists see the glass as being one way or the other: the optimist sees the glass as half full ("Look, I have more to drink!") and the pessimist as half empty ("Look, I have already drunk that much!"). Optimism and pessimism are not so much relationships to truth (the glass is half empty if it is half full, and half full if it is half empty) but ways of perceiving things, in terms of how they may affect us, as well as an orientation toward things, in terms of what they can provide.

But of course the story is not so simple. Say you really didn't like what was in the glass but were being told you must drink it. You look at the glass differently. You might say the glass is half empty as an optimistic orientation toward the object ("Look, I have already drunk that much!" or "Look, I have less to drink!"). In the case of an unwanted drink, the pessimist would be the one who would see the glass as half full ("Look, I haven't drunk that much!" or "Look, I have more to drink!").

Pessimism and optimism are not, then, simply two ways of looking at the same thing: our orientation to the thing itself, whether we take the thing as the cause of happiness or unhappiness, shapes how we apprehend the thing in terms of what it might or might not give us at some future point. Optimism and pessimism are thus evaluations of what we encounter in the present (whether something is good or bad, or causes happiness or unhappiness) and future oriented. On the one hand, optimism and pessimism are ways of apprehending the object's fullness or emptiness, as signs of an occupation (one must have already been occupied with the object for its halfness to be measured as value). On the other hand, they apprehend the object as pointed, where the point of the object is toward a future potential or possibility (how much or how little I have left to drink). Such orientations are both evaluative and anticipatory; they are orientations toward the future as being empty or full, where emptiness and fullness have already been given affective value (it is always emptiness or fullness of something). Given this, both optimism and pessimism involve the temporality of the promise: they see the future in terms of what it promises to deliver or not to deliver, in terms of what there is or is not left to drink from the glass of the present.

Let's turn to a classic philosopher of pessimism from the twentieth century: Alfred Schopenhauer. One of the most interesting aspects of his work is his tendency to read human desire as lack, as a kind of emptiness that cannot be filled (we can see how much psychoanalysis inherits its model of desire from Schopenhauer). For Schopenhauer it is the human being who is empty, which means the promise of happiness is empty. As he argues: "No possible satisfaction in the world can suffice to still its longings, set a goal to its infinite cravings, and fill the bottomless abyss of its heart" ([1818] 1883: 382). The promise of happiness is what does *not keep its word*: "If it has promised [happiness], it does not keep its word, unless to show how little worth desiring were the things desired" (382–83). As soon as one has the object that one anticipates will cause happiness, one is dissatisfied. Happiness for Schopenhauer necessarily does not exist in the present: "The enchantment of distance shows us paradises which vanish like optical illusions when we have allowed ourselves to be mocked by them. Happiness accordingly always lies in the future, or else in the past, and the present may be compared to a small dark cloud which the wind drives over the sunny plain; before and behind it all is bright, only it itself always casts a shadow" (383).

We can certainly see here that Schopenhauer's pessimism anticipates happiness as an unhappiness-cause. The emptiness of happiness is linked explicitly to the negativity of pleasure. As he argues: "We feel pain, but not painlessness, we feel care but not the absence of care, fear, but not security" (384), such that "only pain and want can be felt positively" (384).[9] We might question whether pleasure is simply the absence of feeling. In my previous work, I considered comfort as a nonfeeling: you don't tend to notice comfort until you lose it, until you become uncomfortable (Ahmed 2004: 147–48; Ahmed 2006: 134–35). To become comfortable, which means becoming not uncomfortable, you might notice the feeling of comfort, though such comfort might over time become less noticeable. But perhaps what is in view or not in view is not simply a matter of good or bad feeling. You can have background discomfort too, which comes to your attention only after you get to a certain point (you are concentrating really hard on something, and you realize that you have a pain in your foot, where the feeling of suddenness suspends the very signs of its arrival). In other words, the intensification of affect is what is noticeable: certain affects can hover in the background, as your affective situation, your "around" or surround, which comes to your attention through the accumulation of intensity. A good example is irritation: you might be walking around, and for sure everything irritates you, and then something happens, and you are aware of being irritable and attribute it to something (you search for the cause of the feeling as an effect of being aware of feeling *that way*). Attributing the feeling can direct or "point" the feeling. You might become irritated with x as if x is the cause of the irritation even though x has nothing to do with it but is just who or what you come into contact with at the moment of recognizing your irritation. This background irritation that becomes attributed and directed is close to the affective landscape provided by *Children of Men*.

Another example would be cheerfulness: you could be brimming with it, humming to yourself, and something happens, and you realize your cheerfulness and attribute it to something (this can often involve memory, *oh yes that happened*). In recognizing your cheerfulness you might direct the feeling in the present; you might smile at people who pass by, as if they were the cause of the pleasure, and they might look at you blankly in return. I would not argue that bad feeling is feeling and the good feeling is nonfeeling but rather that good and bad feelings only come into consciousness through processes of intensification, where intensity itself is an object of feeling that is attributed and directed. The very recognition of feeling can generate feeling, which means that once you recognize a feeling, you give that feeling an object, which changes its form.

Happiness gives form to the feeling it recognizes. Schopenhauer's work offers a critique of this form, as a critique of optimism *in its form*. As he suggests rather dryly: "Imagine this race transported to a Utopia where everything grows of its own accord and turkeys fly around ready-roasted, where lovers find one another without any delay, and keep one another without any difficulty: in such a place some men would die of boredom or hang themselves, some would fight and kill one another and thus they would create for themselves more suffering than nature inflicts on them" ([1850] 2004: 5–6). The very expectation of happiness as an overcoming of bad feeling is how happiness can cause unhappiness. Christopher Janaway writes, in his account of Schopenhauer's pessimism, "Part of the wickedness of optimism is that it causes unhappiness by inculcating these false beliefs about happiness, beliefs whose consequences are pain and disillusionment" (1999: 324).

Pessimism might then offer a critique of the optimism we have inherited in the modern world, of how optimism has been confused with neutrality. As Joshua Foa Dienstag argues: "In a relentlessly optimistic world, it is enough to give up on the *promise* of happiness to be considered a pessimist" (2006: xi). The tendency to see the glass as being half full of what has caused pleasure is how we are encouraged to see the glass. It is assumed that a better way of seeing is to see what is better.

Let us suppose the world is our glass. The optimist might constitute the field of political neutrality insofar as politics has a tendency to see the world's resources in terms of fullness rather than emptiness, delighting in what we have left to consume rather than in recognizing what has been depleted. To point to the emptying of the world by overdevelopment is to be a killjoy, getting in the way of a future enjoyment. The pessimist refuses to believe in the promise of the half full. However, this does not mean that we always must see the glass as being half empty. As I will argue later, the point might be that emptiness and fullness are not the point. Or we could see that both optimism and pessimism are directed; there are right and wrong ways of being optimistic as well as pessimistic, where rightness and wrongness are determined as evaluations of objects in terms of their readiness or potential.

We do not have to choose between optimism and pessimism as forms of orientation to the causes of happiness and unhappiness. Indeed, if we turn to the classic optimist, Gottfried Wilhelm Leibniz, we can see that optimism does not necessarily mean focusing only on what's better. Leibniz's optimism involves his belief in the perfection of God, who makes what is possible "possible." There is freedom because many worlds are possible. But only some things come to exist. What comes to exist must be the best, because God is perfect: "divine perfection can never fail to select the most perfect" ([1714] 1965: 128).

But as he shows us, such an argument runs counter to experience: "For the best people often have the worst lives" (91). What exists would appear not as the best but as a "confused chaos." For Leibniz, this chaos is only a false impression, an effect of getting too close to particular goods and bads. By stepping back we can see the order in the chaos: "But on closer inspection, the contrary must be stated. It is certain a priori, by the very reasons we have adduced, that all things, and especially minds, obtain the greatest possible perfection" (91). Leibniz argues that bad feelings—pain, anxiety, and so on—work to increase or even enable the intensity of pleasure: "The auditor, who becomes anxious about what is going to happen; when after a short time all returns to order again, his pleasure will be so more intense" (92). Bad feeling for Leibniz *causes the intensification of pleasure*, such that pleasure without pain is not pleasing: "Who has not tasted bitter food does not deserve sweets and will not even appreciate them. This is the very law of pleasure, that uniformity does not allow it to continue with the same intensity, but produces satiety and dullness instead of enjoyment" (92). Extending from the laws of pleasure, he argues that good people will turn bad things to their "greater advantage," just as "in general, it may be affirmed that afflictions are temporary evils leading to good effects, since they are shortcuts to greater perfection" (93). The point of bad things for Leibniz is certainly to makes things better. Optimism involves a way of reading bad feeling, which takes its point as progress. The cause of pain, or the pain that is caused, becomes the cause of a higher pleasure.

Reading between Schopenhauer and Leibniz is possible and necessary: both speak about the conversion of feeling but read the conversion as going in opposite directions: for the former, the promise of good feeling converts to bad feeling (disappointment, emptiness); for the latter, the existence of bad feeling (pain, misfortune) converts to good feeling (progress, a higher pleasure). Both read the conversion between positive and negative affect as pointed, or oriented toward fullness or emptiness. To be pessimistic would involve a commitment to unhappiness as the endpoint of human action, as being what all promises of happiness lead us toward. To be optimistic would involve commitment to happiness as the endpoint of human action, as what all experiences of bad feeling enable us to reach. Optimism and pessimism are ways of attending to things, which take good or bad feelings as the point, as being the point of human action or what human action points toward, even when they recognize ambivalence and contradiction.[10] Perhaps a more perverse reading would be to refuse to see the ambivalence of affect as pointed: maybe the point is that there is no point that points to some future horizon. Feelings may be perverse because they don't always have a point.

How then can we read the switch between pessimism and optimism in *Children of Men*? Are these conversion points also points of perversion? As I have suggested, we begin with Theo, who expresses bad feeling: his pessimism is about the possibility that a future exists, about the possibility of possibility. We can interrogate the belief in alternatives as a fantasy that defends against the horrors of the present. In other words, the belief that things "will only get better" at some point that is always just "over the horizon" can be a way of avoiding the impact of suffering in the world that exists before us. But we can also interrogate disbelief in the possibility of a different world as a psychic defense against suffering. Perhaps we know this too well: to believe something is possible is to risk being wrong and being disappointed. How better to avoid disappointment than to refuse to believe in the possibility of anything happening at all? Most of us have probably experienced pessimism as a survival tactic: those moments when you prepare for disappointment by avoiding being hopeful, by deciding in advance that there is no hope in achieving the thing one wants even as one "goes for it."[11]

Pessimism becomes here a way of preparing for disappointment, as a kind of habit that accrues its force through repetition. Pessimism can offer a way of inhabiting the world through shielding oneself from possibility. In other words, acts of preparation for disappointment can function as modes of subject formation. The perpetual cynic may be the one who defends hardest against the very possibility of disappointment, enjoying the experience of disappointment before anything bad happens, or enjoying other people's disappointment as a sign of their failure to be prepared. We can examine the cynicism of disbelief as both a defense against contingency, the possibilities kept open by the "hap" of what happens, and as a reasonable response to situations that seem hopeless.

And yet, although Theo's world is shit, there are forms of suffering that exceed the signifiers "too late" uttered in the spirit of pessimism. There is only one point where he is undone by grief: when Julian is killed. His body shows it; he sinks to the ground. He is undone by grief. Throughout the rest of the film his bad feeling is a doing, a way of being in the world in a certain way, rather than an undoing. In fact, we hear about the cause of his grief through the testimony of others: the loss of his child Dylan. This lost cause is telling. Pessimism can be a defense against suffering as well as an expression of suffering: as if to say, "that hurts" or "it hurts" as a way of making the hurt beside oneself, the world is shit, even my life is shit, can be a way of covering over the cause of suffering: in this case, the loss of a child. I will return to the significance of the child as the object of an unspoken grief in due course. What interests me is how pessimism as a mode of subject formation can use suffering to avoid suffering. Oliver Bennett in his reflection on "cultural pessimism" makes this point. He reads pessimism as "a defence against depression and anxiety itself, a projection onto the external world of a negativity which would otherwise be directed towards the self" (2001: 183). Pessimism, by anticipating that what follows is nothing, conceals the something that is at stake in this desire for there to be nothing. While cheerful optimists can overlook suffering by looking on the bright side, seeing fullness instead of emptiness wherever they look, so too pessimists can empty this emptiness of harmful content by seeing emptiness as already there, before anything can happen, before shit happens.

Of course, the film does not allow Theo to remain attached to his own despair, his own "too lateness" that enables his inaction to be self-narrated as wisdom. Theo acts. Well, sort of. In the film, Theo is not the agent with a sense of moral purpose and vision; the film does not show him taking charge. Instead, things happen to him. It is Julian who interpellates Theo as a fellow activist, asking if he can get the papers to help them help a fugi girl to escape the country. He goes along with it, even though he refuses the subject of the address. Julian says, "You should have seen him in the old days where he was a real activist," to which he replies, "You were the activist. I just wanted to get laid." He refuses the identity of activism. And yet he does go along with things. He gets caught up. And things happen. Julian gets killed, and Theo finds out that the fugi girl is pregnant: as his friend Jasper later says, it is "the miracle the whole world has been waiting for."

The pregnancy too just happens; there is no explanation. It is a miracle, and the religiosity of this language has its own affective reality. Pessimism is not an adequate defense against things happening. Or we could say pessimism can defend against the possibility of miracles until they happen. Given this, we cannot defend properly against possibility; we cannot even prepare for it, even if we wait for things to happen. Yes, something happens. The hap that happens involves a certain yes in the becoming actual of what was not possible. It is not that Theo converts from pessimism to optimism in embracing this yes at the level of belief or attitude. Instead he has a very practical task, something he must do: he has to get the pregnant girl to the boat, the *Tomorrow*, so she can join the Human Project. We already know that he does not believe in the Human Project as a symbol of the possibility of a future (before, as it were, the utopianism of an alternative future) and in fact that the possibility of such a project causes for him an intensification of his anger and despair (it's too late, the world was already shit before this happened). And yet he must get her there, *whether or not* he believes in its existence.

The film is not about the availability of belief as a form of optimism ("They do exist!"); nor does it idealize pessimism as a form of wisdom ("They only exist to make you feel better about suffering!"). Something beyond the technology of belief is expressed here. Theo finds out that the Fishes have never spoken to the Human Project; they know where to find the boat on the whim of a whisper: Miriam (Pam Ferris), one of the Fishes, says, "Luke has no way of contacting the Human Project. Nor does anyone else. . . . Contact with the human project is done by mirrors. Julian was our mirror." Theo responds, "What do you mean, mirrors?" And Miriam explains: "Mirrors . . . they contact one of our people and that person contacts someone else, and so on till word gets to Julian." Theo expresses outrage that they can be willing to believe something that might not exist, on the whim of a rumor: "Don't fucking tell me you never actually talked to them." And yet he goes along with the whim. A whim is typically defined as a "capricious idea" or "odd fancy." It is not that you come to believe in something odd but you are willing to keep its oddness going. You act not because you come to believe something is possible that you once disbelieved. You move along as something is asked of you, because you are asked to do something, even if doing something does not correspond to your expectations or beliefs. You do not wait for correspondence.

The pregnancy does not, then, create the future; nor is pregnancy the cause of the future. Rather, the future is what happens through the work required to get close enough to hear the whisper, which is always a whisper that some-body else must have heard. You become the subject of an address that you do not hear. Their arrival at the boat, does not offer an image of a happy future; if anything the arrival is the conversion point or creates the possibility of a future conversion. The arrival is also what takes time. If time is what passes, then the time it takes for something to happen is the time of perversion. We might say that time is what makes the future perverse. In chapter 1, I referred to the game Chinese Whispers, which we can describe as being about the pleasurable per-versity of transmission. We laugh at how the whispering words deviate, so that the words we end up with are not recognizable as the words that were sent out. Deviation is the point and pleasure of the game.

Hope and Anxiety

Optimism and pessimism are not usually described as feelings, although we can certainly feel optimistic and pessimistic. I want to turn to the question of hope as a way of reconsidering the temporality of feeling, how feelings are directed toward objects in the present; how they keep the past alive; and how they involve forms of expectancy or anticipation of what follows (the future is always "the what" that follows, never arriving, always or only tomorrow, even when we have past futures behind us). I have suggested that the promise of happiness is what makes things promising; the promise is always "ahead" of itself. Anticipation is affective as an orientation toward the future, as that which is ahead of us, as that which is to come.

Classically, hope is described as a future-oriented emotion. John Locke, for example, describes hope as an emotion that perceives something that is not yet present as being good, imagining a future enjoyment: "*Hope* is that pleasure in the mind, which everyone finds in himself, upon the thought of a profitable future enjoyment of a thing, which is apt to delight him" ([1690] 1997: 218). Hope is a feeling that is present (a pleasure in the mind) but is directed toward an object that is not yet present. Although of course to place one's hope in something might depend on past experiences: you estimate that something would or will be delightful. I have suggested that happiness is future-oriented even if we experience happiness in the present; you are promised happiness through proximity to objects, which makes happiness "expectant." We could describe happiness as a "hope technology," to borrow Sarah Franklin's term (1997: 203): in hoping for this or that, we attribute this or that as the cause of happiness, which would be a happiness that you would reach at some future point.[12] Or as Zygmunt Bauman describes, we might have happiness as long as we have hope: "*We are happy as long as we haven't lost the hope of becoming happy*" (2008: 15). If we hope for happiness, then we might be happy as long as we can retain this hope (a happiness that paradoxically allows us to be happy with unhappiness).

Hope anticipates a happiness to come. Ernst Bloch described hope as an "anticipatory consciousness"; we are aware of the "not yet" in the unfolding of the present ([1938–47] 2000: 12–13). For Bloch, hope is a "*directing act of a cognitive kind*" (12). Hope, we might say, is a thoughtful way of being directed toward the future, or a way of creating the very thought of the future as going some way. If happiness is what we hope for, when we hope for this or that thing, it does not mean we think we *will be* happy but that we imagine we *could be* happy if things go the right way. We have a certain confidence in outcome premised on the possibility that what comes out might be *just that*. If the future is that which does not exist, what is always before us, in the whisper of the "just ahead," then hope also involves imagination, a wishfulness that teaches us about what we strive for in the present. Hope is a wish and expectation that a desired possibility is "becoming actual."

This is why, for Durkheim, hope's anticipatory logic means that it is a kind of orientation that is past or about the past. In my introduction to this book, I referred to Durkheim's critique of optimism in utilitarian discourse. Durkheim was also a critic of pessimism. As he explores in his classic text on the division of labor, pessimists explain hope as an illusion that sustains the will to "keep going." He argues, "According to them [the pessimists], if, in spite of the deceptions of experience, we hold on to life, it is because we are wrongly hoping that the future will make up for the past" ([1893] 1960: 245). Durkheim refuses to believe that optimism involves this deception of belief or by belief. He suggests that we have hope because of what is in the past, making a calculation about what he calls the average life: in such a life "happiness must prevail over unhappiness. If the relations were reversed, neither the attachment of men to life, nor its continuance jostled by the facts at each moment, could be understood" (245). In other words, he sees the existence of hope as evidence of what he describes as "relative bounty." But we all know that hopeful people can be more and less fortunate. Durkheim suggests that the idea that you can be more and less fortunate can only be meaningful if we have experienced "moments of fortune" as well as "the blow of misfortune."

We do not need to argue that the lessons of history are that of the relativity of good fortune to learn from Durkheim's work.[13] What he shows us is that our history, our arrival, involves moments of fortune and misfortune, and that hope is an orientation toward such past moments as the relativity of fortune. We are hopeful—we can feel fortunate—given that we have experienced moments of fortune, even if we are not fortunate in our life situation at present. Hopefulness in life's persistence might involve a tendency to give affective value to such moments of fortune *as* fortunate.

In the introduction to this chapter, I explained my interest in dystopian forms by reference to Jameson's argument that we need to become anxious about the future. We might assume you would be anxious *rather than* hopeful. To be hopeful as an orientation toward past moments could be a way of avoiding anxiety about the future as what could be lost. I want to suggest an intimacy between anxiety and hope. In having hope we *become* anxious, because hope involves wanting something that might or might not happen. Hope is about desiring the "might," which is only "might" if it keeps open the possibility of the "might not."

I want us to think about dystopian films such as *Children of Men* as object lessons in hopeful anxiety and its translation into a rather anxious hope. *Children of Men* is premised on the belief that we not anxious enough about losing the future, not only showing us that a future can be lost (the world has "gone to ruins") but also suggesting that we will lose the future if we don't think of the future as something that can be lost. The loss of capacity to reproduce becomes a symptom of the loss of the capacity for a future. There will be no humans to witness the past, which means that the past will have no future. Theo asks his cousin why he bothers to preserve the world's treasures: "One hundred years from now there won't be any sad fuck to look at any of this. What keeps you going?" His cousin answers: "You know what it is, Theo. I just don't think about it." The preservation of the past becomes unthinking without the thought of the future. It is what "keeps you going."

Given that all of us face no future as finite beings, the thought of the future might be the thought of the human, or the thought of what Marx calls "species being." Without there being a species, individual being, by implication, becomes pointless, so you "just don't think about it" in doing what you do. Of course, we can question this humanist logic of the next generation being the only point, which returns us to the "reproductive futurism" described by Lee Edelman. Or we can consider how it is the interruption of rather ordinary logics of deferral that are at stake here. As I explored in chapter 1, we have a tendency to endure our struggles in the present by deferring our hope for happiness to some future point. It is not that "no children" simply means "no future" but that "no children" signifies the loss of a fantasy of the future as that which can compensate me for my suffering; it is the very fantasy that there is something or somebody who I suffer for that is threatened. If what it is for is what comes after, in this survival logic of deferral, then the loss of "the after" is experienced as the loss of "the for."

The absence of children is one signifier of the absence of somebody to whom I can defer my hope, for whom I can justify my present suffering. Children, in other words, bear the weight of this fantasy. This is not to say that the idea that lives are pointless without children should not be challenged: many of us who live our lives without having "children of our own" are tired not only of being told we are pointless but also of making the point that lives do not have to involve having children to have a point. However we read this idea of a pointless existence without children, the anxiety expressed is that the future as an idea has been lost, and that we need to retrieve the idea to have a future by becoming anxious about that loss.

How does the conversion from despair to the anxiety of hope take place? What are the conversion points in the narrative? Perhaps the character Kee provides the key. Kee is pregnant, we know this. The project of the film—which becomes Theo's project—is to get her to the boat called *Tomorrow*. I will come back to the significance of the boat shortly. In the film, "getting to the boat" stands for "making the future possible," or "making it possible that there will be a future."

We could describe how Theo's project, his being "caught up" by events, involves a sense of hope. It is not that Theo himself becomes hopeful. If anything, he acts without hope. As Jean-Paul Sartre describes in his defense of existentialism against the charge of quietism, rehearsing what he calls "a time-honoured formula": "One need not hope in order to undertake one's work" ([1946] 1989: 40). In working without hope, you are worked upon. Recall that the Human Project communicates through mirrors: messages are passed between proximate bodies, whereby to keep passing something along requires that each proximity recedes. The recession of a given proximity is the condition of possibility for the creation of another. Perhaps there is hope in the recession of passing. The whispers that pass words create a line from one to another. A line of hope is the hope of a line. You extend the line that passes between bodies, even when you do not know what's what, even if you do not know what you are passing, or whether there is an end to the line. Indeed, the end of the line is not the point of the line: it is no accident that when we say we have reached the end of the line, it means we have lost hope.

There can be hope in passing something on, where the project or task is to keep passing. The film shows us that having a project—something to do for or with others that takes you from the ordinary routines of your life—can energize one and that energy can acquire its own force: if we lack a project, a sense of a purpose, our purpose can be to find one. But having a project can make some things come into view by making other things less visible. Žižek, in his interview, suggests that the film's power inheres in how much the suffering takes place in the background; it is too intense to look at it directly, so we can see it only obliquely, behind the action of the film. We could argue that this is the film's limitation. The very forward direction of the narrative, Theo's "becoming active," which is at once the becoming actual of the possible, is what keeps the suffering in the background. Theo does not see this suffering as he struggles to get Kee to the *Tomorrow*; indeed, if we adopt his gaze, then our "becoming active" also allows us not to see the suffering. In gaining focus, we can lose focus on suffering. At the same time, to lose focus on suffering does not mean that suffering is not there, or that it cannot be behind our action, in the sense of giving us an aim, direction, or purpose. A good question is whether focusing on suffering is always what allows us to do something about suffering—action might require the capacity to lose and gain focus.[14] If it is the case that losing focus makes gaining focus possible at the level of the task, then we can ask what doing something actually does.

Having a task or "something to do" in this film takes a rather conventional gendered and racial form. The white male citizen has to save the black refugee woman, who will bear the burden of giving birth not only to new life but also to humanity as species being. In one scene, Kee calls Theo to the barn (the biblical theme is explicit) and reveals her pregnant body to him. First he is speechless, and then he says, "She's pregnant." He repeats the utterance as if words are needed to confirm the truth. The black woman becomes a means in the film through which he is given words, as a sign of hope, as a kind of reason for doing something, where hope involves an embodied project. In other words, through her, he acquires a sense of purpose. Theo, even as an unwilling hero, helps her, saves her, guides her, and directs her toward the end of the line, which is happy insofar as she gets to the boat, which gives us the possibility of a tomorrow. She is the object of our hope: we hope that she will bear a child. Her hope is to bear a child. Our hope in her hope depends on the white man, who must get her to the boat *Tomorrow*.

I read the film as being about Theo's conversion. He is not so much the conversion point, as Joe was in *Bend It Like Beckham*, the one who promises to convert bad feelings into good feelings. Rather, Theo is the one who is converted, who is converted from despair to hope, and from nonfeeling (the numbness that we can experience as everyday irritability "it is too late, the world is shit") to an intensification of feeling. He converts from indifference—the apparent glibness of the "whatever"—to caring, which means caring for someone, having someone to care for, and thus caring for what happens, caring about whether there is a future or not. Such caring is not constrained as caring for happiness, which is what gives care certain forms, wanting the recipient of care to be a certain way, as I suggested in the previous chapter. It might be a hap care rather than a happiness care: to care for someone is to care about what happens to them. A hap care would not seek to eliminate anxiety from care; it could even be described as care for the hap. There is nothing more vulnerable than caring for someone; it means not only giving your energy to that which is not you but also caring for that which is beyond or outside your control. Caring is anxious—to be full of care, to be careful, is to take care of things by becoming anxious about their future, where the future is embodied in the fragility of an object whose persistence matters. Becoming caring is not about becoming good or nice: people who have "being caring" as their ego ideal often act in quite uncaring ways in order to protect their good image of themselves. To care is not about letting an object go but holding on to an object by letting oneself go, giving oneself over to something that is not one's own.

If the film is the story of Theo's conversion, it becomes more troubling. The film would then be read as being about paternity (unsurprisingly, given its title, but it is easy not to be surprised by the title). It is Theo's lost child that is evoked as the true cause of his pessimism. The first encounter we have with the lost child is through the photographs on the wall in Jasper's house, including a photograph of Theo with a woman and child, as well as happy images of past activisms. The woman and child are not named; but the sadness around this happy image, where happiness is reducible to an image of something that is no longer, that has been lost, lingers. Grief here is unnamed but involves a relation to the loss of the possibility of the happiness contained in the image. The loss of the family becomes the cause of unhappiness, which is then redirected into indifference or apathy: better not to be affected than to be unhappy.

We first hear about this loss through Julian, when she says, "It's hard for me to look at you. He had your eyes." His sees with his sadness. Paternity is here evoked as the sadness of an inheritance; the child inherits the father's eyes, such that to look at the father is to bear witness to the loss of the child. The film can be read as about Theo overcoming his sadness by becoming a father. So, at the very point where he gets Kee to the boat, she turns and says to him: "Dylan. I will call my baby Dylan. It's a girl's name too." The film rewards Theo with paternity. These are the last words he hears before he dies.

So the narrative converts Theo from indifference to caring and rewards him with the gift of paternity. Not much difference: except this time he has a girl, although she bears the same name. As a utopic moment, this is far from ambitious. Reading Theo's conversion shows us how much the conventions of hope are predicated on the becoming father of the white man, where he will "father" not only a new being but a new species being. It is Theo's conversion that gives us a new chance at becoming human. Although Theo dies, the child becomes his child, replacing the dead child through the gift of a name. If the film suggests that it is better to care than not to care, because it allows our anxiety for the future to keep alternatives possible, it leaves us with the question of how caring, even if we care *just or justly* about what happens, can turn us toward the social forms in which hopes for happiness have already been deposited. This failure to offer an alternative that would rescript our narrative of the good life might be telling, not because it suggests that we must disbelieve in alternatives but because it shows how alternatives cannot simply transcend what has already emerged or taken form. The failure of transcendence constitutes the necessity of a political struggle.[15]

I want to conclude this section by contrasting *Children of Men* with another dystopian film, *The Island* (2005, dir. Michael Bay). The nightmare of this film is again predicated on its lack of remoteness. The film is told from the point of view of clones, who do not know they are clones but have been "led to believe" that they are the only humans who have survived an environmental catastrophe. This is the truth they must believe in; their belief becomes the truth, allowing them to persist in the world in which they live. The clones have been created as spare parts, as organ donors for humans who want to buy longevity, and as wombs for women who want to secure their reproductive future.

The nightmare of the film is not so much about cloning or advancements in genetics as about the transformation of human beings into instruments, or even the instrumentalization of species being, as such. Cloning matters as a symptom rather than cause of the instrumentalization of life. The clones come to embody the alienated workers, as well as the slaves, as the others who must be liberated, who must become conscious of their alienation in order to revolt.

The living conditions of the clones are not far from the living conditions of many people under global capitalism: they work but do not know what they are creating or for whom they are creating. It turns out that their work is what sustains their alienation: the liquids they put into tubes is the liquid required to make new clones. The clones are called "products"; they are made to be bought and sold; they are, to use Marx's powerful term, "living capital." Their lives are technologized, scrutinized, monitored by the big Other, whom they encounter in the face of the physician as well as the multiples screens that shape what they can see and do.

The clones, perhaps, are us. Or, the clones are the other, the other who suffers and works in order that we can have "the good life." Their lack of hope is converted into our hope for the future: "The whole reason you exist is that everyone wants to live for ever. It's the new American dream." We have a political economy of hope, as Ghassan Hage (2003) might describe, where hope itself is unevenly distributed, where some not only have more hope than others but acquire their hope by taking hope away from others, which is, at the same time, about making others "be" in order that some can "have" what they hoped for.[16]

Importantly, the clones do not suffer: injustice works here *in the absence of suffering or even by making suffering absent*. The film shows us how optimism, hope, and happiness can be technologies of control. The clones are certainly kept in place through fear, which operates as false memory. As Dr. Merrick (Sean Bean), the psychologist in charge of making the clones, puts it, "We control them with the memory of a shared event, the global contamination that keeps them fearful about going outside." The other mechanism of control is hope: "The Island is the one thing that gives them hope, gives them purpose." The Island is what they hope for; the Island is anticipated as the cause of future happiness. Working as a daily lottery, the Island is presented as a utopic world on the outside, which "chosen ones" will populate. But those who are chosen are really being selected for death; rather than going to the Island, they will have their organs taken, being reduced to parts without a sum. The object of hope participates in suffering and death: not only are the clones hoping for what causes suffering and death (the ticket to the Island) but hope covers over that suffering and death *as* happiness (the bliss of the Island is the horror of the surgeon's table).

Indeed, the clones are made happy by hope; their environment creates happiness. "Our job is to make you happy," says Dr Merrick to the hero, Lincoln Six Echo (Ewan McGregor), so "that things are okay with you." The film provides us with an object lesson on how the promise of happiness keeps things in place; happy and hopeful subjects are well adjusted because they have adjusted to a demand they do not know has been made. Hope is usually considered a transformative emotion, as key to any project that aims to make the world a better place in which to live. In some psychoanalytic literature, hope has been described as a conservative emotion: Anna Potamianou, for example, considers hope "to be stubborn in the extreme" (1997: 4), as a defensive shield against life, with its changes, losses, uncertainties. Hope could be described as a stubborn attachment to a lost object, which stops the subject from "moving on." Hope can even function as a form of melancholia, as a way of holding on to something that has gone, even if hope feels quite different as a relationship to that something. How do we know whether we are holding on to something that has gone, or letting go of something that is present? In a way, all objects of emotion are fantasies of what objects can give us. Hope is a good fantasy of what an object will give us. The Island is just this kind of object; we wish for something that is not present, which is what makes the object present *as* a wish.

This film is also about rebellion; we could even say the narrative is scripted as the revolution of the clones. One clone, Six Echo, is the hero, of course, the one who leads the revolution. Six Echo is an affect alien; he is alienated by his failure to be happy. He is not well adjusted and refuses to adjust to the world. "What's troubling you?" he is asked by Dr. Merrick, to which he replies, "Tuesday night is tofu night. And I ask myself, who decided everyone likes tofu. And what is tofu anyway. And why can't I have bacon. I like bacon. And I'm not allowed to have bacon for breakfast. And let's talk about white. Why do we have to wear white all the time? It's impossible to keep clean. I never get any color. I want to know answers and I want more . . . more than just waiting to go to the Island." Rebellion begins by seeing what is present as not enough, by being anxious about how what is given is given, and by wanting more than what is given.

To question is to be affectively an alien. Six Echo's anxiety is sticky; he is anxious about anything and everything, with the energetic force of the question "but why?" unsettling the blanket warmth of good feeling. Dr. Merrick says of him, "He was the first one to question his environment, his whole existence here," and later says, "We have predicated our entire system on predictability . . . Six Echo has displayed the one trait that undermines it, human curiosity."

It is common to consider wonder and curiosity as positive emotions. In this film, wonder and curiosity, while presented as goods things (as the condition of possibility for freedom), are linked to bad feeling. It is the subject who feels bad who is curious, who wonders.

Six Echo acquires knowledge of what exists outside the horizon of hope, as the purpose of their collective existence. Thrown outside, he does not simply become a revolutionary. He does not just acquire a political will to save the other clones from their happiness. He first searches for the human from whom he was cloned, assuming that his human would care what happens to him: only to find that the human does not care but only wants to protect his investment, which means protecting himself from being faced by the clone, from the evidence that the clone has feelings. In coming to face himself as human, Six Echo witnesses the injustice of what lies behind his existence, or even the injustice of his existence. He acquires the will to revolt through facing his own bodily implication in injustice.

It is also through love that Six Echo acquires this sense of purpose. When his beloved Jordan Two Delta (Scarlett Johansson) wins a place on the Island, he knows she will be going to a certain death. He escapes with her, giving her hope by exposing that the Island is empty of promise. The contrast between the two films is very interesting at this point. Both films involve a man saving a woman, although in *The Island*, this is organized as the romance of the heterosexual couple. In *Children of Men*, Theo acquires his purpose by losing Julian; in effect, he takes her place, by taking up her project of getting Kee to the boat *Tomorrow*. In *The Island*, it is the fact of loving Two Delta that makes Six Echo take charge; liberation begins with his desire to save his beloved. Their love is scripted as rebellion: any proximity is forbidden for clones; their feelings for each other take them "off the program." The heterosexual couple whose love is prohibited are often the agents of social transformation. Heterosexuality becomes the basis for narratives of reconciliation, as if such love can heal the wounds of the past, as I discussed in chapter 4. After they have sex, Two Delta whispers, "The Island is real; it is us."

Six Echo and Two Delta come to embody an alternative hope. They escape and return to free the other clones. It is not that the film embraces hopelessness; if anything it is predicted *on a conversion which sustains an affect*. In other words, the affect is sustained by swapping the object: false hope (the Island) is converted into true hope (love, liberation). It is the white man, clone or no clone, who is the conversion point, who gives the clones true hope by liberating them from the false hope secured by their happiness. At one point, Albert Laurent (Djimon Hounsou) a black man who was appointed to kill the escapee clones, turns around and takes his place alongside Six Echo and Two Delta as liberator. He watches Jordan touch her own brand, with tears falling down her cheeks, and is moved. He recognizes in their struggle for freedom his own history, saying, "My brother and I were branded so that we would know that we were less than human." The brand is a sticky sign; it makes the struggle of the clones adhere to the liberation struggles of black people and all those others declared as less than human by being marked on the skin. I would argue that rather than making the black body a converter, this film, rather like *Children of Men*, uses the black body as the receiver of the gift. Revolution becomes the white man's gift.

We could say that in *Children of Men* and *The Island* the narrative works to contain the revolution that might happen, insofar as revolutionary hope remains predicated on the becoming father or becoming agentic of the white man. And yet in the dystopian form we might witness a potential for other things happening that might not simply be contained by narrative. We witness the creation of solidarity in the face of what happens, a sense of what becomes possible when people are thrown together to overthrow a situation. What happens when the normal rules of engagement are suspended? What do we do with those moments before a new world has begun when the old order is revealed as violence? These moments of suspension are not moments of transcendence, and yet we can still suspend those moments. The moment of suspension creates what Slavoj Žižek calls a "short-circuit between the present and the future" (2005: 247), in which we can act as if the "not yet" is already here rather than being a promise of what might come. In *Children of Men* it is the refugee camp at Bexhill on Sea, where most dread to go, the place where the most wretched reside, that is both the most dangerous and most promising; and it is where an uprising or rebellion is already happening. Žižek describes it as "a kind of liberated territory outside the all-pervasive and suffocating oppression" (2008b: 25). In such places the rules that govern social life are suspended, which means that, at least in the moment, what it means to inhabit specific forms has not been decided. We would no longer be sure what it means to say: a family is *this*, a friend does *this*, a lover means *this*, and a life has *this*. We would not be sure even what it means to admit to being human, or to being alive. If we don't know what it means to be or to have *this*, then we have to work out and work through what it means. A revolution would not simply require that subjects be revolting; it would demand a revolution of the predicate, of what gets attached to the subjects of the sentence. The subjects would be plural, as the "we" is not only called on to make a decision about *this* but is created as an effect of *this* decision. Hap communities take shape in such moments of suspension, where a "we" is assembled by being thrown together, acquiring a sense of purpose in throwing the meanings of *this* into question.

The Freedom to Be Unhappy

To hold on to the moments of suspension we might have to suspend happiness. We might revolt by revolting against the demand for happiness. The dystopian form unsurprisingly then presents us with visions of happiness as a nightmare. We could even name a subgenre of dystopian fiction as "happiness dystopias," from Aldous Huxley's classic *Brave New World* to James Gunn's *The Joy Makers*, or Ursula Le Guin's evocative short story "The People Who Walked Away from Omelas."[17] What can we learn from the nightmares of these books?

Huxley's preface to *Brave New World* gives us a powerful reading of what scientists call "the problem of happiness." He describes the problem of happiness as the problem "of making people love their servitude" ([1932] 1969: xii). The world that is brave and new is the world of happiness, where people "get what they want and they never want what they can't get" (149). Happiness is what holds things together by getting what you desire, and desiring what you get. You must give up desiring what you have not got, and cannot get. "'And that', put in the Director sententiously, 'that is the secret of happiness and virtue — liking what you've *got* to do. All conditioning aims at that: making people like their inescapable social destiny'" (10). To be conditioned by happiness is to like your condition. The happy world is drugged up; the feel-good soma makes people feel good; consensus is produced through sharing happy objects, creating a blanket whose warmth covers over the potential of the body to be affected otherwise.

As with the film *The Island*, which I would describe as a "hope dystopia," the revolutionary is the one who refuses happiness, which means not only failing to be happy but not wanting to be happy. Bernard, who is a psychologist and an outcast, offers the reader the first signs of revolt, of being revolting. "I'd rather be myself. . . . Myself and nasty. Not someone else, however jolly" (59). If "being myself" operates as a challenge to social orthodoxy, it also seems to locate unhappiness with the body of an individual. Bernard doesn't want to be "just a cell in a social body." I am reminded of two animated films about insects, *Antz* (1998, dir. Darnell and Johnson) and *The Bee Movie* (2007, dir. Hickner and Smith). Both of these films are organized around the figure of a revolutionary insect who revolts by not being happy with what he has been given. Indeed, in these films an individual insect is radicalized through unhappiness.[18] The ant or bee that doesn't go along with things is unhappy, curious, and desirous; he wants more than he gets. In turn, these individual heroic insects come to save their hive or colony through their dissent. Their unhappiness becomes an alternative social gift. The imagining of unhappy revolutionaries is limited in its investment of revolutionary hope in the body of an individual.

In *Brave New World* the alternative to happiness is certainly premised on individual freedom. At one level, this freedom is expressed as freedom to be happy in your own way. Bernard's reply to Lenina's expressed desire for happiness is to affirm what she says: "Yes, 'everybody's happy nowadays.' We begin giving the children that at five. But wouldn't you like to be free to be happy in some other way, Lenina?" (61). The book challenges even this idea of freedom to be happy *in some other way* via the figure of the Savage, who comes to this happy world without being conditioned by it. The Savage is the one who articulates the wisdom of the book. "All right then," said the Savage defiantly, "I'm claiming the right to be unhappy" (163). Unhappiness becomes a right in a world that makes happiness compulsory. In James Gunn's later happiness dystopia, *The Joy Makers*, the revolting subject also claims a right to be unhappy: "This is a free country, ain't it," Berns demanded. "A man can be unhappy if he wants to be, can't he?" The Hedonist responds: "No . . . That myth was exploded fifty years ago. The basic freedom is the freedom to be happy" (1961: 63).

The freedom to be happy restricts human freedom if you are not free to be not happy.[19] Perhaps unhappiness becomes a freedom when the necessity of happiness is masked as freedom.

Both *Brave New World* and *The Joy Makers* could be read as critiques of the utilitarian approach to happiness, what is called the science of happiness, with its belief that maximizing happiness is the measure of the social good. The first part of *The Joy Makers* gives us an account of the emergence of the science of hedonics from the point of view of Josh, who is a skeptic: "'The right the Declaration of Independence was concerned about . . . was the *pursuit* of happiness. That was when happiness was an art. Now it is a science. We have pursued it long enough. It's time we caught up with it'" (1961: 22). Hedonics translates the happiness contagion into a happiness duty: "their happiness must lie in making others happy" (37). The horror of hedonics in Gunn's novel is the horror of happiness becoming an endpoint; the story ends with people being turned into embryos, a story of life as womb-to-womb, of the happiest life being the suspension of the distinction between birth and death. It is suggested that the science of happiness is a withdrawal from life: the human being has "built himself a last refuge against life and retreated within it for the slow, happy death" (172).

In contrast, Ursula Le Guin's story "The People Who Walked Away from Omelas" critiques a more robust classical model of happiness as the good and virtuous life. The people of Omelas live happy lives in a meaningful sense: "They were not naïve and happy children—though their children were in fact happy. They were mature, intelligent, passionate adults whose lives were not wretched" ([1973] 1987: 278). Their happiness, you might say, is a good happiness, becoming a sign of worth, of a life and community that is flourishing. They deserve to be happy, we might say. But their happiness has a dark secret. It depends on the misery of one child, a child who is kept in the basement: "The child used to scream for help at night, and cry a good deal, but now it only makes a kind of whining, 'eh-haa, eh-haa' and it speaks less and less often. It is so thin there are no calves to its legs; its belly protrudes; it lives on a half-bowl of corn meal and grease a day. It is naked. Its buttocks and thighs are a mass of festered sores, as it sits in its own excrement continually. They all know it is there, all the people of Omelas. Some of them come to see it, others are content merely to know it is there. They all know that it has to be there. Some of them understand why, and some do not, but they all understand that their happiness, the beauty of their city, the tenderness of their friendships, the health of their children, the wisdom of their scholars, the skill of their makers, even the abundance of their harvest and the kindly weathers of their skies, depend wholly on this child's abominable misery" (281–82).

The story is about the injustice of such a deal: the perversion of a collective happiness that rests on the misery of a single child. If the happiness of the many is caused by the unhappiness of one, then such happiness will always be wrong. We could, following Alan Badiou, describe happiness as a form of nihilism, predicated on the right of some to have protection from misery, and from the causes of misery, or the right to decide just how much misery one can bear ([1993] 2001: 37).[20] In Omelas, the happiness of the world is premised on a necessary indifference to the child's unhappiness. The child's unhappiness provides the moral compass.[21] Like all good dystopias, Omelas asks its readers to recognize our world in the apparently nonexistent world of the story, to recognize the possibility of what seems impossible.

We recognize too much in Omelas. We recognize how much the promise of happiness depends upon the localization of suffering; others suffer so that a certain "we" can hold on to the good life. Returning to the evocative language of *The Well of Loneliness*, the happiness of "everybody" is what keeps misery within walls. The wrong of happiness is that it participates in the localization and containment of misery, the misery of those who cannot inhabit the apparently empty sign of happiness, who cannot populate its form. To walk away from such happiness is to be touched by suffering. To be touched by another would not be premised on feeling the other's suffering. The sympathy of fellow feeling, which returns feeling with like feeling, is a way of touching that touches little, almost nothing. To walk away from happiness would be simply a refusal of indifference, a willingness to stay proximate to unhappiness, *however* we will be affected.[22]

The political will to be affected by unhappiness could be rewritten as a political freedom. We would radicalize freedom *as* the freedom to be unhappy. The freedom to be unhappy is not about being wretched or sad, although it might involve freedom to express such feelings. The freedom to be unhappy would be the freedom to be affected by what is unhappy, and to live a life that might affect others unhappily. The freedom to be unhappy would be the freedom to live a life that deviates from the paths of happiness, wherever that deviation takes us. It would thus mean the freedom to cause unhappiness by acts of deviation.

I am not suggesting here that our aim is to cause unhappiness. It is not that unhappiness becomes our telos:[23] rather, if we no longer presume happiness is our telos, unhappiness would register as more than what gets in the way. When we are no longer sure of what gets in the way, then "the way" itself becomes a question. The freedom to be unhappy might provide the basis for a new political ontology, which, in not taking happiness as an agreed endpoint for human action, would be able to ask about the point of action. We might act politically because we do not agree about the ends of action.

To recognize the causes of unhappiness is thus a part of our political cause. This is why any politics of justice will involve causing unhappiness even if that is not the point of our action. So much happiness is premised on, and promised by, the concealment of suffering, the freedom to look away from what compromises one's happiness. To revolt can hurt not only because you are proximate to hurt but also because you cause unhappiness by revealing the causes of unhappiness. *You become the cause of the unhappiness you reveal.* It is hard labor to live and work under the sign of unhappiness. The unhappy archives that I have discussed throughout this book thus reflect on the collectivity of unhappiness. They resist the individualism that posits the unhappiness of one against the happiness of many. It is not simply that we recognize that unhappiness is collective or shared; it is also that we realize that challenging happiness can only be a shared project. It is too hard to cause unhappiness of the many as a one.

This is why feminist, queer, and antiracist archives are collective weaves of unhappiness even when we struggle for something, even in the moment of aspiration, even when we dance in the gap between inheritance and reproduction. If to challenge the right to happiness is to deviate from the straight path, then political movements involve sharing deviation with others. There is joy, wonder, hope, and love in sharing deviation. If to share deviation is to share what causes unhappiness, even joy, wonder, hope, and love are ways of *living with* rather than *living without* unhappiness.

To share what deviates from happiness is to open up possibility, to be alive to possibility. Political movements are also about opening up possibilities for those who are imagined as unhappiness-causes, as the origin of negation, if, as I have suggested, to be not happy is to be not. To open up possibility for the not happy or the not is not about becoming human—or becoming happy. Political movements are about becoming "not not" becoming something other than not. We work in what we could call an immanent utopia; we live in the present understood, in Lauren Berlant's phrase, as "sensually lived potentiality" (2008b: 272). Political movements imagine what is possible when possibility seems to have been negated or lost before it can be recognized. Political movements involve "freedom dreams," to use Robin D .G. Kelley's powerful language.[24] For Kelley, black politics is utopian because people dreamed of freedom, because they did not allow the restriction of possibility to be the restriction of imagination. Black politics is utopian because it is premised on the idea that "we could possibly go somewhere that exists only in our imagination" (2002: 2). In imagining what is possible, in imagining what does not yet exist, we say yes to the future. In this yes, the future is not given content: it is not that the future is imagined as the overcoming of misery; nor is the future imagined as being happy. The future is what is kept open as the possibility of things not staying as they are, or being as they stay. Revolutionaries must dream; if their imaginations dwell *on* the injustice of how things stay, they do not simply dwell *in* what stays.

To revolt is to be undone — it is not to reproduce an inheritance. And yet, a revolution does not empty the world of significance; it does not create blank pages. The writing might be on the wall, even when the walls come down. Returning to the dystopian films I have discussed in this chapter, it is good to think of how they do and do not imagine revolutions to come. In *Children of Men* we do not have a revolution in quite the same way as *The Island*: the implication of the film is that the world that is left behind — our world — is destroyed (the rebellion is being crushed by the force of greater force as the boat arrives) and that a new world might be created somewhere, out of the ruins of what has been left behind. The task of our hero is not to liberate a people but to save a pregnant girl.

In *Children of Men*, we end with the arrival of the boat *Tomorrow*. The last words are spoken by Key, after Theo has died. She says: "Theo, the boat! Theo, the boat. Its okay, we are safe now. We're safe." The boat signifies the possibility of tomorrow, of a tomorrow whose arrival might save us from today. If the film is hopeful, we could say it is hopeful about possibility, about what is possible if we don't give the future away. For Žižek, the boat provides the film's most convincing political solution. In his interview, he says of the boat: "It doesn't have roots, its rootless, it floats around," from which he concludes: "You cut your roots, that's the solution." However, I contend that such a reading prematurely fills the boat with a meaning, as a kind of optimism (the boat as the cause of pleasure becomes full of potential).[25]

It is noticeable that *The Island* also uses the metaphor of the boat. The boat is in Six Echo's dream. He draws the boat of his dreams for the psychologist. The boat has a Latin word on its side, but no Latin words have been implanted into his consciousness. The boat is a sign of subversion because it is not only a dream but a memory. Six Echo remembers the boat, which means as a clone he remembers what the client has experienced, a sign of the clone becoming human. If the clone is becoming human, then he is becoming other than human or showing the possibility of the human becoming other. Later, when Six Echo has taken the place of the human from whom he was cloned, he acquires the boat. The boat becomes a revolutionary hope for clones, taking the place of the Island as the cause of future happiness, signifying the possibility of becoming other. If the boat is the memory trace, and matters as memory, the boat suggests that hope in the future rests with the objects that are behind us.

We can consider how we are affected by the arrival of something in which we have placed our hopes. The boat that arrives might be empty, or it might be full. We do not know in advance of its arrival whether it is empty or full. So the point might be that we do not point our emotions toward the objects of our cause. Let's think of the happy boat, like the boat *Tomorrow* or the boat with a Latin name: the boat that arrives is the one we expect will cause our happiness in the future. Rather than pointing our happiness toward the boat, by seeing it as full of potential, we would instead accept the happiness as pointless, as a way of responding to the possibility of its arrival. The boat might arrive or not. We have to work hard to get to the point of the boat's arrival, whether or not the arrival happens. If it arrives, we won't know whether the boat will give us what we hope for. The boat will no longer be held in place as a happy object; the prospect of its fullness will not be the point of our journey.

Pointless emotions are not meaningless or futile; they are just not directed toward the objects that are assumed to cause them. Perhaps a revolutionary happiness is possible if we allow our boats to flee.[26] Such a happiness would be alive to chance, to chance arrivals, to the perhaps of a happening. We would not wait for things to happen. To wait is to eliminate the hap by accepting the inheritance of its elimination. To refuse this inheritance is to make things happen. When you make things happen, you make happen as well as make things. A happening is an encounter, the chance of an encounter, or even a chance encounter. Such encounters recreate the ground on which things do happen. To recreate a ground is to deviate from a past that has not been given up. When things go astray, other things can happen. We have a future, perhaps. As Jacques Derrida muses: "What is going to come, perhaps, is not only this or that; it is at last the thought of the *perhaps*, the *perhaps* itself" ([1997] 2005: 29). We might remind ourselves that the "perhaps" shares its "hap" with "happiness." The happy future is the future of the perhaps.

Happiness, Ethics, Possibility

THE WORD *happiness* does things. This much is clear. Throughout this book, I have considered how happiness holds its place as the object of desire, as the endpoint, the telos, as being what all human beings are inclined toward. As Darrin McMahon observes, happiness has often been described as what you reach at the end of a "well marked path" and as "the *summum bonum*, a highest good, happiness remained a *telos*, an end, and virtue the principal means to guide the way" (2006: 137). Happiness describes not only what we *are* inclined toward (to achieve happiness is to acquire our form or potential) but also what we *should be* inclined toward (as a principle that guides moral decisions about how to live well). Happiness provides as it were a double telos: the end of life, and the end of the good life.

Happiness can be what we want, a way of getting what we want, and a sign that we have got what we want. If we are happy, then we are well; or we have done well. Happiness can also be a judgment that others are doing well, even when we do not presume access to another's interiority or presume the other's existence involves interiority. We might say, for instance, that the plant is happy, as a way of saying that the plant is doing well, or flourishing. The association between wellness and feeling can be powerful in such occasions. When I say the plant is happy, I almost imagine that the plant is feeling cheerful, which in turn makes me feel cheerful about the plant, and even with myself for making the plant cheerful. It is as if the word bestows an affect, as if wellness is full of feeling, or a feeling full. Saying happiness can appear to generate the happiness that is said, or at least it provides us with a fantasy that happiness "is" by being said.

The word *happiness* is thus motivated and energetic. Given that happiness is a feeling-state or state-of-being that we aspire toward, then the word is often articulated with optimism and hope, as if saying it might mean having it, as if our feelings will catch up with the word, or even as if we will catch the feeling from the word. Creating happiness might even be a matter of spreading the word. Happiness offers what we could call "a hopeful performative." We hope that the repetition of the word *happiness* will make us happy. We hope that the word *happiness* will deliver its promise.

Positive psychology as a field is predicated on this promise: if you say, "I am happy" or make other positive self-declarations (if you practice being optimistic until it is habitual or routine to look on the bright side), then you will become happy. In such a framework, you can talk yourself *into* being happy by talking about yourself *as* being happy. There can be a certain truth to the promise. The word *happiness* could even be described as a happy word. After all, words can bring things into existence; words can do things, even if we don't always know what it is they will do. And yet, if you say repeatedly "I am happy" it can feel like you are trying to convince yourself about something, such that even if you convince yourself, the very necessity of having to convince yourself demonstrates that you are not really convinced.[1] My question is thus not so much whether we can generate happiness through the repetition of the word but what kind of desire is the desire for happiness in the first place, and what does it mean for subjects to be responsible for generating its effects, or to have a duty to spread the word.

It is the very desire for happiness that is articulated by the repetition of the word. The desire might even censor evidence of its own failure. Given this, to speak happiness is not necessarily to speak of something that exists before us. My own interest in how happiness is put into words was initially sparked by the speech act "I just want you to be happy." We can imagine the speaker giving up, stepping back, flinging up her arms, sighing. I just. The "just" is a qualifier of the want and announces a disagreement with what the other wants without making the disagreement explicit. Statements of desire for "just happiness" imply another unspoken utterance state, "I will be happy if you are happy," which translates into the following: "If you do or are *that*, then you will be unhappy, so I will be unhappy." Such a speech act, which secretly worries that unhappiness will follow *that*, produces the very state that is imagined as being *that* (just happiness = unhappiness). This is what I would call a "perverse performative": the speech act brings into existence what it cannot admit that it wants, or even that very thing that it says that it does not want (the unhappiness that shows you that you would only be happy if you did what I wanted you to do). If happiness is performative, it does not always declare what it wants.

In whatever form it takes, which is the form of the whatever, to speak of happiness is certainly part of the fabric of social life; the weave of reciprocity, of civility, of conflict and antagonism, makes happiness a tool, even a missile, as well as an object of love, that is sent out, returned, such that the word itself circulates, moves around, always going somewhere, always busy. We could describe happiness as a buzzword. It creates a sound through being used, such that when you hear the word *happiness* you are listening to the sound of its busyness.

Happiness as a word is both mobile and promiscuous; it can be articulated lightly, can appear anywhere, even everywhere. Ziyad Marar has argued that "the term *happy* is so dull and ubiquitous that it has been worn thin; rubbed transparent through constant, casual usage" (2003: 7). While happiness can indicate how we feel about our life situation, or what we hope for, whether we are hoping for ourselves or for others, we can also use the word simply to indicate an attitude, feeling, or preference in the present, and we can do so easily, casually, without any tremors of anxiety, or even without much thought: "so happy to meet you," "I am happy that," "this is a happy occasion." The mobility of this word does not always indicate its capacity to generate fullness wherever it goes. The word can also cover over social occasions; happiness as a word might not always do what it says, which is perhaps what allows us to say it, over and over again. In other words, the capacity for the word to move can make it less as well more affective. Indeed, when the word is detached from self-declarations or judgments about others, it can simply hover in the background, saying little, saying nothing.

So even if happiness holds its place as the object of desire, it does not always signify something, let alone signify the same thing. Happiness may hold its place only by being empty, a container that can become quite peculiar as it is filled with different things. Jacques Lacan's description of the history of happiness (rethought as the desire to know whether one's object of desire is worthy) as a secondhand clothes store remains timely: "The result is a kind of catalogue that in many ways might be compared to a second-hand clothes store in which one finds piled up the different judgments that down through the ages and up to our time have dominated human aspirations in their diversity and even their chaos" ([1986] 1992: 14). I have suggested that as a *container* of diverse objects, happiness might also *contain* the forms in which desire can be realized. The idiosyncratic nature of happy object choices, the intimacy of recognizing each other's likes, is how we share a horizon. There is an order to the chaos of happiness. The very diversity of happy objects helps create happiness as a field of choice (do you like this, or that, or whatever), as an illusion of freedom.

If the objects of happiness are diverse, so are the feelings that gather under its name. Happiness as a positive emotion can suggest the warmth and ease of comfort, or the sharp intensities of joy. It can be a momentary feeling, like a bolt of lightning that interrupts the night sky, only to be gone again, or the calm slow sigh of reflecting on something that has gone well. Happiness can be the beginning or end of a story, or can be what interrupts a life narrative, arriving in a moment, only to be gone again. Happiness can be all these things, and in being all of them, risks being none. If happiness does things, then does it do too much? Does happiness stop doings things by doing too much?

We can certainly witness a fidelity to happiness within philosophy, such that the story of happiness seems a story of fidelity. Happiness might even function as philosophy's foundational tautology: what is good is happy and what is happy is good. John Stuart Mill's model of happiness involves such a tautology: happiness is what we desire, so that whatever we desire we desire because it gives us happiness. He suggests that "men do desire happiness" and that "they desire and command all conduct in others toward themselves by which they think their happiness is promoted" ([1863] 2001: 28). He later suggests that happiness is desirable: "The utilitarian doctrine is, that happiness is desirable and the only Thing desirable" (35).[2] We desire what is desirable in desiring happiness. Does this formulation tell us anything at all?

In a way, it may tell us something by not telling us anything. Without the word *happiness*, we would perhaps not have a word that desire could point to: happiness might allow us to avoid the more explicit tautology that we desire what we desire. Of course, we can use other words, in the empty place left by taking out the word *happiness*. We can desire x or y, or any number of perverse combinations. We can be inventive with our object choices. Such combinations won't do quite the same trick. Happiness may be our best trick because it can keep its place, as being what we desire in desiring x or y. We can have confidence in x and y by having confidence in happiness as what x and y will give.

Happiness becomes a stopping point; happiness allows us to stop at a certain point, rather like the word *because*. The child asks you questions, or I ask questions in a way that people might say is "childlike." Why this? If this, then why that? Why that, then why . . . ? Anything can take the place of the dots; the empty place that always marks the possibility of another question, the endless deferral that reminds us that all answers beg questions and that to give an answer is to create the condition of possibility for another question. Eventually, you stop. You must stop. You have to stop to put a stop to the questions because there are other things to do with your time. So you say, "because." Why because? Because "because." When because becomes an answer to a question the conversation can stop. Happiness provides such a because, a "because because." We desire things, because of happiness. Because of happiness, we desire things. Happiness is how we can end the conversation about why it is that we desire what we desire. Happiness provides us with a full stop, a way of stopping an answer from being a question.

We can stop the conversation by taking it as self-evident that happiness is what we want or unhappiness is what we don't want. David Hume focuses more on the latter, providing us with a powerful account of just this kind of conversational stopping point: "Ask a man *why he uses exercise*; he will answer *because he desires to keep his health*. If you then enquire, *why he desires health*, he will readily reply, *because sickness is painful*. If you push your enquiries farther, and desire a reason *why he hates pain*, it is impossible he can ever give any. This is an ultimate end, and is never referred to any other object" ([1748] 1975: 293). You can end the conversion with such a point, as it does not demand another reference point.

To refer to happiness might suspend obligation to refer to anything else in making good an argument. Happiness becomes our defense; you can defend anything by saying it is necessary for happiness, whether that happiness is the happiness of a certain one, or the happiness of many. You can attack anything by saying that it is the cause of unhappiness. Happiness adds weight to arguments. To be on the side of happiness or to be for happiness (as a way of "being for being for") means you are on the side of the good. The language of happiness converts swiftly into missionary language, as we saw in chapter 4, as what we give to others, who in being recipients of a happiness that is not their own acquire a happiness duty.

One could say, in rebuttal, that statements about happiness can be true or false. For example, research might show that feminism causes women to be unhappy (by increasing women's aspirations, by challenging traditional gender roles, and so on), as I discussed in chapter 2. How do we respond? We can respond using the same epistemological commitments implicit in this research by giving evidence that feminism does not cause unhappiness, that feminism makes women happy, or that feminism is indifferent to women's happiness.

I suspect it is not quite that easy. Happiness is a mobile defense in part because happiness is already mobile. It is difficult to pin down; we depend on correlations, expectations, answers, wishes. Much happiness research, as I discussed in the introduction to this book, proceeds by turning correlations into causalities. The correlation between happiness and marriage is used to indicate that marriage causes happiness and thus that we have a moral obligation to promote marriage. Happiness is affective because you can find it even when it is missing, such that the loss of happiness is explained as the loss of this or that thing that causes happiness. To counter an argument by countering a claim to happiness with a counterclaim to happiness hence leaves you with shaky ground to defend a claim to happiness that counters your own. We may need to defend our arguments by not making happiness our ground, while exposing the shakiness of happiness as a ground. Simone de Beauvoir's argument in *The Second Sex* can be described as an exposure of shakiness: "It is always easy to describe as happy the situation in which one wishes to place [others]" ([1949] 1997: 28).

And yet, despite my concluding comments on "pointless emotions" in chapter 5, it seems overwhelmingly the case that the point of life, the meaning of life, the value, ethics, and potential of life is hard to think without thinking about happiness. This is why to be critical of the claim to happiness still has to deal with happiness as a claim. Happiness is weighty not because of its point, as if it simply had a point, but because happiness evokes a point that lies elsewhere, just over the horizon, in the very mode of aspiring for something. Of all the words we can think of as "emotion words," as words that operate as if they are signs of emotion, *happiness* seems the most pointed because happiness has been so closely tied to ethics. For some, the good life is the happy life. Or the virtuous person is the happy person. Or the best society is the happiest society. Happiness becomes not only the thing we want, whatever it is, but a measure of the good, such that happiness becomes a sign that the good must have already been achieved. We need to consider the intimacy of happiness and ethics in order to appreciate more fully the weightiness of happiness as a word.

A Genealogy of Happiness

I offer in conclusion a modest genealogy of happiness by reconsidering how happiness is implicated in what Nietzsche called the genealogy of morals. For Nietzsche, a genealogy of morals teaches us that good and evil as concepts arrive, and they arrive by taking form. To read good and evil we need to give form to their arrival rather than simply read their form. Nietzsche contrasts aristocratic and slave morality as two forms of morality that affirm and negate something. His genealogy of morals could be described as tracking the history of affirmation and negation.

In feminist theory, we are perhaps more familiar with Nietzsche's critique of slave morality, as a critique of the passivity of *ressentiment* and injury-based forms of identity politics (Brown 1995: 73; Skeggs 2004: 181–87).[3] For Nietzsche, slave morality begins by saying no to what is outside, and is locked inevitably in this gesture of negation, as a being that emerges by being against ([1887] 1996: 22), a being that might even take the shape of againstness. The slave revolt is a reaction of the weak and many against the power and happiness of the strong and the few; the moral psychology of its rebellion involves both the internalization of resentment and the desire for revenge.

Nietzsche argues that while slave morality says no to an outside, "the opposite is the case with the aristocratic mode of evaluation: this acts and grows spontaneously, it only seeks out its antithesis in order to affirm itself more thankfully and joyfully. Its negative concept, 'low', 'common,' 'bad' is only a derived, pale contrast to its positive basic concept which is thoroughly steeped in life and passion — 'we the noble, we the good, we the beautiful, we the happy ones!'" ([1887] 1996: 22). For Nietzsche, the gesture of saying "we the happy ones!" is an admirable gesture, a self-affirmation, a creation of something out of nothing.

Does Nietzsche repeat the gesture of affirmation by affirming the gesture? Nietzsche's genealogy shows us how the happiness distinction is a reification of a social distinction. His aim is not to call for a return to aristocratic morality. And yet, quite clearly, he identifies with the gesture "we the happy ones" by describing it as purely creative. He suggests that such self-declarations only later create the unhappy, as those who lack or do not have what it is that we have: "one should not fail to notice the almost benevolent *nuances* present in all the words with which the Greek nobility distinguishes the lower people from itself; how a kind of pity, consideration and forbearance continually intervenes and sweetens, until ultimately almost all the words applied to the common man survive as expressions meaning 'unhappy' 'pitiable'" (23). Nietzsche's own affirmation (which is not necessary or even obvious) is that the aristocratic speech act "we the happy ones" does not require negation: the others are negated only as a kind of afterthought, becoming objects of pity, becoming pitiful and unhappy over time. It is the others, the negated, who begin with negation, who can only act by saying no.

The limitation of this genealogy of morals is not so much that it locates happiness in good fortune (I think this location helps us to understand what happiness is about) but rather that it identifies fortune with creativity. Nietzsche suggests that the fortune is a feeling that allows the "well-bred" to identify happiness with action. "All *this*," he suggests, "is diametrically opposed to 'happiness' as understood on the level of the powerless . . . those for whom happiness appears essentially as narcotic, anaesthetic; calm, peace, 'Sabbath,' the expansion of feeling and the stretching of the limbs, in a word, as *passivity*" (23–24). I challenge the idea that to declare happiness *from* fortune is an affirmation act, or even active, and that it does not *from the very beginning* involve negation (the "un-happy" as the "in-active"). I think the implication of Nietzsche's own genealogy is that the declaration "we the happy ones" does not declare very much at all. Or if it does declare something, then the declaration simply reveals that those who have the power to describe themselves as happy tend to describe themselves as happy (and others as not being so). Such a declaration is not well described as an act of novelty or creation.

We can challenge the assumption that those deemed unfortunate do not act:

that their happiness (as *anaesthetics*) as well as unhappiness (as *ressentiment*) are passive. Throughout this book I have examined unhappiness as a form of political action: the act of saying no or of pointing out injuries as an ongoing present affirms something, right from the beginning. And, if anything, I have suggested that the happiness that is valued or affirmed, as signs of human activity and worth, can be reread as involving *anaesthetics*, a loss of the capacity or will to be affected by anything.

Nietzsche allows us to witness the *history of happiness as a genealogy of self-declaration*, in which the capacity to declare "we the happy ones" is taken as sufficient grounds of the truth of the statement. We could say the genealogy of happiness is inseparable from the history of fortune. If we learn from Nietzsche that the fortunate ones declare themselves as being happy, then we can reread happiness as the *displacement of fortune*. As I pointed out in the first chapter, one of the early meanings of the English word *happiness* relates to the idea of fortune, being fortunate or lucky. And yet, the history of happiness involves anxiety that happiness could simply refer to good fortune. We see this anxiety, for instance, in the Stoic tradition. As Seneca famously described, "Fortune can snatch away only what She has given, but virtue she does not give, therefore, she cannot take it away" (cited in DeBrabander 2007: 22). Fortune is personified as a figure of contingency, of the possibility that what has been given can also be taken away. Happiness becomes virtue, as that which each man can achieve without external goods: "It was nature's intention that there should be no need of great equipment for a good life: every individual can make himself happy" (Seneca 1997: 6). Indeed the happy man is outside the reach of fortune: "No man has been shattered by the blows of Fortune unless he was first deceived by her favours" (7).

The exclusion of fortune from happiness might operate at the same level as the exclusion of the empirical and contingent: all those things that *happen to us*, that cannot as it were be under our control, are excluded from the conditions of happiness. What do contingency, fortune, and the empirical have in common? They all operate under the sign of "the hap." One history of happiness could be described as the history of the removal of the hap from happiness. In *The Theory of Moral Sentiments*, Adam Smith suggests that we must place our happiness not in the hope of winning but in playing the game well: "If we placed our happiness in winning the stake, we place it in what depended upon causes beyond our power and out of our direction. We necessarily exposed ourselves to perpetual fear and uneasiness, and frequently to grievous and mortifying disappointments. If we placed it in playing well, in playing fairly, in playing wisely and skilfully, in the propriety of our own conduct, in short, we placed it in what, by proper discipline, education, and attention, might altogether be in our own power, and under our own direction. Our happiness was perfectly secure and beyond the reach of fortune" ([1759] 2000: 410).

We can explore the narrative of "happiness beyond the reach of fortune" in terms of what it promises: it promises that we can secure happiness. We can secure happiness when happiness is under our own direction, as a reference to our own conduct. This fantasy of happiness is a fantasy of self-control, as if we could control happiness by not placing our hopes for happiness in what is outside of our control. The wise and virtuous person will not be fearful, uneasy, or disappointed as his happiness rests on being wise and virtuous. The gene-alogy of happiness teaches us how happiness is found in the qualities of the fortunate: as Smith describes, in playing well we must have "proper discipline, education, and attention." Fortune may then *accumulate at the very moment it is displaced*, becoming simply the capacity to play well, to be the happy and virtuous ones. To put fortune back into happiness is not to say that the fortu-nate ones are *really* the happy ones but rather to show how happiness allows the fortunate to think of themselves as good, virtuous, and wise *despite* their fortune. It is hard now to think of fortune without thinking about wealth. We might want to return to the early meanings of fortune, as a form of luck and chance, in theorizing the intimacy of happiness and fortune. Happiness might be as chancy as fortune.

Happiness, Passivity, Activity

Perhaps the genealogy of morality offered by Nietzsche stops too quickly: a genealogy of happiness might also need to offer a genealogy of activity and pas-sivity.[4] Such a genealogy of happiness would not simply explore the reification of the distinction between good and evil, and between lower and higher goods but also how that distinction is aligned with the distinction between active and passive, as well as between action and reaction. The distinction between active and passive accumulates force by being detached from bodies, such that it can be reattached to bodies in the form of different qualities or capacities.

In the first instance, all forms of passion have been viewed as passive; indeed, the word *passion* and the word *passive* share the same root in the Latin word for suffering, *passio*. The active/passive can function quite simply as a distinction between action and passion/emotion. But some forms of emotion become read as "active" in comparison to others. Happiness becomes a form of activity through being contrasted with negative emotions; to be happy would be to be active in the determination of your fate, while to be unhappy would be to suffer your fate. The distinction becomes sharper. Some forms of happiness become seen as more active than others. In Nietzsche's *Thus Spoke Zarathustra*, the superman is described as both the most joyful and the "happiest man," whose joy is described as "free from the happiness of serfs" ([1883–85] 1961: 127), and who "smashes their table of values" as "the breaker—the lawbreaker—but he is the creator" (51).[5] The perpetual refinement of the distinction between active and passive allows activity and passivity to become properties of bodies.[6] The unfortunate are the emotional ones, the ones who suffer, and if they feel happiness, then their happiness is weak, as *anaesthetics*.

We can challenge the binary opposition between active and passive by focusing on how the qualities of activity and passivity are distributed. Passivities tend to be located in the bodies of those on whom we have given up. To give something up can be not to see the quality of an action. I would even speculate that the description of the passive voice as a grammatical error involves a kind of giving up. The passive voice is ordinarily applied to that form of the verb in which "the action denoted by it is treated as an attitude of the thing toward which the action is directed." We learn that we must say that the chicken crossed the road. We must not say that the road was crossed by the chicken. In such a case, the road does nothing, and yet is the grammatical subject of the sentence. We must preserve the fantasy that the subject, even the animal-subject, is the one who acts. The chicken must come first in the sentence.

But does the road do nothing in the event of the crossing? The road is a provider; it provides the point at which we can cross, at which we can go from one side to the other. The road is an effect of past actions, of decisions taken to allow crossing points. Rather than hold on to the binary opposition active/passive, we can challenge the opposition, and we can do so by showing how that which has been deemed as passive, as just there doing nothing, is doing something and even provides the conditions of possibility for doing something. The task is not to redescribe passivity as activity (creating as it were a generalized field of action) but to think of passivities as involving different kinds of action.

One of my projects in this book has been to show how suffering is a kind of activity, a way of doing something. To suffer can mean to feel your disagreement with what has been judged as good. Given this, suffering is a receptivity that can heighten the capacity to act. To move from happiness to suffering—or we might even say to suffer the loss of an idea of happiness through disappointment—can even spring you into action. And happiness can be a way of going along with what you are being asked to do, as Nietzsche himself describes. This is not to say that unhappiness has to be installed as the active against which happiness is passive. No, not that. Not that, at all. We need to develop a language to describe qualitative differences in how we experience activities and passivities. To do this, we must challenge the very separation of active and passive, and how that separation works to secure different classes of being, from happy persons and crossing chickens to suffering souls and inert roads.

We can challenge the distinction between happiness as activity and unhappiness as passivity by showing how the active and passive can switch sides. Consider the Deleuzian reading of Spinoza. For Deleuze, Spinoza belongs in the same affirmative horizon as Nietzsche: "Spinoza's all-out struggle, his radical denunciation of all the passions based on sadness" is what "places him in a great lineage that goes from Epicurus to Nietzsche" ([1970] 1998: 72). The radical denunciation of sad passions becomes an alternative line of descent within philosophy. By implication, this line of descent is also a line of dissent from those who do not renounce sad passions. And yet, despite this, we have seen how consistently philosophers present happiness as on the side of the good, although happiness is not always defined in terms of passion. If Epicurus, Nietzsche, and Spinoza share a commitment to happiness as that which is good, then such shared commitments would seem to agree rather than disagree with a philosophical inheritance.

For Deleuze, Spinoza's ethics is ethnology, a description of power, of capacity, of how bodies are affected by other bodies. Deleuze asks: "What can happen if my body is made this way, a certain relation of movement and rest which subsumes an infinity of parts? Two things can happen: I eat something that I like, or else another example, I eat something and collapse, poisoned. Literally speaking, in the one case I had a good encounter, and in the other I had a bad one" (1978: 6). As I discussed in chapter 1, John Locke also considers what it means to like what you eat. He uses the example of loving grapes because they taste delightful, offering a model of the diversity of tastes as "the agreeability to this or that palate" ([1690] 1997: 247). For Deleuze the bad encounter takes us beyond the horizon of likes. He does not suggest "I eat something that I like" followed by "I eat something I don't like." He creates instead a rather more drastic and dramatic image. The bad encounter is when the subject is poisoned, collapses, and dies. That the "bad encounter" is represented as death tells us something. The encounter with something you like achieves a retrospective optimism as a form of survival (you are not poisoned). I have also suggested that when subjects suffer a radical disagreement which takes us beyond the horizon in which likes can gather as a shared form, they risk their lives.

Deleuze does more than describe the unpalatable effects of disagreement. What is disagreeable about disagreement is that you suffer from it: disagreement is itself framed as a form of passivity. This is why Deleuze says that, for Spinoza, those in power such as the despot or the priest "need the sadness of their subjects" (4). The masses must be weakened through suffering. They must be poisoned by what is disagreeable. So if I suffer a disagreement, it is my life at stake: we could say that death is the failure of the subject to persist in his or her own being; death by eliminating the subject altogether is the radicalization of the threat of passivity.

For Deleuze the good encounter increases the capacity for action: we could describe the good encounter as the agreeable effects of agreement. A good encounter would depend on "relations of agreement between such and such body and my own" (11). In a bad encounter, "this body does not agree with mine" (5). There is no doubt that some things more than others will agree with us. Our likes might be determined at least in part by what *can* agree with us given what we are already like.

We can still ask how it is that we come to be like what we are like. Deleuze in considering "an encounter" asks what might happen if so and so meets with so and so. In another example from the same lecture, I might "walk down the street," where I happen upon Pierre and Paul: "I run into Pierre" and "I suddenly see Paul" (3). I meet them by chance on the street and the encounter might be a good or bad encounter. Whether it is a good or bad encounter would depend on how I am affected by Pierre and Paul: when I am pleased or displeased an idea of Pierre and Paul is given to me. I am tempted to ask whether this encounter is chance; sure, we might happen to meet, but we might happen to meet because we are walking along the street. We have already witnessed the agency of the street. The street provides not only a crossing point (for chickens and other others) but also a meeting point. Even chance encounters, you might say, depend on certain grounds being available for action. We are directed by what grounds our action: the paths that allow us to find our way, even if we don't know what we will find on our way.

However we encounter each other, I meet Pierre and Paul and the meeting is either agreeable — or not. What does it mean for an encounter to be agreeable? How do some become agreeable for others? My analysis of happiness has offered an alternative vocabulary for describing what is at stake in an agreement. Happiness can involve an immanence of coercion, the demand for agreement. Coercion is usually thought of as an external force that requires the obedience of subjects through the use of threats, intimidation, or pressure. When we think of being coerced we might think of being forced to do something "against our will." But coercion can shape the very direction of the will, as *the will to will*. What is agreeable to our will might not always be available as an object of consciousness. Arthur Schopenhauer argues in *On the Suffering of the World* that "we never really notice or become conscious of what is agreeable to our will" ([1850] 2004: 3). We might not notice others if they are in agreement with our will. An agreement might stop an encounter from being recognized as an encounter. When things are in agreement, they are even behind us. Agreements might take place before such and such a body encounters such and such a body. Each body carries with it a history of agreements, not all of which are revealed, which incline it in a certain way, as the way of the will.

We can return to the example of the palate. Even a philosopher such as John Locke, who embraces the diversity of happy objects, suggests that the palate is correctible. We can acquire good tastes, as I discussed in chapter 1. The possibility of acquisition is a field of immanence, of not only what you can become but what you should become, translated as the duty of the subject to do better. Pleasure or joy might involve not just finding such and such agreeable but the experience of being affirmed *because* you find the right things pleasing. Those around you "agree" with your agreement. After all, agreement can mean not only "the action of pleasing or contenting" but also "the act of consenting." The good encounter might involve submission, in the sense of being willing to like one's condition, as I explored in my reflections on happiness dystopias in chapter 5. Agreement also describes "accordance in sentiment." When accordance in sentiment is a goal of social and political life, it would require you to accord with what already exists. Harmony would be a demand for accordance. This is why I would argue that the powers-that-be might want their subjects happy rather than sad.[7] And in wanting our happiness, they might forbid recognition of sadness as that which gets in the way, not just of happiness but its want.[8]

We can thus offer a different slant on the Deleuzian example of the good encounter. The good encounter could be read as being how bodies stay in place, or *acquire a place in which they can stay,* by agreeing with what they receive. The bad encounter can be read as how bodies refuse to be placed by disagreeing with what they receive. This book has considered unhappiness as judgmental, as an affective point of disagreement. If acts of revolution, of bringing the walls down, can be understood as protests against happiness, we can also describe such acts as *protests against the costs of agreement.* If to agree is to submit, then good encounters can involve submission—though not necessarily, and not only. We can learn from how that which has been deemed active can be read as passive, and that which has been deemed passive can be read as active. Activities and passivities are ways of framing an encounter rather than describing an encounter as such.[9]

My reading of happiness offers a reframing of an encounter. We could redescribe the social threat of the killjoy in these terms. The killjoy is the one who comes between bodies that would be, or should be, in agreement.[10] The killjoy is the one who gets in the way of an organic solidarity. Or we might say that solidarity becomes organic by locating the disagreement in what gets in the way of an encounter. Solidarity might even take shape by agreeing on what is disagreeable in advance of an encounter. The example of the killjoy teaches us that the nature of organic agreement depends on the localization of disagreement to "whatever" gets in the way. My task in this book has been to refuse the indifference of this whatever.

If ethics is to preserve the freedom to disagree, then ethics cannot simply be *about* affirmation, or *for* affirmation, understood as good encounters, as what increases the capacity for action. I would thus extend my critique of happiness to include what we could describe as "the affirmative turn." The affirmative turn is not reducible to the happiness turn. Much of this literature is at odds with the kind of work within happiness studies; this is philosophical writing that does not have normative commitments to happiness as the good and virtuous life, and that writes itself in opposition to the moralizing frames of reference that characterize happiness studies. Indeed, many writers working in this vein explicitly refuse the "weighty" language of happiness and privilege instead the positivity of joy (Massumi 2002a; Colebrook 2008). So why speak of the affirmative turn as belonging within the same horizon as the happiness turn? I do so for one simple reason: the affirmative turn shares a commitment to positive feelings—which does not mean in any simple way "good feelings"—as sites of potentiality and becoming.

The affirmative turn has posited what we might call "an affirmative ethics." Affirmative ethics turns the Deleuzian example of the good encounter into a call for good encounters. In other words, affirmative ethics does not only describe what happens when bodies are in agreement, it also calls for good encounters as giving "more to life," as more, perhaps, than misery and suffering. Brian Massumi suggests: "Ethical, empirical—and creative, because your participation in this world is part of a global becoming. So it's about taking joy in that process, wherever it leads, and I guess it's about having a kind of faith in the world which is simply the hope that it continue. . . . But again it is not a hope that has a particular content or end point—it's a desire for more life, or for more to life" (2003a: n.p.). Massumi argues carefully that good feelings aren't necessarily about feeling good. But the word *joy* evokes experiences of pleasure and delight. Words are sticky; they retain associations even if we use them differently. In a way, by redefining joy as good feeling, as what increases capacity for action, we also increase the power of the word: feeling good becomes good feeling; feeling good becomes what increases your power for action.

Massumi writes here about taking joy in a process. And yet, joy also gives affective shape to this "more to life." In the affirmative turn, joy is what opens up the potentiality of life. What does it mean to be for joy? Is being for joy different from being for happiness? We need to take care not to collapse joy with happiness; there is no doubt these words have different histories that are attached in some way to what they have been used to refer to. *Joy* is a less weighty word; it is often used to signify an intensity of feeling that is transitory and must be transitory if it is to be experienced as intensity. But if joy is put in the place of happiness as being what we should aim for, then they might have similar effects. Rosi Braidotti, for example, suggests that "joyful or positive passions and the transcendence of reactive affects are the desirable mode"

(2006b: 4).[11] There is so much to admire in Braidotti's visionary feminism. And yet, I wonder what it means for joy to become a desirable mode, a way of transcending negative passions, which are assumed to be reactive. Braidotti does recognize the importance of pain and suffering within her ethics. For Braidotti, "taking suffering into account is the starting point; the real aim of the process, however, is the quest for ways of overcoming the stultifying effects of passivity, brought about by pain" (8). We can ask whether pain is best described as stultifying passivity (or whether pain is only experienced in such terms) and whether all passivity is stultifying. My aim in even asking such questions is not to affirm pain or other bad feelings in response to this affirmation of good feeling. I would simply suggest that we cannot know in advance what different affects will do to the body before we are affected in this or that way. As I argued in chapter 5, being affected involves the perversity of being twisted and turned.

The affective economy which associates joy with good things and pain with bad things might prematurely hold things in place. If we aim for joy, we aim to move beyond pain. Bad feelings are in the way of what gets beyond: they are described by Braidotti as "black holes" (13). Rather than describe bad feelings as obstacles, as being "in the way," I have described in this book *what follows* from bad feelings being understood in such terms. Some more than others are associated with bad feeling, as getting in the way of the promise of happiness. We learn from blockages, and the where and how of their distribution. So rather than presuming "random access to the phenomena the cause pain" (13), I have described how those who refuse the promise of happiness become the causes of bad feeling, which causes unhappiness to take form in specific ways. While sometimes bad things simply happen, while you can be unlucky or misfortunate (as implicit in the saying "to be in the wrong place at the wrong time"), I would argue that our access to the causes of pain is far from random.

We can return to Audre Lorde's work discussed in chapter 2. As she shows us, the very idea that violence is random is what stops us from seeing what is at stake in an encounter: her mother says to her that the woman who spits is spitting into the wind not spitting at her, a black child, as a way of protecting the child from the pain of racism. It is a desire for protection that is understandable — but it fails to protect. Lorde argues throughout her work that we should not be protected from what hurts. We have to work and struggle not so much to feel hurt but to notice what causes hurt, which means unlearning what we have learned not to notice. We have to do this work if we are to produce critical understandings of how violence, as a relation of force and harm, is directed toward some bodies and not others. While we can and should follow Raymond Williams (1977) to explore "structures of feeling," my suggestion here is that we might also want to explore "feelings of structure": feelings might be how structures get under our skin.

The desire to get over suffering is of course an understandable desire, one that might express a longing to do more than describe social relations of force and harm.[12] I have explored throughout this book the limits of this desire (which is not and will not be all that can be said about this desire). To recover can be to re-cover, to cover over the causes of pain and suffering. Rosi Braidotti suggests that "repugnant and unbearable events do happen" but then concludes that "ethics consists however in reworking those events in the direction of positive relations" (13). She argues that "paradoxically, it is those who have already cracked up a bit, those who have suffered pain and injury, who are better placed to take the lead in the process of ethical transformation" (14). Perhaps the relationship between leadership and suffering is only paradoxical if we assume that suffering is stifling. We learn from what Braidotti rightly points out: those who have been undone by suffering can be the agents of ethical transformation.

We might need to attend to bad feelings not in order to overcome them but *to learn by how we are affected by what comes near*, which means achieving a different relationship to all our wanted and unwanted feelings as an ethical resource. I think what is underestimated by affirmative ethics is the *difficulty* of giving our attention to — and sustaining our attention on — certain forms of suffering. The desire to move beyond suffering in reconciliation, the very will to "be over it" by asking others to "get over it," means that those who persist in their unhappiness become causes of the unhappiness of many. Their suffering becomes transformed into our collective disappointment that we cannot simply put such histories behind us. Ethics cannot be about moving beyond pain toward happiness or joy without imposing new forms of suffering on those who do not or cannot move in this way.

The affirmative turn creates a distinction between good and bad feelings that presumes bad feelings are backward and conservative and good feelings are forward and progressive. Bad feelings are seen as oriented toward the past, as a kind of stubbornness that "stops" the subject from embracing the future. Good feelings are associated with moving up, as creating the very promise of a future. This assumption that good feelings are open and bad feelings are closed allows historical forms of injustice to disappear. The demand that we be affirmative makes those histories disappear by reading them as a form of melancholia (as if you hold on to something that is already gone). These histories have not gone: we would be letting go of that which persists in the present. To let go would be to keep those histories present.

My aim in this book has been to explore how bad feelings are not simply reactive; they are creative responses to histories that are unfinished (see also Ahmed 2004: 200–202). I am not saying that we have an obligation to be unhappy—it is important to avoid creating a romance or duty out of feelings that can be experienced as unbearable. I am simply suggesting that we need to think about unhappiness *as more than a feeling that should be overcome*. Unhappiness might offer a pedagogic lesson on the limits of the promise of happiness. If injustice does have unhappy effects, then the story does not end there. Unhappiness is not our endpoint. If anything, the experience of being outside the life-worlds created by passing happy objects around gets us somewhere. We might go further with happiness, if we don't follow its objects around.

Hap-pier Happiness

Where can we go with happiness? I do not want to offer an alternative definition of happiness (a good happiness that can be rescued from bad happiness), as this would keep in place the very idea that happiness is what we should promote. I want to conclude with a reflection on how happiness can acquire significance if it is taken outside the domain of ethics. Happiness has been weighed down as a sign of the good—of the virtuous subject or of the good life.[13] As I have suggested, happiness becomes an exclusion of possibility, and thus a good defense against crisis, as if the decisions about the future are already made. Happiness as a form of duty is written in the language of freedom, as if want follows freely from wanting to cause happiness or not to cause unhappiness.

If happiness is a defense against crisis, this book has attended to moments in which happiness fails, when a subject does not go along or get along, when the way someone is going becomes a direction she does not want to go. When there is a crisis, we have to ask the question "which way?" When the way turns into a question, you become aware of possibility. You become aware of how much living the life you live is not necessary. Happiness can be used as a shield against this recognition of possibility. I was struck while doing the research for this book how rarely crisis points are resolved in narrative by the use of the speech act "I must leave this life for happiness," though it is and will remain possible to speak in this way. I have learned so much about happiness by wondering how it is possible for crisis points to be resolved as "leaving happiness for life."

The unhappy archives I have read in this book teach me what it means for ethics to be a crisis. You are living a life, and you realize you do not want to live the life you are living. The act of leaving a life can be an ethical act, even if it involves causing unhappiness. You might have to be willing to be the cause of unhappiness. This is not to say that causing unhappiness should become an ethical right or a necessary good. It can be right or wrong for this person or that—depending. Dependence involves the necessary task of asking what we should do, without turning to happiness as if it provides the answer to the question.

If we do not assume that happiness is what we must defend, if we start questioning the happiness we are defending, then we can ask other questions about life, about what we want from life, or what we want life to become. Possibilities have to be recognized as possibilities to become possible. This is why embracing possibility involves going back or even "feeling backward," as Heather Love (2007) describes very well. Embracing possibility involves returning to the past, recognizing what one has, as well as what one has lost, what one has given, as well as what one has given up. To learn about possibility is to do genealogy, to wonder about the present by wondering about the how of its arrival. To learn about possibility thus involves a certain estrangement from the present. Other things can happen when the familiar recedes. This is why affect aliens can be creative: not only do we want the wrong things, not only do we embrace possibilities that we have been asked to give up, but we create life worlds around these wants. When we are estranged from happiness, things happen. Hap happens.

I would not say that unhappiness is necessary. But I would say that unhappiness is always possible, which makes the necessity of happiness an exclusion not just of unhappiness but of possibility. As Søren Kierkegaard describes so beautifully: "This possibility that is said to be so light is commonly regarded as the possibility of happiness, fortune etc. But this is not possibility. . . . No, in possibility all things are equally possible, and whoever has truly been brought up by possibility has grasped the terrible as well as the joyful" ([1844] 1980: 156).[14] Possibility means grasping terror as well as joy. Possibility for Kierkegaard is where equality is actual.

A stance toward possibility might be a *happenstance*. As Jean-Luc Nancy describes poetically: "Neither happiness nor unhappiness, there is *happenstance*, the sense of the *happenstance* [*Ni bonheur, ni malheur, il y autrait* l'heur, *le'sens de l'heur*], of the good and bad encounter or confrontation, of the possibility— incessantly renewed—that there could be a good or bad happenstance, that it could be necessary to choose one against the other, but, first of all, to choose to have this choice *and* not to have it, not to master the sense of the happenstance, the fractual combinatory of events that make up the world" ([1993] 1997: 151).[15] To have a sense of the happenstance would involve being open to the possibility of good and bad things happening. We could say that happiness would be a possibility kept open by happenstance, such that the condition of possibility for happiness includes other possibilities. If we think of happiness as a possibility that does not exhaust what is possible, if we lighten the load of happiness, then we can open things up. When happiness is no longer presumed to be a good thing, as what we aim for, or as what we should aim for, then we can witness happiness as a possibility that acquires significance by being a possibility alongside others. We can value happiness for its precariousness, as something that comes and goes, as life does.[16]

When I think of what makes happiness "happy" I think of moments. Moments of happiness create texture, shared impressions: a sense of lightness *in* possibility. Just think of those moments where you are brought to life by the absurdity of being reminded of something, where a sideways glance can be enough to create a feeling that ripples through you. Two people burst out with laughter by the recollection of an event.[17] Just a word can prompt such recollection, a gesture, anything. As Clarissa, who inherits the sadness of Mrs. Dalloway as well as taking her name, describes in *The Hours*: "I remember one morning. Getting up at dawn. There was such a sense of possibility. You know that feeling. So this is the beginning of happiness. This is where it starts and of course there will always be more. It never occurred to me that it wasn't the beginning. It was happiness. It was a moment right then." Happiness might not simply provide a sense of possibility; it is a sense of possibility. To turn happiness into an expectation is thus to annul its sense of possibility. When happiness is not something that we promise to another, is not something that we imagine is due to us or which we have a duty toward, is not something that we anticipate will accumulate from certain points, other things can happen, which involves a certain kind of openness to the possibility of an encounter.

A rethinking of happiness as possibility might also allow us to care for those forms of happiness that are directed in the wrong way. I explored misdirected happiness in my reflections on being happily queer in chapter 3. Some forms of happiness are viewed as less worthy because they do not involve the accumulation of points, creating a line that can be followed. Silliness might be another example of a worthless happiness. The etymology of silliness is striking. It comes from the word *sael*, originally meaning blessed, happy, or blissful. The word mutates over time; from blessed to pious, to innocent, to harmless, to pitiable, to weak and feeble. From the blessed to the feeble: we learn from the depressing nature of the genealogy of silliness.

An example of an attempt to revalue silly forms of happiness is offered by the film *Happy-Go-Lucky* (2008, dir. Mike Leigh). This film follows the life of Poppy (Sally Hawkins), as she cycles around London, has fun with her female flatmate Zoe (Alexis Zegerman), her unconventional sister Dawn (Andrea Riseborough) and her assortment of friends, teaches kids she loves at her primary school, learns to drive, and visits her rather more conventional sister Suzy (Kate O'Flynn) in the suburbs. Poppy is a "happy-go-lucky" character; she seems (at least in the first instance) quite annoyingly persistent in her cheerfulness, chattering to strangers who do not want to have a conversation, who might want to be alone in their misery, or laughing and giggling when unpleasant things happen. We learn from her encounters that "inappropriate" expressions of happiness are far from contagious, that being cheerful in a certain way, at a certain moment, can cause irritation (as an irritation with happiness). Poppy seems at first to embody the cost of happiness, of the labor or effort to persist in happiness, as a way of covering over bad things. But over time, the film encourages us to identify with Poppy, through her responsiveness to the suffering around her: she reaches out to a schoolboy who has been bullied; she listens to her violent racist angry driving instructor; she strikes up a conversation with a homeless man with uncanny ease. In all these examples, she refuses to keep her distance from suffering. The film shows that passivity can be an ethical capacity: you have to be willing to be affected by others, to receive their influence.

We can ask whether the film promotes happiness through idealizing the example of Poppy's cinematic life. The director Mike Leigh has spoken about how he wanted to direct a film that was "anti-miserabilist." And yet, by following Poppy around, the film does not suggest that the response to unhappiness is to be happy or to persist in an idea of happiness. To persist in such an idea would be to remove yourself from what is around you. After all, Poppy's life is not shaped by what I have called happy objects (she does not own her house, she is not married, and she does not have children). Poppy goes to see her sister Suzy in the suburbs (who has or is about to have all these things). Suzy asks her when she is going to become responsible, saying, "I just want you to be happy, that's all," to which Poppy replies, "I am happy." When her sister doubts her right to describe herself in this way, Poppy explains, "I love my life. Yeh, it can be tough at times, that's part of it. I've got a great job, brilliant kids, got lovely flat, got her to look at, got amazing friends. I love my freedom. I'm a very lucky lady, I know that." Her sister becomes upset at this life-affirmation, saying that Poppy is "rubbing it in." Suzy might be upset not because she is unhappy with Poppy's happiness but because Poppy exposes the unhappiness of Suzy's happiness.[18] We are shown what you give up by doing the right thing, in aspiring to have a good life, to reach its points of ceremony.

At one level, this film seems limited by its preoccupation with psychology as a solution (as if change is simply about having a better attitude). So Poppy asks her angry and unhappy driving instructor about his family, taking on the role of therapist who seeks to explain unhappiness by returning to a primal scene, as an explanation which can also explain unhappiness away. And yet *Happy-Go-Lucky* reflects on how the promotion of an idea of happiness, of the good life, means giving up a certain freedom, a certain sense of being able. After all, the happy-go-lucky person is not a conventional figure of happiness. Poppy is happy with her life not despite not following happy objects around but because she does not; she goes wherever her desire, interest, or curiosity takes her. To live life in such a way is to be creative and inventive with your object choices. Indeed this film is quite remarkable for its presentation of the longevity of female friendship, which is not depicted as a route to a heterosexual future, nor a supplement, but as a life world, a world with its own rhythms and contingencies. The film thus gives most value to ties of affection that are outside conventional forms of intimacy. Returning to my discussion in chapter 5 of boats as utopic forms, it is noteworthy that the final scene of *Happy-Go-Lucky* ends with a boat, with Poppy on a boat with Zoe. The film's utopia is expressed in terms of the ease and good humor of their intimacy.

We can thus recognize how a critique of happiness can be offered as an affirmative gesture. We would not be calling for an affirmative approach to life, or calling for affirmation as an ethics. Rather we would be affirming the possibilities of life in whatever happens; we would be opening up possibilities that are negated by the very demand that we live our lives in the right way. Silliness — and all those forms of happiness that are deemed superficial — can thus be instructive. In coming to value that which is not valued, and in finding joy in places that are not deemed worthy, we learn about the costs of value and worth. The happy-go-lucky character might seem unweighed by duty and responsibility; she might seem light as a feather. She might seem careless and carefree. But freedom from care is also a freedom to care, to respond to the world, to what comes up, without defending oneself or one's happiness against what comes up.

I am not suggesting here that a response to my critique of happiness is to become happy-go-lucky. Rather, we can recognize that the figures of the feminist killjoy, unhappy queer, and melancholic migrant have a rather queer kinship with being happy-go-lucky. Unhappiness with and rage about injustice may even be on a continuum with good feelings that are read as careless and silly. To embrace silliness is to embrace affects that would not ordinarily participate in an affirmative or happiness ethics. Our unhappy archives are unsurprisingly full of silliness and other inappropriately positive affects, as Lauren Berlant's reflections on the "counterpolitics of the silly object" might suggest (1997: 12).[19] The freedom to be unhappy, which I explored in the last chapter, would thus include the freedom to be happy in inappropriate ways. Such freedoms would lighten the happiness load. The freedom to be unhappy would thus not leave happiness behind us. We would aim to put the hap back into happiness.

We have to struggle for such freedoms, and we inherit the labor of such histories of struggle. The struggle against happiness as a necessity is also a struggle for happiness as a possibility. I now think of political movements as hap movements rather than happiness movements. It is not about the unhappy ones becoming the happy ones. Far from it. Revolutionary forms of political consciousness involve heightening our awareness of *just how much* there is to be unhappy about. Given that the desire for happiness can cover signs of its negation, a revolutionary politics has to work hard to stay proximate to unhappiness. And yet, a politics of the hap does not simply hold on to unhappiness or turn unhappiness into a political cause. Just recall that one of the definitions of the wretch is "a poor or hapless being." Perhaps we could separate the hapless from the wretched. The wretched ones might be full of hap, might be hapfull, *because* they deviate from the paths of happiness, because they live in the gaps between its lines. To be full of hap is to make happen. A politics of the hap is about opening up possibilities for being in other ways, of being perhaps. If opening up possibility causes unhappiness, then a politics of hap will be thought of as unhappy. But it is not just that. A politics of the hap might embrace what happens, but it also works toward a world in which things can happen in alternative ways. To make hap is to make a world.

NOTES

Introduction

1   There are so many articulations of this belief that it is difficult to choose whom
    to quote. I open with this quote as it uses everyday language to describe an
    idea that is both everyday and philosophical: that happiness is what we aim
    for. Probably one of the most dramatic philosophical articulations of the prin-
    ciple was offered in the seventeenth century by Blaise Pascal, who argued:
    "All men seek happiness. This is without exception. Whatever different means
    they employ, they all tend to this end. The cause of some going to war, and of
    others avoiding it, is the same desire in both, attended with different views.
    The will never takes the least step but to this object. This is the motive of every
    action, of every man, even of those who hang themselves" ([1669] 1910: 138).
    This rather extraordinary insistence on the universality of happiness as a mo-
    tive of the will involves an equally extraordinary discussion of the necessary
    failure of happiness, which clearly anticipated the psychoanalytic enterprise:
    "What is it then this desire and this inability proclaim to us, but that there
    was once in man a true happiness of which there now remain to him only the
    mark and empty trace, which he in vain tries to fill from all his surroundings,
    seeking from things absent to help he does not obtain in things present? But
    these are all inadequate, because the infinite abyss can only be filled by an
    infinite and immutable object, that is to say, only by God Himself" (138–39).
2   The following are some of the key books published in the last few years: Layard
    2005; McMahon 2006; Nettle 2006; Gilbert 2006; Haidt 2006; Schoch 2006;

de Botton 2006. See the collection of essays on happiness that I edited in *New Formations* (2008) for some perspectives from cultural studies, as well as the humanities more broadly.

3 Examples of recent books on happiness that we could describe as popular psychology or "how-to" manuals include Summers and Watson 2006, Seligman 2003, Holden 1998, Ricard 2007. One of the most popular books on happiness is based on a series of interviews between the Dalai Lama and Howard C. Cutler (1998).

4 For example, the *Independent on Sunday* had a special, "The Secrets of Happiness: Why the Ancients Hold the Key," March 17, 2006. Information about the BBC program *The Happiness Formula* can be accessed at http://news.bbc.co.uk. Last visited February 11, 2009.

5 See: http://www.happyplanetindex.org. The results of global surveys of happiness are debated in the journal *Happiness Studies*. Last visited February 11, 2009.

6 See http://www.nriol.com. Last visited February 11, 2009.

7 For details of David Cameron's speech about happiness, see http://news.bbc .co.uk. Last visited February 11, 2009.

8 GPI was first coined by three Californian researchers in 1995. Along with 400 leading economists, business leaders, and professionals, they stated: "Since the GDP measures only the quantity of market activity without accounting for the social and ecological costs involved, it is both inadequate and misleading as a measure of true prosperity. Policy-makers, economists, the media, and international agencies should cease using the GDP as a measure of progress and publicly acknowledge its shortcomings. New indicators of progress are urgently needed to guide our society . . . The GPI is an important step in this direction." For further information about GPI and the genealogy of the term, see http://www.gpiatlantic.org. Last visited February 11, 2009.

9 One study reveals what should be obvious: if you ask subjects how happy they are after asking them about positive topics, you are more likely to get higher happiness levels reported than if you ask them how happy they are after asking them questions about negative topics: "Subjects who had previously been induced to think about positive aspects of their present life described themselves as happier and more satisfied with their life-as-a-whole than subjects who had been induced to think about negative aspects" (Schwarz and Strack 1991: 28).

10 We can see the problems with such an approach when feelings become measures of rights and wrongs. Richard Layard, for example, argues that what makes something wrong is that it makes people unhappy, or even offends peoples' feelings. For Layard, the science of happiness is "inherently" pro-poor and for the redistribution of wealth as inequalities increase unhappiness (2005: 120–21): though the unfortunate implication of his argument is that if

inequalities did not increase unhappiness, then he would not be against them. As he describes: "American slaves wanted their freedom, not because it would give them higher incomes, but because of the humiliation of being a slave. Slavery offended their feelings, and that is why slavery is wrong" (121). The idea that slavery was wrong because it hurt people's feelings shows us what is wrong with this model of wrong. It individuates and psychologizes social wrongs. See Lauren Berlant's (2000) important critique of the conflation of pain and injustice, as well as my conclusion to *The Cultural Politics of Emotion* (2004) for a reflection on the relationship between social wrongs and hurt. Note in particular that one of the problems of the conflation of injustice with hurt is that it presumes access to the other's feelings. Any forms of wrong that are not accompanied by consciously felt suffering that can be spoken about to others would become invisible in such a model.

11   The implication of my suggestion here is that the contemporary moment of the "financial crisis" in which I have completed this book will not mean a withdrawal of public or private concern with happiness but if anything may heighten the cultural preoccupation with happiness (perhaps as an uneasiness in the want of the good life for those who feel they did have and should still have a good life).

12   See http://www.ppc.sas.upenn.edu. Last visited February 11, 2009.

13   Take the following comment from Fay Weldon's book on women and happiness. She argues, "The fight for gender equality is bad for the looks. It makes no one happy, unless you find some reward in struggling for a justice that evolution failed to deliver. It will just develop your jaw, wrinkle your brow beyond the capacity of Botox to unravel, muddy your complexion so much that no amount of Beauty Flash will clear it, and in general do you no good" (2006: 52). Weldon argues that unhappiness will make you look bad, and that unhappiness is caused by fighting for equality. To be happy is to look better. For Weldon happiness means not fighting for equality in order to be more attractive, in order for women to get better men. Happiness becomes a technique for self-promotion (redescribed as evolutionary fitness). As I explore in chapter 2, research into happiness and women tends to promote a return to traditional forms of femininity. Happiness is linked to passivity, which challenges the conventional association of happiness with activity. I discuss the alignment of happiness and activity in the conclusion to this book.

14   I am not suggesting here that the Aristotelian approach to *eudaimonia* can be reduced to this critique. I am simply questioning *the gesture* that idealizes classical happiness over contemporary happiness. The long Aristotelian traditions of writing on happiness as virtue offer alternative concepts of the good life that arguably are based on a less exclusive or particular concept of life. Alasdair MacIntyre's work, for example, describes virtue as "an acquired human quality the possession and exercise of which tends to enable us to

achieve those goods which are internal to practices and the lack of which effectively prevents us from achieving any such goods" (1981: 178). See also MacIntyre's preface to the revised tradition of *The Unconscious: A Conceptual Analysis* (2004), where he develops a defense of an Aristotelian concept of a "teleologically structured life" against psychoanalytic models. Indeed, he suggests that a psychoanalytic critique of neurosis is "not only compatible with but in need of just such a conception of human flourishing." However, MacIntyre's subsequent redefinition of human flourishing as "the actualization of [human] distinctive potentialities issues in reason-informed activity" might still rely on an exclusive model of what counts as life worth living (34–35). Thanks to David Glover for suggesting this clarification.

15 Aristotle argues that the "man engaged in Contemplative Speculation" needs less external goods than other kinds of virtuous men (1998: 193). He suggests that external goods could even be a hindrance to the speculative philosopher in terms of doing the work of speculation but are nevertheless necessary: "he will need such things for maintaining his character as Man though not as a speculative philosopher" (193). Herein lays the political economy: the reproduction of the capacity to live the good life of the philosopher subject, which is to be maintained in your character as Man, may depend upon other people's labor. Such labor would support the philosopher and would thus stay in the background, rather like furniture. See my reading of Husserl, the labor of philosophy, and the "background" of domestic labour in *Queer Phenomenology* (2006).

16 However, within queer cultural studies there has been a turn to theorizing positive affects and emotions, as can be seen in the work of Lauren Berlant (2008a, 2008b) and Michael D. Snediker (2009) on optimism, as well as José Esteban Muñoz (2007) on hope and utopia.

17 I should acknowledge here that in following the word *happiness* around, I am in some cases following a translation into English from other languages, including classical and modern languages (for example *eudaimonia*, *le bonheur* and *glück*). There is no doubt we lose things in translation, including an ability to track the specific histories of association for each of these words. To acknowledge this loss is not however to make the act of translation impossible. In following happiness in translation, I am also accepting a convention: I am accepting how others have translated words into this word.

18 Colebrook uses Nietzsche's new philosophical concept of happiness to exemplify this distinction: "Happiness is the capacity or power to live one's life *actively*-affirming the particularity or specificity of one's moment in time" (2002: 19). It is noticeable, however, that this "new concept" does not look very different from old concepts of happiness, many of which are predicated on the idea of happiness as "activity," as I discuss in my conclusion to this book. We can learn from the inheritance of the old in the language of the new:

philosophy is not beyond habits in refusing to learn from the everyday but has its own habits.

19   Two books were published in 2008 that offer substantial critiques of happiness, although both are from outside philosophy: Eric G. Wilson's *Against Happiness* and Zygmunt Bauman's *The Art of Life*, representing the disciplines of literature and sociology respectively. I wonder (writing in early 2009) whether the tide of happiness is turning, and whether this tide will also turn (in) philosophy.

20   I will engage with ethics throughout this book, especially in chapter 1 and the conclusion. In terms of political philosophy it is useful to note that Giorgio Agamben makes happiness crucial to his definition of the political nature of the human being as "the only beings for whom happiness is always at stake in their living, the only beings whose life is irremediably and painfully assigned to happiness. But this immediately constitutes the form-of-life as political life" ([1996] 2000: 4). In making happiness what is at stake, Agamben does not make happiness into an end but a question, even a painful question. The question of the human becomes a happiness question, as a question of how to live, a question of how to live well.

21   It should be obvious how much of my work is shaped by my interest in psychoanalysis in part through the vocabularies I use (displacement, conversion, etc.). However, this book does not offer a psychoanalysis of happiness: my questions are not posed at the level of the subject. I am interested in the distribution of happiness in psychic and social fields and have theoretical commitments that include phenomenology and Marxism as well as feminist, antiracist, and queer theories. If anything this book involves a messy sort of empiricism: I am interested in describing our experience of the world in the very forms of its emergence. I cannot have a system in place before I get to the point of description without losing the possibility of description. Psychoanalysis demands too much from me: it is a school of thought I draw on eclectically but will always fail to reproduce. There are places readers can go for a psychoanalysis of happiness: think not only of Freud's *Civilization and its Discontents* ([1930] 2004) (which was originally proposed as *Unhappiness in Civilization* [McMahon 2006: 442]) and Lacan's *The Ethics of Psychoanalysis* ([1986] 1992), but also Slavoj Žižek's critiques of happiness in *Welcome to the Desert of the Real* (2002) and *In Defence of Lost Causes* (2008a) and Jonathan Lear's *Happiness, Death, and the Remainder of Life* (2000), which reads Freud alongside Aristotle.

22   As Mark T. Conard suggests in relation to philosophy, "There is comparatively little discussion about unhappiness, except as it's seen as simply the result of someone's having failed to achieve happiness" (2007: 53) There are of course exceptions. Jean-Luc Nancy's *The Sense of the World* offers a powerful consideration of unhappiness that does not make happiness its reference point:

"There is nothing to be said of happiness, as the idyllic version of sense, the immanence of sense bought at a discount, the simple denegation of unhappiness" ([1993] 1997: 145). Nancy not only refuses the sublimation offered by happiness but also implies unhappiness is what "makes sense." See also my conclusion for a brief discussion of Nancy on happenstance.

23 It is worth commenting on the relationship between my argument and Hegel's thesis that periods of happiness are "the empty pages of history" as "times when the antithesis is missing," ([1837] 1988: 29), which seems to imply that the very activity of history depends upon unhappiness and negation. I am writing about the history of happiness as a concept-word: happiness provides a horizon for thought. The overdetermination of happiness as a concept-word is not unrelated to how happiness appears and disappears in history. I would argue that happiness in history is not blank or that the blankness is an illusion that preserves the regulative power of happiness as an idea. In other words, the blankness of happiness is not the sign of the absence of struggle or negativity. We just cannot see the signs of struggle or negation when happiness is given. Happiness only appears blank—or as a blank—because we have learned not to notice what happens when things "go along" and we "get along." This book explores what is erased by signs of "getting along" including the labor which creates the impression of blankness.

24 These definitions are all taken from the *Oxford English Dictionary* (OED). All subsequent definitions and etymological references in this book are drawn from the OED.

1. Happy Objects

1 This chapter will offer an approach to thinking through affect as "sticky." Affect is what sticks, or what sustains or preserves the connection between ideas, values, and objects. My argument that affect is a form of stickiness contrasts with Brian Massumi's work, which suggests that affects are autonomous and distinct from emotions. For Massumi emotion is "qualified intensity" or "a subjective content, the sociolinguistic fixing of the quality of experience which is from that point onward defined as personal" while affects are "intensity" that is unqualified and beyond narrative (2002b: 28). I think that the distinction between affect/emotion can under-describe the work of emotions, which *involve* forms of intensity, bodily orientation, and direction that are not simply about "subjective content" or qualification of intensity. Emotions are not "after-thoughts" but shape how bodies are moved by the worlds they inhabit (see Ahmed 2004). I would also argue that the intensities that Massumi describes as affect are "directed" as well as "qualified" or even "congealed": this directedness is not simply about subjects and interior feeling states but

about how things cohere *in a certain way*. While you can separate an affective response from an emotion that is attributed as such (the bodily sensations from the feeling of being afraid), this does not mean that in practice, or in everyday life, they are separate. In fact, they are contiguous; they slide into each other; they stick, and cohere, even when they are separated. The "fear affect" can be separated from the self-conscious recognition of being afraid (the flicker in the corner of the eye signalling the presence of the stranger, which registers as a disturbance on the skin before we have recognized the stranger as a stranger). However, this does mean the "fear affect" is autonomous. Before we are affected, before something happens that creates an impression on the skin, things are already in place that incline us to be affected in some ways more than others. To read affect we need better understandings of this "in place," and how the "in place" involves psychic and social dimensions, which means that the "in place" is not always in the same place. For example, the flicker is more likely to become an emotion that we retrospectively recognize as fear in places that are already given affective value as fearsome (the "rough neighborhood" is one that we anticipate to be frightening), or for somebody whose body remembers other flickers becoming frightening. See Clare Hemmings (2005) and Imogen Tyler (2008) for related critiques of the "autonomy of affect." See also Sianne Ngai, who offers a contrasting approach to the difference between affect/emotion as "a modal difference of intensity or degree, rather than a formal difference of quality or kind" (2005: 27).

2   For an analysis of the contingency of sensations, see chapter 1 of my *The Cultural Politics of Emotion*. Pleasure and pain could be described as sensations caused by objects (for example the sensation of pain in my foot might be caused by a nail), although as I will argue, via Hume and Nietzsche, such causalities might involve habitual forms of association that are retrospective as well as anticipatory. However, even if we were to assume that sensations were caused by objects, it does follow that sensations can be easily separated from other aspects of human experience. Pleasure has been understood as a complex feeling. For David L. Perry, pleasure is described as a "sort of a feeling" and as having specific kinds of intentional qualities: we receive pleasure from things that give us pleasure (1967: 98). For J. C. B. Gosling, pleasure "belongs to the class of things which are modifications of our awareness, like sensations and feelings" (1969: 29). Interestingly, the philosopher who offers the queerest definition of pleasure that I have found in my research for this book is the one who is often evoked in quite somber terms as a stark utilitarian: Jeremy Bentham. He describes pleasures as "interesting perceptions" and suggests that "by the bent of a man's inclinations may be understood the propensity he has to expect pleasure and pain from certain objects, rather than from others" ([1789] 2007: 49). He then suggests that a person could be described as having "such or such a bent" if "he is apt to expect more pleasure

from one particular sort, than from another particular sort" (49). If pleasure is how we turn toward certain things, then pleasure is always bent. Pleasure for Bentham is a bodily orientation that reveals a social orientation, a tendency to have a certain tendency. The importance of thinking about happiness as contiguous with pleasure sensations is that it allows us to keep our attention on the bodily dimensions of happiness. I do not want to take the body out of happiness.

3   I should acknowledge here that Spinoza suggests that being affected, even joyfully, is a form of passivity, in which the idea formed is inadequate or confused. An affect "is a passion" which thus "ceases to be a passion as soon as we form a clear and distinct idea of it" ([1677] 2001: 231). The ethical task for Spinoza is thus to become free from "the bondage" of passions through reason: "It is therefore most profitable to us in life to make perfect the intellect or reason as far as possible, and in this one thing consists the highest happiness or blessedness of man" (217). To be blessed would be to have adequate ideas, or to be the cause of your own ideas: "he is led adequately to conceive himself and all things which can be conceived by his intelligence" (217). See my conclusion for some further discussion of Spinoza (or to be more accurate, Deleuze's Spinoza), with specific reference to the passive/active distinction.

4   This book draws on phenomenology but I would not say it offers a phenomenology of happiness, as my own points of reference here are primarily outside this intellectual tradition. Or if it does offer a phenomenology of happiness, it would be a rather queer phenomenology (see Ahmed 2006). A phenomenology of happiness is perhaps yet to be written, although of course there is considerable literature on phenomenology and emotion more generally (a classic essay would be Sartre [1939] 2002; see also Solomon 2006 for further references). A phenomenology of happiness might draw on Husserl's later work, in particular his approach to the living body (*Leib*), affect and value, and the life-world, which is often represented as his shift from a static to a genetic and then generative phenomenology (see Thompson 2007: 28–36). I should note here that Husserl's model offers a quite different model of affect and value than we find in Locke's empirical psychology in which "to be affected" is to give value to things. Henning Peucker suggests that Husserl would be critical of any sentimentalism that would describe feelings as "giving things specific value properties" (2007: 312). Peucker's own task is to show how Husserl critiques the Kantian presumption that all moral feeling is pathological. According to Peucker, Husserl mediates between Kant and the sentimentalists by arguing that things already have value properties: "the ego is thus affected by objects with value properties" (316).

5   In David Hume's discussion of the relationship between ideas and impressions in *A Treatise of Human Nature* ([1739–40] 1985: 49–55), he suggests that impressions are more lively. Memory and imagination are described as the two

faculties in which we "repeat our impressions" (56) involving the connection or association between ideas in the form of contiguity and resemblance. Hume offers a rich reflection on what we might call empirical psychology and the habits of sense making. See Deleuze's excellent analysis ([1953] 1991) of Hume's contribution. Also note how much the Freudian concern with displacement and condensation and the Lacanian concern with metaphor and metonymy are consistent with Hume's associationism. English empiricism and psychoanalysis can be described as potentially productive bedfellows.

6 See the second section of chapter 5 for an extension of this argument with reference to irritability and cheerfulness.

7 The precarious nature of happiness as a feeling is described very well by John Stuart Mill in his autobiography in an often cited sentence: "Ask yourself whether you are happy and you cease to be so" ([1873] 2003: 100). It is Mill's own unhappiness that leads him to the recognition of precarity, which he also describes as a disillusionment with utilitarianism, and an awareness that "some end external to happiness" needs to be "the purpose of life" (100). For a discussion of happiness as precarious, see also my conclusion, note 16.

8 Although classical and utilitarian traditions are often represented as very different, they share a teleological conception of happiness. For Aristotle, happiness is the end point for individuals, defining what it would mean to have lived a virtuous life. For utilitarians, happiness is the end point for government, defining what it would mean to have the best society.

9 The way in which a teleological model of happiness makes "all other things" "happiness means" is explicit in John Stuart Mill's utilitarianism. As he puts it, "The utilitarian doctrine is that happiness is desirable and the only thing desirable, as an end; all other things being only desirable as means to that end" ([1863] 2001: 35). While there is considerable scholarship on the significance of happiness as a *telos* or end, there has been less attention given to what this means "for all other things," that is, to what it means when other goods *become good as means to the happiness end.*

10 I am not suggesting that Aristotle makes happiness instrumental. Happiness is not an end in the sense of being something imposed from the outside to govern the emergence of life. Rather, for Aristotle, to achieve happiness would be to actualize your potential; the happy man is the man who achieves his ideal form, who flourishes in a biological as well as ethical sense. I am simply suggesting that if happiness is understood organically as the end of life, then other things become instrumental to the achievement of happiness, to actualizing your potential. It would be useful to consider further the relationship between Aristotle's teleological model of biology and his teleological model of happiness. See Challenger 1994: 75–76 and Annas 1993: 139 for some relevant observations.

11 I will be exploring the relationship between freedom and happiness throughout the book and in particular how the freedom to be happy is a fantasy of

freedom that conceals how happiness directs us toward some life choices and not others. In the final section of chapter 5, I explore an alternative freedom as the freedom to be unhappy.

12 Nietzsche is drawing on David Hume, who argues that causal thinking is itself a form of habit: "This transition of thought from the cause to the effect proceeds not from reason. It derives its origin altogether from custom and experience" ([1748] 1975: 54). I might also suggest here a relationship between the attribution of causality and identification. My sister and I always argued about the causes of road accidents. She would say that slower drivers caused accidents, because they caused fast drivers to feel impatient. I would say that fast drivers caused road accidents because they were impatient. Where we attribute the cause related to our own self-identification as fast drivers (my sister) or slow drivers (myself), which in turn allows us to establish ourselves as occupying the sphere of normality or neutrality. I thought she went "too fast" and she thought I went "too slow." Note also that attributions of causality are stopping devices: you go back "so far" to establish causality, and you go back as far as you need to go to protect yourself from becoming attributed as the cause of something that is evaluated as negative. So for my sister, her impatience was caused (by drivers who wanted to go slow like me), and for me, her impatience was the cause (because she wanted to go faster than she should).

13 As I will show in due course, this is why the experience of affirmation is not always conscious but takes place in the background, as it allows subjects to keep going the way they are going.

14 Clearly, to describe objects as happiness-causes is a stronger claim than to describe them as happiness-means. The latter implies that doing or having certain things will enable you to approach happiness without necessarily causing happiness. For an object to be a happiness-cause is to say that happiness is a necessary effect of doing or having something. I will extend my argument by thinking about the desire to be a happiness-cause in chapter 3.

15 The promise of happiness imposes (implicit or explicit) conditions: you are promised happiness in return for fulfilling certain conditions. For an extension of the argument about how happiness involves conditions (what I call simply conditional happiness), see the first section of chapter 2.

16 Earlier on in How To Do Things with Words, Austin suggests that even an insincere promise is still a promise: it is not void even if it is given in bad faith (11). He later describes any failure of intention as an infelicity (40): so a promise can not promise even if it has been worded as a promise. A promise can thus be an explicit performative and be unhappy if the right conditions are not in place. I should note here that in this book, I will consider happiness and unhappiness in language not simply in terms of the effects that words have, whether they succeed or fail in doing what they say, but also as being in the words; happiness when named in speech is in on the act.

17   It is useful to compare Locke and Kant on this point. Locke, despite his emphasis on happiness as intrinsically good, offers an empirical psychology that
makes uneasiness more compelling. Kant, despite his refusal of the relationship between happiness and the good, describes happiness as the basis of the
pragmatic law, as what is most compelling. Kant thus has a stronger thesis on
happiness as the motor of human action than Locke. This is one of the reasons I find the Lacanian alliance with Kant somewhat perplexing (see Lacan
2006: 645–70, Zupančič 2000), even though I understand that they share a
thesis that ethics must be thought outside happiness and that this requires
a certain formalism (whether defined in terms of the law of duty or desire).
Even if Kant defines the moral law as beyond happiness, he does so only by
making an overly strong thesis of happiness as a pragmatic law, which does
not really allow us to go beyond the pleasure principle. See also my conclusion, note 13.

18   I find Hobbes's definition of desire in *Leviathan* helpful for its emphasis on
bodily motion. He defines desire as a motion-endeavor that "is toward something which causes it" ([1651] 1968: 119). I consider affects as evaluation that
turn us toward and away from objects that are attributed as the cause not only
of the affect but also of the motion. So I turn toward or away from the other
given how they have affected me, where the turning is assumed to be caused
by the other.

19   I am reminded here of Adorno and Horkeimer's critique of the empty promises of the culture industry. They argue that "the culture industry perpetually
cheats its consumers of what it perpetually promises. The promissory note
which, with its plots and staging, it draws on pleasure is endlessly prolonged;
the promise, which is actually all the spectacle consists of, is illusory" ([1944]
1997: 139). One might be tempted to wonder whether the location of false
promises within the culture industry allows us to sustain the fantasy that
there is a full promise, a promise that can keep its promise that resides elsewhere. My reading of the promise of happiness will question this fantasy of
fullness, suggesting that promises are always in some sense empty; they can
never keep their word, as what is sent out does not simply return.

20   Narratives after all are "directed." The narrative "moves forward" toward
something: the ending. The shape of the narrative could be described as its
plot; events are sequenced in time to explain how things happen; how as it
were one thing leads to another. As Peter Brooks argues, plot is "what shapes a
story and gives it a certain direction or intent of meaning" (1984: xi); it is "the
activity of shaping" which allows us to "read forward" (xiii). Indeed, Brooks
relates the act of plotting to a form of desire that moves us through the text:
"Narratives portray the motors of desire that drive and consume their plots,
and they also lay bare the nature of narration as a form of human desire: the
need to tell as a primary human drive that seeks to seduce and to subjugate the

listener, to implicate him in the thrust of a desire that never can quite speak its name—never can quite come to the point—but that insists on speaking over and over again its movement toward that name" (61). This rather thrusting language of desire gives us a very specific version of the movement of narrative. Putting this point aside for one moment, however, we can see the forward movement of narrative is what might give us its point, even when we don't reach that point. Reading for narrative is reading for the direction of its point. If happiness is the point, then it must always be deferred. As D. A. Miller argues in his classic account of narrative and its discontents: "The narrative of happiness is inevitably frustrated by the fact that only insufficiencies, defaults, deferrals, can be 'told.' Even when a narrative 'prepares for' happiness, it remains in this state of lack, which can only be liquidated along with the narrative itself. Accordingly, the narration of happiness might be thought to exemplify the unhappiness of narrative in general" (2002: 272). See Colebrook 2008 for a discussion of narrative happiness. In this book, I am interested in happiness not only as a narrative ending but as a conversion point within narrative. In particular, I will attend to how happiness speech acts such as "I just want you to be happy" are crucial to the twists and turns of narrative.

21   In *The Cultural Politics of Emotion*, I examined happiness as a form of waiting. Happiness might be how waiting for something can acquire a sense of meaning or purpose and can thus be endured, as it points toward something (see Ahmed 2004: 196–97). The failure to achieve happiness in the present can even extend one's investment in a certain path of action: if the more one waits, the more one gives up, then *the more one waits, the harder it is to give up.* The more one persists unhappily on a path of happiness, the harder it is to give up on that path. Unhappiness can thus be what makes happiness harder to give up.

22   My qualification of the chanciness and contingency of happiness suggests that happiness involves a way of being directed, such that we will find happiness in some places more than others. However, I am not arguing that happiness does not involve contingency. Even if you have been directed a certain way, we do not always know what will happen, how we will be affected, by what comes near. The hap of happiness does matter. See my conclusion for more reflections on the politics and ethics of the hap. We might need to recognize how the hap has been taken out of happiness before we can put the hap back in.

23   See chapter 4, where I explore the civilizing mission in terms of giving the other good habits. I note in this chapter how bad habits of the natives are identified with their confusion of the object that causes pleasure with the good. Good habits are thus distinguished from primitive fetishism. What we could call civilized happiness projects fetishism onto the other, failing to recognize how much it still locates the promise of happiness in proximity to objects,

even if those objects are valued through their apparent refusal of insistence on proximity.

24   Annas also provides a very useful discussion of Kant's rejection of the model of habituation. She shows how Kant equates habit formation with moral passivity, such that to form habits would be to lose your freedom (1993: 52). Annas argues that Kant presumes habituation is purely mechanical and thus fails to acknowledge the role of activity, purpose, and agency in virtue-based ethics. I am suggesting that the Kantian contrast between habit and freedom is what allows freedom to be secured as a fantasy: the moral subject is the one for whom freedom has become a habit, such that the habitual nature of this freedom disappears from view.

25   We could ask some speculative questions here about the relationship between moral feeling and action. To feel bad about what is bad would be a sign of virtue in this model. But feeling bad can also be a way that people allow themselves to do what they otherwise know they should not do. Someone can feel bad about something even as a way of giving him/herself permission to do something. Bad feeling thus can allow someone to maintain a good idea of him/herself (I felt bad or guilty about doing x, which shows that I am "really" not bad in doing x). Bad feeling can lead to a moral permissiveness: you can do anything as long as you feel bad about it! Such uses of bad feeling could be described in terms of the politics of good feeling: you can feel good about yourself because you feel bad about x. So, for example, a nation could feel good, or retain its ego ideal as being good, because it feels bad about its racist history.

26   The idea that we have a moral duty to be happy can rest on a contagious model of happiness: because others can catch happiness *from us*, we must be happy *for them*. For an early argument that links contagion and duty, see Daniel Garrison Brinton's *The Pursuit of Happiness*, published in 1893. Brinton argues that we have a moral duty to promote our own happiness in order to be able to promote the happiness of others: "Mental moods are contagious and a man who enjoys little will prove a killjoy to others . . . But as a rule people are not happy whose pleasures are assigned them by others. . . . Before we are qualified to make others happy we must compass happiness in some degree for ourselves; and our success with others will be just to that degree and no more. The quality and intensity of enjoyment which we ourselves have is alone that which we are able to impart to others" (12–13). I will take up this association between the killjoy and the joyless in the following chapter. For a more recent example which links contagion with duty, see Gretchen Rubin's website (http://www.happiness-project.com; last visited February 9, 2009), which is dedicated to her research on happiness. As she describes: "'Emotional contagion' is the psychological phenomenon by which we 'infect' each other with our moods. The fact that my friend was so happy to be at the concert lifted all of us up. Remember the Second Splendid Truth: One of the

best ways to make *yourself* happy is to make *other people* happy; one of the best ways to make *other people* happy is to be happy *yourself*." I should also note here that the happiness duty does not necessarily rest on a contagion model: we can have a happiness duty if it is assumed that through being happy we can better influence or promote the happiness of others (through suggestion, inspiration, compassion, as moral leadership, or by example). As I will explore in the following chapters, the happiness duty can involve not only the duty to be happy in order to cause the happiness of others but also the duty to be happy in order to fulfill one's debt to others.

27 My model of sociable emotion is quite different because I think of affects as already directed toward and shaped by contact with objects. I thus place a strong emphasis on reception as a form of conversion: I might be affected in quite different ways by your happiness, or what I feel is your happiness, depending on my mood, depending on my relation to you, depending on my view of what you are happy about (which may or may not be consciously held), and so on. So your happiness does not necessarily make me happy, even if I love you and I imagine that my happiness is conditional on yours. I will be exploring the complex relation between love and happiness in the following three chapters, especially in the first section of chapter 3.

28 Hume argues in his *Enquiries Concerning the Principles of Morals* that we are more likely to catch happiness from others because happiness as such is agreeable to us: the happy person "is a more animating spectacle; his presence diffuses over us a more serene complacency and enjoyment; our imagination, entering into his feelings and disposition is affected in a more agreeable manner than if a melancholy, dejected, sullen, anxious temper was presented to us" ([1748] 1975: 251). I should acknowledge here that Hume does not rest his theory of compassion on contagion or infection: rather he emphasizes the role of imagination, involvement, and interest (for a good discussion, see Swanton 2000, especially 162–63). David Hume's use of affective contagion as the basis for sympathetic happiness does contrast in interesting ways with Adam Smith's *A Theory of Moral Sentiments*. In Smith's model, sympathetic happiness is more explicitly conditional: even if happiness is agreeable, and even if it is agreeable to be sympathetic, you enter into another's happiness only if you agree with it, in the sense that you think such happiness is appropriate and is expressed appropriately. As he describes quite dramatically: "It gives us the spleen, on the other hand, to see another too happy, or too much elevated, as we call it, with any little piece of good fortune. We are *disobliged even with his joy*; and, because we cannot go along with it, call it levity and folly" ([1759] 2000: 13; emphasis added). For Smith, to be affected sympathetically is dependent on whether emotions "appear to this last, just and proper, and suitable to their objects" (14). His model of conditional happiness thus derives from his model of conditional sympa-

thy. I would also argue that sharing emotion involves conditional judgment. Rather than saying that we share happiness if we agree with its object (which makes the agreement secondary), I would say that to share in the happiness of others is how we come to have a direction toward something, which is *already* an agreement that the object is appropriate. To get along is to go along with a certain direction.

29 Brennan explains this tension between these two aspects of argument by suggesting that if I am picking up on an affect, "the thoughts I attach to that affect, remain my own" (7). The distinction between feeling and thought exercised here suggests that even if feelings are social or shared, thoughts will remain individual and private. I am interested in what follows when this distinction does not hold: when affects are not shared or picked up by others, and when thoughts are shared with others. For example you and I might have the same thought "come to mind" but be affected differently by that very thought; the affects attached to it "remain our own." Memory can work like this: we might both be reminded of somebody by what a third party says, but the thought of that person will affect us differently, depending on our relation to that person. To explore this opacity of social thought and feeling we need to think more about our models of the social. We might assume that affects are social and even sociable insofar as they are shared, or transmitted from one to another. But we need to think about the social as an experience, as well as object of experience, that is not always shared: feelings of tension, antagonism and even "apartness" can be understood as part of the fabric of social life rather than a sign of its failure or absence. What "remains my own" in the sense of not being given or available to others (although what "remains my own" is not necessarily given or available to myself as psychoanalysis would teach us) would be what connects us to others. My reading of *Mrs. Dalloway* in chapter 2 offers such a model.

30 Of course that it is the bride who must be happy, who must bear the burden of the happiness of the day, teaches us something about gender and its uneven distributions of what we might call "happiness hopes." It teaches us to notice what might seem obvious. If we search for the happiness of the bride to confirm the happiness of the day, then happiness hopes for women remain tied to marriage, even if the scripts of gender have become more flexible. See the following chapter for further discussion of the relationship between happiness scripts and gendered scripts. I also want to recognize here the importance of Arlie Hochschild's *The Managed Heart* to my own project. Hochschild stresses the role of "feeling rules" and "emotional labor." Feeling rules are "what guide emotion work by establishing the sense of entitlement or obligation that governs emotional exchanges" ([1983] 2003: 56; see also Hochschild 2003). My own model, which focuses on how we are directed by the promise of happiness, shares key premises with her work, as we can see for instance in my description of happiness as a good habit. But rather

than considering emotions in terms of rules that govern behavior (by being enforced by others and eventually incorporated by subjects), I will be focusing on the more subtle processes of affirmation, encouragement, and support through which subjects are turned toward certain objects, which become social goods that circulate and accumulate value, thus acquiring the "capacity" to turn subjects. I would describe the difference as a difference in emphasis rather than a difference in argument. Further work on happiness as a project or technique of management (including the management of organizations as well as self-management) that draws on Hochschild's model would provide a major contribution to the literatures of happiness studies.

31 Affect aliens are those who do not desire in the right way. As I suggested earlier, classical conceptions of happiness involve the regulation of desire. Appropriate desire is expressed in an appropriate way toward appropriate objects. Of course, desire is regulated precisely because we often fail to desire in the right way. You might want to want x. But as soon as you want to want something you are admitting that you don't really want that thing. You cannot always make yourself want what you want to want (just as you cannot always make the other want what you want or what you want them to want). Rather than simply becoming disappointed, or full of wretchedness, affect aliens might give up wanting what one wants to want, and want other things.

32 Happiness can convert very quickly into anger in political as well as psychic life. One discourse of citizenship, for example, turns happiness into an entitlement. The failure of the nation to deliver its promise of happiness converts very swiftly into anger toward others (foreigners, migrants, asylum seekers) who have stolen the happiness that is assumed "by right" to be ours. This conversion is often expressed through the language of deprivation: the other has deprived us of the good life. This narrative of stolen happiness is what allows the fantasy of happiness (as what would have come to us if only they had not arrived) to be preserved.

33 As I argued earlier, via Nietzsche, objects can lag behind feelings (in the sense that one might feel pain and then look for the object, which becomes the pain cause after the event), and feelings can lag behind objects (once we associate the object with an affect, then the object can cause the affect). Feelings and objects can switch places in this causal economy. The point of the lag is that it teaches us about the temporality of what we might call affective mediation.

34 The word *passing* is of course also used to refer to death (to "pass away"). Passing can thus describe a cessation: when something passes it ceases to exist. Perhaps there is a little death in each moment of passing if what passes ceases to be itself in passing. A little death is also a little birth of something, an emergence of something that was not there before.

35 The name of this game is of course problematic. Rosalind Ballaster argues that "the sinophobic name points to the centuries-old tradition in Europe of

representing spoken Chinese as an incomprehensible and unpronounceable combination of sounds" (2005: 202–3). In the United States, the game is typically called "Telephone," reminding us perhaps of the role of technology in the perversion of affect.

36 Of course, the threat of contagions resides not only in transmission but also in mutation; as the virus spreads (through touch), it can reproduce itself such that it becomes other.

37 Nostalgia involves affective conversion. Nostalgia is an affective state that resisters the presence of a happy object that is no longer or that imagines something as being happy insofar as it is no longer. Things can be happy not only as projections of the future but also as imaginings of what has been lost (if only things are as they were, we would be happy). I will discuss the relation between happiness and utopianism in chapter 5.

38 Tolstoy famously opens *Anna Karenina* with the sentence "All happy families are alike; but an unhappy family is unhappy after its own fashion" ([1875–77] 1985: 13). Perhaps the likeness of the happy family relates to how families are predicated on likeness. When things go happily, the family recedes into the background, as that which is familiar.

39 Of course, sometimes when we are nervous, unsure or lacking in confidence, then we wait for affirmation, we wait for "the yes." In this case, affirmation is audible as it allows us to embrace what we are doing with greater confidence. Hesitant subjects might quicken their pace at the sound of the "yes" although they would still be going the way they were going.

40 The violence of the image of the killjoy is significant. As R. D. Laing shows us, those who do not preserve the idea of the family within themselves, who do not identify with the family, are represented as the cause of violence: "To destroy the 'family' may be experienced as worse than murder or more selfish than suicide" (1971: 14). To break with the family is to risk breaking everything up: "In some families, parents cannot allow children to break the 'family' down within themselves, if that is what they want to do, because this is felt as the breakup of the family, and then where would it end?" (13). The demand that we reproduce the family thus reveals the vulnerability of its form: it is because the family is *not* fully secure (to break up the family is imagined as anarchic) that there is a demand that we retain "it" as our happy object through acts that demonstrate our love and loyalty. Not to do so is to risk being perceived as killing the family by killing its association with joy.

2. Feminist Killjoys

1 Although as Robin Barrow points out happiness and education do not necessarily involve each other: "one can be educated and miserable" (1980: 1).

2   However, as Jane Roland Martin discusses, *Republic* and *Émile* provide very different models of education for women: "The question naturally arises of how such radically different accounts of the education of women could be given by philosophers who make the same fundamental assumptions about education" (1995: 59).

3   I am particularly interested in the influence of *Émile* on Immanuel Kant. Famously, the one occasion on which Kant was reported to have forgotten his routine of a daily walk was when he was reading this book. In the "Fragment of a Moral Catechism," which appears within the first section of his "Doctrine of the Method of Ethics" in *The Metaphysics of Morals*, Kant writes about how to teach ethics, which is immediately translated into classical terms of teaching the pupil how to be virtuous: "The very concept of virtue already implies that virtue must be acquired (that is it is not innate). . . . That virtue can and must be *taught* already follows from its not being innate; a doctrine of virtues is therefore *something that can be taught*" ([1797] 1996: 221). The style of the conversation between teacher and pupil has clear resonance with *Émile*. Kant seems to offer a different account of the relationship between happiness and virtue, given that he separates the pragmatic law of happiness from the moral law of virtue. And yet both Rousseau and Kant suggest that the virtuous subject does not pursue happiness but will get happiness in return for following nature's path (Rousseau) or becoming worthy of happiness (Kant), although Kant describes this as a hope rather than guarantee. See also note 13 in my conclusion for a further discussion of Kant's "Fragment of a Moral Catechism."

4   I would like to acknowledge that I first developed this argument about conditional happiness as a result of reading *Émile*. Conditional happiness usually refers to the process whereby individuals define for themselves various conditions that need to be in place before they can be happy. The clinical psychologist Alan Gettis argues that "the conditional happiness notion doesn't really work" and cites Joan Borysenko's work to show how such a model for happiness will always lead to disappointment, as new conditions will always be set: "How many times has your mind told you that you could be happy if you lost ten pounds. Made more money? Then, even if these things come to pass, you just move on to the next set of conditions for happiness. The conditions are like the proverbial carrot that dangles in front of the donkey. You never reach them" (Gettis 2006: 41). I want to offer a different angle on the idea of conditional happiness by describing how conditions of happiness include the happiness of others, such that we will only be happy on condition that they are happy. I will not be evaluating whether or not we should make our happiness conditional in this way but rather will be exploring what follows when other people's happiness becomes a condition of our own.

5   For more reflection on happiness and compromise, see the final section of chapter 4.

6   You might be asked to disregard your views on x in order to make someone happy. I have found this especially true in the case of weddings. You are asked or even instructed to join the happy event of the wedding because it would make someone happy for you to share in their happy occasion even if they know that you are not happy with the very idea of marriage that is celebrated in weddings. You are often judged as selfish when you refuse the demand to participate in the happiness of others, especially in cases when such happiness is sanctioned by law, habit, or custom.

7   More recent feminist critiques of *Émile* exist, although they do not attend specifically to Rousseau's arguments about happiness and gender. See, for example, Penelope Deutscher's (1997) analysis of sexual difference within *Émile*.

8   In thinking of happiness as a technology one might consult Foucault's essay "The Political Technology of Individuals." Foucault begins this essay by reflecting on a historical coincidence between World War II and public welfare and public health, suggesting that "life insurance is connected with a death command" (1988: 147). He then considers the police as "the specific techniques by which a government in the framework of a state was able to govern people as individuals" (154), offering an analysis of the manual or "systematic encyclopedia" written in France in the early eighteenth century by N. Delamare (156). Foucault analyzes how this document conceives of happiness as "a requirement for the survival and development of the state. It is a condition, it is an instrument, and not simply a consequence. People's happiness becomes an element of state strength" (158). Happiness can be a technique of governance: life insurance could be described as happiness insurance. When individuals assume responsibility for their own happiness, and the happiness of others, they are adopting such a technique. As Nikolas Rose argues: "The regulation of conduct becomes a matter of each individual's desire to govern their conduct freely in the service of a maximization of a version of their happiness and fulfillment that they take to be their own" (1996: 58–59).

9   Lynne Segal's wonderful book *Making Trouble: Life and Politics* (2007), about the history of her involvement in feminist politics, is thus very appropriately named.

10 *The Mill on the Floss* was one of my favorite texts from the nineteenth-century women's writing course that I took in 1988 at Adelaide University, which was the first course in which I was introduced to feminist theory. I wrote my honors dissertation about the narrative ending of this book in 1990. When I thought more about the figure of the female troublemaker in relation to killing joy, this was the first book that came to my mind. When I reread it, I was struck by how explicitly it engages with happiness in the dialogue between characters as well as in its narrative development. This of course should not surprise us: the genre of bildungsroman, with its focus on moral development, is inevitably bound up with ideas of happiness.

11 Rousseau links the danger of reading for girls to their inability to distinguish between imagination and reality. Sophy becomes unhappy, the narrative suggests, because she has fallen in love with a character from a book (440). The implication here is that girls lack the epistemic skills to distinguish fantasy from reality; they have a tendency to fancy the fanciful. But we could also read this narrative differently. Sophy's unhappiness might be caused by an infatuation with a fictional hero, but the infatuation is also what causes her to be disappointed with what life has to offer: in reference to her suitors, she says to her mother, "I am dissatisfied with every one" (439). The danger of reading for girls is a danger not so much to their own happiness but to the happiness of others: it is reading which leads to a refusal to be satisfied with reality. The happiness of the ending thus requires Sophy to give up her books so that she can be satisfied with the prospect of marriage to Émile. It is also interesting to note that a sequel was published to *Émile* after Rousseau's death, in which the happiness of their fate is rewritten. Sophy commits adultery (with the implication that she was a victim of a crime) and Émile abandons her and their children. See Rousseau 1783.

12 I should point out here that the novel is presenting Maggie's solution in a paradoxical way by showing her as *willfully giving up her will* or as *desirously giving up desire* rather than fully renouncing her will or desire (see Shuttleworth 1984: 104). Maggie has her epiphany after reading Thomas à Kempis's *Imitation of Christ*, a book whose spirit George Eliot reportedly much admired (see Cooke [1884] 2007: 236). The implication of the novel might even be that true renunciation of the kind called for by *Imitation of Christ* is an ethical ideal. For an extended discussion of this episode and the idea of renunciation in *The Mill on the Floss*, see Carroll 1992: 123–39. I should note as well that the idea that happiness can be achieved through the renunciation of desire has a long history. Despite their differences, both Epicurean and Stoic models of happiness rest on the strict limitation of desire. For a discussion, see McMahon 2006: 55–56. See also my reflections on happiness and fortune in the conclusion to this book. The idea that we should give up desire (as a desire for something that exists outside one's self) relates to the perceived necessity of becoming indifferent to that which is beyond our control. Happiness becomes tied to self-control: you have self-control if you make your happiness conditional upon only what is within your control.

13 Maggie's identification as racially other makes sense of an earlier episode, where she runs off to be with the gypsies, with whom she feels a sense of kinship. Her kinship with gypsies functions to express her lack of kinship feeling for her family. For a good discussion of race within Victorian novels, including the significance of the figure of the gypsy, see Meyer 1996. Clearly, the use of racial trouble to describe female trouble does involve an act of appropriation

that can vacate the whiteness of the troublemaker. We can also see how to trouble one category can also put others into trouble.

14 I say Kantian subject, as the opposition that Maggie shares with Kant is between duty and inclination—as if without duty all we have is inclination. But note here that Maggie says she cannot sacrifice others for her own happiness. The paradox that I will explore is how happiness becomes a duty *as* a duty to promote the happiness of others.

15 Writing this book on happiness has sparked my interest in theorizing the sociality of the will and the ways in which people are described as willful insofar as they will too much, or too little, or in "the wrong way." In other words, the willful subject is the one who makes explicit her disagreement.

16 See Rita Felski's excellent description of feminist killjoys in her *Literature after Feminism* (2003: 1–2). She reads various caricatures of feminists as puritanical, bitter, and mean in writing by male literary critics intent on defending the value of literature against feminism. I will suggest that the figure of the feminist killjoy can be exercised in a wide variety of contexts, wherever there is a perception of a need to hold onto forms of power that are challenged by feminism.

17 Feminists are regularly diagnosed within popular culture as sublimating their disappointment through politics. This is why there is a kinship between the feminist and other figures such as the spinster or lesbian, who likewise embody the risk of disappointment (which is presumed to be the proper affective consequence of the "failure" to achieve heterosexual happiness). It is absolutely necessary that we continue to discuss the sexism and homophobia of such figurations.

18 I am using the very recognizable figure of "the angry black woman" as referring to all women of color. Sometimes words can fail to capture the complexities of history, especially in translation. In the UK context, to talk about "black feminism" would automatically reference work by all feminists of color, and I am aware that this is not the case in the United States. But the figure of "the angry black woman" has been written about in different contexts. See, for example, Suneri Thobani's reference to this figure in relation to women immigrants of color in the Canadian context (2003: 401), and Aileen Moreton-Robinson in relation to indigenous women in the Australian context (2002: 6). When discussing the figure, I keep the shorthand of "angry black woman," and when discussing our relation to that figure, I have adopted the U.S. term "of color."

19 It might seem here that I am placing my hope in capacity, as that which is restricted by gender. Capacities are not simply about the joy of opening things up. Capacities also make some things possible at the expense of others—even if we don't know yet what a body can do, we can recognize there is only so much this body can do at a given point in time. There is a little misery and

loss in every capacity—which does not make capacity miserable. I have been very struck in my participation in conferences by how much "opening up the body's capacity to act" as a kind of weak inheritance of Spinoza has become a mantra in affect studies, as if such openings are necessarily good, or as if they should be installed as an agreed *telos* for politics. We always need to ask: capacities for what, and capacities to do what? See the first chapter of my book *Queer Phenomenology* (2006) for a reflection on capacity as a mode of directionality.

20 Mrs. Dalloway's stream of consciousness offers itself as a consciousness of death: "Did it matter, then, she asked herself, as she walked towards Bond Street, did it matter that she must inevitably cease completely; all this must go on without her; did she resent it; or did it not become consoling to believe that death ended absolutely?" (12). I am offering my own slant by associating consciousness of death with consciousness of gender: so Clarissa in becoming Mrs. Richard Dalloway "must inevitably cease completely."

21 To be hopeful can defer recognition that one is not experiencing happiness by following a certain path. You can feel sad but be hopeful that "along the way" things will get better. The more you are hopeful the more you give up by not giving up. In recognizing that situations are hopeless, all those forms of deferred sadness can hit you. Recognition of loss can thus be one of the hardest forms of recognition. It often means being prepared to be undone.

22 Another, more recent book which could be described as an ode to *Mrs. Dalloway* is Rachel Cusk's *Arlington Park* (2006). This book approximates the form of *Mrs. Dalloway*: we have multiple points of consciousness, a sense of an unhappiness that is worldly, that is around; the action of the book takes place on a single day; there is a party, and the different characters of the book meet at the party.

23 This sense of how realizing possibility does not make things possible haunts Kate Chopin's *The Awakening*. The heroine becomes aware of a life outside the confines of domestic happiness, which is redescribed as an "indescribable oppression" ([1899] 1993: 6), only to realize that what is outside that life would also involve becoming a possession. You recognize that what you gave up was not necessary but that you cannot take back what you have given up without giving yourself up. Her awakening to life thus leads her to death. Her death could be considered as liberation from happiness, a feminist refusal to be taken, to be given away by happiness scripts. For the significance of unhappy endings in women's writing, especially in the genres of romance, see Radway 1984 and DuPlessis 1985.

24 I am indebted to Sarah Schulman for this point.

25 I am not saying here that Richard's inheritance of sadness does not matter. It does. The injustice of his sadness needs to be recognized. Throughout history, women who deviate from the paths of happiness (who do not care in the

right way by preserving "family happiness" at all costs, whatever their own un-happiness) have paid high prices: they have lost access to their children, they have lost their freedom, and they have lost their lives. The unhappy conse-quences for their children are part of this history. It is wrong to blame mothers for such unhappy consequences. The work of feminist critique is not to deny the unhappy consequences of acts of deviation but to offer better explanations of how they happen. When thinking about Richard's sadness, I was reminded of the relatively happy ending of the lesbian novel *The Price of Salt*, which was first published in 1952 (see chapter 3, note 2, for a discussion of its ending). This ending is happy in the sense that the lesbian lovers Therese and Carol get to stay together; or at least plan their lives as if they are staying together. But the cost of their happiness is high: Carol loses the custody battle for her child. Beyond the frame of this ending, her child might inherit the unhappiness of the life they leave behind. We should also remember here that children often bear the burden of the desire to maintain the appearance of family happiness. When parents stay in unhappy relationships "for the sake of the children," the consequences for children are often unhappy. Some forms of inherited unhappiness are less visible because they challenge the myth of where and how happiness should be given.

26 In describing Claudia as an affect alien, I am not suggesting that she simply persists in her feeling of alienation; such persistence could, after all, compro-mise her capacity to live. In order not to be compromised by alienation one might learn to compromise, to be strategic about how one lives. Claudia's own survival strategy is love: "The best hiding place was love. Thus the conversion from pristine sadism to fabricated hatred, to fraudulent love. It was a small step to Shirley Temple. I learned much later to worship her, just as I learned to delight in cleanliness, knowing, even as I learned, that the change was adjust-ment without improvement" (16). I would describe such learning as falling short of an identification: she might learn to find the right things delightful, but in describing such self-learning as adjustment without improvement, she is not "really" agreeing that the cause of delight is what is most delightful, nor is she considering herself as having become more delightful. Some adjust-ments are not about becoming well-adjusted by accepting what exists and be-lieving in the good of its existence; they can involve pragmatic reorientations to what does exist in order to make an existence possible. The word *adjustment* suggests not only to get used to, but also to bring near. Claudia's compromise allows her to become a subject of knowledge; she learns about whiteness — by tracking its genealogy through domesticated objects — through what is brought near. There is hope generated by the very proximity of an adjustment. For good discussions of the complexity of Claudia's relationship to whiteness see Cheng (2001: 18) and Yancy (2008: 214–16).

27 The ending gives Pecola her blue eyes, at the cost of her sanity. It takes away

the potential of her child. And yet, there is hope in this ending, expressed in Claudia's conversion from rage against white dolls to care for an unwanted black baby: "More strongly than my fondness for Pecola, I felt a need for some-one to want the black baby to live — just to counteract the universal love for white baby dolls, Shirley Temples and Maureen Peals" (149). Of course, to convert deficiency into desire does not necessarily rescript unhappy lives into happy ones. As Claudia acknowledges: "The soil is bad for certain kinds of flowers. Certain seeds it will not nurture, certain fruits it will not bear, and when the land kills of its own volition, we acquiesce and say the victim had no right to live. We are wrong, of course, but it doesn't matter. It's too late. At least on the edge of my town, among the garbage and the sunflowers of my town, it's much, much, much too late" (164). It might be too late for a happy ending, too late even for possibility, but at least someone wanted that child. To want the unwanted is a moment of political hope, however much the moment passes by.

28 See also Barbara Ehrenreich's "Welcome to Cancerland" (2001) for a related critique of the requirement that cancer patients be cheerful. Ehrenreich sug-gests that "so pervasive is the perkiness of the breast-cancer world that un-happiness requires a kind of apology" (48) as if "the disease offers more than the intangible benefits of spiritual upward mobility" (49). What Ehrenreich offers, dissenting from this obligation to be cheerful, is an account of her "purifying rage" (53).

29 I develop this argument about happiness and false consciousness in chap-ter 5.

30 For a good critique of affirmative feminism, see McRobbie 2008. See also my critique of affirmative ethics in the conclusion of this book.

3. Unhappy Queers

1 Anxiety about happy queers is crucial to the enforcement of heterosexuality. For instance, the Section 28 Law in the UK, which was introduced in 1988 and repealed in 2003, forbade any "promotion" of homosexuality by local authori-ties. By "promotion" the law included "the publishing of materials with the in-tention of promoting homosexuality" or "of the acceptability of homosexuality as a pretended family relationship." It is interesting to note that a children's book, *Jenny Lives with Eric and Martin*, was a key reference point in the moral panic leading to Section 28: in 1983 the *Daily Mail* reported that a copy of the book was in the collection of a school library. This novel begins: "Jenny is a little girl. Martin is Jenny's dad and Eric is Martin's lover. They all live happily together" (Bösche 1983: 1). Happiness is read here as a form of promotion: to tell the story of a queer family as "happy" is read as promoting homosexuality.

That some stories of happiness are visible as forms of promotion shows how happiness is already presumed to reside in specific ways of living: in this case, in the form of the nuclear family. It may also involve an anxious belief that there is something dangerously promotable about queer family forms.

2 One novel stands out as quite exceptional for giving its lesbian characters a relatively happy ending: Patricia Highsmith's *The Price of Salt*, first published in 1952 under the pseudonym Claire Morgan. In her reflections on the significance of the book in an afterward to the new edition, Highsmith explains: "The appeal of *The Price of Salt* was that it had a happy ending for its two main characters, or at least they were going to try to have a future together. Prior to this book, homosexuals male and female in American novels had to pay for their deviation by cutting their wrists, drowning themselves in a swimming pool, or by switching to heterosexuality (so it was stated), or by collapsing—alone and miserable and shunned—into a depression equal to hell" ([1952] 2004: 261). However, the costs of this happiness are high: Carol loses custody of her child.

3 The happiness duty thus becomes a duty not to cause unhappiness by speaking about your disappointment (your failure to be made happy by x). For example, say you are out having a meal with someone you love, someone whose happiness matters to you. You really want her to enjoy her meal. You don't want her to be disappointed. If she is disappointed, you will be disappointed. Her disappointment will even cause your disappointment. She might experience this anxiety about the possibility of her disappointment as a pressure not to be disappointed. She might have to perform enjoyment to avoid causing you disappointment. Your desire for the happiness of your beloved can create an illusion of happiness ("false impressions"), which involves the negation rather than expression of desire. In raising questions about the intimacy of love and happiness, I am not saying that we do not experience love as a care for what happens to loved others (whether in the form of wanting their happiness, wanting what is good for them, wanting them to get what they want, wanting good things to happen to them). We can, and we do. I am just raising concerns about some of the less happy effects of love as wanting happiness for the beloved. Of course, having another want your happiness can also generate happiness.

4 This principle that to love makes the other's happiness essential to your own is widely articulated. But does this principle always hold true? I would say that there is a desire for this principle to be true but this desire does not make the principle true, as a psychoanalytic approach might suggest. If love is to desire the happiness of another, then the happiness of the subject who loves might depend upon the happiness of the other who is loved. As such, love can also be experienced as the possibility that the beloved can take your happiness away from you. This anxious happiness, you might say, forms the basis of an

ambivalent sociality in which we love those we love, but we might also hate those we love for making us love them, which is what makes us vulnerable to being affected by what happens to them: in other words, love extends our vulnerability beyond our own skin. Perhaps fellow-feeling is a form of social hope: we want to want happiness for those we love; we want our happy objects to amount to the same thing. Even if we feel guilty for wishing unhappiness upon our enemies, it is a less guilty wish than wishing unhappiness upon our friends. In other words, our presumed indifference toward the happiness of strangers might help us to sustain the fantasy that we always want the happiness of those we love, or that our love wants their happiness.

5   Leibniz (following unnamed philosophers and theologians) differentiates between "concupiscence," as the "desire or feeling we bear towards what gives pleasure to us," and "benevolence," as "the feeling we have for something by whose pleasure or happiness we are pleased or made happy" ([1765] 1981: 163). Let us assume that such feelings are addressed toward another person. We would have a distinction between the other as causing my pleasure or happiness, or the other's pleasure as causing my pleasure or happiness. In both cases, the other occupies the same position as the cause of my pleasure or happiness whether or not my pleasure or happiness is made conditional upon the other's. The inclusion of the other's happiness in a discourse of benevolence does not necessarily involve a shift of position and may even keep the other in the same position. These definitions are offered in Leibniz's *New Essays on Human Understanding*, where he participates in an imaginary dialogue with Locke. He exposes what he clearly perceived to be the weaknesses of Locke's empiricism in An *Essay Concerning Human Understanding*, a book I used to develop my thesis on happy objects in chapter 1. It is very noticeable in this section of the text, which corresponds to Locke's account of modes of pleasure and pain (162–69), Leibniz represents himself as pretty much in agreement with Locke.

6   When articulated in a certain way, this "whatever" can be an expression of scorn, a "whatever" we associate, perhaps harshly and prematurely, with adolescence. Indifference can present itself as caring (I will care for you no matter what you do), or as a form of uncaring (I don't care what you say or do). There is difference within indifference, for sure. Indifference can also be a fantasy. So parents might say that they "just want" the child's happiness when they disagree with the child but cannot afford (for one reason or another) to make their disagreement explicit. I would argue that speech acts are more likely to take this form when the person who speaks is in a position of relative power to decide or command the conditions of happiness. One critic who considers such parental speech acts is Raymond Angelo Belliotti. He argues, "Parents often say that what they want most for their children is happiness. Typically, parents utter this bromide self-satisfied that they are open-minded

and accepting of the paths their children choose: 'I may disagree with what my children are doing, it is not for me, but if it makes them happy I cannot say they are wrong'" (2004: 1). Belliotti's reading of the speech act is helpful. He shows us that the desire for the child's happiness involves an implicit disagreement with what the child does. The speech act thus appears indifferent as it *withholds the judgment it makes* (I think they are wrong but cannot say it).

7 Voon Chin Phua, in *Icelandic Lives: The Queer Experience*, discusses how her mother's response to coming out involved the dread of unhappiness: "Also, she thought if I was a lesbian, I would be unhappy. That's just the image she had of gay and lesbian people who were out. They were all unhappy. She assumed that lesbian and gay people are all unhappy, always struggling, never happy with family and no kids" (2003: 107).

8 There are so many examples of this. In addition to *Annie on My Mind*, another very good example is Julie Anne Peter's *Keeping You a Secret*, when a mother says to her daughter's friend: "I want her to be happy. That's all Tom and I ever wanted for our kids. I am sure your mother feels the same way, Holland. We want so much for our kids to grow up and have things we never had. We have high hopes for you. Expectations, dreams. Then, something like this" (2003: 190). To become a lesbian is to disappoint your parents; they want you to be happy, which means wanting you to live according to an idea of their happiness, or their idea of your happiness. A very different version of this speech act is offered in the lesbian film *Imagine Me and You* (2000, dir. Ol Parker), where a girl falls in love with another girl whom she first encounters at her wedding. Here it is the husband who speaks: "I want you to be happy. I wanted to be the cause of the happiness in you. But if I'm not, then I cannot stand in the way." Here, the husband lets his wife go when he realizes that she has fallen in love with a woman, as he recognizes that he cannot be the one to cause her happiness. If you desire your loved one to be happy, and you recognize that you cannot make your loved one happy, then you can let her go to pursue happiness in her own way, even if that makes you unhappy (because what would have made you happy would have been to cause her happiness). In most of the examples I encountered doing the research for this book, the desire for the other's happiness does not involve such recognition. Such desire usually insists upon what another's happiness does involve, or should involve, rather than hesitating on the question of whether the subject can or cannot contribute to another's happiness. Indeed, expressions of the desire *to make* another happy are not usually articulated with much anxiety as to whether one *can make* another happy. However, the following section of this chapter discusses some of the problems for queer politics when love is made dependent on causing happiness.

9 However, we could also read Sharon Fairbanks's desire for her daughter to be straight as melancholic, as being not so much about wanting her daugh-

ter to be happy as wanting her daughter to give up happiness, or, to be specific, to sacrifice desire and queer happiness for the good life. In this episode
the opening "flashback" scene involves two girls with their horses, which, we
later come to realize, were the young Sharon and her female friend. Sharon
tries to kiss her friend in a queer moment of stable intimacy (there are many
queer stories to tell about girls and horses) and her friend is horrified, saying,
"People have all kinds of feelings, it doesn't mean we are supposed to act upon
them." Later, when Sharon refuses to accept Dana's coming out, she repeats
her girlfriend's words to Dana, with a difference: "We all have feelings for
our girlfriends, Dana. It doesn't mean we have to act on them." So behind her
mother's unhappiness with her daughter being queer is her grief that she had
to sacrifice the possibility of queer desire in order to act on the right kind of
feelings, or in order to be directed in the right way by choosing what feelings
to act upon. I will return to the perverse possibility of being happily queer in
the final section of this chapter.

10 In books like *How to Be a Happy Homosexual* it is unsurprising that the promotion of happy homosexuality involves a commitment to "de-queer" gay life.
The book includes criticisms of practices such as cottaging, asserting that
"for the isolated and insecure gay man it fosters the idea that contact with
gay people is of necessity dirty, undignified, nerve-wracking and dangerous.
It can do nothing for the self-image of those gay men who already have a bad
opinion of their sexuality" (Sanderson 1999: 64). Cruising is also criticized
as it can "increase the sense of isolation in those who are already unhappy
with their sexuality" (67). Sanderson criticizes the hedonism of queer culture, suggesting that homosexual men need to develop an ethics premised
on making other people happy (145). Although Sanderson does not describe
such ethics in terms of conservative family values (or in terms of mimicking
straight relationships or family forms), it is clearly linked to the promoting
of a sociability premised on fellow-feeling, or what he calls "finer feelings,"
which is contrasted to the superficiality and hedonism of queer cultures (145).
I am indebted here to Vincent Quinn for an excellent paper which reflected
on *How to Be a Happy Homosexual* as a sexual conduct manual.

11 The perception of inherently unhappy queers can have extremely violent and
devastating consequences. See, for example, Michael Schroeder and Ariel
Shidlo's analysis of how clinicians have used this argument—that gay people
will inevitably be unhappy—to justify sexual conversion therapy (2002: 134–
35). By implication, gay patients are asked to give up desire for happiness.
Many of these homophobic discourses in psychiatry aimed to debunk what
they call "the myth of the happy homosexual" in order to argue for "cure"
rather than "adjustment" (see Conrad and Schneider 1980: 191). They are
deeply invested in the necessity and inevitably of queer unhappiness. So although we might want to question the promotion of happy homosexuals dis-

cussed in note 10, we might also want to remember that disbelief in the very possibility of queer happiness is crucial to the violence of homophobia.

12   Derived from sexology, inversion was used as a way of interpreting lesbian sexuality (if she desires women, she must be a man). Given this, the invert both stands for and stands in for the figure of the lesbian, a way of presenting her that also erases her, which is not to say that we should assume the invert can only signify in this way. See Ahmed 2006 for a discussion of the relation between the figure of the lesbian and the invert in *The Well of Loneliness*, as well as Prosser 1998, which reads the invert as the transsexual. See Bland and Doan 1998 for an excellent collection of sexological writing from the late nineteenth and early twentieth centuries, as well as Doan and Prosser's edited collection on *The Well of Loneliness* (2002), which includes articles on the relations between inversion, transsexuality, and homosexuality.

13   I am extending my analysis of the concept of contagion offered in the first chapter by suggesting that very possibility that feelings are contagious becomes a point of antagonism or social pressure. Also note the implications for our understanding of suffering. It is a truism that sharing suffering eases the pressure of suffering by sharing its burden. But we can also consider how the very possibility of sharing suffering becomes a social bind. If another suffers in response to my suffering, then I might fear that I can cause suffering by sharing my suffering. I might also fear that if that person suffers my suffering, then my suffering no longer refers to me. In other words, the possibility that another whom I love might suffer if I suffer can create a burden on me not to cause the loved one's suffering or to give my suffering way. The concealment of suffering can be done in the name of love.

14   Recent research on happiness provides "happiness maps" by looking at "happiness clusters" and rests at least in part on a model of affective contagion. For example, the study by James H. Fowler and Nicholas A. Christakis study published in the *BMJ* in 2008 (which was widely reported in the global media under the heading "happiness is contagious" in December 2008 — maybe it is the idea that happiness is contagious that is most contagious) examines how happiness can spread from person to person within social networks, creating "clusters of happy and unhappy people" (1). In their analysis of happiness distributions, the authors suggest that "people at the core of their local networks seem more likely to be happy, while those on the periphery seem more likely to be unhappy" (6). The happiness of the center is presumed to be a sign that happy people are drawn to each other. This fantasy that happiness resides within the center might allow those in the center not to recognize the relationship between their happiness and the unhappiness of those relegated to the margins. The authors admit that the data does not allow them to make conclusions about the causal mechanisms behind happiness clusters. They speculate that happy people might "share their good fortune" or "change their

behavior towards others" or "merely exude an emotion that is genuinely contagious." Although contagion is described as one possible causal mechanism among others, I would argue that contagion provides a central model of causality in much happiness research. So it is assumed that we have happiness clusters because happiness can spread more easily. My aim is not to deny the existence of happiness and unhappiness clusters (although we might want to remember that these are clusters of those who are more and less likely to describe themselves as being happy). Rather I want to suggest they are effects of complex social mechanisms, whereby those who are associated with unhappiness are kept at a distance, at the margins of social life, which allows happiness and unhappiness to be deposited in certain places. In other words, the idea that happiness is contagious becomes crucial to forms of social regulation that creates the very clusterings that are then taken up as proof that happiness is contagious! Contagion offers a weak model of social causality, which fails to account for the complex mechanisms through which certain qualities, materials, and attributes (whether they are tangibles or intangibles) accumulate for some and not others. The weakness of contagion as a model of social causality would be self-evident if we used it to explain the distributions of tangibles (for example, to explain the concentration of wealth as an effect of contagion—that people catch money from people with money—would be self-evidently absurd); we need also to recognize its weakness as a model for explaining the distributions of intangibles.

15   Both Hemmings and Newton are addressing how *The Well*'s focus on "the mannish lesbian" means that the position of the femme or feminine lesbian is left vacant. My reading concurs with theirs and suggests that this vacation could be reread in terms of happiness: the femme's desire is not presented beyond the desire for happiness, which is assumed to lead her back into the straight world. Such readings are in sympathy with the novel, recognizing the force of its own revelation of the injustice of the straight world, even if they suggest that femme desire outside the happiness economy needs to be spoken.

16   In *Feeling Backward*, Heather Love offers a useful reflection on the ending of the novel, showing how "Stephen comes face to face with the pain—including her own and Mary's—that she has disavowed over the course of the novel" (2007: 125). My reading offers a more optimistic slant on the sharing of Stephen's pain with the pain of other inverts. I think of the ending as revolution: the walls that contain suffering are brought down.

17   The film replays a common narrative within lesbian fiction: two girls fall in love; but one cannot bear giving up on the straight world and thus gives up her love. In Nancy Toder's classic *Choices* (1980), for example, Jenny is scared by loving Sandy and leaves her to get married. Sandy witnesses Jenny's fear as based on the presumption that happiness requires marriage: "What made me angry was that you acted as though married people were the only happy and

successful people. That makes single people — a category which, by the way, includes most gay people — implicitly unhappy" (242).

18 As I will discuss in the next section, care for sick birds can function as a queer kinship story.

19 http://www.popmatters.com. Last visited June 25, 2008.

20 We have an interesting contrast to the film *Bend It Like Beckham* discussed in chapter 4, where I suggest that it is the agency of the white man that converts unhappy racism to multicultural happiness. So where we locate "the conversion point" between bad and good feeling does matter: not only does it involve different arguments about history (and how social change happens), but it also involves distributions of agency that might challenge or support existing distributions of power. For instance, in some depictions of queer happiness within the mainstream media, the implicit narrative is that queers now have recognition because the straight world has given it to them, which locates the conversion point between the unhappy and the happy queer with happy heterosexuals.

21 I am reminded of an impossibly sad scene in *The L Word*, when Bette is speaking to her father about her mother. He says to her: "You must have experienced the bond of marriage to appreciate how much I hurt your mother." I think one of the most powerful representations in *The L Word* is Bette's relationship with her father. His refusal to recognize her lesbian relationship is a grief that nothing can cover over. Achieving relative proximity to the conventional forms of the good life (a stable relationship, a successful job, a beautiful house, a child) cannot compensate for this grief.

22 See Duggan 2003 and Halberstam 2005 for important critiques of the new homonormativity. My argument supports theirs while also suggesting that the desire to stay close to the scenes of the normative is not simply about the desire for the good life, as a form of assimilation, but is also shaped by histories of struggle for a bearable life.

23 See chapter 2, note 26, in the present work.

24 The social investment in unhappy queer lives can thus exist alongside envy for queer enjoyment: queer enjoyment bypasses the duty to reproduce social form and is thus given without being earned. By living outside the logics of duty and sacrifice, queer pleasures embody what is threatening about freedom. See the final section of chapter 5 for a discussion of the radicalization of freedom as the freedom to be unhappy, which I suggest includes the freedom to enjoy life without being bound by the happiness duty.

4. Melancholic Migrants

1 Information about the BBC program *The Happiness Formula* can be accessed at http://news.bbc.co.uk. Last visited February 14, 2009.

2 Commission for Racial Equality, *Good Race Relations Guide*, 2005: http://www
.cre.gov.uk. This commission merged with other equality commissions in 2007
and is now named the Equality and Human Rights Commission; see http://
www.equalityhumanrights.com. Last visited February 14, 2009.

3 Paul Gilroy describes how "multiculturalism was officially pronounced dead
in July 2005" in his lecture "Multi-Culture in Times of War," Inaugural Lecture, London School of Economics, May 10, 2006.

4 The argument that diversity causes unhappiness does appear to withdraw social hope from the very idea of diversity—or, indeed, multiculturalism as an
imagined community of diverse cultures. But the narrative then involves a
certain acceptance of diversity and the possibility of unhappiness by evoking
a horrifying image of happy sameness: the Ku Klux Klan. The KKK is evidence
that apparently happy communities—communities that have the ingredients deemed necessary for good community life—can cause racism. In other
words, they embody the possibility that communities can be happily racist or
even happy insofar as they are racist. The program cannot afford to give moral
approval to racism, even if the logical consequence of the argument thus far
is that racist communities are happier. The program thus concludes that our
moral task, and the task of government, is to make what causes unhappiness
cause happiness in the future, where making happiness is premised on concepts such as building bridges and integration.

5 Please note that I am using *football* in the British sense, to refer to the sport
that is called *soccer* in the United States. I will not be considering the relation between football and multiculturalism beyond considering the symbolic
function of football in the film *Bend It Like Beckham*. For an important analysis
of football in relation to racism and national identity, see Back, Crabbe, and
Solomos 2001. I acknowledge here the significance of football as a local and
international sport even though I am focusing on how football provides a national ideal.

6 We might expect a substantive postcolonial literature on the intersection of
utilitarianism and empire (and thus on the role of the greatest happiness principle in justifying the imperial mission), but there is not. We do have some key
historical works on this intersection that have influenced postcolonial critics,
such as Eric Stokes's *The English Utilitarians and India* (1959) upon which Homi
Bhabha drew in *The Location of Culture* (1994). However, as Bart Schultz and
Georgios Varouxakis point out in their introduction to the important edited
collection *Utilitarianism and Empire*, postcolonial and poststructuralist writers
have not emphasized utilitarianism in their critiques of colonial discourses
(2005: 3). Schultz and Varouxakis suggest that this relative absence might be
explained by the tendency to focus on liberalism rather than utilitarianism as
the primary object of critique. It is noteworthy that Bhabha (1994) does offer
a reading of John Stuart Mill but only in terms of liberalism.

7 James Mills and Jeremy Bentham are often represented as more moderate in their support for empire, in comparison to John Stuart Mill, who is described as the first of the major utilitarians "to develop a more or less unqualified defence of empire" (Jones 2005: 183). However, as Jennifer Pitts argues in her valuable study of imperial liberalism (2005), the historical records in turn suggest that Bentham did not support James Mill's own justifications of empire, especially as presented in *The History of British India*, which I will discuss later. She quotes from Bentham's description of Mill's book: "This book on British India abounds with bad English which made it to me a disagreeable book. His accounts of the superstitions of the Hindoos made me melancholy" (105). Given that Mill's own focus is on what is disagreeable with Hindu culture, the significance of Bentham's critique of Mill is clear.

8 For a good account of the history of the company, see Mia Carter's introduction to the volume, "Company to Canal: 1756–1860," in *Archives of Empire* (2003), as well as the volume itself, which contains fascinating archival materials. I should note here that James Mill was offered his position in the East India Company, which he held for seventeen years, partly as a result of the publication of *History of British India*. John Stuart Mill began his work for the company as his father's unpaid servant. He later served as an examiner in its Office of Correspondence and defended the company's policies before Parliament in 1857. It is interesting to note for historical record that in his autobiography Mill describes his father's *History of British India* as "a book which contributed largely to my education" ([1873] 2003: 17). I will be concentrating in this chapter on James Mill's role as a utilitarian defender of empire. For an account of John Stuart Mill's role in the East India Company, see Zastoupil 1994. See also Anderson 1998 for a study of John Stuart Mill's philosophy of moral education which also describes the differences between James Mill and John Stuart Mill on educational policy in India, and Sullivan 1983 for analysis of the relationship between John Stuart Mill's views on India and liberalism.

9 I want to acknowledge here my debt to Man To Leung (1998) for his important paper on James Mill's utilitarianism and empire, which helped direct my thinking. It refers to the Bruce report, although incorrectly attributing it to Mill himself.

10 We can also consider the significance of the production of the myths of happiness, such as the myth of the happy slave, which is a myth that finds happiness in the violence of colonial subjection. The myth of the happy slave has a powerful ideological function, suggesting that slavery liberates the other to happiness. Consider Fredrick Douglass's debunking of this myth: "I have often been utterly astonished, since I came to the north, to find persons who could speak of the singing, among slaves, as evidence of their contentment and happiness. It is impossible to conceive of a greater mistake. Slaves sing most when they are most unhappy. The songs of the slave represent the sorrows of his

258 NOTES TO CHAPTER FOUR

heart; and he is relieved by them, only as an aching heart is relieved by its tears. At least, such is my experience. I have often sung to drown my sorrow, but seldom to express my happiness" ([1845] 2003: 26). In his later *My Bondage and My Freedom* Douglass powerfully extends his reflection on slave songs in the following way: "Slaves sing more to *make* themselves happy, than to express their happiness" ([1855] 2005: 86). The very necessity of making one-self happy is a sign of unhappiness. We can also turn to W. E. B. Du Bois's *The Souls of Black Folk* for a description of slave songs as "songs of sorrow": "They are the music of an unhappy people, of the children of disappointment: they tell of death and suffering and unvoiced longing toward a truer world, of misty wanderings and hidden ways" ([1903] 2003: 179). See also Saidiya V. Hartman's powerful *Scenes of Subjection* for a critique of this myth of happiness which reads slave songs not only as "songs of sorrow" but as involving opacity of feeling (1997: 48). The defense of slavery insists not only on mishearing misery as happiness but also on descriptions of the unhappiness of the to-be-enslaved others. A Pennsylvania surgeon, William Chancellor, wrote in 1751: "It is accounted by numberless people that a voyage to Africa in regard to the purchasing Slaves is very vile, but in my opinion, and I think I know, it is not in the least so, tis redeeming an unhappy people from inconceivable misery" (cited in Blassingame 1992: 28). The first edition of Encyclopedia Britannica in 1798 describes "the Negros" as an "unhappy race" (Feagin 2000: 81). Descriptions of "the others" as unhappy peoples in need of liberation saturate the colonial archive. The Aboriginal peoples in Queensland were also described as "that unhappy race" (see Reid 2006).

11 Note that misery derives from the Latin word *miseria*, referring to wretchedness. I am not suggesting that the colonial archives are full of misery (we should not read such archives as evidence that "the natives" were sad, as I suggest above in note 10). I am arguing simply that we can read in colonial archives an investment in the wretchedness of natives, in how they are unfortunate and cause misfortune. Colonial rule is thus justified in terms of good fortune (for the ruled). I would describe *History of British India* as invested in the cultural misery of "Hindoos" in a quite extraordinary manner. I will not be able to offer a reading of this vast series, which was republished by Routledge in 1997 in ten volumes. For a masterful reading which attends to the complexity of the volumes as well as the political context in which they were written, see Majeed 1992.

12 This is particularly the case in Bentham's model even though he has a rather queer definition of pleasure (see chapter 1, note 2). Martha Nussbaum argues, in contrasting Bentham with John Stuart Mill, that for Bentham "nothing else is good but pleasure; pleasure and the good are the same thing" (2005: 111).

13 This speech is available on the Commission for Racial Equality website, http://83.137.212.42/sitearchive/cre/Default.aspx.LocID-ohgnew07y.RefLoc

ID-ohg00900c002.Lang-EN.htm. Last visited September 3, 2008. Note the apparent contradiction between this happy presentation of imperial history as "mixing and mingling" and Trevor Phillips's comments about unhappy diversity with which I opened my chapter. By implication, the white British community is happily diverse (willing and able to mix with others), while other communities (perhaps those with whom they mixed and mingled) become the ones who are happier with people like themselves. So although the nostalgic vision of the French village where people stay put over generations is the happiness fantasy offered by the BBC program on which Trevor Phillips made his comments, it seems that likeness is more associated in present time with minority cultures. To become happy they must give up their likeness and become diverse "like us."

14 I undertook a research project on diversity work in 2003–6 which involved interviewing diversity practitioners from Australian and British universities. One of my findings was that diversity was seen as a happy and appealing notion which works to conceal inequalities. As one practitioner described so astutely: "Diversity is like a big shiny red apple right, and it all looks wonderful . . . but if you actually cut into that apple there's a rotten core in there and you know that it's actually all rotting away and it's not actually being addressed. It all looks wonderful but the inequalities aren't being addressed." Speaking to diversity practitioners reminded me of the second wave feminist critique of the figure of the happy housewife discussed in chapter 2: Betty Friedan describes an infection underneath her smile. Diversity offers a smiling surface which creates the illusion of equality and thus works to conceal and reproduce inequalities. See Ahmed 2007a, 2007b for articles that draw on this research.

15 The book does mention Atlantic slavery as "an evil side to this commercial expansion and prosperity" (31) and then moves quickly to discuss British involvement in abolitionism, allowing the national subject to reappear as the liberator of slaves rather than a perpetrator of the slave trade. Not even slavery is allowed to disturb the happiness of imperial history. Slavery becomes, in Frantz Fanon's astute observation, "no longer even mentioned, that unpleasant memory" ([1952] 1986: 115). I could also note here that abolitionism is the name taken up by a biomedical organization that promotes happiness through science: "Abolitionists promote a rational/scientific approach towards minimizing involuntary suffering and maximizing voluntary happiness leading to the abolition of involuntary suffering and the capacity for infinite voluntary happiness as the prime ethical directive for humanity." See http://www .abolitionistsociety.com. Last visited February 9, 2009.

16 Pride is also being used as a defense against extremism: "We need to ensure that all citizens feel a sense of pride in being British and a sense of belonging to this country and to each other, and ensure that our national symbols, like the Union Jack, and the flags of the nations, are not the tools of extremists,

260 NOTES TO CHAPTER FOUR

but vividly demonstrate our unity as we saw through the Golden Jubilee celebrations" (United Kingdom Home Office, 2005a). The message here is that we must be proud in order not to give up the signs of pride to fascism. So the flag itself has returned as a happy object, a way of reclaiming being British and a refusal to have one's love for the nation be prohibited by concerns about political correctness or other political ideologies that constrain our right not only to free speech but to express happiness about the nation.

17 Such contrasts might seem in tension with my argument that happiness has become a duty for migrants, as here I seem to be placing happiness and freedom in opposition to duty. I would argue that happiness appears to be about freedom rather than duty. The happiness duty is a duty that conceals itself under the sign of freedom.

18 We are encouraged to read the film in such terms. Not only does the film play with the metaphor of "bending the rules of femininity"; it also suggests a relation of equivalence between Jess's and Jules's stories. Both are presented as girls who love football; both have conflicts with their mothers, who worry they are risking their femininity; both fall in love with their coach; both go to America. This mirroring functions as a way of making their friendship "real" within the diegesis of the film. But I think it also works to suggest that their story is somehow the same story: that "really" this is a story of girls bending the rules. But accepting the equivalence of their stories would require that we overlook some key differences: as I will show, moving up for Jess is coded as leaving her culture behind. In a way, this sacrifice disappears by scripting the story as female disobedience. See also note 23, for a reading of the use of equivalence between Jess and Joe.

19 This is not to say that the death of a stranger cannot become an event, in the sense of achieving significance. Indeed, the media can make the death of strangers an event for you. The mediation of death, however, might still rely on discourses of love. So the death of some strangers becomes more significant than the deaths of other strangers insofar as some are made present as others that you *could have* loved, that you *would have* an affinity with, as sharing some form of kinship, likeness, or proximity with you. For a reflection on the kinship of stranger death, see Eng 2002 and Butler 2004. See also a short discussion of death and identification in Ahmed 2004: 156–61.

20 In considering the production of the melancholic migrant as a figure doing certain kinds of work, I will not reflect in detail on melancholia as a lived experience of inhabiting a body that is marked as other. For an excellent account of racial melancholia, see Cheng 2001, which offers an astute analysis of the "psychic implications of the haunting negativity that has not only been attached to but has also helped to constitute the very category of the racialized" (25). See also Eng and Han's analysis of the complexity of immigration as a form of mourning: "The experience of immigration itself is based on a

structure of mourning. When one leaves one's country of origin, voluntarily or involuntarily, one must mourn a host of losses both concrete and abstract. These include homeland, family, language, identity, property, status in the community" (2003: 352). What is specific about my own contribution might be my emphasis on the *figure* of the melancholic migrant, as what allows the nation to locate soreness at a certain point, and also my concern with how consciousness of racism *as such* becomes diagnosed as melancholic.

21 For an excellent consideration of the affectivity of the turban, see Puar 2007. We can relate the anxiety about the turban to the burqa. Take Jack Straw's comments about the burqa made in 2006 when he was British home secretary: that the burqa made him feel uncomfortable and that the failure of the covered woman to show her face was a refusal to communicate. When defending his comments to a Muslim woman, he said, "If we bumped into each other in the street, you would be able to say hello to me. I would not be able to do the same. The obvious reason is that I cannot see your face. Chance conversations make society stronger." The Muslim woman becomes the stranger; she prohibits our capacity to say hello, as a happily weak signifier of social solidarity. We might say that the Muslim woman is constituted as unfriendly, as refusing the very grounds of friendship. Unhappy difference becomes the blockage point; the point where things stop, where community fails to deliver its social promise. Note also how discomfort is used here as a demand: for the white body to be comfortable, others must unveil. Such differences become unhappy; they become the origin of national unhappiness, such that unveiling is imagined as liberation to happiness.

22 I should note here that the father's speech (which is addressed to Joe) supplements his account of her refusal to let Jess play, with a comment about racism in sport *in the present*, referring to the lack of Asian male footballers. That his memory of racism becomes a critique of racism as ongoing lived reality for British Asians is crucial, suggesting not that the memory is a false memory but that consciousness of racism becomes a form of preoccupation with injury that gives up on the possibility of playing at all.

23 By reading Joe's speech act in terms of identification and whiteness, it could appear that I am negating the significance of his Irishness, with its postcolonial history, as not quite being white in the white/right way. It is of course significant that empathy is offered by an Irishman, as a kind of shared recognition of what it means to be the butt of an insult. That Joe's actual comment allows us to pass over the moment of Jess's insult does matter. In terms of the narrative, this speech act operates to create a relation of equivalence between Jess and Joe, which is perhaps one way in which it aims to restore universality to the experience of injury. By implication, both Jess and Joe share a common ground as the recipients of racist insults. But the analogies go further. The film also centers on their scars as forms of injury they have in common. Jess has a

scar on her leg, which is a source of shame. Joe has a scar on his knee. In one
scene, they talk about their scars. They share a mutual confession about past
hurts, which is also the moment that the love story begins to take shape. Jess
relays to Joe how her injury was caused. She was at home as her mother was
at work at Heathrow. She was cooking herself baked beans, slipped, and got
burnt. Note how the injury is associated with being at home, and with the absence of the mother. The airport is an unhappy object that must be converted
into a happy object by the plot of the film. For Joe, the injury comes not only
from playing football but also from his bad relationship with his father. He
played with an injury as his father had put him under pressure to succeed. So
the scars have histories, each linked to a parent of the same sex, as uncanny
reversals of the other (the mother's absence, the father's presence). The act of
identification, of sharing forms of hurt, allows those injuries to be healed.

24 For a discussion of this decision, see Warn 2003.

25 Hybrid familiality can also be a queer familiality—interracial queer love can
offer its own reconciliation fantasy. A useful contrast with *Bend It Like Beckham* is the film *Chicken Tikka Masala* (2005, dir. Harmage Singh Kalirai), which
is about two men falling in love: Jimi (Chris Bisson), a British Asian, and
Jack (Peter Ash), from a white working-class background. Jimi is supposed to
marry Simran (Jinder Mahal). In a comedy of errors, his parents think the reason he is not happy about the marriage is because he is in a relationship with
Vanessa (Sally Bankes), who is Jack's aunt, and the father of her child Hannah
(Katy Clayton). They then arrange for Jack and Vanessa to be married, which
Jimi and Jack go along with, as it means they could still share a house as a
queer family. What is extraordinary about this film is the extent of its reliance
on happiness as a speech act. Let me quote from the dialogue. At the engagement party with Simran, his grandmother says: "Jimi why are you making
such a glum face? Smile it's your engagement. You spoil the photos with that
sulk." His father says, "This is for your happiness, son." His grandmother later
says, "I'm so proud of you. This has been a happy day," to which Jimi replies,
"That's great grandmother, at least one of us is really happy." When Jack finds
out about the engagement, he says, "This is not just about your life or your
happiness. I mean what about the girl you are marrying? Have you thought
about her happiness? You really think your parents want you to be unhappy?"
When Jack then asks Jimi what he wants, he replies, "I just want to be happy,
but unfortunately I am only happy when you're all happy and that includes
my parents," to which Jack replies, "Tell them what makes you happy." When
Jack and Jimi go to his parents, Jack makes a queer joke to Simran out of frustration: "He bends over backwards to keep people happy." When the parents
think that Vanessa is Jimi's girlfriend, Simran's father says to them, "You must
forgive Jimi. After all he is the only one. Our future is in his happiness." When
they arrange for Jimi, Vanessa, and Hannah to go to their house [for what

turns out to be a second engagement party], his father says, "We just thought we would swap brides. If this is what makes you happy, this is what makes us happy." After the party, Jimi's father asks his wife, "Just tell me one thing, did Jimi look happy to you?" She answers, "Did he look happy? Of course he looked happy. This is what he wants." On the wedding day, Jimi's mother says to Vanessa, "All we want is for you and Jimi to be happy." When Jimi's father shouts out "stop the wedding," he asks Jimi, whom he loves, and he says Jack. When he asks Jimi, "Why all this?" Jimi answers, "I have always wanted to do good by you. To make you happy. To make you proud of me. When you wanted me to be a doctor, I studied for that. But when and how I fell in love I do not know. What I know is I love Jack more than life itself. But for you, I could even sacrifice that." His father replies, in what becomes the true reconciliation moment of the film, "Son, you are my flesh and blood, I seek your happiness not your sacrifice." Happiness eventually binds father and son together, allowing them to overcome difference and antagonism, as a reconciliation of want premised on the parents wanting their child's happiness above all wants. In representing queer desire in happiness terms, the film straightens that desire. We do not see any queer intimacy between Jack and Jimi, and they speak in a language that seems more akin to straight forms of romance. One wonders whether queerness can be incorporated into happiness only by being made to approximate signs of heterosexuality. See the first section of chapter 3 for a discussion of what it means when queers must be happy in order to gain recognition as queers.

26 For a longer explanation of the ethics of proximity in multiculturalism, see Ahmed 2004: 133–41.

27 In an interview on the Jonathan Dimbleby program in 2006, Trevor Phillips argued that freedom of speech means the freedom to be offensive. He directed his comments specifically against Muslims in part in response to the controversy over the Danish cartoons. The very "offendability" of Muslims becomes a restriction of our freedom. Freedom of speech, rather like freedom to be happy, becomes compulsory. It also becomes a quality attached to some rather than others. They "must" accept our freedom and happiness or leave. See http://news.bbc.co.uk/2/hi/uk_news/4752804.stm for more information about this discussion. Last visited January 7, 2009.

28 This is a tricky point. It remains (and will remain) politically important to represent domestic violence wherever and whenever it happens. And yet we also need to expose the racism in how violence within immigrant families and communities is represented. In many cases, violence is depicted as intrinsic to immigrant culture. The violence of the Muslim father is attributed to the violence of Islam. In cases of violence within majority cultures, that violence is usually represented as individual and exceptional.

29 When considering Muslim families, the investment in the happiness of the

second generation is heightened because of the "sticky" association of Islam with terror (Ahmed 2004). Indeed, the possibility of home-grown terrorism has even been described as the failure to protect the second generation from the transmission of melancholia, making them easy targets for radical Islam, which steals the affections of the second generation, recruiting them into hate or turning them from happiness to hate. As one newspaper article describes: "a section of the Muslim young . . . faces these problems with only the support of parents whose world view and values might arguably be better suited to the hamlets of Waziristan . . . When the problem of indoctrination is seen also as a problem of exploitability, a clearer picture emerges of the dynamic that aids Islamists in their targeting of individuals. But while the problem might be better understood, the job to be done suddenly gets harder, since the discussion is now about how parents, extended families, and wider communities raise their children" (Rahman 2007). The exploitability of the second generation is attributed to the failure of the first generation to raise their children in the right way, which I would argue rests on a wider perception of the first generation as melancholic, as failing to let their children go (let their children be happy) in the very desire to hold onto cultural identity.

30　Many thanks to Ali Rattansi, whose helpful comments on an earlier version of this chapter helped me to realize that I needed to pose this question. A more sympathetic reading of how Jess is portrayed within *Bend It Like Beckham* is possible that would recognize in her embodied situation some of the pressures, conflicts, and anxieties of second-generation daughters. At the same time, I acknowledge that I have experienced some of the unhappy consequences of being a happy sign of diversity, of being rather "oddly" a conventional form of social hope. Once when I was speaking about whiteness while delivering a paper, a member of the audience responded, "But you're a professor": as if to say, when women of color become professors the whiteness of the world recedes. If you embody the hope of overcoming the unhappy history of racism, you can be interpellated as a sign of its overcoming. When you are a happy sign of diversity, the very talk about racism or whiteness becomes a form of ingratitude, a failure to receive the hospitality by sharing in the happiness you have been given.

31　I suspect I am offering here an overly happy version of the compromise. A classic saying about compromises is that they are decisions no one is happy with. In reaching a compromise everyone might lose "such and such" amount of happiness. The key would be to make this "such and such" as equal as possible such that we would all happily give up happiness. A happy compromise might rest upon the perception of an equality of unhappiness. Note also that a compromise is a joint promise. We might speculate that the promise of happiness, as a joint promise, also rests on the distribution of unhappiness. Happiness might become a social or personal crisis when that distribution seems unfair, that is, when some people appear to give up more happiness than others. In such situations the promise of happiness would be regarded as too compromising.

32 I am oversimplifying for the sake of argument here or suggesting that this oversimplification is part of the problem with how generational and cultural conflicts are aligned. In *Bend It Like Beckham*, the words "who wants to cook *alo gobi* when you can bend the ball like Beckham" do narrate conflict in this way, where "bending the ball like Beckham" is read as wanting something different from cooking *alo gobi*, which itself becomes a culinary metaphor for the reproduction of culture. However, I would argue that the film "wants" to say that these wants are not in collision: that you can do and have both, or that you can have it both ways. I have questioned whether the film succeeds in offering such a happy resolution, by suggesting that some wants are given more value as signs of freedom to be happy. Our task in reading such mainstream narratives about migration is to read for the location and distribution of social wants.

33 This was certainly my experience of being in a mixed-race migrant family. The only time my father brought up our failure to be Muslim was during moments of conflict or when he had already made a judgment that we were doing something wrong. I understood this at the time and so was never especially upset by being found wanting. And the only time others brought up his Muslim identity was when something went wrong. When my father and mother separated, one of his white friends said to my mother, "This is what happens when you marry a Muslim." I found this kind of speech act much more upsetting. We must learn to think about what I would call forms of "lazy racism," when racist attitudes that are part of the background and which go unnoticed are brought to the foreground as (often retrospective) explanations of conflict.

34 My own memories of going to Pakistan and hearing of Pakistan as a child were not simply about the unhappiness of not being from where I lived or of being asked to identify with what I was not (although I did experience the unhappy effects of being recognized as a stranger, as a body out of place, by those with whom I shared my place of residence) but also about a sense of excitement about intimate histories that are not woven into the fabric of where I lived. See the final chapter, "The Orient and Other Others," from *Queer Phenomenology* for an explanation of this excitement and its relation to secrecy (to what cannot be revealed from a viewing point).

35 The problem of this fantasy is that it locates unhappiness within the white working classes. This problem was exacerbated by the film version of the novel, which for me was almost unwatchable for how it ridiculed white working-class culture and the sharp contrast it set up between cultured migrants and the uncultured white working classes.

36 In *My Son the Fanatic* the father, Parvez, wants his son to achieve relative prox-

imity to the good life: "Was it asking too much for Ali to get a good job now, marry the right girl and start a family? Once this happened, Parvez would be happy" ([1994] 2008: 6). The father's happiness rests on the son being integrated into English society. The son, Ali, cannot bear this Western idea of happiness and becomes a fanatic, refusing to identity with "the mix" of English culture. The novella maintains the place of "home-grown" Islamic fundamentalism as an enigma or mystery (how could this happen?) but offers a rather different account of its emergence as a form of disobedience to the parental wish for happiness. At the same time, I would suggest that Kureishi's novella rests on a reduction of Islam to fundamentalism (which implicitly idealizes liberal secularism as a horizon that admits to the diversity of likes).

37 This quote is taken from the Home Office report *Secure Borders, Safe Haven: Integration with Diversity in Modern Britain* (United Kingdom 2002). This document reported on what was called (problematically) "the race riots" that took place in the north of England in 2001. The metaphor of parallel lines implies that proximity between communities is what is lacking and that proximity can generate national happiness. It does not recognize ordinary proximities that do exist; nor does it recognize that a lack of proximity might be an effect of racism and the power of whiteness to secure its haven. For further discussion of this report, see my chapter, "In the Name of Love" (Ahmed 2004).

38 The nation becomes the universal through being imagined as the bearer of the promise of happiness. It is no accident that V. S. Naipaul's (1990) identification with universal culture proceeds through asserting the ideality of happiness: "It is an elastic idea; it fits all men. It implies a certain kind of society, a certain kind of awakened spirit. I don't imagine my father's Hindu parents would have been able to understand the idea. So much is contained in it: the idea of the individual, responsibility, choice, the life of the intellect, the idea of vocation and perfectibility and achievement. It is an immense human idea. It cannot be reduced to a fixed system. It cannot generate fanaticism. But it is known to exist, and because of that, other more rigid systems in the end blow away" (n. p.). The universality of happiness is one that is shaped around particular bodies: it cannot admit fanatics who appear outside the horizon of the human. I would describe Naipaul's identification with universality as melancholic; it cannot grieve for the loss the grandparents who can appear only as the ones who do not understand happiness, who suffer from what we might call "happiness illiteracy." Nor can it cover over his inability to inhabit this universal, given that the family has already left its trace. To draw on Douglas Crimp's analysis of melancholia (2004: 13), identifying with universal happiness as a migrant subject might involve *identifying with that which repudiates you.*

5. Happy Futures

1   Rather ironically this utterance, "no future," is also made by one of the fore-
runners of the positive psychology movement, Robert Holden. He argues that
"there is no future" and that you should "give your best now," offering a critique of the very futurity of happiness discourse, which he argues involves a
fear of happiness or a "happychondria" (1998: 44). He claims "*now* is sacred"
and that "*now* is an eternal treasure chest" (5–6). We can witness how "no
future" can mean different things as an utterance, just as forms of politics
which affirm the present can affirm quite different things, or forms of politics
which negate the present can negate different things. The point might be the
kinds of orientations we have toward the past, present, and future, which are
irreducible to yes-saying or no-saying.

2   Optimism and pessimism are ways of directing affect toward the future, so our
question becomes not so much *whether* we feel hope or despair but *in what*
do we feel hope and despair. Some forms of good feeling and some forms of
bad feeling can create points of alienation. As I explored in the final section
of chapter 3, queers can also be affectively alien insofar as they direct positive
feeling in the wrong way. I called this "happily queer." This is why I would not
describe queer pride as normative. To be proud about what others recognize
as shameful is a form of affective disobedience. Queer pride events, where
queers populate the streets and celebrate signs of queerness, remain subver-
sive and politically important as well as enjoyable. Inappropriate good feelings
can still create spaces for political action.

3   I agree with Lee Edelman's reading of the novel: as he suggests, the novel
attributes infertility to sexual freedom (2004: 11–13). The film offers a more
progressive account of infertility, even if it makes infertility into a problem.
In one scene, Theo is on the bus, which passes by a familiar sight: a group of
people chanting, protesting, activists of some kind, with boards and logos.
They are the called "repenters" and resemble Christian fundamentalists.
Placards read: "Infertility is god's punishment"; "He has taken away his most
precious gift to us." The camera refuses identification with them. Theo turns
away, and sixties music signifying sexual freedom is playing. In other words,
the film speaks back to the novel by refusing to attribute infertility to sexual
freedom. Perhaps the kind of world that attributes infertility to sexual freedom is the kind of world that has no future.

4   I will be exploring "silly" forms of happiness in the conclusion to this book.

5   So if we describe happiness as false consciousness, we would not be challenging happiness at the level of belief: we would not be saying that such and such
happiness is wrong or false or that so and so is wrong when he describes himself as happy. We would be describing happiness as a veil that does not simply

conceal unhappiness but reproduces a certain order of things, defining the very conditions of intelligibility and truth. We would witness the interested nature of the belief rather than suspending belief. A good example of this would be the happy signs of diversity discussed in chapter 4; not only do they conceal the struggles and antagonism of racism but they reproduce racism at the very moment that racism is no longer "believed" in. To recognize happy diversity as a veil would not mean the exposure of the truth. The veil is not what the truth hides behind; it participates in the production of the truth. We have to learn to see things otherwise over time. The labor of antiracism is thus very much about learning to recognize racism and the how and where of its reproduction. Antiracism is not about seeing through racist beliefs but reading how those beliefs are sustained through disappearance.

6 Happiness or unhappiness can become compulsive in this way, such that you encounter what happens as a threat to a feeling that must persist. My suspicion is that we tend to notice when people cling onto their unhappiness (and see them as stubborn in their persistence). We don't tend to notice so easily when people cling onto happiness, perhaps because we assume that such persistence can only be a good thing, because it is persistence with a good thing. But persistence in happiness can have problematic effects. You can overlook or look over what gets in the way of your happiness. You can also act in quite problematic ways to ensure its persistence. Both happiness and unhappiness can be a way of getting stuck. So although in my reflections on melancholia and conversion in chapter 4 I challenged the reduction of unhappiness to stuckness, I do not deny that unhappiness can involve getting stuck. The reduction might be an expression of the ease with which unhappiness is noticeable whether or not it gets stuck. It is because of this ease that one might have to persist in one's unhappiness: there is such a compulsion to convert unhappiness to happiness (even when the object of unhappiness persists) that we might have to hold on even harder, which might mean being as stubborn as we are perceived.

7 We could also refer here to Žižek's distinction between subjective violence and objective violence (including systematic and symbolic violence). Žižek suggests that our cultural preoccupation with subjective violence (where there is an agent who performs the violence who can be clearly identified) allows us to overlook objective violence, which becomes a background, defining what Žižek calls "the non-violent zero level" (2008b: 2). I think Žižek misses some nuances here: some agents of violence are visible precisely because other forms of subjective violence recede into the background, becoming inseparable from the social and symbolic system. The figure of the killjoy teaches us this: the killjoy destroys the "objective peace" only if the violence performed by certain subjects remains concealed, or their violence remains concealed by identifying the agent who exposes this violence as violent. The killjoy could

also be considered through the figure of the whistle-blower: in exposing the misconduct of an organization, the one who blows the whistle is often perceived as causing a problem rather than exposing a problem. To blow the whistle is an act of institutional disloyalty: suggesting that the very demand for loyalty is a demand that subjects "agree" to cover over misconduct, for which they will get something in return. Happiness is promised to those who agree to cover over the causes of unhappiness: the promise of happiness is a promise of return. To speak out about violence and injustice is to refuse this promise.

8   Indeed, one might say that Theo is better described as a rebel without a cause, although maybe he is not even quite that. I am well aware that my analysis of this film is not an analysis of revolution, which, as Hannah Arendt shows so well, requires more than individual or collective rebellion: "only where this pathos of novelty is present and where novelty is connected with the idea of freedom are we entitled to speak of revolution" ([1961] 1973: 34). This is not a film *about* revolution, although like many dystopias, it is a film about the nightmare of the present world (a vision of a future predicated on its lack of remoteness), and thus it is in a way about the need for revolution. So why evoke the figure of the revolutionary? I do so for strategic reasons: I want to consider what Michel Foucault calls "the enigma of revolt" (1979: 132) in ways that do not locate revolutionary hope in traditional models of revolutionary action. Arendt does reflects on emotion and revolution, suggesting that revolutionary passion has some relation to compassion: "The words *le peuple* are the key words for every understanding of the French revolution, and their connotations were determined by those who were exposed to the spectacle of the people's sufferings, which they themselves did not share. For the first time, the word covered more than those who did not participate in government, not the citizens but the low people. The very definition of the word was born out of compassion and the term became the equivalent for misfortune and unhappiness" (75). The implication of Arendt's reflection is not that the revolutionary task is to feel compassion but that the revolutionary task involves a reorientation toward the causes of sufferings that are not shared. My interest in Theo is in what happens when he takes up his task. Thanks to Elena Loizidou for her encouragement to think with Arendt.

9   Schopenhauer's argument about the positivity of pain can be linked to the role he gives to compassion and sympathy in his ethics. He argues in *On the Basis of Morality* that although we may be pleased by another's happiness, "the fortunate and contented man *as such* leaves us indifferent" ([1840] 1995: 146). Our "immediate sympathy" is stirred "by the suffering, privation, and misfortune of another *purely as such*" (146). Although I do not agree that we are morally indifferent to another's happiness, I think Schopenhauer offers us useful insights into the relationship between compassion and identification.

He suggests that identification takes place through "weal and woe." In the case of woe, "I feel *his* woe just as I ordinarily feel only my own" (143). Given woe is what is positive, for Schopenhauer, identification takes place primarily through unhappiness, such that I come to feel the blows to the other's happiness as blows to my own. See also chapter 1, note 28, for a related discussion of sympathy and happiness with reference to David Hume and Adam Smith.

10 Given this, we can see that many texts that are read as pessimistic can be read as a form of optimism at least in terms of their points of affective conversion. For instance, Lee Edelman's critique of reproductive futurism discussed in the introductory section of this chapter could be considered not only "optimistically motivated" (Snediker 2009: 15) but also optimistic in a more precise sense. By "embracing" the negation of queer from normative culture, Edelman turns the "no" into a "yes": in other words, converting bad feeling into good (which would go something like: we are happy to be unhappy for you, such that your unhappiness with us makes us happier to be us, to be not you, or not). This affective conversion is closer to Leibniz than Schopenhauer even though Edelman explicitly critiques ideas of hope and progress. We can see how the queer negativity might function as utopic in a later statement by Edelman in his contribution to the *PMLA* special issue "The Anti-Social Turn in Queer Theory." He argues that "*No Future* . . . approaches negativity as society's constitutive antagonism, which sustains itself on the promise of resolution in futurity's time to come, much as capitalism is able to sustain itself only by finding and exploiting new markets. As the figure of nonproductivity, then, and of the system's ironic incoherence, the queer both threatens and consolidates the universal empire of the Futurch. But what threatens it most is queer negativity's refusal of positive identity through a drivelike resistance to the violence, the originary violation, effected as Adorno writes, 'by the all-subjugating identity principle'" (2006: 822). If queer becomes a figure of nonproductivity, then such nonproductivity is also contained by the figure, which as a figure might remain attached to some more than others (the subject who are the subjects of queer theory, one wonders). Note how the idea that queer "threatens and consolidates" the universal empire of the Futurch, in the second sentence, turns into an emphasis on queer as that which "threatens" the violence of identity in the third sentence. I would say that queer as the figure of absolute negativity, as that which threatens the violence of identity, might offer a dream of a more perfect order. Such a dream might be available to those who can resist the violence of identity, which is arguably dependent on the capacity to transcend identity categories, that is, on the unmarked and unremarkable nature of privilege.

11 Of course, such tactics do not always work: we can be hopeful, perhaps even "secretly hopeful," simply as an effect of going for something. To dedicate time to something is after all to become invested in something. Hope can be pro-

duced simply as an effect of going for something. Even if you have prepared yourself for disappointment you can still feel disappointed if you do not get what you want. I would even say, perhaps counterintuitively, that you can be disappointed without being hopeful. You can still want something even if you have already given up hope of getting it. To give up the belief you can acquire something does not suspend wanting something and can be a way of wanting something without admitting your want. And to give up something in case you lose it might allow the subject to achieve a sense of mastery. You would master a potential loss by making that loss actual: as if you would say to the object "go away" rather than let it simply be taken away. Freud's analysis of the child's game in *Beyond the Pleasure Principle* ([1920] 1964)—described as the *fort-da* game where the child throws away a cotton reel and occasionally pulls it back—might be redescribed in these terms. If the child seems to repeat the trauma of the mother's departure by throwing the object away, it also gives the child a certain pleasure in mastery and even revenge, of being able to make it/her "go away" (see Caruth 1996 and 2001 for a good analysis of the dynamics of departure and loss in Freud's description of the game). We could reread the game in terms of hope: you would give up the object of hope rather than have it be lost, as if it is better to throw things way than have them be taken away, to be active rather passive in the face of loss. You might give up something before you lose something, or "just in case" you might lose something, a dynamic which could be related to what Lauren Berlant calls "cruel optimism" (2008a). You give up hoping for something *because* you are hopeful about what would follow proximity to that thing. You have not then really given up hope but expressed an attachment: you want it, and thus you want to give up hope of getting it. So when you don't get the thing you have given up hope of getting you can still be disappointed. You might live with this disappointment by the pleasure of being able to say to yourself or to others: "See, I told you there was no hope!"

12   However, I would not argue, as Immanuel Kant does, that "all *hoping* has happiness for its object" ([1781] 1990: 452). I think you can hope for other kinds of things. Hope does make things good—insofar as to hope for something is to want that thing to come—although of course getting what you hoped for does not necessarily retain the goodness of the thing. To get what you hoped for can even mean to lose hope.

13   See Neves 2003 for an excellent analysis of optimism, pessimism, and hope in Durkheim's sociology.

14   We could return to *Bend It Like Beckham* and offer a more sympathetic reading of Jess's situation. We could recognize the capacity to lose focus on racism as a way of dealing with racism rather that refusing to deal with racism. Such recognition does not mean we have to suspend our critique of how the narrative conversions within the film posit this overcoming of racism as a debt to

the white man. And we still need to attend to the risks of overlooking racism for minorities — even as a survival tactic. See chapter 4, note 30, for a related discussion.

15 The figure of the revolutionary is perhaps difficult to separate from the desire for white men to be heroic. For example, a conference on communism took place at Birkbeck College in May 2009 in which all the speakers were white, and all the speakers bar one were male. Feminists of color must stay killjoys of the left: the body of the (self-identified) revolutionary can be hard to separate from the body of privilege.

16 This is one way of describing a political economy of hope. Hope will do different things depending on who is hoping for what. I am completing the final revisions to this book in February 2009 just after the inauguration of Barack Obama as president of the United States. Obama speaks eloquently about hope and his election has come to embody a certain moment of hope. We can give value to such moments: hope or any other positive emotions do not need to be understood as necessarily uncritical. It is interesting to note that Obama's own hope in hope dramatizes how hope can offer an affective disobedience. Those who are presumed to be hopeless — perhaps Frantz Fanon's "wretched of the earth" — disobey by hoping for a different future in which they will no longer be wretched. In his keynote address at the Democratic Convention in 2004, Obama asked: "Do we participate in a politics of cynicism, or do we participate in a politics of hope? . . . I'm not talking about blind optimism here, the almost willful ignorance that thinks unemployment will go away if we just don't think about it, or the health care crisis will solve itself if we just ignore it. That's not what I'm talking about. I'm talking about something more substantial. It's the hope of slaves sitting around a fire singing freedom songs; the hope of immigrants setting out for distant shores; the hope of a young naval lieutenant bravely patrolling the Mekong Delta; the hope of a millworker's son who dares to defy the odds; the hope of a skinny kid with a funny name who believes that America has a place for him, too. Hope in the face of difficulty, hope in the face of uncertainty: the audacity of hope." We can see here that hope, however disobedient, can still work as a form of assimilation: hoping for freedom is converted into hoping to have a place in the nation, in a way that keeps the nation in place as the distributor of hope. We can see how audacious hope can slide into something rather less audacious by thinking about how Obama inserts his own story into the story of hope. The hope that we can overcome racism (that a "skinny kid with a funny name" can have a place in America, can participate in the American dream, and, projecting forward, that such a kid could even become president) can also offer a fantasy that racism has been overcome. In other words, Obama's hope of becoming postracist can be translated into a fantasy of being postracial. It might be helpful to place this speech alongside his more recent speech in Philadelphia

NOTES TO CHAPTER FIVE 273

in 2008 (now often referred to as "the race speech"), in which Obama spoke of how anger and hurt about racism cannot be wished away: "For the men and women of Reverend Wright's generation, the memories of humiliation and doubt and fear have not gone away; nor has the anger and the bitterness of those years. . . . The anger is real; it is powerful; and to simply wish it away, to condemn it without understanding its roots, only serves to widen the chasm of misunderstanding that exists between the races." In speaking of anger and bad feeling as antagonisms that cannot be wished away (we can think of such a wish as the happiness wish), we can make more sense of hope's audacity. We have hope *because* of anger; we have hope if we do not and will not allow our hope for a different world be taken as a sign of overcoming.

17　Thanks to Michael Rothberg and those who participated in my workshop at the Unit of Criticism, University of Illinois, who directed me to this short story via an essay by Elizabeth Povinelli. This short story is based loosely on William James's essay "The Moral Philosopher and the Moral Life," in which he asks the question: "Or if the hypothesis were offered us of a world in which Messrs. Fourier's and Bellamy's and Morris's utopias should all be outdone, and millions kept permanently happy on the one simple condition that a certain lost soul on the far-off edge of things should lead a life of lonely torture, what except a specifical and independent sort of emotion can it be which would make us immediately feel, even though an impulse arose within us to clutch at the happiness so offered, how hideous a thing would be its enjoyment when deliberately accepted as the fruit of such a bargain?" ([1891] 1956: 188).

18　One could contrast both of these films with *Happy Feet* (2006), in which the penguin who ends up saving his community is happy. When he is born, his father notices he is doing something "odd" with his feet. He asks why, and his son says it is because his feet are happy. To have happy feet is to be a deviant: in this film, happiness for penguins is supposed to reside in the voice (that sings) and not the feet (that dance). Our hero thus has a misdirected happiness, which is what leads to his alienation from the community and his eventual capacity to save the day by acquiring knowledge of what lies beyond the horizon of happiness. However, as Judith Halberstam has argued, the narrative is limited by individualism, its organization of deviance as the struggle of the individual against the conformity of the collective (2008: 272).

19　We can listen to Winston's weary thoughts in *1984* as he anticipates the arguments of the Party: "That the choice for mankind lay between freedom and happiness, and that, for the great bulk of mankind happiness was better. That the Party was the eternal guardian of the weak, a dedicated sect doing evil that good might come, sacrificing its own happiness to that of others" (Orwell [1949] 1985: 26). Weariness in proximity to words can teach us about words: to hear wearily here is to learn how happiness requires giving up freedom.

20　Badiou offers a concrete description of such nihilism: "When a prime min-

274 NOTES TO CHAPTER FIVE

ister, the political eulogist of a civic ethics, declares that France 'cannot welcome [*accueillir*] all the misery of the world,' he is careful not to tell us about the criteria and the methods that will allow us to distinguish the part of the said misery that we welcome from that part which we will request—no doubt from within detention centres—to return to its place of death, so that we might continue to enjoy those unshared riches which, as we know, condition both our happiness and our 'ethics.' And in the same way, it is certainly impossible to settle on stable, 'responsible,' and of course 'collective' criteria in the name of which commissions on bio-ethics will distinguish between eugenics and euthanasia, between the scientific improvement of the white man and his happiness, and the elimination 'with dignity' of monsters, of those who suffer or become unpleasant to behold" ([1993] 2001: 37).

21 The miserable child is often evoked within humanitarian discourse in a way that appeals to our sympathy. That our capacity for identification rests on the figure of the child is no accident. The child is already imagined as innocent; the child who is unhappy thus cannot deserve its unhappiness. Henry Jenkins argues that the ideological presumption of the child's innocence "allows us to direct anger against any social force that makes our children unhappy" (1998: 9). The use of the figure of the child exposes our reliance on a distinction between deserved and undeserved unhappiness, a distinction which makes explicit the violence of happiness as being about "just deserts." The idea that you must deserve happiness turns unhappiness into a sign of being undeserving. According to this logic, the undeserving are the ones who deserve their unhappiness.

22 It is interesting to consider Kant on this point. In *The Metaphysics of Morals* Kant uses the idea of the contagion (defined as natural sympathy) to argue that sympathy cannot be a duty. He advances the rather odd argument that to be sympathetic to someone's misery cannot be turned into a duty as such sympathy would create more suffering and it cannot be a duty to increase suffering. So rather than one person suffering x, two people would suffer x, although the first person would only be the one "really" affected by x. For Kant, to be sympathetic would thus "increase the ills in the world" ([1797] 1996: 205). However, Kant also argues that while we do not have a duty to share suffering, we have an indirect duty to cultivate the faculty of sympathy or compassion, which he describes in quite practical terms of where the moral subject should not "not go": "It is therefore a duty not to avoid the places where the poor who lack the most basic necessities are to be found but rather to seek them out, and not to shun sickrooms or debtor's prisons and so forth in order to avoid sharing painful feelings" (205). Although Kant suggests that we do not want to increase human suffering by sharing suffering, he does argue that we have an indirect duty not to avoid proximity to the scenes of suffering. He refuses to participate in what I described in chapter 3 as the self-regulation of feeling

worlds where you would refuse proximity to unhappiness in order to protect your happiness.

23 As I have already suggested, Schopenhauer's pessimism offers unhappiness as a telos, as being the endpoint of all human action. My critique of happiness does not involve such pessimism. I am not calling for optimism (the happiness telos) or pessimism (the unhappiness telos) as a foundations of politics. I would call instead for a politics without foundation, a politics without endpoints that are assumed to govern action. Such a politics will offer a queer mix of optimism and pessimism, hope and despair: what we mix up will depend on what gets thrown up.

24 My thanks to Tony Birch for an inspirational paper delivered at the Australian Critical Race and Whiteness Studies conference in 2007. Birch referred to *Freedom Dreams*, and his paper encouraged me to be more hopeful about hope.

25 Žižek's optimism about the boat recalls Foucault's own reflection on the boat as "heterotopia *par excellence*" (1986: 27). As Foucault explained, "The boat is a floating piece of space, a place without a place, that exists by itself, that is closed in on itself and at the same time is given over to the infinity of the sea and that, from port to port, from tack to tack, from brothel to brothel, it goes as far as the colonies in search of the most precious treasures they conceal in their gardens, you will understand why the boat has not only been for our civilisation, from the sixteenth century until the present, the great instrument of economic development (I have not been speaking of that today) but has been simultaneously the greatest reserve of the imagination" (26). We learn from Foucault's description how much the technologies of utopia are also technologies of capital and empire.

26 It is useful to note here that Daniel Gilbert's reflection on happy futures turns to the boat in the following way: "We want—and we *should* want—to control the direction of our boat because some futures are better than others," although he suggests that "the truth is that much of our steering is in vain" as "the future is fundamentally different than it appears through the prospectiscope" (2006: 23). An instrumental relationship to the future—and to happiness—might involve a fantasy that we can control our boats: that we know where we are going, where we want to be going, and how to get there.

Conclusion

1 Jean-Paul Sartre describes this process of convincing yourself of feeling in more phenomenological terms. He argues, "If I make myself sad, it is because I *am* not sad—the being of the sadness escapes me by and in the very act by which I affect myself with it" ([1965] 1993: 170–71). Even though you can

make yourself sad, the value of such a feeling "stands as a regulative meaning of my sadness, not as its constitutive modality" (171). So you make yourself happy insofar as you are not happy—and in becoming happy or being affected happily the being of happiness escapes. Happiness becomes a regulative meaning and not a modality.

2   Despite this, happiness remains quite slippery for John Stuart Mill. After all, he argues that some forms of happiness are better than others, which he describes as a "difference of quality in pleasures" ([1863] 2001: 8), a controversial idea some would argue takes him outside a utilitarian and hedonic framework (for a good discussion of Mill's "qualitative hedonism," see West 2004). It is interesting to note how quickly these different qualities of feeling become attached to different qualities of persons: "a being of higher faculties requires more to make him happy" (9), which leads Mill to his famous conclusion that "it is better to be a human being dissatisfied than a pig satisfied; better to be Socrates dissatisfied than a fool satisfied" (10). Such a statement could be read as a rejection of the principle that happiness is necessarily good (it is better to be wise and unhappy than happy and foolish) and also points to some limitations of happiness, perhaps as a way of being satisfied with what exists (a lowering of horizons). But we should note how quickly the moral distinction between good and bad happiness becomes a social distinction between those who are worth more and less.

3   For an excellent essay on feminist uses of *ressentiment* to describe feminism's own attachments, see Stringer 2000. I have articulated some concerns about the critique of feminist *ressentiment* in chapter 8 of *The Cultural Politics of Emotion* (2004).

4   It is interesting to consider the role of the passive/active distinction in Kant's arguments about inclination and the moral law. In *Critique of Practical Reason* Kant describes all feelings as passive and pathological, as ways of being affected or under influence ([1788] 2004: 79). But he qualifies this argument by describing respect as a moral feeling which is produced simply by reason (80). Respect is moral insofar as it is respect for the moral law (83). In a footnote in *Groundwork for the Metaphysics of Morals*, Kant defends this distinction in the following way: "It might be here objected to me that I take refuge behind the word *respect* in an obscure feeling, instead of giving a distinct solution of the question by a concept of reason. But although respect is a feeling, it is not a feeling *received* through influence, but is *self-wrought* by a rational concept, and, therefore, is specifically distinct from all feelings of the former kind, which may be referred either to inclination or fear" ([1785] 2005: 62). Passive feelings—those that are received through influence—refer to inclination or fear. Respect is "self-wrought." Respect provides Kant with a fantasy that the rational subject is not affected or under influence. I would argue that this subject is precisely under the influence of the law.

5 I challenge the idea that the happiness of the over-man can transcend the happiness of serfs. As Mari Ruti has observed, authenticity is often defined against the "auspices of conformity" (2006: 121). The philosopher-subject might aim to disassociate an "I" from the horror of "they." Authentic happiness would here be the happiness of one defined against the many. This fear or hatred of conformity against which an "I" can appear might return us to the question of equality. I noted in the introduction to this book that the origins of political economy are premised on happiness: the move from the equality of what Adam Smith called "the miserably poor" to a division of labor in which ever the poorest have more than what "any savage" could acquire ([1776] 1999: 105). I would suggest that in contemporary political discourse we have an inheritance of this view in the very perception of equality and equal opportunity as misery devices or leveling devices: a way of bringing others down (the mediocre and the miserable are conflated), of getting in the way of a happiness that is presumed by right to belong to those above (their happiness is naturalized as merit). The struggle for equality is rewritten as the *generalizing of the state of misery*. Redressing inequality thus already functions as a challenge to happiness and the terms of its appeal.

6 I am well aware that this is a counter-intuitive argument. The refinement of the distinction between active/passive surely depends on the mobility of the terms *activity* and *passivity* and thus upon their detachment from specific bodies? I would suggest that the more such terms are detached from bodies, the more they move around, *the stickier they become*. So we can take up these terms "as if" they do not have a referential function, which allows words to acquire more rather than less affective force. We can then have an elitism that does not locate its referent in literal bodies or in social categories: in my view, such an elitism is as "embodied" as the forms of elitism that explicitly attach the value system of active/passive (and with it higher/lower) to different kinds of bodies. Perhaps the desire for Nietzsche that we can witness in some contemporary theory is also a form of identification, a way of being in "an elite" that does not rely on social categories of privilege: identifying with Nietzsche is a way of being among "the higher ones." We could safely describe this kind of politics as an avant-gardism (see Bauman 2008: 121 for a rather cryptic but related reading of Nietzsche's "present-day popularity"). Please note in describing such an elitism I am not suggesting that Nietzsche is not an important and helpful philosopher to think with: in this book I have drawn on his work on affect and causality and his genealogical method, as well as his critique of utilitarian happiness.

7 To follow Deleuze and Spinoza more loyally one might say here that my argument in this book suggests that happiness might be sanctioned as a positive emotion, and social good, but that it can be a sad affect insofar as happiness decreases the capacity for action (although see chapter 1, note 1, for a dis-

cussion of the problems of relying on an affect/emotion distinction). It is my view that at this moment in time we need to challenge the very association of positive and negative affects with increasing and decreasing powers of action. Having said this, and turning to Spinoza directly, I would not deny that sad affects play a role in governance. Spinoza focuses on the use of fear (and hope, which he relates to fear) in rule by superstition, which "rail[s] at vice" rather than teaches virtue ([1677] 2001: 210). Such focus is understandable given the context in which he was writing. For contemporary readers, we need an understanding of governance as operating not only through fear and hope but also as an incitement to be good, joyful, and happy. Another history of affect would thus be a history of joy as decreasing capacities for action, though there will be and should be other "other histories" of joy (see, for example, Ehrenreich 2007). At one point in *Ethics* Spinoza hints at how joy and sorrow can operate similarly as forms of governance: "Parents, by reprobating what are called bad actions, and frequently blaming their children whenever they commit them, while they persuade them to what are called good actions, and praise their children when they perform them, have caused the emotions of sorrow to connect with the former, and those of joy with the latter" (152). For me, this is a wonderfully astute analysis of the relation between affect, habit, and custom: and we can follow Spinoza here in thinking about how sorrow and joy are caused (in a confused and inadequate way) by being assumed to be caused by specific actions.

8 Theodor Adorno exposes how "admonitions to be happy" can be a form of dominance in *Minima Moralia* ([1951] 1978: 62). He describes how "it is part of the mechanism of domination to forbid recognition of the suffering it reproduces" (63). Or we might say that forms of suffering and sadness are permitted as long as they do not involve recognition of domination.

9 I offer this reading as a reframing of the good encounter described in Deleuze's encounter with Spinoza (which is not the only way we can encounter Spinoza). It is not intended as a negative critique but instead a different angle on the processes Deleuze is describing. For other ways of encountering Deleuze and Spinoza that turn specifically on the question of joy and good encounters, see Macherey 1996 and Hardt 1993. Macherey asks whether Deleuze is true to Spinoza in his suggestion that joyful passions can help "leap" to adequate ideas insofar as all passions are based on inadequate ideas (153). Hardt suggests that "become joyful" is the "Spinozian mandate" (95), although I think "becoming blessed" would be the more accurate description.

10 Another example of the killjoy as the one who gets in the way of an organic agreement is "theory." How many times when I was a student of literature in the late 1980s did we have discussions in classroom about how theory gets in the way between readers and their enjoyment of texts! Theory "stops" the organic nature of such and such a reader liking such and such a text. Theory

gets in the way of the rhythm of reading. Theory becomes like poison, leading to indigestion, leading even to the death of literature.

11 For another example, see the work of Ben Anderson. He argues that "being political *affectively* must therefore involve building a protest against the affectivities of suffering into a set of techniques that also aim to cultivate 'good encounters' and anticipate 'something better'" (2006: 749). Good encounters are something we must cultivate, as a set of techniques. When ethics aims for good encounters, suffering might be located in those who do not submit to this aim, those who have not cultivated the right techniques. I should note here that Anderson has a caveat to his argument which acknowledges that affirmation is not always positive. As he carefully describes, "There are numerous occasions when the enactment of hope catalyses relations of injustice" (749).

12 Eric G. Wilson's argument "against happiness" is that "to desire only happiness in a world undoubtedly tragic is to become inauthentic" (2008: 6). Although he says that he does not want to romanticize clinical depression (7), he also suggests that unhappiness can make us creative (106). I share some of Wilson's concerns but my argument does not rest on concepts of authenticity or inauthenticity, which lead to Wilson becoming scathingly critical of those whom he calls "happy types" who come to represent the inauthenticity he ascribes to happiness. I submit that if unhappiness cannot be willed away by the desire for happiness, then the desire for happiness can conceal signs of unhappiness or project them onto others who become symptoms of the failure to be happy. To desire only happiness in a world that involves tragedy is to ask others to bear the burden of that tragedy.

13 I should signal how my argument is different from Kant's given that he questions the good of happiness. Kant separates inclination from duty and suggests that happiness is the basis of a pragmatic law. All men have "already the strongest and most intimate inclination to happiness, because *it is just in this idea that all inclinations are combined in one total*" ([1785] 2005: 60; emphasis added) The pragmatic law based on "the motive of happiness" tells us "what we have to do, if we wish to become possessed of happiness" ([1781] 1990: 452). The moral law, based on motives presented by reason alone, tell us "how we ought to act in order to deserve happiness" (452) or how to "*do that which will render thee worthy of happiness*" (454). For Kant, happiness becomes a meta-inclination, combining all inclinations in one total, and is thus separated from the moral law. My argument has explored how happiness works not only as inclination but also involves the language of duty. Indeed, I would describe happiness as a "switching point" between duty and inclination. While Kant argues that you cannot make a duty out of an inclination, I suggest that happiness becomes a duty because happiness is not simply or only an inclination. Kant does qualify his separation of happiness and duty by suggesting

that we have an indirect duty to promote the happiness of others. Given that I have an indirect duty to promote the happiness of others, Kant makes two further qualifications. First, he suggests that others can decide what belongs to their happiness: "It is for them to decide what they count as belonging to their happiness" ([1797] 1996: 151). And second, he suggests that I can disagree with their decision: "It is open to me to refuse them many things that *they* think will make them happy but that I do not" (151). We learn about happiness by noticing how quickly the duty to promote the happiness of others is translated into a duty to promote my idea of their happiness for them. I have found Kant's "Fragment of a Moral Catechism" especially useful for considering the relationship between virtue and happiness. Here, the Teacher tells the Pupil that what we want is happiness and then demonstrates how duty must be separated from happiness. The Teacher explains how promoting the other's happiness would not be acceptable if that person's happiness conflicts with the good, asking rhetorical questions: "Would you really give a lazy fellow soft cushions so that he could pass his life away in sweet idleness? Or would you see to it that a drunkard is never short of wine and whatever else he needs to get drunk? Would you give a swindler a charming air and manner to dupe other people? And would you give a violent man audacity and strong fists so that he could crush other people? Each of these things is a means that somebody wishes for in order to be happy in his own way" (224). So Kant suggests that you would not promote happiness of others if their happiness is not good, if their happiness compromises their virtue. The catechism concludes with the argument articulated by the (now wise) Pupil that the good can still hope for happiness: "For we see in the works of nature, which we can judge, a wisdom so widespread and profound that we can explain it to ourselves only by the inexpressibly great art of a creator of the world. And with regard to the moral order, which is the highest adornment of the world, we have reason to expect a no less wise regime, such that if we do not make ourselves *unworthy of happiness*, by violating our duty, we can also hope to *share* in happiness" (225). The good can hope for a share in happiness by not being unworthy of happiness. Kant thus restores the relationship he severs between happiness and the good. For an excellent discussion of Kant on happiness and ethics, see Chalier 2002.

14 It might seem ironic that I am aiming to lighten happiness by associating happiness with possibility rather than duty, given that Kierkegaard argues for possibility as a heavy rather than light category ([1844] 1980: 156). Kierkegaard is defending possibility as heavy in order to show how possibility is not simply about good things happening. Possibility is thus more serious than actuality, which might or might not involve bad things (bad things are always possible but not always actual). What makes possibility heavy for Kierkegaard is what makes it light for me. Possibility is light in the sense that in possibility one is

open to being blown this way or that, to being picked up by what happens, which can include being picked up in a good or bad way.

15 My thanks to a member of the audience at the last paper I gave on happiness before completing this book, at the Center for Lesbian and Gay Studies, CUNY, February 6, 2009, who suggested I think about the *stance* of happenstance. Thanks also to my good friend Elena Loizidou, who recommended on February 8, 2009, that I read Jean-Luc Nancy on unhappiness, in which, it turns out, he develops the idea of happenstance. It is thus happenstance that I stumbled on happenstance: not just a chance event (or coincidence of events) but the chance of an event. The word *happenstance* derives from the amalgamation of *happening* ("an event, occurrence, a chance") and *circumstance* ("standing around, surrounding condition, to stand"). A philosophy of the *happenstance* (such as offered by Nancy) would thus be one of accounting for how our surroundings happen to surround us, which would at once offer a stance or orientation toward our surroundings as happenings in which certain things become possible (or not).

16 The idea of happiness as precarious has a long history. Precariousness would most commonly be described as "dependent on chance or circumstance; uncertain; liable to fail; exposed to risk, hazardous; insecure, unstable." So we would be saying that happiness is as chancy as life, always exposed to what happens, which makes the idea that you can secure your happiness a fantasy. Another (now rare) meaning of precarious refers to "Esp. of a right, tenancy, etc.: held or enjoyed by the favour of and at the pleasure of another person; vulnerable to the will or decision of others." Happiness that is dependent on the will of others is viewed as precarious. The OED offers two eighteenth-century uses of this idea: "This little Happiness is so very precarious, that it wholly depends on the Will of others" and "As a precarious loan may be recalled at the lender's pleasure, even at a time that may prove hurtful to the borrower." To value precarity in this sense would be to give value to how others can affect our happiness, to allow ourselves to be recalled by the other's pleasure. We would not make our happiness dependent on others (which may require a coincidence of will) but would be willing to be affected by what happens to others.

17 Thanks to Eileen Joy for helping me to rethink the affirmative in happy moments.

18 The relationship between happiness and envy is complex. It is interesting to note that Spinoza defines envy as hatred at that which disposes a man "so that he rejoices over the evil and is saddened by the good which befals another" ([1677] 2001: 117). Arguably, envy is a disposition that is attuned to the competitive logics of capitalism (or to be more accurate that capitalism encourages such an attunement), in which fortune is translated from chance to wealth, as something that is not only distributed but finite: such that someone

having more fortune means someone else having less. Envy would refer to the experience of the fortune of others as a theft of one's own fortune (you want their misery, and you don't want their happiness as a way of holding on to your own). I contend that in this film there is a relationship between the experience of happiness and the desire for the other to be envious (as a desire for the other to want what one has). It is Suzy who "wants" Poppy to be envious (which is how her speech act "I just want you to be happy" can be translated) because her own happiness is precarious, because it rests on what she has given up. Certain forms of happiness might depend on both emulation and envy of others who don't have the "right things" and are assumed to want "the right things" for themselves. In other words, the "have nots" are understood as necessarily envious and unhappy as a way of keeping the value of "having" intact. When Poppy refuses to be envious (about the mortgage, the house, the baby-to-be, the pension, the husband) and is confident about her own good fortune ("I am a lucky lady, I know that"), Suzy's happiness turns into rage ("stop rubbing it in"). Poppy has not taken Suzy's happiness away but exposed how Suzy's happiness depends on others to confirm its value. Perhaps the desire for another to be envious becomes envy of that other's refusal to invest in the competitive logics of envy.

19   My appreciation to Judith Halberstam, whose lecture "Bees, Bio-Pirates, and the Queer Art of Cross-Pollination" delivered at Birkbeck College, May 15, 2008, explored the silly nature of queer archives.

REFERENCES

Abraham, Julie. 1996. *Are Girls Necessary? Lesbian Writing and Modern Histories*. New York: Routledge.

Adorno, Theodor W. [1951] 1978. *Minima Moralia: Reflections from Damaged Life*. Trans. E. F. N. Jephcott. London: Verso.

Adorno, Theodor W., and Max Horkheimer. [1944] 1997. *Dialectic of Enlightenment*. Trans. John Cumming. London: Verso.

Agamben, Giorgio. [1996] 2000. *Means without End: Notes on Politics*. Trans. Vincenzo Binetti and Cesare Casarino. Minneapolis: University of Minnesota Press.

Ahmed, Sara. 2000. *Strange Encounters: Embodied Others in Post-Coloniality*. London: Routledge.

————. 2004. *The Cultural Politics of Emotion*. Edinburgh: Edinburgh University Press.

————. 2006. *Queer Phenomenology: Orientations, Objects, Others*. Durham, N.C.: Duke University Press.

————. 2007a. "The Language of Diversity." *Ethnic and Racial Studies* 30 (2): 235–56.

————. 2007b. "'You End Up Doing the Document Rather than Doing the Doing': Diversity, Race Equality and the Politics of Documentation." *Ethnic and Racial Studies* 30 (4): 390–609.

————, ed. 2008. "Happiness." *New Formations* 63.

Aidoo, Ama Ata. 1977. *Our Sister Killjoy: or, Reflections from a Black-Eyed Squint*. Harlow: Longman.

Anderson, Ben. 2006. "Becoming and Being Hopeful: Towards a Theory of Affect." *Environment and Planning D: Society and Space* 24:733–52.

Anderson, Elizabeth. 1998. "John Stuart Mill: Democracy as Sentimental Education." *Philosophers on Education: New Historical Perspectives*, ed. Amélie Oksenberg Rorty, 333–52. New York: Routledge.

Annas, Julia. 1993. *The Morality of Happiness*. New York: Oxford University Press.

Arendt, Hannah. [1961] 1973. *On Revolution*. Harmondsworth: Penguin.

———.1972. *Crises of the Republic: Lying in Politics, Civil Disobedience, on Violence, Thoughts on Politics and Revolution*. New York: Harcourt Brace.

Argyle, Michael. 1987. *The Psychology of Happiness*. London: Methuen.

Aristotle. 1998. *Nicomachean Ethics*. Trans. William Kaufman. New York: Dove Publications.

Austin, John Langshaw. [1962] 1975. *How to Do Things with Words*. Ed. J. O. Urmson and M. Sbisà. Oxford: Oxford University Press.

Back, Les, Tim Crabbe, and John Solomos. 2001. *The Changing Face of Football: Racism, Identity and Multiculture in the English Game*. Oxford: Berg.

Badiou, Alain. [1993] 2001. *Ethics: Essays on the Understanding of Evil*. Trans. Peter Hallward. London: Verso.

Ballaster, Rosalind. 2005. *Fabulous Orients: Fictions of the East in England, 1662–1785*. Oxford: Oxford University Press.

Barrow, Robin. 1980. *Happiness*. Oxford: Martin Robertson.

Baudrillard, Jean. [2001] 2006. *Utopia Deferred: Writings from Utopie, 1967–1978*. Trans. Stuart Kendall. New York: Semiotexte.

Bauman, Zygmunt. 2008. *The Art of Life*. Cambridge: Polity Press.

Beauvoir, Simone de. [1949] 1997. *The Second Sex*. Trans. H. M. Parshley. London: Vintage.

Belliotti, Raymond Angelo. 2004. *Happiness Is Overrated*. Lanham, Md.: Rowman and Littlefield.

Bend It Like Beckham. 2002. Dir. Gurinder Chadha. Helkon SK.

Bennett, Oliver. 2001. *Cultural Pessimism: Narratives of Decline in the Postmodern World*. Edinburgh: Edinburgh University Press.

Bentham, Jeremy. [1776] 1988. *A Fragment on Government*. Cambridge: Cambridge University Press.

———. [1789] 2007. *An Introduction to the Principle of Morals and Legislation*. Mineola, N.Y.: Dover.

Berlant, Lauren. 1997. *The Queen of America Goes to Washington City*. Durham, N.C.: Duke University Press.

———. 2000. "The Subject of True Feeling: Pain, Privacy and Politics." *Transformations: Thinking Through Feminism*, ed. Sara Ahmed, Jane Kilby, Celia Lury, Maureen McNeil and Beverley Skeggs, 33–47. London: Routledge.

———. 2002. "Two Girls, Fat and Thin." *Regarding Sedgwick: Essays on Queer Cul-

ture and Critical Theory, ed. Stephen M. Barber and David L. Clark, 71–108. New York: Routledge.

———. 2008a. "Cruel Optimism: On Marx, Loss and the Senses." *New Formations* 63:33–51.

———. 2008b. *The Female Complaint: The Unfinished Business of Sentimentality in American Culture*. Durham, N.C.: Duke University Press.

Bhabha, Homi. 1994. *The Location of Culture*. London: Routledge.

Blackman, Lisa. 2008. "Is Happiness Contagious?" *New Formations* 63:15–32.

Blackman, Lisa, and Valerie Walkerdine. 2001. *Mass Hysteria: Critical Psychology and Media Studies*. London: Palgrave Macmillan.

Bland, Lucy, and Laura Doan, eds. 1998. *Sexology Uncensored: The Documents of Sexual Science*. Cambridge: Polity Press.

Blassingame, John W. 1992. "Some Precursors of the *Amistad* Revolt." *The Connecticut Scholar: Occasional Papers of the Connecticut Humanities Council* 10:26–36.

Bloch, Charlotte. 2002. "Moods and the Quality of Life." *Journal of Happiness Studies* 3 (2): 101–28.

Bloch, Ernst. [1938–47] 2000. *The Principle of Hope*, vol. 1, Trans. Neville Plaice, Stephen Plaice, and Paul Knight. Oxford: Blackwell.

Bösche, Susanne. 1983. *Jenny Lives with Eric and Martin*. London: Gay Men's Press.

Bourdieu, Pierre. [1979] 1986. *Distinction: A Social Critique of the Judgment of Taste*. Trans. Richard Nice. New York: Routledge.

Braidotti, Rosi. 2002. *Metamorphoses: Towards a Materialist Theory of Becoming*. Cambridge: Polity Press.

———. 2006a. *Transpositions: On Nomadic Ethics*. Cambridge: Polity.

———. 2006b. "Affirmation versus Vulnerability: On Contemporary Ethical Debates." *Symposium* 10 (1): 235–54.

Brennan, Teresa. 2004. *The Transmission of Affect*. Ithaca, N.Y.: Cornell University Press.

Brinton, Daniel Garrison. 1893. *The Pursuit of Happiness: A Book of Studies and Strowings*. Philadelphia: David McKay.

Brooks, Peter. 1984. *Reading for the Plot: Design and Intention in Narrative*. Cambridge, Mass.: Harvard University Press.

Brown, Rita Mae. 1973. *Rubyfruit Jungle*. New York: Bantam Books.

Brown, Wendy. 1995. *States of Injury: Power and Freedom in Late Modernity*. Princeton, N.J.: Princeton University Press.

Bruce, John. 1813. "Bruce's Report on the East India Negotiation." *Monthly Review*: 20–37.

Butler, Judith. 1990. *Gender Trouble: Feminism and the Subversion of Identity*. New York: Routledge.

———. 1997. *The Psychic Life of Power*. Stanford, Calif.: Stanford University Press.

————. 2004. *Precarious Life: The Powers of Mourning and Violence*. London: Verso.

Carr, Alan. 2004. *Positive Psychology: The Science of Happiness and Human Strengths*. London: Routledge.

Carroll, David. 1992. *George Eliot and the Conflict of Interpretations: A Reading of the Novels*. Cambridge: Cambridge University Press.

Carter, Mia. 2003. "Company to Canal: 1756–1860." *Archives of Empire: From the East India Company to the Suez Canal*, ed. Barbara Harlow and Mia Carter, 1–15. Durham, N.C.: Duke University Press.

Caruth, Cathy. 1996. *Unclaimed Experience: Trauma, Narrative and History*. Baltimore: Johns Hopkins University Press.

————. 2001. "Parting Words: Trauma, Silence and Survival." *Cultural Values* 5 (1): 7–26.

Chalier, Catherine. 2002. *What Ought I to Do? Morality in Kant and Levinas*. Trans. Jane Marie Todd. Ithaca, N.Y.: Cornell University Press.

Challenger, Douglas F. 1994. *Durkheim through the Lens of Aristotle: Durkheimian, Postmodernist, and Communitarian Responses to the Enlightenment*. Lanham, Md.: Rowman and Littlefield.

Chatterjee, Piya. 2001. *A Time for Tea: Women, Labor, and Post/Colonial Politics on an Indian Plantation*. Durham, N.C.: Duke University Press.

Cheng, Anne Anlin. 2001. *The Melancholia of Race: Psychoanalysis, Assimilation and Hidden Grief*. Oxford: Oxford University Press.

Chicken Tikka Masala. 2005. Dir. Harmage Singh Kalirai. Seven Spice Productions.

Children of Men. 2006. Dir. Alfonso Cuarón. Based on the novel by P. D. James. Universal Pictures.

Chopin, Kate. [1899] 1993. *The Awakening*. New York: Dover Publications.

Colebrook, Claire. 2002. *Gilles Deleuze*. London: Routledge.

————. 2008. "Narrative Happiness and the Meaning of Life." *New Formations* 63:82–102.

Colwin, Laurie. [1982] 1990. *Family Happiness*. New York: Perennial.

Conard, Mark T. 2007. "*Mean Streets*: Beatitude, Flourishing and Unhappiness." *The Philosophy of Martin Scorsese*, ed. Mark T. Conard, 53–71. Lexington: University Press of Kentucky.

Conrad, Peter, and Joseph W. Schneider. 1980. *Deviance and Medicalization: From Badness to Sickness*. Ann Arbor: University of Michigan Press.

Cooke, George Willis. [1884] 2007. *George Eliot: A Critical Study of Her Life, Writing, and Philosophy*. Boston: IndyPublish.

Cowan, J. L. 1968. *Pleasure and Pain: A Study in Philosophical Psychology*. London: Macmillan.

Crimp, Douglas. 2004. *Melancholia and Moralism: Essays on AIDS and Queer Politics*. Cambridge, Mass: MIT Press.

Csíkszentmihályi, Mihály. 1992. *Flow: The Psychology of Happiness*. London: Rider.

Cunningham, Michael. 1998. *The Hours*. New York: Farrar, Straus and Giroux.

Cusk, Rachel. 2006. *Arlington Park*. London: Faber and Faber.

Cvetkovich, Ann. 2003. *An Archive of Feelings: Trauma, Sexuality, and Lesbian Public Cultures*. Durham, N.C.: Duke University Press.

Dalai Lama, and Howard C. Cutler. 1998. *The Art of Happiness: A Handbook for Living*. New York: Riverhead.

Dawesar, Abha. 2005. *Babyji*. New York: Anchor Books.

de Botton, Alain. 2006. *The Architecture of Happiness*. London: Penguin.

DeBrabander, Firmin. 2007. *Spinoza and the Stoics: Power, Politics and the Passions*. London: Continuum.

Deleuze, Gilles. [1953] 1991. *Empiricism and Subjectivity: An Essay on Hume's Theory of Human Nature*. Trans. Constantin V. Boundas. New York: Columbia University Press.

———. [1970] 1998. *Spinoza: Practical Philosophy*. Trans. Robert Hurley. San Francisco: City Lights Books.

———. 1978. "Lecture Transcripts on Spinoza's Concept of Affect." http://www.goldsmiths.ac.uk/csisp/papers/deleuze_spinoza_affect.pdf. 1–28.

Derrida, Jacques. [1997] 2005. *The Politics of Friendship*. Trans. George Collins. London: Verso.

Descartes, René. [1649] 1989. *The Passions of the Soul*. Trans. Stephen H. Voss. Indianapolis: Hackett Publishing Company.

Deutscher, Penelope. 1997. *Yielding Gender: Feminism, Deconstruction and the History of Philosophy*. New York: Routledge.

Dienstag, Joshua Foa. 2006. *Pessimism: Philosophy, Ethic, Spirit*. Princeton, N.J.: Princeton University Press.

Doan, Laura, and Jay Prosser, eds. 2002. *Palatable Poison: Critical Perspectives on "The Well of Loneliness."* New York: Columbia University Press.

Douglass, Frederick. [1845] 2003. *Narrative of the Life of Frederick Douglass, an American Slave*. New York: Barnes and Noble.

———. [1855] 2005. *My Bondage and My Freedom*. New York: Barnes and Noble.

Du Bois, W. E. B. [1903] 2003. *The Souls of Black Folk*. New York: Barnes and Noble.

Duggan, Lisa. 2003. *The Twilight of Equality: Neoliberalism, Cultural Politics and the Attack on Democracy*. Boston: Beacon Press.

DuPlessis, Rachel Blau. 1985. *Writing beyond the Ending: Narrative Strategies of Twentieth Century Women Writers*. Bloomington: Indiana University Press.

Durkheim, Émile. [1893] 1960. *The Division of Labour in Society*. Trans. George Simpson. Glencoe, Ill.: Free Press of Glencoe.

Eagleton, Terry. 2007. *The Meaning of Life*. Oxford: Oxford University Press.

East Is East. 1999. Dir. Damien O'Donnell. Based on the play by Ayub Khan-Din. Channel 4 Films.

Edelman, Lee. 2004. *No Future: Queer Theory and the Death Drive*. Durham, N.C.: Duke University Press.

———. 2006. "Antagonism, Negativity and the Subject of Queer Theory." *PMLA*; 821–22.

Educating Rita. 1983. Dir. Lewis Gilbert. Based on the play by Willey Russel. Acorn Pictures.

Ehrenreich, Barbara. 2001. "Welcome to Cancerland: A Mammogram Leads to a Cult of Pink Kitsch." *Harper's Magazine*, November, 43–53.

———. 2007. *Dancing in the Streets: A History of Collective Joy*. London: Granta Publications.

Elias, Norbert. [1939] 1969. *The Civilizing Process: The History of Manners and State Formation and Civilization*, vol 1. Trans. Edmund Jephcott. Oxford: Blackwell.

Eliot, George. [1860] 1965. *The Mill on the Floss*. New York: New American Library.

Eng, David L. 2002. "The Value of Silence." *Theatre Journal* 54 (1): 85–94.

Eng, David L., and Shinhee Han. 2003. "A Dialogue on Racial Melancholia." *Loss: The Politics of Mourning*, ed. David L. Eng and David Kazanjian, 343–71. Berkeley: University of California Press.

Fanon, Frantz. [1952] 1986. *Black Skin, White Masks*. Trans. Charles Lam Markmann. London: Pluto.

———. [1961] 2001. *The Wretched of the Earth*. Trans. Constance Farrington. London: Penguin.

Feagin, Joe. R. 2000. *Racist America: Roots, Current Realities and Future Reparations—Remaking America with Anti-Racist Strategies*. New York: Routledge.

Felski, Rita. 2003. *Literature after Feminism*. Chicago: University of Chicago Press.

Firestone, Shulamith. 1970. *The Dialectic of Sex: The Case for Feminist Revolution*. New York: Bantam Books.

Foucault, Michel. 1979. "Is It Useless to Revolt?" Trans. James Bernauer. *Religion and Culture*. Ed. Jeremy R. Carette, 131–34. Manchester: Manchester University Press.

———. 1986. "Of Other Spaces." *Diacritics* 16:22–27.

———. 1988. "The Political Technology of Individuals." *Technologies of the Self: A Seminar with Michel Foucault*, ed. Luther H. Martin, Huck Gutman, and Patrick H. Hutton, 145–62. Amherst: University of Massachusetts Press.

Fowler, James H., and Nicholas A. Christakis. 2008. "Dynamic Spread of Happiness in a Large Social Network: Longitudinal Analysis over Twenty Years in the Framingham Heart Study." *BMJ* 337: a2338.

Franklin, Sarah. 1997. *Embodied Progress: A Cultural Account of Assisted Conception*. London: Routledge.

Freeman, Elizabeth. 2005. "Time Binds, or, Erotohistoriography." *Social Text* 23:57–68.

Freud, Sigmund. [1917] 2005. "Mourning and Melancholia." *On Murder, Mourning and Melancholia*, 201–18. Trans. Shaun Whiteside, London: Penguin Books.

———. [1920] 1964. "Beyond the Pleasure Principle." *The Standard Edition of the Complete Psychological Works of Sigmund Freud*, Vol. 18. Trans. James Strachey. London: Hogarth Press.

———. [1920] 1955. "The Psychogenesis of a Case of Homosexuality in a Woman." *The Standard Edition of the Complete Works of Freud*, vol. 18. Trans. James Strachey. London: Hogarth Press.

———. [1923] 1960. *The Ego and the Id*. Trans. Joan Riviere. New York: W. W. Norton.

———. [1930] 2004. *Civilisation and its Discontents*. Trans. David McLintock. London: Penguin.

Frey, Bruno S., and Alois Stutzer. 2002. *Happiness and Economics: How the Economy and Institutions Affect Human Well-Being*. Princeton, N.J.: Princeton University Press.

Friedan, Betty. 1965. *The Feminine Mystique*. Harmondsworth: Penguin.

Frye, Marilyn. 1983. *The Politics of Reality: Essays in Feminist Theory*. Trumansburg, N.Y.: Crossing Press.

Garden, Nancy. 1982. *Annie on My Mind*. New York: Farrar, Straus and Giroux.

Gettis, Alan. 2006. *The Happiness Solution: Finding Joy and Meaning in an Upside Down World*. Victoria, BC: Trafford Publishing.

Gibbs, Anna. 2001. "Contagious Feelings: Pauline Hanson and the Epidemiology of Affect." *Australian Humanities Review*, no. 24 http://www.australianhumanities review.org.

Gilbert, Daniel. 2006. *Stumbling on Happiness*. New York: HarperCollins.

Gilman, Charlotte Perkins. [1903] 2002. *The Home: Its Work and Influence*. Lanham, Md.: Rowman and Littlefield.

Gilroy, Paul. 2004. *After Empire: Melancholia or Convivial Culture?* London: Routledge.

Goodman, Gerre, George Lakey, Judy Lashof, and Erika Thorne. 1983. *No Turning Back: Lesbian and Gay Liberation for the '80s*. Philadelphia: New Society Publishers.

Gopinath, Gayatri. 2005. *Impossible Desires: Queer Diaspora and South Asian Public Culture*. Durham, N.C.: Duke University Press.

Gosling, J. C. B. 1969. *Pleasure and Desire: The Case for Hedonism Reviewed*. Oxford: Clarendon Press.

Graeber, David. 2007. *Possibilities: Essays on Hierarchy, Rebellion, and Desire*. Oakland, Calif.: AK Press.

Greene, Gayle. 1991. *Changing the Story: Feminist Fiction and the Tradition*. Bloomington: Indiana University Press.

Gunn, James. 1961. *The Joy Makers*. New York: Bantam Books.

Gunnell, Barbara. 2004. "The Happiness Industry." *New Statesman*, September 6.

Hage, Ghassan. 2003. *Against Paranoid Nationalism: Searching for Hope in a Shrinking Society*. Annandale, NSW: Pluto Press.

Hai, Yasmin. 2008. *The Making of Mr Hai's Daughter: Becoming British*. London: Virago.

Haidt, Jonathan. 2006. *The Happiness Hypothesis*. London: William Heinemann.

Halberstam, Judith. 2005. *In A Queer Time and Place: Transgender Bodies, Subcultural Lives*. New York: New York University Press.

———. 2008. "Animating Revolt/Revolting Animation: Penguin Love, Doll Sex and the Spectacle of the Queer Nonhuman." *Queering the Non/Human*, ed. Noreen Giffney and Myra J. Hird, 265–82. London: Ashgate.

Hall, Radclyffe. [1928] 1982. *The Well of Loneliness*. London: Virago Press.

Happy-Go-Lucky. 2008. Dir. Mike Leigh. Momentum Pictures.

Hardt, Michael. 1993. *Gilles Deleuze: An Apprenticeship in Philosophy*. Minneapolis: University of Minnesota Press.

Hartman, Saidiya V. 1997. *Scenes of Subjection: Terror, Slavery and Self-Making in Nineteenth Century America*. New York: Oxford University Press.

Heady, Bruce, and Alexander J. Wearing. 1991. "Subjective Well-Being: A Stocks and Flows Framework." *Subjective Well-Being: An Interdisciplinary Perspective*, ed. Fritz Strack, Michael Argyle, and Norbert Schwarz, 49–76. Oxford: Pergamon Press.

Hegel, Georg Wilhelm Friedrich. [1837] 1988. *Introduction to the Philosophy of History*. Trans. Leo Rauch. Indianapolis: Hackett Publishing Company.

Hemmings, Clare. 2001. "'All my life I have been waiting for something': Theorising Femme Narrative in *The Well of Loneliness*." *Palatable Poison: Critical Perspectives on "The Well of Loneliness,"* ed. Laura Doan and Jay Prosser, 179–96. New York: Columbia University Press.

———. 2005. "Invoking Affect: Cultural Theory and the Ontological Turn." *Cultural Studies* 19 (5): 548–67.

Highsmith, Patricia. [1952] 2004. *The Price of Salt*. New York: W. W. Norton.

Hobbes, Thomas. [1651] 1968. *Leviathan*. Harmondsworth: Penguin Books.

Hochschild, Arlie Russell. [1983] 2003. *The Managed Heart: Commercialization of Human Feeling*. 2nd ed. Berkeley: University of California Press.

———. 2003. *The Commercialization of Intimate Life: Notes from Home and Work*. Berkeley: University of California Press.

Holden, Robert. 1998. *Happiness Now! Timeless Wisdom for Feeling Good Fast*. London: Hodden and Stoughton.

hooks, bell. 2000. *Feminist Theory: From Margin to Centre*. London: Pluto Press.

The Hours. 2002. Dir. Stephen Daldry. Based on the novel by Michael Cunningham. Paramount Pictures.

Hudson, Deal Wyatt. 1996. *Happiness and the Limits of Satisfaction*. Lanham, Md.: Rowman and Littlefield.

Hume, David. [1739–40] 1985. *A Treatise of Human Nature*. London: Penguin Books.

———. [1748] 1975. *Enquiries Concerning Human Understanding and Concerning the Principles of Morals*. Oxford: Clarendon Press.

Husserl, Edmund. [1946] 2002. "The World of the Living Present and the Constitution of the Surrounding World That Is Outside the Flesh." *Husserl at the Limits of Phenomenology*, ed. Leonard Lawlor and Bettina Bergo, 132–54. Evanston, Ill.: Northwestern University Press.

———. [1950] 1989. *Ideas Pertaining to a Pure Phenomenology and to a Phenomenological Philosophy, Second Book*. Trans. Richard Rojcewicz and André Schuwer. Dordrecht: Kluwer Academic Publishers.

Huxley, Aldous. [1932] 1969. *Brave New World*. New York: Harper and Row.

If These Walls Could Talk 2. 2000. Dir. Jane Anderson, Martha Coolidge, Anne Heche. HBO.

The Island. 2005. Dir. Michael Bay. Dreamworks, SKG.

James, P. D. 1993. *The Children of Men*. New York: Alfred A. Knopf.

James, Susan. 1997. *Passion and Action: The Emotions in Seventeenth Century Philosophy*. Oxford: Oxford University Press.

James, William. [1891] 1956. "The Moral Philosopher and the Moral Life." *The Will to Believe, and Other Essays in Popular Philosophy*, 184–285. New York: Dover Publications.

Jameson, Fredric. 2005. *Archaeologies of the Future: The Desire Called Utopia and Other Science Fictions*. London: Verso.

Janaway, Christopher. 1999. "Schopenhauer's Pessimism." *The Cambridge Companion to Schopenhauer*, ed. Christopher Janaway, 318–44. Cambridge: Cambridge University Press.

Jenkins, Henry. 1998. "Introduction: Childhood Innocence and Other Modern Myths." *The Children's Culture Reader*, ed. Henry Jenkins, 1–37. New York: New York University Press.

Johnson, Lesley, and Justine Lloyd. 2004. *Sentenced to Everyday Life: Feminism and the Housewife*. Oxford: Berg.

Jones, H. S. 2005. "The Early Utilitarians, Race and Empire: The States of the Argument." *Utilitarianism and Empire*, ed. Bart Schultz and Georgios Varouxakis, 179–88. Lanham, Md.: Lexington Books.

Jullien, François. 2007. *Vital Nourishment*. New York: Zone Books.

Kant, Immanuel. [1781] 1990. *Critique of Pure Reason*. Trans. J. M. D. Meiklejohn. New York: Prometheus Books.

———. [1785] 2005. *Groundwork for the Metaphysics of Morals*. Ed. Lara Denis, trans. Thomas Kingsmill Abbott. Toronto: Broadview Editions.

———. [1788] 2004. *Critique of Practical Reason*. Trans. Thomas Kingsmill Abbott. New York: Dover Publications.

————. [1797] 1996. *The Metaphysics of Morals*. Trans. Mary J. Gregor. Cambridge: Cambridge University Press.

Kelley, Robin D. G. 2002. *Freedom Dreams: The Black Radical Imagination*. Boston: Beacon Press.

Kenny, Anthony. 1993. *Aristotle on the Perfect Life*. Oxford: Clarendon Press.

Kierkegaard, Søren. [1844] 1980. *The Concept of Anxiety*. Trans. Reidar Thomte with Albert B. Anderson. Princeton, N.J.: Princeton University Press.

Kureishi, Hanif. [1994] 2008. *My Son the Fanatic, The Flies*. Germany: Heuber Verlag.

Lacan, Jacques. 1982. "God and the *Jouissance* of The Woman." *Feminine Sexuality: Jacques Lacan and the* école freudienne, ed. Juliet Mitchell and Jacqueline Rose, 137–49. New York: W. W. Norton.

————. [1986] 1992. *The Ethics of Psychoanalysis, 1959–1960*. Trans. Dennis Porter. London: Routledge.

————. 2006. *Écrits*. Trans Bruce Fink with Héloïse Fink and Russell Grigg. New York: W. W. Norton.

Laing, R. D. 1971. *The Politics of the Family*. Middlesex: Penguin Books.

Lang, Kurt, and Gladys Engel Lang. 1969. "The Unique Perspective of Television and Its Effects: A Pilot Study." *Mass Communications: A Book of Readings*, ed. W. Schramm, 544–60. Champaign: University of Illinois Press.

Layard, Richard. 2005. *Happiness: Lessons from a New Science*. London: Allen Lane.

Lear, Jonathan. 2000. *Happiness, Death and the Remainder of Life*. Cambridge, Mass.: Harvard University Press.

Le Bon, Gustave. [1895] 2002. *The Crowd: A Study of the Popular Mind*. Mineola, N.Y.: Dover Publications.

Le Guin, Ursula. [1973] 1987. "The Ones Who Walk Away from Omelas." *The Wind's Twelve Quarters*. New York: Perennial.

Leibniz, Gottfried Wilhelm. [1714] 1965. *Monadology and Other Philosophical Essays*. Trans. Paul Schrecker and Anne Martin Schrecker. Indianapolis: Bobbs-Merrill.

————. [1765] 1981. *New Essays on Human Understanding*. Trans. Peter Remnant. Cambridge: Cambridge University Press.

Levy, Andrea. 1999. *Fruit of the Lemon*. London: Headline Book Publishing.

Locke, John. [1690] 1997. *An Essay Concerning Human Understanding*. London: Penguin Books.

Lorde, Audre. 1982. *Zami: A New Spelling of My Name*. London: Sheba Feminist Publishers.

————. 1984. *Sister Outsider: Essays and Speeches*. Trumansburg, N.Y.: Crossing Press.

————. 1997. *The Cancer Journals*. San Francisco: Aunt Lute Books.

Lost and Delirious. 2001. Dir. Léa Pool. Based on the novel by Susan Swan. Seville Pictures.

Love, Heather. 2007. *Feeling Backward: The Politics of Loss in Queer History.* Cambridge, Mass.: Harvard University Press.

———. 2008. "Compulsory Happiness and Queer Existence." *New Formations* 63:52–64.

Lucas, Bill. 2006. *Happy Families: How to Make One, How to Keep One.* Harlow: Educational Publishers.

Lukács, György. 1971. *History and Class Consciousness.* Trans. Rodney Livingstone. Cambridge, Mass.: MIT Press.

Macaulay, Thomas Babington. [1835] 2003. "Minute on Indian Education." *Archives of Empire: From the East India Company to the Suez Canal,* ed. Barbara Harlow and Mia Carter, 227–38. Durham, N.C.: Duke University Press.

Macherey, Piere. 1996. "The Encounter with Spinoza." *Deleuze: A Critical Reader,* ed. Paul Patton, 139–61. Oxford: Blackwell.

MacIntyre, Alasdair C. 1981. *After Virtue: A Study in Moral Theory.* London: Duckworth.

———. 2004. *The Unconscious: A Conceptual Analysis.* London: Routledge.

Majeed, Javed. 1992. *Ungoverned Imaginings: James Mill's "The History of British India" and Orientalism.* Oxford: Clarendon Press.

Marar, Ziyad. 2003. *The Happiness Paradox.* London: Reaktion Books.

Marcuse, Herbert [1964] (2002). *One-Dimensional Man: Studies in the Ideology of Advanced Industrial Society.* London: Routledge.

Martin, Jane Roland. 1995. *Changing the Educational Landscape: Philosophy, Women and the Curriculum.* New York: Routledge.

Marx, Karl. [1844] 1964. *The Economic and Philosophical Manuscripts of 1844.* New York: International Publications.

Massumi, Brian. 2002a. "Navigating Movements." www.brianmassumi.com/interviews/NAVIGATING%20MOVEMENTS.pdf. Visited August 18, 2009.

———. 2002b. *Parables for the Virtual: Movement, Affect, Sensation.* Durham, N.C.: Duke University Press.

Mbembe, Achille. 2001. *On the Postcolony.* Berkeley: University of California Press.

McCarney, Joseph. 2005. "Ideology and False Consciousness." http://www.marxmyths.org/joseph-mccarney/article.htm. Visited August 28, 2008.

McMahon, Darrin M. 2006. *Happiness: A History.* New York: Atlantic Monthly Press.

McRobbie, Angela. 2008. *The Aftermath of Feminism: Gender, Culture and Social Change.* London: Sage.

Mill, James. [1818] 1997. *History of British India.* London: Routledge.

———. 1828. *Essays reprinted from the Supplement to the Encyclopaedia of Britannica.* London: J. Innes.

Mill, John Stuart. [1863] 2001. *Utilitarianism*. Indianapolis: Hackett Publishing.

———. [1873] 2003. *Autobiography of John Stuart Mill*. Whitefish, Mont.: Kessinger Publishing.

Miller, D. A. 2002. "Problems of Closure in the Traditional Novel" (1981). *Narrative Dynamics: Essays on Time, Plot, Closure and Frames*, ed. Brian Richardson, 272–81. Columbus: Ohio State University Press.

Millett, Kate. 1970. *Sexual Politics*. New York: Doubleday.

Moreton-Robinson, Aileen. 2002. "'Tiddas talkin' up to the White Woman': When Huggins et al. Took on Bell." *Black Lines: Contemporary Critical Writing by Indigenous Australians*, ed. Michele Grossman, 66–78. Melbourne: Melbourne University Press.

Morrison, Toni. [1970] 1979. *The Bluest Eye*. London: Picador.

Muñoz, José Esteban. 2007. "Cruising the Toilet: LeRoi Jones/Amiri Baraka, Radical Black Traditions, and Queer Futurity". *GLQ* 13 (2–3): 353–67.

Munt, Sally. 2001. "*The Well* of Shame." *Palatable Poison: Critical Perspectives on "The Well of Loneliness,"* ed. Laura Doan and Jay Prosser, 199–215. New York: Columbia University Press.

———. 2007. *Queer Attachments: The Cultural Politics of Shame*. Aldershot: Ashgate.

Meyer, Susan. 1996. *Imperialism at Home: Race and Victorian Women's Fiction*. Ithaca, N.Y.: Cornell University Press.

Naipaul, V. S. 1990. "Our Universal Civilization." *New York Times*, November 5. http://www.nytimes.com.

Nancy, Jean-Luc. [1993] 1997. *The Sense of the World*. Trans. Jeffrey S. Librett. Minneapolis: University of Minnesota Press.

Nettle, Daniel. 2006. *Happiness: The Science behind Your Smile*, Oxford: Oxford University Press.

Neves, Carlos M. 2003. "Optimism, Pessimism and Hope in Durkheim." *Journal of Happiness Studies* 4:169–83.

Newton, Esther. 2000. *Margaret Mead Made Me Gay: Personal Essays, Public Ideas*. Durham, N.C.: Duke University Press.

Ngai, Sianne. 2005. *Ugly Feelings*. Cambridge, Mass.: Harvard University Press.

Nietzsche, Friedrich. [1883–85] 1961. *Thus Spoke Zarathustra*. Trans. R. J. Hollingdale. London: Penguin Books.

———. [1886] 1997. *Beyond Good and Evil*. Trans. Helen Zimmern. Mineola, N.Y.: Dover Publications.

———. [1887] 1996. *On the Genealogy of Morals*. Trans. Douglas Smith. Oxford: Oxford University Press.

———. [1889] 1990. *Twilight of the Idols*. Trans. R. J. Hollingdale. London: Penguin Books.

———. [1901] 1968. *The Will to Power*. Trans. Walter Kaufman and R. J. Hollingdale. New York: Vintage Books.

Noddings, Nel. 2003. *Happiness and Education*. Cambridge: Cambridge University Press.

Nussbaum, Martha C. 2005. "Mill on Happiness: The Enduring Value of a Complex Critique." *Utilitarianism and Empire*, ed. Bart Schultz and Georgios Varouxakis, 107–24. Lanham, Md.: Lexington Books.

O'Rourke, Meghan. 2006. "Desperate Feminist Wives: Why Wanting Equality Makes Women Unhappy." http://www.slate.com.

Orwell, George. [1949] 1985. *1984*. New York: Penguin Books.

Packer, Vin. [1952] 2004. *Spring Fire*. San Francisco. Cleis Press.

Pascal, Blaise. [1669] 1910. *Thoughts, Letters, Minor Works*, vol. 8. Trans. W. F. Trotter, M. L. Booth, O. W. Wight. New York: P. F. Collier and Son.

Perry, David L. 1967. *The Concept of Pleasure*. The Hague: Mouton and Co.

Peters, Julie Anne. 2003. *Keeping You a Secret*. New York: Little, Brown.

Peucker, Henning. 2007. "Husserl's Critique of Kant's Ethics." *Journal of the History of Philosophy* 45 (2): 309–19.

Phua, Voon Chin. 2003. *Icelandic Lives: The Queer Experience*. Philadelphia: Hawarth Press.

Pitts, Jennifer. 2005. *A Turn to Empire: The Rise of Imperial Liberalism in Britain and France*. Princeton, N.J.: Princeton University Press.

Plato. 1998. *Republic*. Trans. Robin Waterfield. Oxford: Oxford University Press.

Potamianou, Anna. 1997. *Hope: A Shield in the Economy of Borderline States*. Trans. Phillip Slotkin. London: Routledge.

Probyn, Elspeth. 2005. *Blush: Faces of Shame*, Minneapolis: University of Minnesota Press.

Prosser, Jay. 1998. *Second Skins: Body Narratives of Transsexuality*. New York: Columbia University Press.

Puar, Jasbir K. 2007. *Terrorist Assemblages: Homonationalism in Queer Times*. Durham, N.C.: Duke University Press.

Radway, Janice A. 1984. *Reading the Romance: Women, Patriarchy and Popular Literature*. London: Verso.

Rahman, Zia Haider. 2007. "The Young Can Be Far Too Easy to Exploit." *Daily Telegraph*, November 7.

Reid, Gordon. 2006. *That Unhappy Race: Queensland and the Aboriginal Problem, 1838–1901*. Melbourne: Australian Scholarly Publishing.

Ricard, Matthieu. 2007. *Happiness: A Guide to Developing Life's Most Important Skill*. Trans. Jesse Browner. London: Atlantic Books.

Rose, Nikolas. 1996. "Governing Advanced 'Liberal' Societies." *Foucault and Political Reason: Liberalism, Neo-Liberalism and the Rationalities of Government*, ed. Andrew Barry, Thomas Osborne and Nikolas Rose, 37–64. Chicago: University of Chicago Press.

———. 1999. *Governing the Soul: The Shaping of the Private Self*. London: Free Association Books.

Rousseau, Jean-Jacques. [1762] 1993. *Émile*. Trans. Barbara Foxley. London: Everyman.

———. 1783. *Emilius and Sophia: Or, a New System of Education*. London: H. Haldwin.

Rowbotham, Sheila. 1989. *The Past Is before Us: Feminism in Action since the 1960s*. London: Penguin Books.

Ruti, Mari. 2006. *Reinventing the Soul: Posthumanist Theory and Psychic Life*. New York: Other Press.

Sanderson, Terry. 1999. *How to Be a Happy Homosexual: A Guide for Gay Men*. London: Other Way Press.

Sartre, Jean-Paul. [1939] 2002. *Sketch for a Theory of the Emotions*. Trans. Philip Mairet. New York: Routledge.

———. [1946] 1989. *Existentialism and Humanism*. Trans. Philip Mairet. London: Methuen.

———. [1965] 1993. *Essays in Existentialism*. Ed. Wade Baskin. New York: Citadel Press.

Scheler, Max. [1913] 2008. *The Nature of Sympathy*. Trans. Peter Heath. New Brunswick: Transaction Publishers.

Schoch, Richard N. 2006. *The Secrets of Happiness*. London: Profile Books.

Schopenhauer, Arthur. [1818] 1883. *The World as Will and Idea*, vol. 3. Trans. R. B. Haldane and J. Kemp. London: Routledge and Kegan Paul.

———. [1840] 1995. *On the Basis of Morality*. Trans. E. F. J. Payne. Indianapolis: Hackett Publishing Company.

———. [1850] 2004. *On the Suffering of the World*. Trans. R. J. Hollingdale. London: Penguin Books.

Schroeder, Michael, and Ariel Shidlo. 2002. "Ethical Issues in Sexual Orientation Conversion Therapies: An Empircal Study of Consumers." *Sexual Conversion Therapy: Ethical, Clinical, and Research Perspectives*, ed. Ariel Shidlo, Michael Schroeder, Jack Drescher, 131–66. Philadelphia: Haworth Press.

Schulman, Sarah. [1992] 2006. *Empathy*. Vancouver: Arsenal Pulp Press.

———. 1998. *Stage Struck: Theatre, AIDS and the Marketing of Gay America*. Durham, N.C.: Duke University Press.

Schultz, Bart, and Georgios Varouxakis. 2005. Introduction. *Utilitarianism and Empire*, ed. Bart Schultz and Georgios Varouxakis, 1–32. Lanham, Md.: Lexington Books.

Schwarz, Norbert, and Strack, Fritz. 1991. "Evaluating One's Life: A Judgment Model of Subjective Well-Being." *Subjective Well-Being: An Interdisciplinary Perspective*, ed. Fritz Strack, Michael Argyle and Norbert Schwarz, 27–48. Oxford: Pergamon Press.

Sedgwick, Eve Kosofsky. 2003. *Touching Feeling: Affect, Performativity, Pedagogy*. Durham, N.C.: Duke University Press.

Segal, Lynne. 2007. *Making Trouble: Life and Politics*. London: Serpent's Tail.

Seligman, Martin E. P. 2003. *Authentic Happiness: Using the New Positive Psychology to Realize Your Potential for Lasting Fulfillment*. London: Nicholas Brealey.

Seneca. 1997. "Consolation to Helvia." *Dialogues and Letters*, 3–28. Trans. C. D. N. Costa. London: Penguin Books.

Shine, Darla. 2005. *Happy Housewives*. New York: HarperCollins.

Shuttleworth, Sally. 1984. *George Eliot and Nineteenth-Century Science: The Make-Believe of a Beginning*. Cambridge: Cambridge University Press.

Skeggs, Beverley. 2004. *Class, Self, Culture*. London: Routledge.

Smith, Adam. [1759] 2000. *The Theory of Moral Sentiments* New York: Prometheus Books.

———. [1776] 1999. *The Wealth of Nations, Book 1–3*. London: Penguin Books.

Smith, J. A. 1998. Introduction to *Nicomachean Ethics*, by Aristotle, iii–xviii. Mineola, N.Y.: Dover Publications.

Snediker, Michael D. 2009. *Queer Optimism: Lyric Personhood and Other Felicitous Persuasions*. Minneapolis: University of Minnesota Press.

Solomon, Robert. 2006. "Emotions in Phenomenology and Existentialism." *A Companion to Phenomenology and Existentialism*, ed. Hubert L. Dreyfus, Mark A. Wrathall, 291–309. Cambridge, Mass.: Blackwell.

Spinoza, Benedict de. [1677] 2001. *Ethics*. Trans A. H. White. Ware, Hertfordshire: Wordsworth Editions.

Spivak, Gayatri Chakravorty. 1988. "Can the Subaltern Speak?" *Marxism and the Interpretation of Culture*, ed. Cary Nelson and Lawrence Grossberg, 271–313. Champaign: University of Illinois Press.

Stimpson, Catharine R. 1988. *Where the Meanings Are: Feminism and Cultural Spaces*. New York: Methuen.

Stokes, Eric. 1959. *The English Utilitarians and India*. Delhi: Oxford University Press.

Strack, Fritz, Michael Argyle, and Norbert Schwarz. 1991. Introduction. *Subjective Well-Being: An Interdisciplinary Perspective*, ed. Fritz Strack, Michael Argyle, and Norbert Schwarz, 1–6. Oxford: Pergamon Press.

Stringer, Rebecca. 2000. "A Nietzschean Breed: Feminism, Victimology, *Ressentiment*." *Why Nietzsche Still? Reflections on Drama, Culture, Politics*, ed. Alan D. Schrift, 247–73. Berkeley: University of California Press.

Strong, Tracy B. 2002. *Jean-Jacques Rousseau: The Politics of the Ordinary*. Lanham, Md.: Rowman and Littlefield.

Struik, Dirk J. 1964. Introduction. *The Economic and Philosophical Manuscripts of 1844*, by Karl Marx, 9–56. New York: International Publications.

Sullivan, Eileen. 1983. "Liberalism and Imperialism: John Stuart Mill's Defence of the British Empire." *Journal of the History of Ideas* 44 (4): 599–617.

Summers, Heather, and Anne Watson. 2006. *The Book of Happiness: Brilliant Ideas to Transform Your Life*. Mankato, Minn.: Capstone.

Swan, Susan. 1993. *Wives of Bath*. New York: Alfred A. Knopf.

Swanton, Christine. 2000. "Compassion as a Virtue in Hume." *Feminist Interpretations of David Hume*, ed. Anne Jaap Jacobson, 156–73. University Park: Pennsylvania State University Press.

Syal, Meera. [1996] 2004. *Anita and Me*. London: Harper Perennial.

Tate, Shirley. 2005. *Black Skins, Black Masks: Hybridity, Dialogism, Performativity*. London: Ashgate.

Terada, Rei. 2001. *Feeling in Theory: Emotion after the "Death of the Subject."* Cambridge, Mass.: Harvard University Press.

Thobani, Sunera. 2003. "War Frenzy and Nation Building: A Lesson in the Politics of 'Truth-Making.'" *International Journal of Qualitative Studies in Education* 16 (3): 399–414.

Thompson, Evan. 2007. *Mind in Life: Biology, Phenomenology, and the Sciences of Mind*. Cambridge, Mass.: Harvard University Press.

Toder, Nancy. 1980. *Choices*. Boston: Alyson Publications.

To Leung, Man. 1998. "James Mill's Utilitarianism and British Imperialism in India." http://www.tamilnation.org/Oneworld/imperialism.htm. Visited May 11, 2009.

Tolstoy, Leo. [1875–77] 1985. *Anna Karenina*. Trans. Rosemary Edmonds. London: Penguin.

Tyler, Imogen. 2008. "Methodological Fatigue: The Politics of 'The Affective Turn.'" *Feminist Media Studies* 8 (1): 85–90.

United Kingdom. Home Office. 2002. *Secure Borders, Safe Haven: Integration with Diversity in Modern Britain*. London: Stationery Office.

———. 2005a. "Strength in Diversity: Towards a Community Cohesion and Race Equality Strategy." http://www.homeoffice.gov.uk/documents/cons-strength-in-diverse-170904.

———. 2005b. *Life in the United Kingdom: A Journey to Citizenship*. Norwich: Stationery Office.

Veenhoven, Ruut. 1984. *Conditions of Happiness*. Dordrecht: D. Reidel Publishing Company.

———. 1991. "Questions on Happiness: Classical Topics, Modern Answers, Blindspots." *Subjective Well-Being: An Interdisciplinary Perspective*, ed. Fritz Strack, Michael Argyle and Norbert Schwarz, 8–24. Oxford: Pergamon Press.

Walker, Lisa. 2001. *Looking Like What You Are: Sexual Style, Race and Lesbian Identity*. New York: New York University Press.

Warn, Sarah. 2003. "Dropping Lesbian Romance from *Beckham* the Right Decision." http://www.afterellen.com/Movies/beckham.html. Visited February 12, 2009.

Weil, Simone. [1952] 2002. *Gravity and Grace*. Trans. Emma Crawford and Mario von der Ruhr. London: Routledge.

Weldon, Fay. 2006. *What Makes Women Happy?* London: Fourth Estates.

West, Henry W. 2004. *An Introduction to Mill's Utilitarian Ethics*. Cambridge: Cambridge University Press, 2004.

Williams, Raymond. 1977. *Marxism and Literature*. Oxford: Oxford University Press.

———. 2006. *Modern Tragedy*. Peterborough, Ontario: Broadview Encore.

Wilson, Eric G. 2008. *Against Happiness: In Praise of Melancholy*. New York: Sarah Crichton Books.

Wollstonecraft, Mary. [1792] 1975. *A Vindication of the Rights of Women*. New York: W. W. Norton.

Woodward, Kathleen. 2009. *Statistical Panic: Cultural Politics and Poetics of the Emotions*. Durham, N.C.: Duke University Press.

Woolf, Virginia. [1925] 1953. *Mrs. Dalloway*. New York: Harvest Books.

Yancy, George. 2008. *Black Bodies, White Gazes: The Continuing Significance of Race*. Lanham, Md.: Rowman and Littlefield.

Zastoupil, Lynn. 1994. *John Stuart Mill and India*. Stanford, Calif.: Stanford University Press, 1994.

Žižek, Slavoj. 2002. *Welcome to the Desert of the Real*. London: Verso.

———. 2005. "From Revolutionary to Catastrophic Utopia." *Thinking Utopia: Steps into Other Worlds*, ed. Jörn Rüsen, Michael Fehr and Thomas W. Rieger, 247–62. New York: Berghahn Books.

———. 2008a. *In Defence of Lost Causes*. London: Verso.

———. 2008b. *Violence*. London: Profile Books.

Zupančič, Alenka. 2000. *Ethics of the Real: Kant, Lacan*. London: Verso.

INDEX

Abraham, Julie, 90
activism, 107–8, 169–70. *See also* consciousness, consciousness-raising
activity, 208–17, 276–79 nn. 4–12
Adorno, Theodor, 235 n. 19, 270 n. 10, 278 n. 8
affect: affective value of objects, 21–27, 231–33 nn. 2–10; conversion points of, 44–45, 180, 185–86, 240–41 nn. 33–37; cultural studies of, 13–15; disappointment and anger of, 7, 41–42, 44, 239–40 nn. 30–32; of happy family, 45–49, 241 nn. 38–40; inside-out model of, 39; outside-in model of, 40–41; revolutionary consciousness in, 162–63; self-production of, 43–44; in shared social contexts, 39–45, 162, 237–41 nn. 26–37; stickiness of, 40, 44, 230 n. 1
affect aliens, 41–42, 240 n. 31, 247 n. 26; alternative hopefulness of, 189–91; melancholia of, 141; in migration contexts, 148–59, 263–66 nn. 29–38; revolutionary consciousness of, 164–72, 267–69 nn. 5–8
affirmation of negation, 162
affirmative feminism, 87
affirmative turn, 213–17
Against Happiness (Wilson), 228 n. 18
Agamben, Giorgio, 229 n. 19
Aidoo, Ama Ata, 68
alienation. *See* affect aliens
aliveness, 79
altruism, 9–10
anaesthetics, 207
Anderson, Ben, 279 n. 11
anger, 42, 44, 67–69, 240 n. 32, 245 n. 18, 272 n. 15
Anita and Me (Syal), 149–54, 265 n. 35
Anna Karenina (Tolstoy), 241 n. 38
Annas, Julia, 36–37, 236 n. 24
Annie on My Mind (Garden), 18, 92–93
anticipatory causality, 27–33, 233–36 nn. 11–21
antiracism, 2, 17–19, 267 n. 5. *See also* multicultural happiness

"Antisocial Turn in Queer Theory, The" (Edelman), 270 n. 10

Antz, 193

anxiety: hopefulness in, 183–92, 271–72 nn. 12–16; in outside-in model of affect, 31–32, 40–41; in self-doubt, 42

archives of happiness, 15–18. *See also* feminist archives; future dystopias; migration archives; queer archives

Arendt, Hannah, 29, 269 n. 8

Argyle, Michael, 7–9

Aristotle, 10, 13, 227–28 nn. 14–15; on feelings in habituation, 36–37; on moderation of the good man, 37; teleological conception of happiness of, 26, 233 nn. 8–10

Arlington Park (Cusk), 246 n. 22

Art of Life, The (Bauman), 228 n. 18

aspiration, 120

assimilation. *See* migration archives

atmosphere, 40–41, 67

Austin, John, 29–30, 234 n. 16

authentic happiness, 209, 277 n. 5

Awakening, The (Chopin), 246 n. 23

Babyji (Dawesar), 90, 118–20

Badiou, Alan, 195, 273 n. 19

Ballaster, Rosalind, 240 n. 35

Barrow, Robin, 24–25, 241 n. 1

Baudrillard, Jean, 163

Bauman, Zygmunt, 181, 228 n. 18

bearable lives, 97

Beauvoir, Simone de, 2, 45–46, 73, 204

Beccaria, Cesare, 4

Bee Movie, The, 193

Belliotti, Raymond Angelo, 250 n. 6

Bend It Like Beckham, 18–19; conversion from melancholia in, 141–45, 255 n. 20, 261 nn. 22–23, 271 n. 14; individual freedom as goal in, 133–

38, 260 n. 18; second-generation affect alienation in, 151–54, 263 n. 30, 265 n. 32

benevolence, 250 n. 5

Bennett, Oliver, 179

Bentham, Jeremy, 4–5, 123, 231 n. 2, 257 n. 7, 258 n. 12

Berlant, Lauren, 11, 226 n. 10, 228 n. 16; on cruel optimism, 271 n. 11; on promises of future happiness, 30, 196; on silliness, 222; on zones of privacy, 90

Beyond the Pleasure Principle (Freud), 270 n. 11

Bhabha, Homi, 129–30, 256 n. 6

Bhutan, 3

bird tropes, 105, 255 n. 18

black contexts: of angry black woman, 67–69, 245 n. 18, 272 n. 15; consciousness of racism in, 79–87, 247–48 nn. 26–29; of happy housewife fantasies, 51; of liberation struggles, 191; of utopian dreams of freedom, 196–97. *See also* racial contexts

Black Skin, White Masks (Fanon), 86

Bloch, Charlotte, 169

Bloch, Ernst, 181–82

Bluest Eye, The (Morrison), 79–83, 116, 247 nn. 26–27

boats, 184, 198–99, 222, 275 nn. 25–26

Borysenko, Joan, 242 n. 4

Bourdieu, Pierre, 33–35

Boys in the Band, The (Crowley), 94

Braidotti, Rosi, 87, 214–16

Brave New World (Huxley), 19, 192–94

breast cancer, 83–84, 247 n. 28

Brennan, Teresa, 40, 239 n. 29

brides, 29, 41–42, 239 n. 30, 242 n. 6

Brinton, Daniel Garrison, 237 n. 26

Britain: Commission for Racial Equality of, 122; empire of, 123–33;

Section 28 Law, 248 n. 1; segregation in, 156, 266 n. 37; social well-being agenda of, 3

Brooks, Peter, 235 n. 20

Brown, Rita Mae, 35, 115–18

Bruce, John, 124

Buddhism, 3

burqas, 159, 261 n. 21

Butler, Judith, 60, 97, 104, 115–16

Cameron, David, 3

Cancer Journals, The (Lorde), 83–84

capacities, 71, 245–46 nn. 19–20

capitalism, 4, 277 n. 5

Carr, Alan, 10–11

Carter, Mia, 257 n. 8

cause of happiness, 6–7, 14, 204; anticipatory causality, 27–33, 233–36 nn. 11–21; upward mobility as, 119–20. *See also* object of desire

Chadha, Gurinda, 144–45

Chancellor, William, 257 n. 10

chanciness, 33, 208

Cheng, Anne-Anlin, 260 n. 20

Chicken Tikka Masala, 262 n. 25

children, 48, 59, 183–84, 274 n. 21

Children of Men, 163; anxious hope for future in, 183–87, 191–92; Edelman's critique of, 164, 267 n. 3; optimism and pessimism in, 175, 177–80; revolutionary consciousness in, 169–72, 197–98, 269 n. 8

Choices (Toder), 254 n. 17

Chopin, Kate, 246 n. 23

Christakis, Nicholas A., 253 n. 14

citizenship, 130–34

Civilization and Its Discontents (Freud), 31

civilizing mission, 35, 236 n. 23

civil partnerships, 106

class contexts: of happy housewife fantasies, 51; myth of transcendence of racism in, 153–54, 265 n. 35; of workers, 166–67, 171

classical happiness, 10–12, 36–37, 227–28 nn. 14–15, 233 nn. 8–10; political economy as basis of, 13, 227 n. 14; teleological structure of, 26, 199–200, 233 nn. 8–10

clones, 187–91, 197–98

coercion, 212

Colebrook, Claire, 14, 228 n. 17

Colwin, Laurie, 46–49

comfort, 174–75

Commission for Racial Equality (UK), 122, 256 n. 2

communities of feeling, 56–57

compromise, 149, 264 n. 31

Conard, Mark T., 229 n. 21

concupiscence, 250 n. 5

conditional happiness: empathy in, 95–96; in love contexts, 90–95, 100, 249–52 nn. 3–11; in migration experiences, 133–38; in social and family contexts, 56–58, 90–95, 186–87, 242 n. 4, 242 n. 6

consciousness, consciousness-raising, 53; in black awareness of racism, 79–87, 247–48 nn. 26–29; false, 83–84, 165–66, 168, 267 n. 5; revolutionary, 164–72, 267–69 nn. 5–8; unhappiness in, 64–79, 86–87, 245–46 nn. 16–25

contagion, 39–40, 97–98, 195, 237–39 nn. 26–29, 253 nn. 13–14, 274 n. 22

contingency, 22, 33, 207–8, 236 n. 22

convention, 64

conversion points, 44–45, 180, 240–41 nn. 33–37, 268 n. 7; in alternative hopes, 185–86, 190–91; in migratory melancholia, 138–48, 185, 260–63 nn. 20–29, 266 n. 38; in queer happy families, 107–14, 248 n. 1, 255 nn. 20–22

courtly love, 32
cricket test, 159
Crimp, Douglas, 266 n. 38
crisis in happiness, 7, 41–42, 239–40
nn. 30–31
crisis points, 218
Critique of Practical Reason (Kant), 276
n. 4
crowd psychology, 40–43
Crowley, Matt, 94
Csíkszentmihályi, Mihály, 11–12, 22
Cultural Politics of Emotion, The
(Ahmed), 14, 226 n. 10, 231 n. 2, 236
n. 21
cultural studies, 6
Cunningham, Michael, 75–76
curiosity, 189–90
Cusk, Rachel, 246 n. 22
Cvetkovich, Ann, 114

Dawesar, Abha, 118–20
definitions of happiness, 5–6
Deleuze, Gilles, 14, 210–13, 232 n. 5,
277 n. 7, 278 n. 9
de-queering, 252 n. 10
Derrida, Jacques, 198
Descartes, René, 23
desire for happiness, 1, 30–32, 201,
204–5, 225 n. 1, 234 n. 17; Maggie
Tulliver's renunciation of, 62–64,
244 n. 12; regulation of, 37, 240
n. 31; teleological conceptions of,
26, 199–200, 203, 233 nn. 8–10; in
utilitarianism, 4–5, 15, 193–94, 202,
231 n. 2, 235 n. 18. *See also* object of
desire
"Desperate Feminist Wives"
(O'Rourke), 53
Desperate Housewives, 52
Diener, Ed, 7
Dientstag, Joshua Foa, 176

disappointment, 7, 41–42, 239–40
nn. 30–31
discomfort, 174–75
Distinction (Bourdieu), 33
double alienation, 167
Douglass, Frederick, 257 n. 10
drama of contingency, 22
Du Bois, W. E. B., 257 n. 10
Durkheim, Émile, 5, 160, 182
dystopias. *See* future dystopias

Eagleton, Terry, 12
Eastern traditions, 3
East India Company, 124, 257 n. 8
East Is East, 145–48, 263 n. 28
*Economic and Philosophical Manuscripts
of 1844, The* (Struik), 166–67
economic contexts, 6; of false consciousness, 165–66; growth at the
expense of happiness in, 7–8; happy
inequality of capitalism, 4, 226–27
nn. 10–11, 277 n. 5; in positive psychology, 10–11, 227 n. 13; of progress
measures, 3, 5, 226 nn. 8; purchasing power, 5; of revolutionary consciousness, 164–65
Edelman, Lee, 161, 164, 183, 267 n. 3,
270 n. 10
Educating Rita, 35
education: of colonial subjects, 128–
29; of Rousseau's Sophy, 54–60, 62,
241–43 nn. 2–7, 243 n. 11
Ehrenreich, Barbara, 247 n. 28
Elias, Norbert, 35
Eliot, George, 60–64, 115, 243 n. 10,
244 nn. 12–14
Émile (Rousseau), 54–59, 62, 241–43
nn. 2–7
Empathy (Schulman), 95–96
empire: civilizing philanthropy of,
124–25; double alienation of natives

in, 167–68; Mill's defense of, 126–29; multicultural outcomes of, 130–33; racism underlying, 148; teaching of happiness in, 128–30; utilitarian analysis of, 123–33, 167–68, 256–59 nn. 6–16

empiricism, 15, 22–24, 207–8

Eng, David L., 139, 260 n. 20

Engels, Friedrich, 165

English Utilitarians and India, The (Stokes), 256 n. 6

Enquiries concerning the Principles of Morals (Hume), 238 n. 28

envy, 281 n. 18

Essay concerning Human Understanding, An (Locke), 250 n. 5

Ethics (Spinoza), 277 n. 7

ethics of happiness, 1, 15, 205, 218, 229 n. 19; affirmative turn in, 213–17; Aristotle's examination of, 10, 13, 26, 36–37, 227–28 nn. 14–15, 233 nn. 8–10

Ethics of Psychoanalysis, The (Lacan), 37–38

eudaimonia, 12–13, 36, 227 n. 14

evangelicism, 128, 131–32, 134

everyday habits of happiness, 14–15, 35–37, 128, 178, 236 n. 24

existentialism, 184

false consciousness, 83–84, 165–66, 168, 267 n. 5

families, 7, 10–11; conditional happiness in, 56–58, 90–95, 186–87, 242 n. 4, 242 n. 6; consequences for children in, 78–79, 246 n. 25; education of females in, 54–59, 241–43 nn. 1–7; happy, 21, 45–49, 241 nn. 38–40; of happy queers, 107–14, 248 n. 1, 255 nn. 20–22; influence toward happiness in, 47–48, 241

n. 39; killjoys in, 19–20, 49, 50–87, 241 n. 40; kinship objects of, 46–47; as points of inheritance, 95, 186–87; reconciliation of want in, 149–50; violence in, 146–48, 263 nn. 28–nn. 29; wedding days, 29, 41–42, 239 n. 30, 242 n. 6. *See also* housewives

Family Happiness (Colwin), 46–49

Fanon, Frantz, 86, 167–68, 259 n. 15, 272 n. 16

fear affect, 230 n. 1

fellow-feeling, 56–57, 195

Felski, Rita, 245 n. 16

female friendship, 221–22

Feminine Mystique, The (Friedan), 50–51, 78–79

feminist archives, 2, 17–19, 50–57, 222–23; affirmative feminism, 87; aliveness in, 79; black perspectives of, 67–69, 79–87, 245 n. 18; in Colwin's *Family Happiness*, 46–49; consciousness-raising of unhappiness in, 53, 64–79, 86–87, 245–46 nn. 16–25; consequences for children in, 78–79, 246 n. 25; in Cunningham's *The Hours*, 75–78; Firestone's smile boycott, 69–70; of imagination, 62–63; intergenerational sympathy in, 78; in Lorde's *Cancer Journals*, 83–84; responses to Mrs. Dalloway in, 73; responses to Rousseau's Sophy in, 58–60, 62, 243 n. 7; studies of emotion and affect in, 13–15; of troublemaking and defying convention, 60–65, 115–16, 243–45 nn. 9–15

Feminist Theory (hooks), 50–51

fetishism, 126–27

Firestone, Shulamith, 69–70

football, 122, 256 n. 5, 260 n. 18, 261 n. 22

fortune, 22, 205–8

Foucault, Michel, 243 n. 8, 269 n. 8, 275 n. 25

Fowler, James H., 253 n. 14

"Fragment of a Moral Catechism" (Kant), 279 n. 13

Fragment of Government, A (Bentham), 4–5

Franklin, Sarah, 181

freedom, 27, 233 n. 10; to be unhappy, 192–98, 222–23, 273–75 nn. 17–26; giving up of, 221–22; as object of happiness, 133–38, 260 nn. 17–18

Freeman, Elizabeth, 115

Freud, Sigmund, 15–16; on desire and anxiety, 31; on homosexuality, 95–96; on mourning and melancholia, 132, 138–41, 270 n. 11

Frey, Bruno S., 1, 6, 225 n. 1

Friedan, Betty, 50–51, 78–79, 259 n. 14

friendship, 221–22

Fruit of the Lemon (Levy), 84–86

Frye, Marilyn, 66–67

Fuch, Cynthia, 106

future dystopias, 18, 160, 173–78; alternative forms of hope in, 181–92, 271–72 nn. 12–16; birth and children in, 164, 170–72, 179–80, 183–87, 267 n. 3, 274 n. 21; boats as utopic destinations in, 184, 198–99, 222, 275 nn. 25–26; in *Children of Men*, 163–64, 169–72, 175, 177–80, 183–87, 191–92, 197–98, 267 n. 3; freedom to be unhappy in, 192–98, 222–23, 233 n. 11, 273–75 nn. 17–26; in Gunn's *The Joy Makers*, 192–94; in Huxley's *Brave New World*, 192–94; in *The Island*, 187–93, 197–98; in Le Guin's "The People Who Walked Away from Omelas," 192, 194–95; optimism and pessimism about, 161–63, 172–80,

267 nn. 1–2, 269–70 nn. 9–11; promises of happiness in, 27–33, 38–39, 59, 181, 233–36 nn. 11–21; revolutionary consciousness in, 162–72, 267–69 nn. 5–8; in teleological conceptions of happiness, 26, 233 nn. 8–10

Garden, Nancy, 18, 92–93

gendered scripts, 18; of body's capacities, 71, 245–46 nn. 19–20; of divisions of labor, 53–59; of equality struggles, 227 n. 13; of wedding days, 29, 41–42, 239 n. 30, 242 n. 6

Gender Trouble (Butler), 60

genealogy of happiness: activity and passivity in, 208–13, 220–21, 276–79 nn. 4–12; affirmative turn in, 213–17; of Nietzsche, 205–7; possibility and happenstance embraced in, 217–23, 280–81 nn. 14–18

Genuine Progress Indicator (GPI), 3, 226 nn. 8

geography of happiness, 97–98, 253 n. 14

Gettis, Alan, 242 n. 4

Gibbs, Anna, 39

Gilbert, Daniel, 275 n. 26

Gilman, Charlotte Perkins, 79

Gilroy, Paul, 132, 256 n. 3

good feeling, 13–14, 37–38

good habits, 14–15, 35–37, 128, 178, 236 n. 24

Good Race Relations Guide, 122, 256 n. 2

Gopinath, Gayatri, 144–45

Gosling, J. C. B., 231 n. 2

governance, 3–4. *See also* political contexts

Graeber, David, 165

Greene, Gayle, 70

grief. *See* mourning

Gross National Happiness (GNH), 3

Groundwork for the Metaphysics of Morals (Kant), 276 n. 4
Gunn, James, 192
Gunnell, Barbara, 3

habits, 14–15, 35–37, 128, 178, 236 n. 24
Hage, Ghassan, 188
Hai, Yasmin, 149, 154–58
Halberstam, Judith, 273 n. 18, 282 n. 19
Hall, Radclyffe, 96–106, 252 n. 12, 254 nn. 15–16
Han, Shinhee, 139, 260 n. 20
hap, 31, 33, 41, 179, 218, 236 n. 22; hap cares, 186; hap movements, 192, 198, 222–23
happenstance, 219–20, 281 n. 15
happiness, 14, 200, 228 n. 17, 229 n. 22, 275 n. 1; mobility of, 201–5; original meaning of, 22–26
Happiness (McMahon), 16
Happiness (Layard), 5
Happiness and Economics (Frey and Stutzer), 6
happiness archives, 15–18. *See also* feminist archives; future dystopias; migration archives; queer archives
happiness duty, 7, 249 n. 3, 260 n. 17
Happiness Formula, The (BBC), 3, 121–22
happiness indicators, 6–7
happiness industry, 3
Happiness Mission, 125
happiness profile, 10–11
Happiness Studies, 4
happiness turn, 2–7, 214
Happy Feet, 273 n. 18
Happy-Go-Lucky, 220–22, 281 n. 16
Happy Housewives (Shine), 52
Hardt, Michael, 278 n. 9
Hartman, Saidiya V., 257 n. 10
Heady, B., 10
hedonics, 194
Hegel, G. W. F., 166, 229 n. 22

Heinlin, Robert, 92
Helvétius, Claude Adrien, 4
Hemmings, Clare, 100, 254 n. 15
heterosexual happiness, 2, 18, 97–103, 221–22; assumptions of, 90–95, 108–9, 255 n. 22; as form of injustice, 96; in housewife fantasies, 52; in interracial contexts, 145, 262 n. 25; reproduction in, 112–13
hierarchies of happiness, 12–14
Highsmith, Patricia, 249 n. 2
History and Class Consciousness (Lukács), 162
History of British India (James Mill), 125–29, 257 nn. 7–8, 258 n. 11
Hobbes, Thomas, 235 n. 18
Hochschild, Arlie Russell, 41, 239 n. 30
Holden, Robert, 267 n. 1
homonormativity, 255 n. 22
hooks, bell, 50–51, 67
hope, hopefulness, 178, 181–92, 270 n. 11, 271–72 nn. 12–16
horizons, 24, 47, 76–77, 119, 147–48
Horkheimer, Max, 235 n. 19
Hours, The (Cunningham), 75–78, 219, 246 n. 25
housewife, 50–53, 78–79; conditional happiness of, 55–58, 242 n. 4, 242 n. 6; conventions of duty of, 63–65; obligations of happiness of, 59–60, 259 n. 14; Sophy's education as, 55–60, 62, 241–43 nn. 2–7, 243 n. 11
How to Be a Happy Homosexual (Sanderson), 252 n. 10
How to Do Things with Words (Austin), 29–30, 234 n. 16
Hudson, Deal W., 36
Hume, David, 4, 39, 203, 231 n. 2, 233 n. 12, 238 n. 28
Husserl, Edmund, 23–24, 231 n. 4
Huxley, Aldous, 192–94

Icelandic Lives (Phua), 251 n. 7

Ideas Pertaining to a Pure Phenomenology and to a Phenomenological Philosophy (Husserl), 23–24

idiosyncratic nature of happy objects, 47, 119, 159, 202

If These Walls Could Talk 2, 90, 107–14, 255 n. 20

imagination, 62–64, 243 n. 11

Imagine Me and You, 251 n. 8

Imitation of Christ (Thomas à Kempis), 244 n. 12

influence, 47–48, 241 n. 39

inside-out model of affect, 39

instrumental models of happiness, 10, 59, 227–28 nn. 13–15, 233 n. 10, 243 n. 8

intellectual history of happiness, 16–20

intentionality, 24–26

inversion, 96, 252 n. 12

irritation, 174

Island, The, 187–93, 197–98

James, P. D., 163–64

James, Susan, 23

James, William, 273 n. 17

Jameson, Fredric, 163, 183

Janaway, Christopher, 175–76

Jenkins, Henry, 274 n. 21

Jenny Lives with Martin and Eric, 248 n. 1

Johnson, Lesley, 53

Jones, H. S., 123

joy, 214–15

Joy Makers, The (Gunn), 19, 192–94

Jullien, François, 15

Kant, Immanuel, 1, 15; on aesthetics of pure taste, 34–35; on duty, 64, 244 n. 14; on habituation, 236 n. 24; on hope, 271 n. 12; on moral feeling, 231 n. 4, 276 n. 4, 279 n. 13; on natural sympathy, 274 n. 22; on

pragmatic law, 234 n. 17; Rousseau's influence on, 242 n. 3

Keeping You a Secret (Peter), 251 n. 8

Kelley, Robin D. G., 196–97

Kempis, Thomas à, 244 n. 12

Kenny, Anthony, 26

Kierkegaard, Søren, 218–19, 280 n. 14

killjoys, 19–20, 49, 53, 213, 241 n. 40, 278 n. 10; angry black women as, 67–69, 245 n. 18, 272 n. 15; in black awareness of racism, 79–87, 247–48 nn. 26–29; in conscious choice of unhappiness, 64–79, 86–87, 245–46 nn. 16–25; in political pessimism, 176; troublemakers as, 60–65, 243 nn. 9–15; violence exposed by, 268 n. 7

kinship objects, 46–47, 110

Ku Klux Klan, 256 n. 4

Kureishi, Hanif, 154

labor, 166–67, 171

Lacan, Jacques, 15–16; on courtly love, 32; on happiness, 202; on moral experience, 37–38, 234 n. 17; on transformation through identification, 137

Laing, R. D., 241 n. 40

laughter, 42

Layard, Richard, 5, 7, 226 n. 10

Lear, Jonathan, 32

Le Bon, Gustave, 42–44

Le Guin, Ursula, 192, 194–95, 273 n. 17

Leigh, Mike, 220–21

Leung, Man To, 257 n. 9

Leviathan (Hobbes), 235 n. 18

Levy, Andrea, 18, 84–86

Liebniz, Gottfried, 92, 176–77, 250 n. 5, 270 n. 10

life insurance, 243 n. 8

Life in the United Kingdom, 130–32, 259 n. 15

Literature after Feminism (Felski), 245 n. 16

Lloyd, Justine, 53

Location of Culture, The (Bhabha), 256 n. 6

Locke, John, 15; on blank slate of the child, 54; on desire for happiness, 30–31, 234 n. 17; empiricism of, 22–27, 231 n. 4, 250 n. 5; on futurity of hope, 181; on taste, 33, 35–36, 47, 211–12

Lorde, Audre, 67–68, 82–84, 215–16

Lost and Delirious (Pool), 103–6, 254 n. 17

love: alternative hope through, 190–91; conditional happiness in, 92–95, 100, 249–52 nn. 3–11; queer definitions of, 100–101

Love, Heather, 89, 218

Lukács, György, 162, 165–66

L Word, The, 94, 251 n. 9, 255 n. 22

Macaulay, Thomas Babington, 129–30

Machery, Pierre, 278 n. 9

MacIntyre, Alasdair, 227 n. 14

Making of Mr. Hai's Daughter, The (Hai), 154–58

Making Trouble (Segal), 243 n. 9

Managed Heart, The (Hochschild), 41, 239 n. 30

maps, 253 n. 14

Marar, Ziyad, 201

Marcuse, Herbert, 169

marriage, 6–7, 10–11, 119, 204; gendered scripts of wedding days, 29, 41–42, 239 n. 30, 242 n. 6; same-sex, 94

Martin, Jane Roland, 241 n. 2

Marx, Karl, 167, 171, 183, 188

Massumi, Brian, 214–15, 230 n. 1

Mbembe, Achille, 129

McCarney, Joseph, 165

McMahon, Darrin, 13, 16, 199

means, 10, 59, 227–28 nn. 13–15, 233 n. 10, 243 n. 8

measures of happiness. *See* science of happiness

melancholia, 138–48, 260–63 nn. 20–29, 266 n. 38; hope as form of, 189; of workers, 166–67, 171

memory, 25, 45, 160–61, 241 n. 37

Metaphysics of Morals, The (Kant), 242 n. 3, 274 n. 22

migration archives, 222–23; affect alienation of second generations in, 148–59, 263–66 nn. 29–38; in *Bend It Like Beckham*, 133–38, 141–45, 151–54; conditional happiness in, 133–48; conversion from melancholia in, 138–48, 260–63 nn. 20–29, 266 n. 38; in *East Is East*, 145–48; empire's effect on, 123–33; familial violence in, 146–48, 263 nn. 28–nn. 29; fetishizing of culture in, 154; in Hai's *The Making of Mr. Hai's Daughter*, 154–58; individual freedom achieved in, 133–38, 260 nn. 17–18; multicultural happiness in, 121–23, 130–33, 138, 145, 159, 258–59 nn. 13–15, 267 n. 5; racism and exclusion in, 121–23, 142–47, 151–58, 261 nn. 21–23, 263 nn. 27–29, 265 n. 35, 271 n. 14; in Syal's *Anita and Me*, 149–54

Mill, James, 123–29, 257 nn. 7–8

Mill, John Stuart, 16, 123–24, 202, 233 n. 7, 256–57 nn. 6–9, 258 n. 12, 276 n. 2

Miller, D. A., 235 n. 20

Millett, Kate, 73

Mill on the Floss, The (Eliot), 60–64, 115, 243 n. 10, 244 nn. 12–14

Minima Moralia (Adorno), 278 n. 8

"Minute on Indian Education" (Macaulay), 129–30
Mrs. Dalloway (Woolf), 70–78, 219, 245–46 nn. 19–22
mobility of happiness, 201–5
moderation, 37
Modern Tragedy (Williams), 170
moral distinctions, 14; in classical happiness, 12–13, 227 n. 14; embodied in taste, 33–38, 234 n. 17, 236–37 nn. 22–25; in good feeling, 37–38, 231 n. 4, 276 n. 4, 279 n. 13; in Nietzsche's genealogy of morals, 205–7; in obligation to be happy, 39, 59–60, 237 n. 26
Morality and Happiness (Annas), 36–37
"Moral Philosopher and the Moral Life, The" (James), 273 n. 17
Moreton-Robinson, Aileen, 245 n. 18
Morgan, Claire (Patricia Highsmith), 249 n. 2
Morrison, Toni, 79–83, 116, 247 nn. 26–27
mourning, 260 n. 19; Freud's definition of, 132, 138–41; for loss of an abstraction, 139–40; for loss of possibility, 186–87; melancholia vs., 140–41; in queer contexts, 98–99, 108–11
"Mourning and Melancholia" (Freud), 138–41
"Moving on Up," 137
multicultural happiness, 121–23, 130–33, 138, 145, 159, 256 nn. 3–4, 258–59 nn. 13–15, 267 n. 5
Muñoz, José Esteban, 228 n. 16
Munt, Sally, 89, 102
My Bondage and My Freedom (Douglass), 257 n. 10
My Son the Fanatic (Kureishi), 154, 265 n. 36

Naipaul, V. S., 266 n. 38
Nancy, Jean-Luc, 219, 229 n. 21, 281 n. 15
narrative, 235 n. 20
nationalism, 130–32
New Essays on Human Understanding (Liebniz), 250 n. 5
Newton, Esther, 100–101, 254 n. 15
Nicomachean Ethics (Aristotle), 26
Nietzsche, Friedrich, 15, 228 n. 17; on causality of sensation, 231 n. 2; genealogy of morals of, 205–7; on promises of happiness, 29; on retrospective attribution of causality, 27–28, 233 n. 12, 240 n. 33; on superman, 209, 277 nn. 5–6; on utilitarianism, 123, 125
nihilism, 195, 273 n. 19
1984 (Orwell), 273 n. 18
Noddings, Nel, 54
No Future (Edelman), 161
nostalgia, 160–61, 241 n. 37
No Turning Back (Goodman et al.), 92
Nussbaum, Martha, 258 n. 12

Obama, Barack, 272 n. 16
object of desire, 14, 202–3; as affective points of conversion, 44–45, 240–41 nn. 33–37; affective value of, 21–27, 230–33 nn. 1–10; end-oriented intentionality in, 24–27, 34; good living embodied by, 33–38, 236–37 nn. 22–25; happy family as, 45–49, 241 nn. 38–40; instrumental value of, 10, 26, 227–28 nn. 13–15, 233 n. 10; positive value of, 33; promises of happiness in, 27–33, 38–39, 119, 233–36 nn. 11–21; shared social affects regarding, 38–45, 237–41 nn. 26–37. *See also* desire for happiness
On the Basis of Morality (Schopenhauer), 269 n. 9

On the Suffering in the World (Schopenhauer), 212
oppression, 2
optimism: in dystopic visions, 172–80, 269–70 nn. 9–11, 275 n. 23; in positive psychology, 9–10, 200; in queer theory, 161–63, 267 nn. 1–2; utilitarianism's critique of, 182
orientation toward an object, 24, 34, 54–59
O'Rourke, Meghan, 53
Orwell, George, 273 n. 18
Our Sister Killjoy (Aidoo), 19, 68
outside-in model of affect, 40

Packer, Vin, 88–89
pain, 23, 174, 231 n. 2, 240 n. 33, 269 n. 9
Pascal, Blaise, 225 n. 1
passion, 209
passivity, 208–17, 220–21, 276–79 nn. 4–12
past happiness, 160–61, 241 n. 37
"People Who Walked Away from Omelas, The" (Le Guin), 192, 194–95, 273 n. 17
Perry, David L., 231 n. 2
personal characteristics, 10
perversion, 44–45, 180, 240 n. 36
pessimism, 161–63, 172–82, 267 nn. 1–3, 269–70 nn. 9–11, 275 n. 23
Peter, Julie Anne, 251 n. 8
Peucker, Henning, 231 n. 4
phenomenology of happiness, 23–24, 232 n. 4, 275 n. 1
Phillips, Trevor, 121–22, 130, 258 n. 13, 263 n. 27
philosophical contexts, 1, 202–3; affirmative ethics, 213–17; Aristotle's classical views, 10, 12–13, 26, 36–37, 227–28 nn. 14–15, 233 nn. 8–10; everyday usage vs., 14–15, 228 n. 17;

happiness archives of, 15–18, 228 n. 18; unhappiness archives of, 17–20, 229–30 nn. 21–23. *See also* utilitarianism
Phua, Voon Chin, 251 n. 7
Pitts, Jennifer, 257 n. 7
Plato, 38, 54–55, 241 n. 2
pleasure, 22–27, 177, 212–13, 231 n. 2, 232 n. 5. *See also* affect; taste
pointless happiness, 197–98
political contexts, 2–4, 17–19, 207; of classical happiness, 13, 227 n. 14; of freedom to be unhappy, 195–98, 222–23, 273–75 nn. 20–23; hap movements in, 192, 222–23; in killjoy pessimism, 176. *See also* consciousness, consciousness-raising; future dystopias
"Political Technology of Individuals, The" (Foucault), 243 n. 8
Pool, Léa, 103–6
positive psychology, 3, 7–9, 200, 226 n. 3; Carr's happiness profile in, 10–11; flow promoted in, 11–12, 169; sacred *now* in, 267 n. 1
possibility, 186–87, 217–23, 280–81 nn. 14–18
postcolonial melancholia, 132
Potamianou, Anna, 189
Povinelli, Elizabeth, 273 n. 17
precariousness of happiness, 219, 281 n. 16
present happiness, 161
Price of Salt, The (Highsmith), 246 n. 25, 249 n. 2
pride, 259 n. 16
Probyn, Elspeth, 89
progress, 3, 5, 226 nn. 8
promises of happiness, 27–33, 38–39, 59, 160–61, 181, 233–36 nn. 11–21
promotion of happiness: moral distinctions in, 13–14; in positive psychol-

promotion of happiness (*continued*)
ogy, 10–12; value in, 5–7, 26, 226
n. 10

Prosser, Jay, 99–100

Psychic Life of Power, The (Butler), 104

psychoanalytic theory, 6, 15–16,
229 n. 20, 232 n. 5; on desire and
anxiety, 31–32; on hope, 189

Psychology of Happiness, The (Argyle),
8–9

Pursuit of Happiness, The (Brinton), 237
n. 26

queer archives, 2, 17–19, 222–23; activism in, 107–8; in Brown's *Rubyfruit
Jungle*, 90, 115–18; conditional happiness in, 90–95, 100, 249–52 nn. 3–
11; conversion into happy families
in, 107–14, 248 n. 1, 255 nn. 20–22;
definitions of love in, 100–101;
Freud's reading of, 95–96; in Garden's *Annie on My Mind*, 92–93; grief
and mourning in, 98–99, 108–11; in
Hall's *The Well of Loneliness*, 89–90,
96–106, 108; happily queer pleasures in, 115–20, 220, 255 n. 24; in
If These Walls Could Talk 2, 90, 107–
14; legal contestation of family in,
109–11; optimism and pessimism in,
161–63, 267 nn. 1–2; as points of rebellion, 144–45, 262 n. 25; in Pool's
Lost and Delirious, 103–6; pregnancy in, 112–14; presumptions of
unhappiness in, 88–90, 94–95, 228
n. 16, 248–49 nn. 1–2; risks of promotion of happiness in, 105–6, 248
n. 1; same-sex marriage, 94; silliness
in, 222–23, 282 n. 19; unhappiness
of causing unhappiness in, 95–106,
252–55 nn. 12–18

Queer Phenomenology (Ahmed), 14, 18,
71, 228 n. 15, 245 n. 19

racial contexts: of angry black woman,
67–69, 245 n. 18, 272 n. 15; consciousness of racism in, 79–87,
247–48 nn. 26–29; creation of
paranoia in, 84; of empire, 123–33,
148; fantasy of postracism in, 272
n. 16; gypsy figures in, 244 n. 13;
happy housewife fantasies in, 51;
lazy racism in, 265 n. 33; liberation
struggles in, 191, 272 n. 15; migration in, 121–23, 142–47, 151–58, 261
nn. 21–23, 263 nn. 27–29, 265 n. 35,
271 n. 14; multicultural happiness
in, 121–23, 130–33, 138, 145, 159,
256 n. 4, 267 n. 5; parallel worlds
of segregation in, 156, 266 n. 37;
of slavery, 2, 80, 127, 226 n. 10, 257
n. 10, 259 n. 15

reconciliation of want, 149–50, 216

Republic (Plato), 38, 54–55

responsibility to be happy, 9

ressentiment, 207, 208. *See also* unhappiness

revolutionary consciousness, 164–65,
171, 267–69 nn. 5–8; anxiety and
alternative hopefulness in, 181–
92, 271–72 nn. 12–16; in Fanon's
double alienation, 167–68; fixation
and violence in, 169–70; in Marx's
analysis of labor, 166–67; optimism
and pessimism in, 172–80, 269–70
nn. 9–11; unhappiness as alternative
social gift in, 192–98

Rose, Nikolas, 8, 243 n. 8

Rousseau, Jean-Jacques, 53–59, 62,
241–43 nn. 2–7, 243 n. 11

Rowbotham, Sheila, 51

Rubin, Gretchen, 237 n. 26

Rubyfruit Jungle (Brown), 35, 90,
115–18

Ruti, Mari, 120, 277 n. 5

Sanderson, Terry, 252 n. 10

Sartre, Jean-Paul, 184, 275 n. 1

Sassen, Saskia, 164

Scenes of Subjection (Hartman), 257 n. 10

Scheler, Max, 56–57

Schoch, Richard, 12

Schopenhauer, Arthur, 15, 163, 174–77, 212, 269–70 nn. 9–10, 275 n. 23

Schroeder, Michael, 252 n. 11

Schulman, Sarah, 95–96

Schultz, Bart, 256 n. 6

science of happiness, 2, 4, 193–94; analysis and indicators in, 6–7, 11–12; basis in feelings of, 6; happiness profile in, 10–11; hedonimeters as units in, 5; positive psychology in, 7–12, 169, 200, 226 nn. 3; self-reporting in, 5–6, 8–9, 226 nn. 9–10; surveys in, 3, 226 nn. 5

Second Sex, The (Beauvoir), 204

Secrets of Happiness, The (Schoch), 12

Section 28 Law (UK), 248 n. 1

secular evangelism, 128, 134

Sedgwick, Eve Kosofsky, 39, 89

Segal, Lynne, 243 n. 9

self-help discourses, 3

Seligman, Martin, 9–10

Seneca, 207

sensation, 23, 231 n. 2

Sense of the World, The (Nancy), 229 n. 21

sentimentalism, 231 n. 4

September 11 attacks, 157

sexual conversion therapy, 252 n. 11

Shidlo, Ariel, 252 n. 11

Shine, Darla, 52

Shirley Temple dolls, 116, 247 nn. 26–27

Sidgwick, Henry, 123

silliness, 165, 220–21, 282 n. 19

Skeggs, Beverley, 34

slavery, 2, 80, 127, 226 n. 10, 257 n. 10, 259 n. 15

Smith, Adam, 4, 207–8, 238 n. 28, 277 n. 5

Snediker, Michael D., 161–62, 228 n. 16

social bonds, 2, 7, 10–11, 38; conditional happiness through, 56–58, 242 n. 4, 242 n. 6; contagion of feelings in, 39–40, 97–98, 195, 237–39 nn. 26–28, 253 nn. 13–14, 274 n. 22; conversion of affect by, 44–45, 240–41 nn. 33–37; in crowd psychology, 40–43, 239–40 nn. 29–31; future alternatives of, 191–92; happy family, 21, 45–49, 241 nn. 38–40; through multiculturalism, 121–22. *See also* families

Socrates, 38

Souls of Black Folks, The (Du Bois), 257 n. 10

speech acts, 19–20, 29–30, 218, 234 n. 16; perverse performative in, 200–201; reciprocal aspirations and antagonisms in, 91–94, 250 n. 6, 251 n. 8

Spinoza, Baruch, 23, 210–12, 231 n. 3, 245 n. 19, 277 n. 7, 278 n. 9, 281 n. 18

Spivak, Gayatri, 127

Spring Fire (Packer), 88–89

Stoicism, 207

Stokes, Eric, 128, 134, 256 n. 6

Straw, Mack, 261 n. 21

stress, 169

Struik, Dirk J., 166–67

Stutzer, Alois, 1, 6, 225 n. 1

Subjection of Women, The (Mill), 16

suffering, 210. *See also* unhappiness

surveys of happiness, 3

Swan, Susan, 103

Syal, Meera, 149–54
sympathy, 39–40, 97–98, 195, 237–39
  nn. 26–29, 253 nn. 13–14, 274 n. 22

taste, 33–34, 47, 213, 236 n. 22, 237
  n. 25; civilizing mission of, 35, 236
  n. 23; habituation of, 14–15, 36–37,
  236 n. 24; Locke on, 33, 35–36, 211–
  12; moral injunctions for, 35–38
teleological conceptions of happiness,
  26, 199–200, 203, 233 nn. 8–10
temporal contexts, 26; past happiness,
  160–61, 241 n. 37; present happiness, 161. See also future dystopias
terrorism, 144, 157, 169–70, 263 n. 29
Theory of Moral Sentiments, The
  (Smith), 207–8, 238 n. 28
Thobani, Suneri, 245 n. 18
Thus Spoke Zarathustra (Nietzsche),
  209
Toder, Nancy, 254 n. 17
Tolstoy, Leo, 241 n. 38
Tomkins, Silvan, 39
Transmission of Affect, The (Brennan),
  40
Treatise of Human Nature, A (Hume),
  232 n. 5
troublemakers, 66–69, 243 n. 9, 243–
  44 n. 11, 245 n. 15; convention defied
  by, 64–65, 115–20; Eliot's Maggie
  Tulliver as, 60–65, 243 n. 10, 244
  nn. 12–14; among second-generation
  migrants, 150
turbans, 143, 159, 261 n. 21
Twilight of the Idols (Nietzsche), 29

unattributed happiness, 25–26
unbearable lives, 97
Unconscious, The (MacIntyre), 227 n. 14
unhappiness, 17–20, 210, 229–30
  nn. 21–23; in affirmative turn,
  213–17; in black feminist contexts,

79–87; of causing unhappiness in
  others, 95–106, 252–55 nn. 12–18;
  consciousness-raising of, 69–79,
  245–46 nn. 16–25; conversion from
  happiness to, 44–45, 241 n. 37; feminism saturated by, 64–69, 86–87;
  freedom to be unhappy, 192–98,
  222–23, 233 n. 11, 273–75 nn. 17–26;
  future promises of happiness in, 32–
  33; getting stuck in, 138–48, 166–67,
  169, 171, 189, 260–63 nn. 20–29,
  266 n. 38, 268 n. 6; postcolonial
  melancholia, 132; presumptions in
  queer contexts of, 88–90, 94–95,
  248–49 nn. 1–2; telos of, 195–96,
  275 n. 23
utilitarianism, 4, 15, 193–94, 202–3,
  231 n. 2, 276 n. 2; critique of optimism in, 5, 182; defense of empire
  in, 123–33, 167–68, 256–59 nn. 6–
  16; on desire, 235 n. 18; teleology
  of, 233 n. 8. See also science of happiness
Utilitarianism and Empire (Schultz and
  Varouxakis), 256 n. 6
utopia, 163

values. See moral distinctions; promotion of happiness
Varouxakis, Georgios, 256 n. 6
Vindication of the Rights of Women
  (Wollstonecraft), 58–59
violence, 268 n. 7
virtue, 12–13, 55–56, 227 n. 14, 242
  n. 3. See also moral distinctions

Walker, Lisa, 89
Waves, The (Woolf), 73
wealth, 7
Wealth of Nations, The (Smith), 4
Wearing, A., 10
Wedderburn, Alexander, 4

wedding days, 29, 41–42, 239 n. 30, 242 n. 6

Weil, Simone, 100

"Welcome to Cancerland" (Ehrenreich), 247 n. 28

Weldon, Fay, 227 n. 13

Well of Loneliness, The (Hall), 18, 89–90, 96–106, 108, 195, 252 n. 12, 254 nn. 15–16

what(ever) of happiness, 2, 22, 250 n. 6

will, willfulness, 30, 64, 244 n. 12, 245 nn. 15–16

Williams, Raymond, 170, 216

Will to Power, The (Nietzsche), 27–28

Wilson, Eric G., 228 n. 18, 279 n. 12

Wives of Bath, The (Swan), 103

Wollstonecraft, Mary, 58–59

Woolf, Virginia, 70–78, 245–46 nn. 19–22

workers, 166–67, 171

World Happiness Survey, 3

wretchedness, 17, 98, 168, 223, 240 n. 31

Wretched of the Earth, The (Fanon), 167–68

Žižek, Slavoj, 31, 164, 185, 191, 197, 268 n. 7, 275 n. 25

SARA AHMED is a professor of race and cultural studies at
Goldsmiths College, University of London. She is the author
of *Queer Phenomenology: Orientations, Objects, Others* (2006),
The Cultural Politics of Emotion (2004), and *Strange Encounters:
Embodied Others in Post-Coloniality* (2000).

Library of Congress Cataloging-in-Publication Data
Ahmed, Sara.
The promise of happiness / Sara Ahmed.
p. cm.
Includes bibliographical references and index.
ISBN 978-0-8223-4666-1 (cloth : alk. paper)
ISBN 978-0-8223-4725-5 (pbk. : alk. paper)
1. Happiness. 2. Social norms. 3. Social control. I. Title.
B187.H3A36 2010
170 — dc22   2009047829